SOCCER YEARBOOK 1984/5

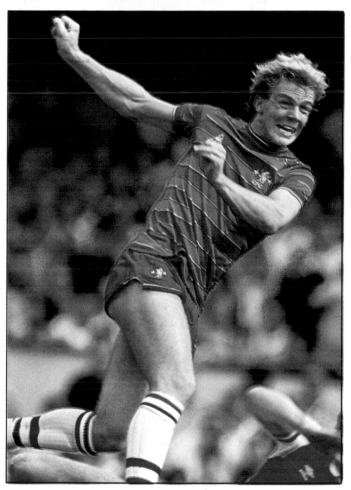

SOCCER YEARBOOK 1984/5

Edited by Dave Brenner

Front cover *FA Cup Final, 1985: Manchester United stars Gary Bailey, Kevin Moran and Norman Whiteside on the lap of honour at Wembley.*

Back cover *Main picture: Mike Channon (Norwich City) tangles with Sunderland skipper Barry Venison during the Milk Cup Final at Wembley. Inset: Everton's Gary Stevens, Trevor Steven, and Kevin Sheedy parade the League Championship Trophy at Goodison Park.*

Half-title *Kerry Dixon (Chelsea), who made a sparkling debut in the full England side on the 1985 summer tour of America.*

Title spread *Peter Shilton saves Andreas Brehme's penalty kick in England's victory against West Germany in Mexico City, June 1985.*

This spread *FA Cup Final, 1985: Everton's Derek Mountfield beats Manchester United's Gary Bailey, Paul McGrath (5), and Norman Whiteside (4) at a corner kick. Smaller pictures on opposite page: (left) the shambles in Brussels' Heysel Stadium before the European Cup Final; (right) the acceptable face of English football, with Everton supporters celebrating victory in the European Cup-Winners' Cup Final at Amsterdam.*

First published in 1985 by Octopus Books Limited 59 Grosvenor Street London W1

ISBN 0 86273 216 6

Printed in England by Severn Valley Press

CONTENTS

INTRODUCTION

The general rule when writing an introduction to a book is to say how good you think it is and to hand out bouquets to all concerned for their efforts. As it happens, I *do* think the St Michael *Soccer Yearbook 1985* is the most colourful and entertaining in its field – and everyone involved deserves to take a bow. At the same time, as Chairman of a Football League club, I'd like to make the most of this opportunity to reach thousands of soccer fans all over the country.

Everyone involved in football realises that, thanks to the scenes of crowd violence we all saw on television last season, the game's reputation isn't exactly sky-high at present. Of course, all the clubs want to clean up football and make soccer grounds safe and enjoyable places to visit – but we need the help of you, the fans, to make that happen.

I know it's not always easy to avoid trouble at matches. But by deliberately turning your back on aggravation you'll help us to isolate the real trouble-makers and drive them out forever. I really believe that we can make World Cup year in 1986 a memorable one by working together to show that British football and British football fans are once again the best in the world.

In the meantime, here in the *Soccer Yearbook* you'll find all the action and atmosphere of our greatest game at home and abroad, with exciting first-hand accounts of the English and Scottish league season, the great domestic and Continental cup competitions, and the vital qualifying matches for the World Cup.

Elton John

REVIEW OF SEASON 1984/5

DIVISION 1

Preceding two pages *Steve Foster (Luton Town, left) beats Everton's Graeme Sharp to a high ball during the FA Cup Semi-final at Villa Park.*

Below *Brave and combative as always, Andy Gray (Everton) challenges Martyn Bennett (West Bromwich Albion) in the air during a League match.*

A season which should have been made memorable by the remarkable achievements of Howard Kendall's Everton, who finally overshadowed even their famous neighbours on the other side of Stanley Park, will live on in vastly different images: fire 'raging through the main stand at Bradford; a youth falling beneath a mounted police charge at Chelsea; the wild-eyed mob advancing down the pitch at Luton; and then the appalling carnage of the European Cup Final in Brussels.

Those were the images most often used to sum up the state of soccer in 1985. They rightly and inevitably overshadowed such matters as who won what, how, and why. Yet taken in context, these matters were not without interest: far from it. Everton threatened to make history (as, indeed, did poor Stoke); other Wembley Cup finalists found themselves facing relegation;

while Chelsea and Sheffield Wednesday moved straight from Division 2 to the top six in the Big League. All this in a season extended to such a degree by two severe bouts of snow and ice that its last Division 1 match had still not begun as the England squad flew out of Heathrow on their summer tour of Mexico. By that time, sadly, most people had had more than enough.

There was little doubt from the start that the title would be won again by a Big City club. Only real romantics could see the limited resources of Nottingham Forest or Southampton stretching far enough to keep the trophy away from London, Merseyside or Manchester.

Everton's Charity Shield victory over Liverpool, courtesy of Bruce Grobbelaar's own goal, was proof to some that the balance of power in that little corner was changing. How much so was graphically illustrated by the Division 1 table on Sunday morning, 28 October. It showed Everton, having beaten Manchester United 5-0 the previous day, now holding second place, and Liverpool, with two wins from 11 league games, in the bottom three!

The gap between them was never as wide again, but that did not stop Evertonians having a hugely enjoyable winter. Their team was beginning to confirm its promise, while Liverpool found themselves without not only Graeme Souness, transferred to Sampdoria, but also Ian Rush, missing for the first two months of the season because of a knee injury. Being Liverpool, they then moved from 20th place to 7th in the space of a month with the ease of a team content to give the others a start.

The 'hares' who had leapt ahead only to fall back almost as quickly, included newly-promoted Newcastle United, Nottingham Forest and West Ham United. Arsenal stayed at the top for rather longer, including Everton among their victims after a disputed penalty at Highbury; but in the first week-end of November the changing fortunes of the two clubs finally hoisted Everton to the top for the first time in almost six years.

They had won at Anfield (for the first time since 1970) before routing Manchester United and seeing off Leicester to take over from Don Howe's team, whose 2-4 defeat at Old Trafford was their third loss in eight days. So the top positions read:

	P	Pts	Diff
Everton	13	26	+9
Arsenal	13	25	+8
Man. Utd	13	23	+8
Tottenham	13	23	+13

Arsenal were never to be convincing again. Graham Rix insisted on an operation; Charlie Nicholas looked in vain for some form. Tentative inquiries for Steve Williams began after he and

Mark Wright had been dropped by Southampton, and his transfer was eventually concluded just before Christmas – without having the desired effect.

By the end of November, Everton could have opened up a six-point lead. But after Spurs had been held to a home draw by Chelsea (who themselves threatened at times to join the contenders), Everton lost 2-4 in an exciting game at Norwich. Coming a few days after their extraordinary Milk Cup defeat at home to Grimsby Town, this raised the hopes of other challengers, as did an extraordinary 3-4 home reverse by Chelsea, who until then had not won a single away game. Gordon Davies, recently signed from Fulham in acrimonious circumstances to cover for David Speedie's suspensions, scored a hat-trick.

That defeat dropped Everton to third place, below Spurs and a Manchester United side hanging on gamely despite a tendency to lose away games after taking the lead and dominating the play. It was a low point for Everton which served only to set them off on another long run without defeat: away wins at Sunderland and Ipswich in the last week of 1984 rounding off a wonderful year for manager Howard Kendall, who had looked a candidate for the sack at the same time the previous season.

They maintained their form through all the interruptions for snow, as did Tottenham, who strangely were much happier away from White Hart Lane, where they did not play a League game from 29 December until 12 March. The

How They Stood at Half-Way

	P	W	D	L	F	A	Pts	*
Tottenham	21	12	4	5	43	22	40	(3)
Everton	21	12	4	5	45	28	40	(1)
Man. Utd.	21	11	5	5	42	26	38	(4)
Arsenal	21	11	3	7	39	27	36	(7)
WBA	21	10	4	7	36	30	34	(12)
Southampton	21	9	7	5	27	23	34	(5)
Nottingham F.	21	10	3	8	33	31	33	(9)
Chelsea	21	8	8	5	37	25	32	(6)
Sheffield Wed.	21	8	8	5	32	23	32	(8)
Liverpool	21	8	7	6	27	21	31	(2)
Norwich C.	21	8	6	7	29	28	30	(20)
Leicester C.	21	8	4	9	40	39	28	(15)
West Ham Utd	21	7	7	7	27	30	28	(16)
Sunderland	21	7	5	9	28	30	26	(21)
Watford	21	6	7	8	40	40	25	(11)
Newcastle Utd	21	6	7	8	33	41	25	(14)
Aston Villa	21	6	7	8	26	34	25	(10)
QPR	21	5	8	8	25	36	23	(19)
Luton Town	21	5	6	10	26	40	21	(13)
Ipswich Town	21	4	7	10	19	31	19	(17)
Coventry C.	21	5	4	12	20	40	19	(18)
Stoke C.	21	2	5	14	17	46	11	(22)

*Final positions

first Saturday in March, with the weather relenting at last, provided Spurs with a good opportunity to bridge the gap, which had now reached four points, as they visited the bottom club Stoke City while Manchester United and Everton collided at Old Trafford. United were badly under strength, with Moran, Robson, Moses, Muhren

One of the revelations of the season, Mark Hughes (Manchester United) turns Neil Orr (8) inside out in a League match against West Ham United.

and Stapleton all injured, but could in the end have either won or lost the game, which finished 1-1. Gordon Strachan missed his fifth penalty in six attempts (after having scored a hatful from the spot earlier in the season), and Mountfield equalised Olsen's fierce volley before Gary Bailey did the rest of the division a favour by saving Kevin Sheedy's late penalty.

Spurs duly improved their already impressive away record, Garth Crooks's goal beating his old club, so with almost two-thirds of the race run, the standings were:

	P	Pts	Diff
Everton	27	56	+29
Tottenham	27	54	+26
Man. Utd	28	49	+19
Liverpool	28	48	+17

That fixture at Old Trafford was the first of a series of critical games between the top clubs. Ten days later United visited Spurs and deservedly won 2-1 to revive their own challenge. Tottenham not only lost their chance to go back to the top but, more seriously for the long term, lost England midfielder Gary Stevens for the rest of the campaign: 'He was my man of the season', lamented manager Peter Shreeves. Steve Perryman, not as frisky as he once was, was pushed into midfield for the next match at Liverpool, where they had not won for 73 years. Amazingly, Garth Crooks knocked in the only goal to keep

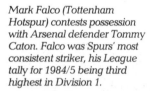

Mark Falco (Tottenham Hotspur) contests possession with Arsenal defender Tommy Caton. Falco was Spurs' most consistent striker, his League tally for 1984/5 being third highest in Division 1.

the pot boiling and keep Spurs believing. (It took one more home defeat before Liverpool could be counted out with any conviction. This time it was achieved by Manchester United, when Frank Stapleton was left unmarked to head a second-half goal.)

So to another crunch match – Spurs against Everton at White Hart Lane on Wednesday, 3 April. Tottenham went into it after a bad Saturday on which, with six internationals missing, they were well beaten at home by Aston Villa, coming off to hear that Everton had won at Southampton to go three points clear with a game in hand.

Cliché or not, it was a game Tottenham had to win, for the sake of morale as much as the points. But two defensive errors undid them, giving goals to Gray and Steven; and after Roberts had pulled one back, Southall made a stupendous save to keep out Falco's header. Many would say the championship was decided in that split-second.

Certainly Spurs went from poor to worse to worse still, losing a third successive home game to Arsenal and a fourth to struggling Ipswich. Manchester United moved into second place, but then were pegged back by odd-goal defeats at Sheffield Wednesday and Luton on each side of their epic FA Cup-ties against Liverpool. At Hillsborough Stephen Pears, deputising for Gary Bailey,

was blamed for the only goal; at Kenilworth Road, Mick Harford scrambled a winning goal in the last minute after Foster's thunderous free-kick had struck the bar.

Everton simply kept on winning: 4-1 against Sunderland, 4-1 against West Bromwich (to go seven points clear), 2-0 at Stoke (10 points clear). The bookmakers had long since stopped taking bets when, on the May Bank Holiday weekend, further victories over Sheffield Wednesday, away, and Queen's Park Rangers, at home, made the title mathematically certain. Even then, the celebrations both on and off the pitch, were restrained: Everton's thoughts were already turning to two Cup finals in the space of four days....

The bottom end of Division 1 provided more sustained interest. With postponements and consequent games in hand complicating matters considerably, the only certain outcome as winter eventually turned into spring was the relegating of Stoke City. Those most perilously involved in the dogfight were the south-eastern clutch of Luton Town, Ipswich, Watford and West Ham United (early-season League leaders !), plus Milk Cup finalists Sunderland and Norwich City and, almost inevitably, Coventry City. QPR, Leicester City and Newcastle United hovered above this unhappy little group, knowing that any one of them could easily suffer a sudden fall.

Coventry, with fewest quality players, fought their way clear for a while as Don Mackay took over from his erstwhile boss Bobby Gould: then they fell from 17th to 21st by early April. West Ham, again deprived of Bonds and Devonshire through injury, would have been in worse trouble but for an unexpected win at Nottingham Forest, where they had failed even to score a goal since 1969. Unable, like Spurs, to beat anyone at home, the Hammers achieved another important victory away to Sunderland, who were having to contend with the disappointment of a Wembley defeat and the knowledge that they had fewer games in hand than anyone else.

The Wembley victory did not do Norwich any good, either. A desperate run of only one league win in 14 games, with defeats by Ipswich, Luton and Leicester, put them down among the strugglers, while those who beat them were inspired to greater things. Luton, surrounded by the ballyhoo of their Cup game against Millwall and a subsequent extremely unlucky semi-final defeat by Everton, recovered quickly

Paul Allen (left) and Norman Whiteside in action at Old Trafford. Allen, on the right of midfield, was perhaps West Ham's most consistent success in 1984/5, but in the close season he was lured away to the bright lights of Tottenham.

enough to beat Norwich and then Manchester United in the space of five days. The same weekend Ipswich's success at Tottenham lifted them out of the bottom three. The basement now read thus:

	P	Pts	Diff
Norwich City	36	42	-15
Luton Town	34	41	- 9
West Ham Utd	34	41	-12
Ipswich Town	35	39	-14
Sunderland	37	39	-14
Coventry C.	34	37	-18
Stoke City	35	17	-53

Sunderland's position as favourites to join Stoke was confirmed when their next four games yielded just one point; the 0-4 drubbing at home by an Aston Villa side with ostensibly nothing to play for suggested that they deserved little better, even if their long-suffering supporters did.

The same unpredictable Villa then provided one last heave out of trouble for

Striking contrasts: Peter Withe (Aston Villa, centre) chased by Watford's Luther Blissett. At season's end Withe was disposed of by Villa to make way for Andy Gray; but Blissett had recovered from his unhappy Italian stint, scoring goals with all his old regularity, and once again trying to catch Bobby Robson's eye.

Luton, who won there with Brian Stein's goal two days after rubbing Arsenal's noses in the Kenilworth Road dust. West Ham won a critical victory at home to Norwich, who appealed at length but in vain (Mark Barham being sent off for dissent) for a last-minute penalty which might have prevented them falling below the Hammers into the bottom four. They were then five points ahead of Coventry, but had played three games more.

West Ham finally made themselves safe by beating Stoke and Ipswich, while Norwich's rain-soaked 3-1 win away to Chelsea meant they would be safe unless Coventry could win their last three matches: away to Stoke then at home to Luton and Everton.

On Cup Final eve they scrambled a 1-0 victory in the potteries after Stoke's Ian Painter missed a penalty six minutes from the end. That condemned his team to Division 1's worst points total under any system since 1894.

Six days later there was again a dramatic finish, centre-half Brian Kilcline's goal beating Luton at Highfield Road with just seven minutes to play. Suddenly the Sky Blues were one win away from survival; and if Everton had to provide the opposition, this was unquestionably the best time for them to do so: a late crop of injuries meant they turned up on Sunday, 26 May without Stevens, Mountfield, Reid, Gray, Atkins and Bailey. Steven and Sharp had been sent south to take part instead of playing in the Scotland-England international, but their annoyance proved less significant a factor than Coventry's desperation. The champions were two goals down in 17 minutes and eventually lost 1-4, their heaviest defeat since losing to Spurs at Goodison on the opening day of the season. Coventry's Houdini act doomed Milk Cup-winners Norwich to relegation.

Of greater importance to Everton was a 1-0 win which brought them their first double for 20 years over Liverpool, who had nevertheless made sure of finishing runners-up – a rise of 18 places since October 1984. The whole of Merseyside should have had reason to derive immense pride and satisfaction from the season. But Brussels was still to come.

Leading Scorers	League	FA Cup	Milk Cup	Europe	Total
Dixon (Chelsea)	24	4	8	0	36
Sharp (Everton)	21	2	3	4	30
Falco (Tottenham)	22	1	2	4	29
Lineker (Leicester)	24	3	2	0	29
Blissett (Watford)	20	6	1	0	27
Wark (Liverpool)	14	7	0	5	26
Hughes (Man United)	16	4	3	2	25

Final Table

	P	HOME W	D	L	F	A	AWAY W	D	L	F	A	Pts	Leading League Scorers	Average Home Gates 1984/5	Diff. from 1983/4
Everton	42	16	3	2	58	17	12	3	6	30	26	90	Sharp 21	32,131	+12,778
Liverpool	42	12	4	5	36	19	10	7	4	32	16	77	Wark 18	34,131	+2,491
Tottenham H.	42	11	3	7	46	31	12	5	4	32	20	77	Falco 22	28,932	+231
Manchester Utd	42	13	6	2	47	13	9	4	8	30	34	76	Hughes 16	43,010	+506
Southampton	42	13	4	4	29	18	6	7	8	27	29	68	Jordan 12	18,032	−56
Chelsea	42	13	3	5	38	20	5	9	7	25	28	66	Dixon 24	23,061	+1,942*
Arsenal	42	14	5	2	37	14	5	4	12	24	35	66	Allison, Talbot, Woodcock 10	31,305	+2,189
Sheffield Wed.	42	12	7	2	39	21	5	7	9	19	24	65	Varadi 16	27,779	+5,009*
Nottingham For.	42	13	4	4	35	18	6	3	12	21	30	64	Davenport 16	16,777	−921
Aston Villa	42	10	7	4	34	20	5	4	12	26	40	56	Rideout 14	18,318	−3,052
Watford	42	10	5	6	48	30	4	8	9	33	41	55	Blissett 21	18,366	+1,856
West Bromwich	42	11	4	5	36	23	5	3	13	22	39	55	Thompson 19	13,827	−741
Luton Town	42	12	5	4	40	22	3	4	14	17	39	54	Harford 15	10,825	−1,113
Newcastle Utd	42	11	4	6	33	26	2	9	10	22	44	52	Beardsley 17	26,046	−3,764*
Leicester C.	42	10	4	7	39	25	5	2	14	26	48	51	Lineker 24	14,530	−393
West Ham Utd	42	7	8	6	27	23	6	4	11	24	25	51	Cottee 17	18,402	−2,984
Ipswich Town	42	8	7	6	27	20	5	4	12	19	37	50	Gates 13	17,054	−410
Coventry C.	42	11	3	7	29	22	4	2	15	18	42	50	Gibson 15	12,862	+290
QPR	42	11	6	4	41	30	2	5	14	12	42	50	Bannister 17	14,171	−1,199
Norwich C.	42	9	6	6	28	24	4	4	13	18	49	49	Deehan 13	16,058	−399
Sunderland	42	7	6	8	20	26	3	4	14	20	36	40	Walker 10	18,341	+2,262*
Stoke C.	42	3	3	15	18	41	0	5	16	6	50	17	Painter 6	10,477	−3,423

* Division 2 in 1983/4

CLUB BY CLUB: HOW THEY RAN

1 EVERTON

Defeats by Spurs at home and West Bromwich away to start the season did not mark the FA Cup holders out as potential champions; even by mid-October, when a run of 10 successive wins was well underway, bookies were offering 22-1 against them. The odds decreased sharply after their victory at Anfield, and once Tottenham began to falter they became everybody's favourites. They were lucky with injuries: Adrian Heath's was the only serious one, and Andy Gray deputised so well that he earned a recall for Scotland, alongside Graeme Sharp. Another splendid unbeaten run, from 22 December to 11 May, ensured that no-one got anywhere near them.

2 LIVERPOOL

Took no great pride in finishing second, especially to Everton: but for a team in the bottom three at one stage it was a considerable achievement. Loath to admit that the loss of any individual was of much significance, they nevertheless found the absence of Souness and then of Rush (out for eight weeks with a knee injury) too much. Dalglish, dropped for the first time in October, gave some masterly performances later; but his elevation to player-manager when Joe Fagan retired amidst the mayhem of Brussels astonished many people.

3 TOTTENHAM HOTSPUR

An extraordinary disparity between home and away form was the feature of a season in which they should have got much closer to their first championship title for 24 years. Unbeaten away from 20 October to the finish, they suffered a catastrophic run in front of the demanding White Hart Lane crowd, losing six games out of seven as the defence, lacking the elegant Gary Stevens, was caught out time after time. All the more odd that Chris Waddle, another striker, was the man they pursued most enthusiastically as soon as the season ended.

4 MANCHESTER UNITED

Cup wins against Everton and Liverpool proved they were as good as anyone on their day: league defeats by Stoke and Sunderland (after they had been ahead in both games) illustrated why their championship challenge was again inadequate.

With Ian Rush injured at the start of the season, John Wark (seen here with Manchester United's Graeme Hogg) finished up as Liverpool's top League goal marksman and also scored prolifically in the European Cup.

Above *Peter Shilton continued to make Southampton's defence one of the more parsimonious in the League, and his place in England's goal remained unchallenged.*

The revamped team, with Whiteside often effective in midfield, Strachan and Olsen down the flanks, and Hughes wreaking havoc up front, was often exciting. The defence, with Hogg still learning, Moran often injured, and Duxbury out of sorts, too often failed to stand up to pressure away from home; but McGrath stamped himself as a defender of power and skill.

5 SOUTHAMPTON

Fifth place was another substantial achievement on gates of 18,000; but at season's end manager Lawrie McMenemy decided that 12 years of Hampshire football was enough. Internal rows involving Agboola and Williams (who both left) and Wright, plus a poor start, made the season's achievement all the more creditable. Jimmy Case looked a value-for-money signing in the run-in, which would have meant European football again but for the ban on English clubs.

6 CHELSEA

Headlines about hooliganism and electric fences tended to obscure a successful return to Division 1 despite a failure to win an away game until Christmas, when they beat Everton 4-3 (!). They were unbeaten in London derbies, which also meant a lot. Kerry Dixon made a fool of those who predicted he wouldn't score at this level. The club need a dominant midfielder. And the greatly gifted Speedie should spend more time on the field and less on suspension.

7 ARSENAL

Four points clear at the top and looking good after 11 games, they then lost their way. Manager Don Howe, suddenly under pressure in his first full season in charge, publicly criticised his biggest names for lack of character when the going got tough. Arsenal gained more home points than anyone except Everton, but defeats at places like York and Stoke emphasised their fragility away from Highbury; and even when they were winning their play conspicuously lacked charm or coherent style.

8 SHEFFIELD WEDNESDAY

The unexpected sale of Bannister, Megson and Cunningham – linchpins of their promotion team – didn't hinder their progress, built on straightforward long-ball play appreciated by the Hillsbrough crowd (up almost 25 per cent on the previous season). Lee Chapman, unsuccessful at Arsenal and Sunderland, took over from Bannister as the goal-scoring foil to talented Imre Varadi. Unpopular visitors, their away games produced far fewer goals (43) than any other club's.

9 NOTTINGHAM FOREST

Down from third the previous season, they left it until the end of the season before spending what little money was available. Gary Birtles' long absence through injury gave Peter Davenport the chance to impress not only Brian Clough but also Bobby Robson, who had capped him by the end of March. Johnny Metgod brought much pleasure with his elegant defensive work and powerful shooting.

10 ASTON VILLA

A 0-5 defeat at home to Forest early on suggested a difficult season – but ultimately showed only the inconsistent nature of both teams. Villa rose from 17th at half-way stage after Graham Turner sorted out the personnel. Brendan Ormsby emerged as a useful defender, Mark Walters and Paul Rideout represented the England under-21s. But gates down by 5,500 in two years reflected the locals' disenchantment with the product.

11 WATFORD

The division's great entertainers again, their 42 games yielded an amazing 152 goals. They stuck to their guns despite lying bottom after failing to win any of the opening nine games. Luther Blissett returned (and rediscovered his scoring touch) as Maurice Johnston went back to Scotland, while Colin West usefully replaced George Reilly just before the transfer deadline.

Below *David Speedie (left), seen here with Spurs' Steve Perryman and team-mate Pat Nevin, formed a dangerous partnership with Kerry Dixon in Chelsea's front line and earned himself a Scottish cap.*

12 WEST BROMWICH ALBION

Never the same team after Bob Wilson tipped them to win the FA Cup! They lost at Orient in the third round and fell from fifth place at Christmas to the fringe of the relegation fight. They had looked capable earlier on of reviving interest in the depressed West Midlands, but flattered to deceive.

13 LUTON TOWN

Like all the teams below them, they finished too close to relegation for comfort and might have gone down (which they wouldn't have deserved) if they had they reached the Cup Final (which they did deserve). Manager David Pleat shrewdly toughened the team's spine, buying Foster, Preece, Nicholas and Harford (whose goals were crucial in the end).

14 NEWCASTLE UNITED

Roared out of Division 2 to the top of the league after three games: it was the other 39 which were the problem. Their final position was a more realistic one: they suffered – like many Newcastle teams in the past – from chronic incompetence away from home. Waddle was a source of entertainment, getting his first England cap and eventually signing for Spurs; Beardsley, too, proved an accomplished performer at the top level.

15 LEICESTER CITY

Fifteenth for the second season running, they were often an engaging side to watch and only five teams scored more league goals. Gary Lineker contributed 24 of them (sharing top spot with Chelsea's Dixon) but, at season's end, took the chance to better himself at Everton.

16 WEST HAM UNITED

The bubbles popped even earlier than usual, plunging them from joint top to 13th by the new year and into relegation trouble by Easter. Billy Bonds, hoping to phase himself out, remained first-choice when fit; Alan Devonshire was again unlucky with injury; Tony Cottee scored consistently; as always, Paul Goddard was short of height but never short of class.

17 IPSWICH TOWN

They stemmed the flow of leading players away from Portman Road and also the drift towards Division 2 as youngsters like Brennan, Dozzell and Cranson found their feet. Eric Gates was again leading scorer – and again he deserved much more help.

18 COVENTRY CITY

One point away from going down, for the third successive season. This was the most remarkable escape yet, requiring three wins from their last three games. Bobby Gould was the club's sixth manager in 18 years to depart. At season's last gasp, Cyrille Regis's long-lost form showed signs of returning.

19 QUEEN'S PARK RANGERS

Traumatic season as Alan Mullery failed to win over Terry Venables' protégés, who managed to lose a four-goal lead in the UEFA Cup and had scored only four away goals by Christmas. Mullery transfer-listed four players, bought John Byrne and Robbie James, but was sacked on 4

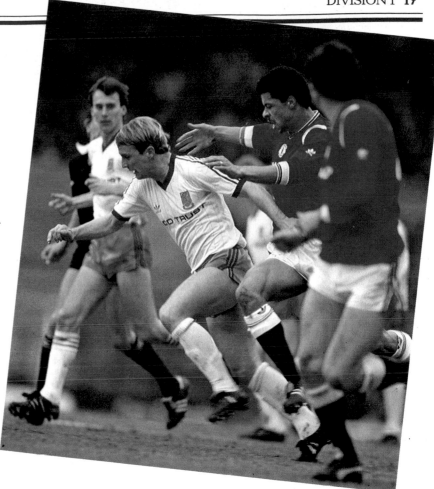

December, an hour after QPR's victory over Stoke. Frank Sibley kept heads above water thereafter – if only just.

20 NORWICH CITY

Danger signs were visible even before the Milk Cup final as they won only two games out of 11 – though the seriousness of their plight did not become apparent until much later. Even then, a win away to Chelsea in the final match looked good enough. But Coventry produced their late flourish, and a season already marred by fire in the main stand at Carrow Road was ruined completely by relegation and the ban on their UEFA Cup début.

21 SUNDERLAND

A disastrous second half of the season produced just 12 goals and 14 points in 21 games, and a return to Division 2 after five unconvincing years – plus the sack for Len Ashurst only two months after he had led them out at Wembley. Victory over Manchester United in October marked the high point, from which it was downhill all the way except for the Milk Cup interlude.

22 STOKE CITY

There was ghoulish statistical interest in a season of 3 wins, 21 goals, 17 points and 31 defeats (all Division 1 records in modern times). Just six of the goals came away from home. Poor Bill Asprey had to stop work through exhaustion at Christmas and was 'suspended' in April before leaving the club altogether. Long before the end, supporters were already worrying about the prospect of following Wolves and Notts County straight through to Division 3.

Paul Goddard (West Ham) evades Paul McGrath's attentions in a match against Manchester United. A gifted player often plagued by injury, Goddard has sometimes proved too quick in thought and deed for his colleagues. McGrath, meanwhile, has emerged as one of the strongest defenders in the League.

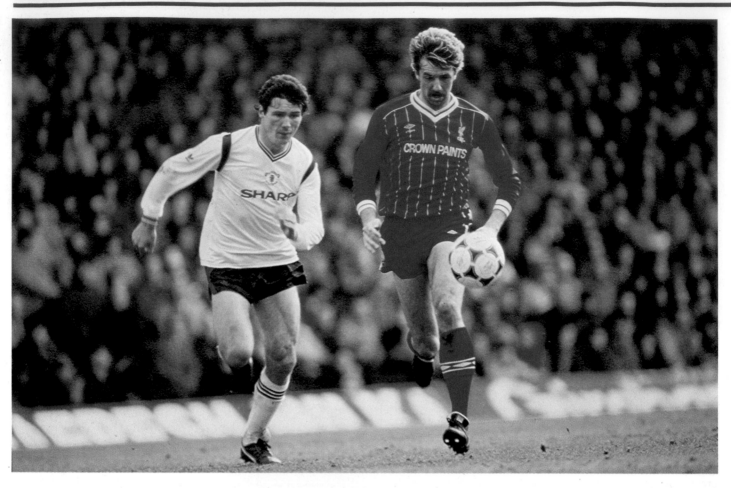

Mark Lawrenson regularly shows true international class whether as a central defender or as a midfield ball-winner. Here (right) he races for the ball with fellow Irish Republic star Frank Stapleton.

PFA TEAM

Six changes in the 'team' selected by fellow-professionals reflected the changing balance of Division 1, with four Evertonians included and young strikers Chris Waddle and Kerry Dixon picked after playing only seven months in the top echelon. Missing from the previous year's selection were Mike Duxbury, Alan Hansen, Glenn Hoddle, Graeme Souness (playing abroad), Frank Stapleton and Kenny Dalglish; but, in hindsight, the most surprising absentee was Mark Hughes. Clubs given are those at time of the awards:

PETER SHILTON (Southampton)
Still the greatest in the view of his fellow-pros, although Neville Southall must have pushed him very close, Ray Clemence had a vintage year and Gary Bailey finally won an England cap. He faced the challenge of remaining England's number one for the World Cup at the age of 37 – the same age as Pat Jennings had been in Spain (1982) and a mere stripling compared to Italy's Dino Zoff.

GARY STEVENS (Everton)
One to watch from the day of his debut at West Ham in September 1981, within 3½ years of which he was called into the England squad. Adventurous and not a man to leave unmarked within shooting range, he scored from right-back in only his second League game and got two in six minutes against Watford last season.

MARK LAWRENSON (Liverpool)
Many were surprised he was not pushed permanently into midfield once Souness had left. Enormously accomplished, and strong as well as elegant, he is comfortable in both positions and would have won a formidable tally of England caps if the Republic of Ireland had not snatched him at the age of 19.

KEVIN RATCLIFFE (Everton)
Not a bad year, 1984: an outstanding captain of Wales when they beat England, he led Everton to the FA Cup and the Charity Shield before captaining the club in their three-pronged assault in 1984/5. Very quick, he is a fine man-to-man marker, but usually plays a covering role alongside Derek Mountfield in central defence.

KENNY SANSOM (Arsenal)
Unchallenged in this position ever since he became a Division 1 player with Crystal Palace in 1979. Experience gained as stand-in captain at Arsenal and as one of the senior members of the England squad (he already has half a century of caps) has helped him become one of the best left-backs in Europe.

BRYAN ROBSON (Manchester United)
United may have proved they can live without him but England do not look the same team in his absence. The complete modern player, like Lawrenson equally at home in midfield and defence, he is also a ferocious poacher of goals. The number and variety of injuries he collects remain a worrying problem for club and country but are an almost inevitable legacy of his boundlessly aggressive style.

PETER REID (Everton)
The first non-international to be voted Player of the Year. Survived Bolton's rapid descent in the

League and two major injuries to become a creative playmaker in centre-midfield for Everton, who paid only £60,000 for him.

KEVIN SHEEDY (Everton)

Liverpool demanded £100,000 from their greatest rivals for Sheedy's transfer in the summer of 1982 even though he had played only one full League game for them after impressing at Hereford. Born in Wales, he was another player quickly latched onto by the Republic of Ireland. Unlucky to miss the last two months of 1983/4 season, including the FA Cup Semi-Final and Final.

IAN RUSH (Liverpool)

One of the most down-to-earth of superstars, feet kept firmly on the ground by his large family in North Wales, all of whom have nevertheless advised him to take the opportunity of moving to the continent. Missed the start of the 1984/5 campaign with a serious knee injury, but since then has shown he is still one of the most clinically efficient finishers in Europe.

CHRIS WADDLE (Newcastle United)

His characteristically hunched-shoulder style and rare dribbling ability add to his appeal as a genuine individualist. Essentially left-footed, he scores some of his best goals by cutting in from the right-hand side. He was tipped last season as a future England player by Kevin Keegan — though both must have been surprised at how soon he won a cap.

KERRY DIXON (Chelsea)

The obvious choice to play Roy of the Rovers if the movie is ever made. Tall, blond and handsome, he was allowed to leave Spurs and missed by his local club Luton, becoming a goalscorer to rival Rush (if not Roy Race) at every level he has played.

Above Kevin Ratcliffe, the inspirational captain of both Everton and Wales in a splendid year for club and country, allies technical skill as a marker with the ability to move faster than perhaps any other central defender in the League.

Left Chris Waddle is never afraid to take on and beat defenders. His dribbling and goal-scoring skills took him into the England team and, at the end of the season, from Newcastle to Tottenham.

DIVISION 2

After the excellence of 1983/4, with Chelsea, Sheffield Wednesday and Newcastle United all possessing teams of undoubted quality, Division 2 experienced a levelling out last year. It could not even be said that the greater openness of the promotion race provided real compensation, for (Oxford United apart) it looked as if none of the contenders sincerely wanted to be promoted: all continually spurned opportunities to grab a place. That it was not until the final week that a decision was reached on who claimed the third place owed more to the contestants' failings than to their successes.

Oxford did not quite match the glories of 1983/4, although the defeat of Arsenal, then Division 1 leaders, in the Milk Cup revived memories of them. But they were the most consistent of the contenders, and often the most exciting, certainly in the months up until Christmas when the rampaging Irish international Billy Hamilton and Ian Rush-lookalike John Aldridge (ironically from Liverpool) proved to be the most lethal striking partnership in the division. Hamilton's injury, very slow to mend, was a severe blow to the club, already deprived of their exciting young midfield star Andy Thomas. Aldridge missed his strike partner

noticeably and, as the ice and snow caused postponements, Oxford's previously smooth progress began to falter. Hamilton, although not fully fit, returned temporarily to help steady things, and although Oxford never recovered their earlier fluency, they made few mistakes on the run in.

Birmingham's success, by contrast, was built on their solid away record. Their team, much changed from the one relegated the previous season, showed all the Ron Saunders characteristics of organisation, ceaseless running and a tough – sometimes too tough – competitiveness as they recovered their Division 1 place at the first time of asking, their flying start and a sound late run, after a few hiccups in mid-season, being enough to see them home. There was, however, precious little to suggest that Division 1 will be better for their presence.

The same could be said of the rivals for the third spot – mainly Manchester City (who succeeded at the last gasp), Portsmouth (who failed only on goal difference), Blackburn Rovers, and Leeds United.

Portsmouth, who spent money with abandon – the sale of Mark Hateley to AC Milan in the summer bringing in abundant lire – several times seemed poised to take over as leaders, only to decline the opportunity,

Neil Webb, seen here (centre) scoring for Portsmouth against Fulham keeper Gerry Peyton, was perhaps the most sought-after star in Division 2 in 1984/5. Brian Clough signed him to Nottingham Forest in the close season, and few doubted that this goal-poaching midfielder would flourish in Division 1.

most especially on the final lap in April, when it mattered most. Their performances were as inconsistent as their results, sometimes impressing neutrals with their Division 1 credentials, at others looking like 'ale-house footballers' (in Bob Paisley's memorable phrase). Yet in Neil Webb they had probably the hottest property in the division, a midfield player with a stamp of quality who infiltrated forward to score an impressive number of goals.

The other candidates had their qualifications. Manchester City, the biggest club, with a ground and support which deserve Division 1 football, were an attractive team in the club's best tradition. But they seemed a bit lightweight, lacking power in front of goal; and the club's financial straits, a lingering result of past extravagances by Malcolm Allison and John Bond, left their first team squad a bit short of quality and the club vulnerable to a series of injuries.

Blackburn were a tight, well-organised team, best described as hard to beat, with three strikers, Jimmy Quinn, Simon Garner and Chris Thompson, all capable of conjuring something out of nothing, and a promising young midfield player in Simon Barker. But after leading the table at Christmas their lack of real quality caught up with them.

The team which seemed the best equipped for a long stay in Division 1, Leeds United, until the end made the least serious assault on the target. Always on the fringe of the race, they frequently looked as if they were gathering pace for a determined surge – but each time it failed to materialise. Some felt that their young team would benefit from a further year in Division 2. Peter Lorimer and Frank Gray showed all their old class in midfield roles, where John Sheridan and Scott Sellars showed a subtlety and touch which marked them out as outstanding prospects. Equally exciting on occasion was their young goalscorer Tommy Wright. But until Ian Baird arrived late in the season they lacked physical presence at the front and (ironically for a club with their history) in midfield. But if the days have gone when teams wore three pairs of shinpads to play at Elland Road, the yobs among Leeds supporters continued to earn notoriety, with Oxford, Huddersfield, Barnsley and Birmingham all suffering the loathsome activities of their fans.

At the other end of the table there was the increasingly familiar sight of famous names in trouble. A year previously it had been Swansea City on a downward crash as dramatic as their rise had been. In 1984/5 Wolves and Notts County plunged straight to the Division 2 basement. The fall of Wolves under Tommy Docherty was the more astonishing, for until mid-season they had managed to keep their heads a little above the waterline; but in the end 'the consequences of 15 years of neglect' (in Docherty's words) proved unavoidable.

Notts County's demise had seemed the more likely before the season began, and they lost little time in fulfilling the gloomy prophecies, settling into the bottom three from the beginning. By November they looked doomed, but the change in management – with Jimmy Sirrel reassuming direction and Dave Watson arriving as coach – signalled something of a revival. They jostled with Middlesbrough and Cardiff City, their companions in distress for most of the season, for the place on the lifeboat vacated by Wolves, the matter not being decided until the last week of the season. The other club to face the drop for most of the season, Crystal Palace, escaped thanks to a convincing late run, to ensure that a traumatic first year in management for Steve Coppell at least had a happy ending.

Several of these themes were to be glimpsed on the opening day itself. Oxford gave notice of their intention that Division 1 was to be a staging post rather than their ultimate objective with a comprehensive 3-0 victory at injury-riddled Huddersfield. Notts County began their venture in the lower division inauspiciously, two goals from Tommy Wright bringing Leeds an encouraging victory at Meadow Lane. Portsmouth and Middlesbrough's meeting at Fratton Park ended predictably in hindsight, although Portsmouth's 1-0 margin hardly suggested the ultimate gap between the clubs. Manchester City and Blackburn could both be satisfied with draws in south London, Blackburn in a typically unexciting 1-1 draw at Palace, while City survived a barnstorming opening by newly promoted Wimbledon, the Wednesday and Watford disciples of Division 2, to escape with a commendable 2-2 scoreline.

The most revealing result of all, though, was at Boundary Park, where Birmingham

Above *Jimmy Quinn proved to be one of Blackburn Rovers' liveliest strikers of recent seasons. He was drafted into Northern Ireland's team when Billy Hamilton was injured, and played well enough to earn a place in Billy Bingham's long-term plans.*

Below *Tommy Wright (Leeds United) proved to be one of the best of the younger strikers in a team capable of reaching greater heights than most clubs in the division.*

Wayne Clarke (centre), seen here avoiding Wolves' Nicky Sinclair, spearheaded Birmingham City's drive for an instant return to the League elite, taking fifth place among Division 2 strikers.

won few friends but three points thanks to an own goal by Oldham's Kenny Clements. That was to set the pattern for Birmingham in the early stages. Their first home game was somewhat out of character as Wimbledon's open approach persuaded Ron Saunders' roundheads into a goal extravaganza, Birmingham winning 4-3; but more cautious away victories over Fulham and Crystal Palace were more typical, and in mid-September they led the table with 15 points from five games.

Brighton, with four wins, had also made a bright start to stand second; Leeds were third, but their slip was already showing, and although three more goals from Wright had helped in wins over Fulham and Wolves, successive defeats at Cardiff (the Welshmen's first points of the season) and at home to Portsmouth had undermined them. Oxford were already in the frame with three wins and a draw from four matches.

If Birmingham's start was surprisingly good, Manchester City's was horrifically bad. After beating Grimsby (fellow promotion candidates the previous season) in their opening match at Maine Road, City found themselves on the skids. They swiftly dropped to 14th position (their lowest for 20 years), and although a scrambled win over a still-weakened Huddersfield halted the slide, even their loyal fans could see little reason for optimism.

Birmingham's stride was soon to be checked. Portsmouth, who had won at Leeds on 15 September, completed a notable away double at St Andrew's three days later, a Neil Webb goal bringing them the points and setting Pompey on the first of their own good runs. At the end of that week they had reached fourth place. Blackburn, who had also been quietly advancing,

were ahead of them on goal difference behind Birmingham and Oxford; the latter had a game in hand on all their rivals.

The first Saturday in October is often a sign, in the Football League, that winter is coming; it is a time for early promise to be fulfilled or a bad start to be put behind one. Oxford somewhat unluckily lost their unbeaten record before 24,755 fans at Maine Road, a Steve Kinsey goal in the 87th minute suggesting that Manchester City's autumn of discontent might yet lead to a winter of fulfilment. On the same day Birmingham went down 0-2 at Brighton, while Blackburn continued their unheralded advance with a 3-1 win over Shrewsbury, whose Barker and Stevens were sent off. The following Saturday two goals from Chris Thompson brought Blackburn the points at St Andrew's which took them to the top, while a pair for Billy Hamilton restored Oxford's spirits with a 2-1 defeat of Brighton.

Blackburn's leadership was to be short-lived. Oxford, still with their game in hand, went to the top by thrashing Sheffield United, while Blackburn were held to a scoreless draw by Oldham. Oxford themselves were scoreless on the last Saturday in October, drawing a bad-tempered, scrappy match at Birmingham before the day's largest Division 2 crowd of 20,416. The loss of the points made no difference to Oxford's position. Manchester City had lapsed again after beating Oxford, going down to Shrewsbury and then to Middlesbrough; but they showed they could rise to the occasion by beating Blackburn 2-1 with the help of a John Lowey own goal. Blackburn's lack of self-belief against their big-city neighbours angered their normally calm manager Bobby Saxton. Blackburn lost again the following week as another two goals from Billy Hamilton gave Oxford the points in a much better game.

It seemed, however, that Blackburn could afford such frailties, for nobody seemed capable of punishing them. Leeds lost hard-fought Yorkshire derbies scarred by crowd trouble at both Barnsley and Huddersfield. Wolves interrupted Portsmouth's progress with a 1-0 win at Fratton Park. The performance of Jim Melrose, on loan from Celtic, suggested that he might be the goalscorer Tommy Docherty wanted. Docherty agreed – but was unable to buy him. Birmingham were also sliding, in popularity as well as points – only 9,807 people turning up to see them draw 0-0 with Shrewsbury; the gate suggested that their fans were some way from being convinced about their promotion potential. The point was confirmed the following week as Manchester City, with Clive Wilson in superb form in midfield, beat them far more easily in front of 25,369 Maine Road fans than was reflected in the

PFA Divisional Team of the Season
Gennoe (Blackburn) Parker (Fulham), McCarthy (Manchester City), Gilbert (Portsmouth), McDonald (Oxford), Webb (Portsmouth), C. Wilson (Manchester City), D. Wilson (Brighton), Aldridge, Hamilton (Oxford), Wilkinson (Grimsby).

League Table Before Christmas Matches 1984

	P	W	D	L	F	A	Pts
Blackburn	20	13	4	3	42	17	43
Portsmouth	20	11	6	3	33	23	39
Birmingham	20	12	3	5	25	15	39
Oxford	18	11	4	3	41	18	37
Leeds Utd	20	11	2	7	37	25	35
Manchester City	20	10	5	5	29	18	35
Barnsley	19	9	6	4	23	13	33
Grimsby	20	10	3	7	39	32	33
Huddersfield	20	9	4	7	27	26	31
Fulham	20	10	1	9	35	35	31
Brighton	20	8	5	7	20	15	29
Shrewsbury	20	6	7	7	34	32	25
Carlisle	20	7	4	9	37	44	25
Wimbledon	20	7	4	9	37	44	25
Oldham	20	6	4	10	22	39	22
Wolves	20	6	3	11	27	41	21
Sheffield Utd	20	4	8	8	28	34	20
Charlton	19	5	5	9	25	31	20
Crystal Pal	19	4	7	8	25	28	19
Middlesbrough	20	5	4	11	25	37	19
Notts County	19	4	1	14	19	41	13
Cardiff	20	3	2	15	24	46	11

1-0 score. Birmingham lost again a week later at Charlton. Oxford had to settle for draws in consecutive away matches at Shrewsbury and Oldham; but Blackburn – with successive wins over Brighton and Middlesbrough – Portsmouth and Leeds were again on the up, as were Manchester City.

It was all very tight, and by mid-November only six points separated Oxford (top on goal difference from Portsmouth) and Fulham who were in ninth place. A week later the gap widened again. Oxford after being two goals down, rallied to beat Leeds 5-2, Hamilton grabbing two and Aldridge a second-half hat-trick in a thrilling game marred by the sending off of Peter Lorimer and a riot by the rabble masquerading as Leeds fans. Blackburn also won, while Birmingham and Barnsley and Manchester City and Portsmouth could only share the points and so lost ground. A week later it was Oxford's turn for a surprising upset as they lost 1-2 to Notts County. Own goals from Mick Tait and Noel Blake gave Blackburn the points at Portsmouth which took them to the top of the table, and the Lancashire surge was carried on by Manchester City. Jim Melrose had indeed left Celtic, but for Maine Road instead of Molineux, and he immediately began to repay his fee with a flurry of goals to help them win consecutive away matches at Oldham and Charlton. Birmingham, who had made a profitable exchange in selling goalkeeper Tony Coton to Watford and acquiring England Under-21 cap David Seaman from Peterborough to replace him (with no noticeable detriment to their stern defensive qualities), got back on the right track with a 1-0 success at Elland Road to push Leeds further away from the top as Christmas approached. And when Oxford suffered the first of a series of idle Saturdays when their fixture at Barnsley was postponed, Blackburn took full advantage, a 3-0 win at Wolves opening up a three-point lead.

The weekend before Christmas confirmed Blackburn's position. City lost 2-3 at Fulham in an exciting game from which they should have rescued at least a point. Two goals from David Geddis, their signing from Barnsley, gave Birmingham the points at Wimbledon, and Alan Biley (then still in favour at Portsmouth) scored with two dramatic headers in injury time to beat

Oxford 2-1. Blackburn's match at Carlisle was on the Sunday, and they duly won with a Derek Fazackerly penalty to spend Christmas Day firmly at the top. Barnsley,

Probably the classiest full-back in the division, Paul Parker (Fulham) was a member of the divisional team of the season and an almost automatic choice for the England Under-21 side.

Above *Clive Wilson, Manchester City's most creative midfielder, seen here taking on Wimbledon's John Kay (2), proved capable on more than one occasion of turning a match on his own.*

Below *Billy Hamilton's season was blighted by injury and his absence for long periods proved even more damaging to Northern Ireland than to Oxford United. It will be interesting to see how this inspirational veteran fares in Division 1.*

who had not been beaten since September, saw their 15-match run finally ended by Oldham on the same day.

With snow and ice ahead to play havoc with fixtures, Blackburn's tenure at the top was to continue for some weeks. But in retrospect we can see that the holiday period marked the start of their slow decline. The result on Boxing Day did not reveal it, for Blackburn beat Leeds 2-1 before an impressive 20,149 holiday crowd. The scoreline was deceptive for Leeds dominated the match, their football persuading Bobby Saxton to proclaim them the best footballing team in the division. Blackburn had escaped from that somewhat luckily unscathed, but their unbeaten home record lasted only three more days before falling to the next Yorkshire invaders, Huddersfield Town. With only half a team available in the early weeks of the season, Huddersfield had sunk to 19th by the end of September; but as their injured players returned they had begun an impressive surge up the table under Mick Buxton's canny stewardship, and they dominated the Blackburn game for long periods before winning 3-1. To neutrals, Huddersfield looked far the likelier promotion candidates, but their rise was ended promptly on New Year's Day as they went to Grimsby and were torn apart by the Mariners' exciting young strike force of Paul Wilkinson and Gary Lund, going down 1-5.

Oxford had enjoyed a fruitful holiday against struggling teams, beating Cardiff 4-0, Palace 5-0, and earning a much tighter 1-0 victory at Middlesbrough. Birmingham could also be sat-

> **Highest Gate** 47,285: Manchester City v. Charlton Athletic, 12 May '85.
> **Lowest Gate** 2,337: Wimbledon v. Shewsbury Town 27 March '85.

isfied, a home draw with Fulham punctuating a respectable 2-1 win over Grimsby and an eventful match at Bramall Lane, where they beat Sheffield United by the odd goal in seven after a scoreless first half. Portsmouth, however, were going through one of their silly periods after beginning soberly enough on Boxing Day by drawing a typically hard-fought south coast derby away to Brighton. From then on they seemed to imbibe an overdose of goodwill to all men as they crashed 1-4 at Bramall Lane, and returned to Fratton to play like drunken sailors on New Year's Day, drawing 4-4 with Fulham after holding a 4-0 lead at half time. That, it seemed, said much about Portsmouth; but to be strictly fair it was typical of most of the division's leading teams, all of which displayed inconsistency, with the conspicuous exceptions of Oxford and Birmingham.

Although their defeat at Fulham on the Saturday before Christmas had interrupted Manchester City's smooth progress – and their cause was not helped by draws with a dour Barnsley at Maine Road and with Leeds in a more open match at Elland Road – they were still moving promisingly; and as the snow and ice began to bite, and FA Cup matches also intervened, City were to bless their foresight in installing undersoil heating. The weather was kind to them in away matches, too, and on 19 January, with all their rivals except Portsmouth idle, a 3-0 win over Wimbledon took them into third place, two points behind Blackburn and equal on points with second-placed Oxford and fourth-placed Birmingham; they had, however, played more games than all their rivals. Portsmouth were four points further adrift in fifth place; Leeds, who that day had beaten Notts County 5-0 with a Wright hat-trick, were a further two points worse off.

As the weather began to relent, these positions were not to fluctuate markedly, although all the contenders still had wayward moments: Oxford, who lost Hamilton virtually for the rest of the season during their cup defeat by Blackburn, lost at Crystal Palace to give the struggling south Londoners an important boost. City's improving run was ended in embarrassing fashion by Carlisle in front of the TV cameras at Maine Road. And Portsmouth began February by being beaten at home by Charlton.

City's failure proved to be a mere hiccup. At the beginning of March they moved into first place: a goal from Steve Kinsey gave them victory at Blackburn, while on the same day Oxford were comprehensively beaten at the Manor Ground by Birmingham in another match revealing there was little love lost between the two sides. By the middle of the month the bit was firmly between Manchester City's teeth as they thrashed Shrewsbury 4-0 to demolish the Shropshire club's growing belief that they could have a say in the race; then City drew 0-0 at St Andrew's to give themselves a six-point lead over Blackburn, Portsmouth and Birmingham. Oxford were a point further away and many wondered whether they had at last shot their bolt, even though their three games in hand put even City within their range.

Oxford ended such speculation abruptly as they tore City to shreds, two goals from Aldridge giving them a 3-0 victory and City only their second defeat in 12 games. This time, with City's injury crisis growing, the damage inflicted was considerable. City managed to take only two points from five games; these included an Easter Monday defeat by Leeds, who played splendidly before the division's largest crowd of the season, 33,553 at Maine Road, to revive their own fading hopes. Although Oxford had had their own setback, losing 0-3 at Barnsley, they clearly were not to be thwarted. By the end of the Easter programme Portsmouth were on their heels, with City hanging on in third place. But everything was to change yet again, as 13 April proved unlucky for several contenders. Oxford were unaffected, a narrow win at Wolves putting them four points ahead of the field (and making their victims' relegation look a formality). Birmingham, however, stressed their own challenge by winning 3-1 at Portsmouth, while City crashed 1-4 at Grimsby. Blackburn gathered new hope by winning at Cardiff, and Leeds hung on by beating Palace 4-1. The table now read:

	P	Pts
Oxford United	35	70
Birmingham City	36	66
Portsmouth	37	65
Blackburn Rovers	36	64
Manchester City	37	64
Leeds United	37	61

Birmingham and Oxford were in no mood to be halted, and six points apiece in the course of the next week made their promotion almost a formality. Who went up with them was still anybody's guess. Manchester City revived their hopes by at last finding a win and beating Sheffield United; and then they suggested that they had turned the corner finally by winning at Portsmouth — who in the meantime had also lost to the fast-recovering Crystal Palace. Blackburn were still in a topsy-turvy state, beating Middlesbrough, then losing in turn to Palace and Charlton.

Suddenly, Manchester City faltered again over the May Bank Holiday weekend. A frustrating 0-0 draw with Oldham Athletic was followed by a 2-3 defeat at Notts County, their fans rioting as the home side made a brave but unavailing bid to avoid relegation. Portsmouth at last got back into their stride, gaining six points over the weekend, three of them at the expense of Blackburn in a bitterly contested encounter at Ewood Park. Leeds also dropped vital points at Wimbledon. But on the last Saturday of the season five clubs — Manchester City, Portsmouth, Blackburn, Leeds, and Brighton — all stood a chance of joining Oxford and Birmingham in promotion. City, however, had matters in their own hands, and although Portsmouth did all they could by winning at Huddersfield, City's superior goal difference took them through as they thrashed Charlton Athletic 5-1.

It was equally tense at the bottom, as Cardiff City, Notts County, and Middlesbrough waited to see which one would escape joining poor doomed Wolves in Division 3. Middlesbrough made it with an impressive 2-0 win at Shrewsbury, while Cardiff and Notts County lost at Wimbledon and Fulham.

Hamilton's fellow striker at Oxford United, John Aldridge temporarily lost form in his partner's absence. But he soon regained his appetite for goals and finished not only as top scorer in the Division but as his club's highest-ever scorer in a season.

Final Table

	P	HOME					AWAY					Pts
		W	D	L	F	A	W	D	L	F	A	
Oxford Utd	42	18	2	1	62	15	7	7	7	22	21	84
Birmingham C.	42	12	6	3	30	15	13	1	7	29	18	82
Manchester C.	42	14	4	3	42	16	7	7	7	24	24	74
Portsmouth	42	11	6	4	39	25	9	8	4	30	25	74
Blackburn R.	42	14	3	4	38	15	7	7	7	28	26	73
Brighton	42	13	6	2	31	11	7	6	8	23	23	72
Leeds Utd	42	12	7	2	37	11	7	5	9	29	32	69
Shrewsbury T.	42	12	6	3	45	22	6	5	10	21	31	65
Fulham	42	13	3	5	35	26	6	5	10	33	38	65
Grimsby T.	42	13	1	7	47	32	5	7	9	25	32	62
Barnsley	42	11	7	3	27	12	3	9	9	15	30	58
Wimbledon	42	9	8	4	40	29	7	2	12	31	46	58
Huddersfield T.	42	9	5	7	28	29	6	5	10	24	35	55
Oldham Ath.	42	10	4	7	27	23	5	4	12	22	44	53
Crystal Pal.	42	8	7	6	25	27	4	5	12	21	38	48
Carlisle Utd	42	8	5	8	27	23	5	3	13	23	44	47
Charlton Ath.	42	8	7	6	34	30	3	5	13	17	33	45
Sheffield Utd	42	7	6	8	31	28	3	8	10	23	38	44
Middlesbrough	42	6	8	7	22	26	4	2	15	19	31	40
Notts County	42	6	5	10	25	32	4	2	15	20	41	37
Cardiff C.	42	5	3	13	24	32	4	5	12	23	37	35
Wolves	42	5	4	12	18	32	3	5	13	19	47	33

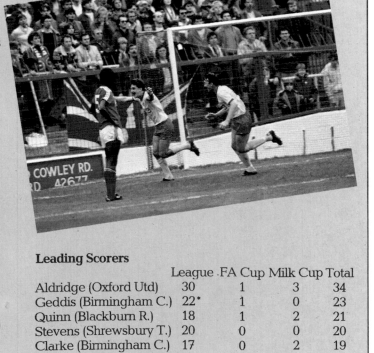

Leading Scorers

	League	FA Cup	Milk Cup	Total
Aldridge (Oxford Utd)	30	1	3	34
Geddis (Birmingham C.)	22*	1	0	23
Quinn (Blackburn R.)	18	1	2	21
Stevens (Shrewsbury T.)	20	0	0	20
Clarke (Birmingham C.)	17	0	2	19
Harkouk (Notts County)	14	1	4	19

*includes 10 for Barnsley

DIVISION 3

The events of another exciting and satisfying Division 3 season were almost obliterated by the fire which engulfed the stand of the champions, Bradford City, on the last Saturday of the season. The ghastly inferno claimed over 50 lives, with many others receiving terrible burns, and turned what should have been a triumphant celebration into the starkest day of tragedy in English football history. It was first and foremost a human tragedy for the victims, their friends and families, and any account which failed to acknowledge that would be failing in its duty. It also had worrying implications for the majority of the clubs in the two lower divisions, which had not been required to conform to the Safety of Sports Grounds Act, but who now were faced with the fact that vast expenditure would be vital if they were to make their own, equally vulnerable grounds safe. It was also another stunning blow for a game under pressure from all sides as a result of another wave of hooliganism, in which, sadly, the good name of one of the other promoted clubs, Millwall, had again suffered grievously at the hands of thugs, claiming to be Lions supporters, who rioted at Luton during the 6th round FA Cup tie.

It was impossible not to feel sympathy for the officials and players of both clubs. Bradford had received the championship trophy before the game against Lincoln, a prize which testified to the great efforts of their go-ahead chairman Stafford Heginbotham (who had rescued City from liquidation two years earlier) as well as to the efforts of their

players and their impressive young management team of Trevor Cherry and Terry Yorath. With Hull the second team to claim a promotion spot it had seemed like a good season for Yorkshire until the catastrophe of 11 May. Millwall, whose late run took them through to claim second place, deserved better than the continuing notoriety over which they had no control.

Bradford had dominated the division for much of the season. They went to the top in November and moved implacably on to promotion, which they had made certain of by mid-April. They wre returning to Division 2 for the first time since 1937. With Bobby Campbell – whose sale to and return from Derby had shown a healthy, and much needed, profit – upsetting every defence in the division with his aggressive, physical presence; with the promising midfielder Stuart McCall, who was picked for the England Under-21 squad before deciding to throw in his lot with Scotland; and with wise guidance form Cherry and Yorath, City were a formidable team, never allowing opponents to settle, and going for the killing thrust at every opportunity.

Another raw-boned centre-forward, Billy Whitehurst, played an equally important part in East Yorkshire's accompanying success at Hull City. After the heart-ache of the failure by one goal to win promotion the previous season, and then manager Colin Appleton's possibly ill-fated decision to go to Swansea, it would have surprised no-one if Hull had spent 1984/5 season suffering a monumental hangover. In his first year as manager, however, Brian Horton ensured that this time there would be no mistakes, and his well-drilled outfit kept their nerve with total conviction on the run-in. Peter Skipper lived up to his name, proving a rock at centre-half and scoring the goal which made promotion certain at Walsall in May. Steve McLaren and Billy Askew showed a touch and imagination few rivals could match in midfield, and in goal Tony Norman fully deserved his selection as the best in the division.

Millwall manager George Graham's shrewd activity in the transfer market, as he quickly built virtually a new team after deciding the squad he had inherited was not good enough, paid off rapidly. Anton Otulakowski added subtlety to the midfield; John Fashanu, the more-famous Justin's younger brother, ensured that the London sophisticates had a powerhouse centre-forward to rival any in the hard north; and Dave Cusack's power in the air was as dangerous in opposing penalty

Peter Skipper, Hull City's aptly named captain, led by forceful example in the club's most impressive season for years, and he fully earned his place as a member of the PFA divisional team.

areas as it was reliable in Millwall's own. But Graham's most rewarding decision was, as he willingly confessed, born of desperation: the switching of the Welsh Under-21 midfielder Steve Lovell to a striking role. Lovell, whose career had been going backwards after his early promise with Crystal Palace, took to his new position with relish, and his goals were a major factor in Millwall's exciting season. The club certainly needed Lovell's contribution, for Gillingham and the two Bristol clubs proved powerful adversaries. Gillingham, who had neither the resources nor the potential (nor, be it said, the embarrassment of visits by the Receiver) of some of their rivals, were carefully managed by Keith Peacock, and made the early running, Tony Cascarino quickly catching the attention of Division 1 scouts with his goals and heading ability. Gillingham, though, were not able to establish any sort of lead. The two promoted clubs, York and Doncaster, who subsequently had to settle for cup exploits, gave an early indication of Yorkshire's determination to have a major say in events.

The West Country, too, found much promise in Bristol. Rovers made the initial thrust, their autumn form persuading such an august personage as the Bradford City chairman to proclaim them far and away the outstanding team in the division. By the end of September they were still undefeated and led the division, with Bradford City the most notable of the scalps on their belt. They were not the only West Country team creating headlines, Swansea City already being in dire trouble and soon to dismiss Colin Appleton and turn in desperation to John Bond, a most unlikely manager for a club with their financial restrictions. Plymouth Argyle, too, were attracting headlines; and they deserved to attract crowds, for no-one could accuse them of being dull as they followed a 2-7 thrashing by Bolton with a 6-4 victory over Preston and, most surprising of all, a 3-3 draw at Gillingham as October arrived. By then Hull had inflicted Gillingham's first defeat and, on the same day, York ended Bristol Rovers' apparently unstoppable progress by the only goal of an excellent game.

October was to prove a significant month. Millwall took up the running, raising further doubts about Gillingham's defence with a crushing 4-1 win at Priestfield Road. Bristol City announced their arrival on the scene with a 2-0 win over Gillingham and another by the same margin at York, who also dropped home points to Millwall in a 1-1 draw, and then succumbed to a Bobby Campbell goal at Valley Parade. On both 20 and 27 October point-sharing was in vogue. On the first date Bradford City and Bristol City, Bristol Rovers and Doncaster, York and Millwall all ended up one goal

apiece as Gillingham leaked 5 goals at Brentford and Hull lost 1-3 at Derby before 13,422 fans. A week later the tightness of the struggle showed again. Bristol Rovers and Hull drew 1-1 at Eastville; Millwall and Bristol City had the same result at the Den, thanks to Steve Lovell's 87th minute equaliser; and Bradford City had to wait almost to the final minute for Garry Jackson's equaliser in a 2-2 draw at Gillingham. But all the leaders except Rovers – who went down 0-1 at Wigan – had won in midweek.

As October gave way to November, the jostling for position intensified. A Keith Houchen hat-trick helped York to expose Gillingham's defensive limitations in the most savage manner, the Gills subsiding in tatters 1-7 on the first Saturday of the month. That pushed Gillingham down to 11th. But there was little daylight above them: Hull, in 9th position led Gillingham only on goal difference; the first seven were almost inseparable.

By the end of the month things were becoming a little clearer. Bristol City, showing that their own recovery from liquidation was healthy, gained the most satisfying individual result of the month, beating Rovers 3-0 as Glyn Riley claimed two goals to outshine the more vaunted Rovers striker Paul Randall before 18,672 spectators. It was just like old times at Ashton Gate. But it was the Yorkshire duo of Bradford and Hull who made the more permanent progress, Hull going through the month with a string

Ian Snodin, in whom many big clubs have shown an interest, continued to run Doncaster's midfield to good purpose. He was ever-present in England's Under-21 side, for whom he is seen here in the match against Romania in May 1985.

PFA Divisional Team of the Season
Norman (Hull), Forrest (Rotherham), Skipper (Hull), Cusack (Millwall), Mower (Walsall), I. Snodin (Doncaster), McCall (Bradford), Williams (Bristol Rovers), Campbell (Bradford), Davison (Derby).

Leading Scorers	League	FA Cup	Milk Cup	FRT*	Total
Tynan (Plymouth A.)	31	1	0	0	32
Senior (Reading	22	4	1	0	27
Lovell (Millwall)	21	4	2	0	27
Walsh (Bristol C.)	19	1	2	4	26
Davison (Derby Cty)	24	0	0	2	26
Campbell (Bradford C.)	23	3	0	0	26

*Freight Rover Trophy

League Table Before Christmas Matches 1984

	P	W	D	L	F	A	Pts
Bradford C.	20	13	4	3	31	14	43
Hull	21	10	8	3	34	20	38
Rotherham	20	11	5	4	32	19	38
Gillingham	20	11	3	6	36	33	36
Millwall	20	10	5	5	35	24	35
Bristol R.	19	10	5	4	30	19	35
Bournemouth	20	9	5	6	22	15	32
Derby County	20	9	5	6	30	24	32
York	20	9	4	7	37	31	31
Bristol C.	20	8	6	6	30	25	30
Doncaster	20	8	4	8	34	30	28
Walsall	19	7	7	5	25	21	28
Reading	20	8	4	8	26	31	28
Brentford	20	7	5	8	24	26	26
Wigan	20	6	8	6	22	25	26
Newport	21	6	7	8	24	28	25
Plymouth	20	6	6	8	32	38	24
Bolton	20	7	2	1	34	32	24
Lincoln	20	5	7	8	27	25	22
Burnley	20	5	7	8	29	33	22
Preston	20	6	2	12	26	50	20
Swansea	20	4	3	13	24	42	15
Orient	20	4	2	14	23	41	14
Cambridge Utd	20	2	4	14	18	39	10

Rumbustious striker Bobby Campbell made a welcome return to Bradford City's colours. He put himself about to good effect in the Bantams' triumphant campaign, finishing sixth in the divisional League goal tally.

of victories, including a see-saw 5-4 defeat of struggling Orient at Brisbane Road, to move into third place, if only temporarily. Bradford did even better, a brace from Greg Abbot taking them to the top as they beat erstwhile leaders Millwall 3-1 at home.

No-one could match their consistency as they dismissed Bournemouth, Reading and Lincoln in subsequent weeks. Millwall recovered long enough to beat Burnley, but then a home draw with Hull provided their only point in three games leading up to Christmas. Rotherham showed more resilience, and Hull refused to be shaken off. In the aftermath of the Bristol derby Rovers responded to the spur, but City failed to build on their victory. Bradford began the Christmas matches with a five-point lead.

The holiday period began inauspiciously for them as a Glyn Snodin goal gave Doncaster's youngsters an encouraging win at Bradford. Rotherham stumbled, giving Swansea a Christmas box of three points at Vetch Field before going down to Bradford on New Year's Day. Gillingham wasted the advantage gained by their see-saw 3-2 win over Derby and an impressive 4-1 defeat of Bristol Rovers by a poor performance at Bournemouth. Hull, however, proved sterner foes, 2-1 wins over York and Bristol City maintaining their momentum. But even

Hull could not match the pace Bradford were setting. By the end of January Bradford's lead had stretched to seven points. Hull were second, with Gillingham and Rotherham still on their tails, and Millwall (caught up in Cup-ties and the bad weather) six points behind second place.

The first week of February did nothing to encourage Bradford's pursuers, only Millwall winning. Gillingham gained a point at home to Swansea thanks to a 90th-minute equaliser from Martin Robinson. The two Bristols, Hull and Rotherham all lost, Rotherham by a humiliating 0-7 margin to struggling Burnley. With a defeat the previous week by Bolton, Rotherham's challenge was beginning to run out of steam. Two weeks later, Bradford ended any question about their mastery of the division. In mid-week Bristol Rovers were brushed aside, and on the Saturday they travelled to Hull to give probably their most authoritative display of the season. Before 14,752 fans at Boothferry Park they rode the loss of goalkeeper Eddie McManus after only five minutes, and goals from Don Goodman and Peter Jackson brought a victory which opened their lead at the top to 12 points.

Although Millwall brought them down to earth with a bump the following Saturday, two goals from John Fashanu contributing to a 0-4 defeat, and a week later Gillingham matched them before the TV cameras at Valley Parade, Bradford were never to be caught; they recovered their balance to stride on impressively. The only hiccup came after promotion was assured – a 2-5 home defeat

Final Table

	P	HOME					AWAY					Pts
		W	D	L	F	A	W	D	L	F	A	
Bradford C.	46	15	6	2	44	23	13	4	6	33	22	94
Millwall	46	18	5	0	44	12	8	7	8	29	30	90
Hull C.	46	16	4	3	46	20	9	8	6	32	29	87
Gillingham	46	15	5	3	54	29	10	3	10	26	33	83
Bristol C.	46	17	2	4	46	19	7	7	9	28	28	81
Bristol R.	46	15	6	2	37	13	6	6	11	29	35	75
Derby Cty	46	14	7	2	40	20	5	6	12	25	34	70
York C.	46	13	5	5	42	22	7	4	12	28	35	69
Reading	46	8	7	8	31	29	11	5	7	37	33	69
Bournemouth	46	16	3	4	42	16	3	8	12	15	30	68
Walsall	46	9	7	7	33	22	9	6	8	25	30	67
Rotherham Utd	46	11	6	6	36	24	7	5	11	19	31	65
Brentford	46	13	5	5	42	27	3	9	11	20	37	62
Doncaster R.	46	11	5	7	42	33	6	3	14	30	41	59
Plymouth Argyle	46	11	7	5	33	23	4	7	12	29	42	59
Wigan Ath.	46	12	6	5	36	22	3	8	12	24	42	59
Bolton W.	46	12	5	6	38	22	4	1	18	31	53	54
Newport Cty	46	9	6	8	30	30	4	7	12	25	37	52
Lincoln C.	46	8	11	4	32	20	3	7	13	18	31	51
Swansea C.	46	7	5	11	31	39	5	6	12	22	41	47
Burnley	46	6	8	9	30	24	5	5	13	30	49	46
Orient	46	7	7	9	30	36	4	6	13	21	40	46
Preston N.E.	46	9	5	9	33	41	4	2	17	18	59	46
Cambridge Utd	46	2	3	18	17	48	2	6	15	20	47	21

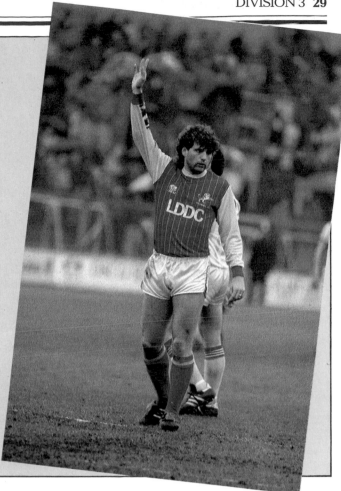

Millwall's promotion prospects took on a rosier glow when manager George Graham gave midfielder Steve Lovell a striking role in partnership with John Fashanu. Lovell (above) scored consistently in League and Cup matches, finishing third on goal tally in the division.

by Reading briefly raising Hull's hopes of grabbing the championship on the first Saturday in May. That hope was dashed immediately, Bobby Campbell fittingly scoring the goal which put Bradford in command at Bolton and made the championship theirs.

Bradford's win at Boothferry Park in February had raised a few doubts in Hull minds, and consecutive away matches with Rotherham and Gillingham produced only one point. By the middle of March Rotherham were beginning to fade; but Millwall (especially after their impressive performance against Bradford), Gillingham and Bristol City were all firmly in contention. But now dog began to eat dog in earnest: as March gave way to April, Gillingham lost to both Bristol City and Millwall, compounding matters with a home draw against Burnley and defeat at Derby; Millwall, too, began to stumble, being beaten by Hull and suffering frustrating goal-less draws at the Den against Rotherham and Reading.

On Easter Monday Hull fell in their turn, going down 0-2 to Bristol City. The following Saturday was to prove eventful. City went down to Rovers in the Bristol derby at Eastville to a goal by Ian Holloway, the outstanding player on the pitch; Millwall and Gillingham also lost, at Preston and Rotherham respectively, while a Whitehurst hat-trick took Hull to a 5-1 win over Orient. This gave them a five-point lead over third-placed Millwall, who however had two games in hand. Hull now had the wind in their sails, and a win at Walsall (Brian Horton's first club) on the first Saturday in May gave them promotion. Millwall made no mistake in joining them, although Bristol City pushed hard until their cause was lost.

At the bottom of the table things were even tighter. Cambridge United, of course, were doomed; but the names of the other three victims were still in doubt on the final Saturday. Orient, who spurned their chance of escape with a 0-0 home draw with Bournemouth, and Preston, in spite of a 1-0 win at York, then joined Cambridge. The final place, however, had still to be decided between John Bond's former and present clubs, Burnley and Swansea City. Both clubs had 46 points, the same as Preston and Orient. Burnley had the better goal difference but Swansea had a game in hand, and if they took a point they would be safe. On the night before the Cup Final, in front of 10,000 spectators, Bristol City were held to a tense 0-0 draw at Vetch Field, and Swansea had avoided falling from Divisions 1 to 4 in successive seasons. Instead, Burnley went down, and John Benson immediately lost his job as manager. It was a sad season for Lancashire, as two of the most famous names in English football tumbled into the basement of the League.

Highest Gate 18,672: Bristol City v. Bristol Rovers, 10 November '84.
Lowest Gate 1,307: Newport County v. Lincoln City, 30 March '85.

DIVISION 4

It was not to be a dramatic year in Division 4, but it provided some heart-warming stories. Romantics were delighted to see once-great Blackpool well on the mend under Sam Ellis after the embarrassment of a re-election bid two years earlier; and there were unmistakable signs of life in the often-linked but dissimilar north-east towns of Darlington and Hartlepool; the success enjoyed by John Duncan at Chesterfield was all the sweeter after his scurvy treatment at Scunthorpe; and memories of happier days at Burnley were evoked by the performances of Martin Dobson and Leighton James in Bury's colours.

There was some cup glory for the division too. Hereford and Stockport could take pride in holding Arsenal and Liverpool to draws in the FA and Milk cups, even if Hereford paid dearly in the replay.

No-one would begrudge Chesterfield their championship, confirmed with a draw at Peterborough on the May Bank Holiday as Bury, the only team which could catch them, slipped to defeat at Tranmere, victims of the division's most prolific striking duo of John Clayton and Colin Clarke. Chesterfield had few individual stars, as the absence of any of their players from the divisional team of the season suggests; but they were an impressive and experienced team. If one individual stood out it was Bob Newton, the club's player of the year, whose goals and aggressive leadership played an important part in their success.

Bury's success was equally pleasing. Player-manager Martin Dobson, in the new role of sweeper, stamped his style on the team throughout, and with the other two Burnley cast-offs Yanek (Joe) Jakub and Leighton James adding a further touch of class, they were probably the best footballing side in the division.

Both will be welcomed back to Division 3; so too will Blackpool, whose attacking commitment gave the Bloomfield Road fans an exciting and ultimately rewarding season after an inconsistent autumn. They had their nervous moments later as a series of injuries meant that the defence, built around the commanding figure of Steve Hetzke, was unsettled. The signing of Eamonn O'Keefe, the Republic of Ireland international forward, proved invaluable on the run in: as the other teams showed signs of faltering, Blackpool got stronger and stronger.

Darlington, the fourth promoted team, were the least experienced, and suffered the greatest tension. But they, too, made it in the end, to give ex-Spurs star Cyril Knowles a fine start to his management career.

The unlucky ones were led by Hereford, who had been in the frame for most of the season and had headed the pack during the early weeks. At the end of September they led on goal difference from Bury, with Chesterfield a point behind, and Darlington and Blackpool in mid-table. As October began Darlington lost the north-east derby at home to Hartlepool, who had already shown that this year they were not going to be involved in the re-election stakes, and whose fans were responding enthusiastically to the first signs of success. That was a rare failure by Darlington, however, as they held out for a point from a 0-0 draw at Chesterfield, won thrillingly 4-3 at Aldershot, and put four past one of the pre-season favourites, Colchester, without reply. By the beginning of November Darlington had moved up to fourth place with 27 points from 14 games, two less than Chesterfield and Hereford and three behind leaders Bury. Blackpool were still four points adrift, but a 4-1 win at Southend was a sign that their illuminations were beginning to flicker on. Temporarily, however, they blacked out as John Wile's Peterborough beat them and they also lost at Hereford for the gap between them and the leaders to increase to nine points by the end of the month. Bury had also dropped surprising points in draws with local rivals Rochdale and Crewe Alexandra, and Chesterfield had taken over the top spot when they ended Tranmere's promising run with

Eamonn O'Keefe's signing during the season proved an excellent investment for Blackpool, who made a welcome return from the basement of the League. Here O'Keefe, awarded a cap for the Republic of Ireland, tangles with Terry Butcher in the friendly against England at Wembley.

a 4-2 victory at Saltergate.

Darlington were now the form team, however, and another tight performance saw them win 1-0 at Hereford. By the end of November they were only one point behind Chesterfield and on 15 December they moved to the top with a 2-0 win at Port Vale (never an easy place for visitors) as Bury crashed 0-3 at Wrexham and Chesterfield could only draw at Crewe. Blackpool again showed their taste for visits to rival seaside resorts with a 2-0 win at Torquay.

Hereford were still keeping Darlington company, and with the prize of a cup ticket for the match with Arsenal as an incentive, 8,536 people (the biggest crowd at Edgar Street for seven years and more than double their average attendance) turned up to see Stuart Phillips score the winner against Aldershot on Sunday before Christmas to take them back to the top of the table.

At the other end of the table there was the extraordinary sight of Wrexham propping up the rest, with the perennial strugglers Halifax, Rochdale, Hartlepool and Crewe all out of the bottom four.

Steve Kendal (centre) was an important cog in Chesterfield's well-oiled machine, which was ably managed by John Duncan.

League Table Before Christmas Matches 1984

	P	W	D	L	F	A	Pts
Hereford	20	13	3	4	33	14	42
Darlington	20	11	8	1	29	12	41
Bury	20	12	5	3	33	18	41
Chesterfield	19	11	6	2	36	18	39
Blackpool	21	11	5	5	33	22	38
Tranmere	20	11	1	8	38	32	24
Peterborough	20	10	4	6	28	22	34
Colchester	20	9	5	6	38	33	32
Crewe	21	10	2	9	32	33	32
Hartlepool	20	6	7	5	24	23	31
Swindon	20	8	5	7	26	26	29
Port Vale	20	7	6	7	23	22	27
Scunthorpe	19	6	7	6	32	27	25
Southend	21	6	7	8	31	39	25
Mansfield	19	6	6	7	13	13	24
Stockport	20	6	5	9	25	34	23
Rochdale	20	4	7	9	19	28	19
Halifax	18	6	1	11	13	28	19
Aldershot	19	5	3	11	24	31	18
Torquay	20	4	6	10	17	29	18
Northampton	20	4	6	10	17	29	18
Exeter	19	3	7	9	20	30	16
Chester	20	3	6	11	18	32	15
Wrexham	18	4	2	12	27	35	14

Whether or not it was the Christmas celebrations or thoughts of their upcoming clash with Arsenal, Hereford could not retain top spot, beginning the holiday period with two draws before beating Southend 3-0. Blackpool and Bury took advantage with three wins, but Darlington fell from grace, losing at Mansfield after their match with Crewe had to be postponed as the season of bad weather arrived. Halifax, of all unlikely candidates, then threw their oar

in, drawing 1-1 at Blackpool and thrashing Bury 4-1 with a Simon Lowe hat-trick before an incredulous Shay.

Bury were also to lose at Colchester in January, but with Chesterfield also dropping points and Darlington's fixtures interrupted by the weather, they were still leading the table at the end of the month on goal difference from Chesterfield, with 50 points from 25 games. Hereford, with a game in hand, and Blackpool were two points behind. Darlington trailed by six, but had played three matches fewer. Peterborough, with 44 points from 26 games, could still be considered in touch, but Colchester and Tranmere, both 10 points adrift, were already dropping out of contention.

February, with a plethora of postponements, did little to clarify the picture, although it began promisingly for Bury as Wayne Entwistle's goal brought them a win over Chesterfield at Saltergate. Darlington crashed out of the FA Cup to non-leaguers Telford United, but bounced back, winning 1-0 at Scunthorpe and, more satisfyingly, 2-1 before 5,950 spectators at Hartlepool, where Carl Airey showed why he was attracting the scouts with the winner in the last minute. Postponements were also hampering Chesterfield's progress in February, and when they did manage to play they wished they hadn't, as they succumbed to a Tony Adcock hat-trick at Colchester. Darlington also suffered on the same day, going down 2-5 to Chester City in one of the most surprising upsets of the season. Both, however, soon recovered.

Highest Gate 8,586: Blackpool v. Hereford Utd, 20 April '85.
Lowest Gate 890: Halifax Town v. Torquay Utd, 30 March '85

Freight Rover Trophy Final: Wigan's Tony Kelly slots in the second goal in the victory against Brentford at Wembley.

back Steve Whitworth his first League goal after more than 600 games).

At Christmas Halifax had been the giant-killers. As Easter approached, Rochdale took over that mantle, beginning by holding Bury 2-2 at Gigg Lane, while Darlington and Hereford drew at Feethams. In mid-week Rochdale went one better, putting the skids under Hereford with a 2-1 away win; and on Easter Saturday they completed their sniping at their betters by taking a point off Blackpool. Chesterfield and Bury were also held to draws at Mansfield and Port Vale, while Darlington collapsed ignominiously at Tranmere, 0-3. Only Hereford gained any encouragement at the beginning of the Easter weekend, beating Colchester 2-1, so virtually extinguishing the Essex club's lingering hopes. Easter Monday and Tuesday were more rewarding for the leaders as Bury and Darlington beat Hartlepool and Mansfield. Blackpool, with two goals apiece from Dave Windridge and John Deary, beat Crewe 6-1, while an 89th minute strike by Greg Walker against Swindon kept Chesterfield at the top. They retained that position the following Saturday as Walker struck again to take the points at Tranmere, while Bury lost to an own goal at Crewe and Darlington rescued a point at Wrexham by the same means.

Then, with rapid finality, things changed. Swindon's players were celebrating the reinstatement of their manager Lou Macari, who had been sacked for disagreements with coach Harry Gregg, and they plunged a knife into Hereford's heart with a 3-0 win at Edgar Street. Wrexham were also showing signs of life and they halted Chesterfield's progress with a 2-0 victory, but another own goal by the home team at Torquay immediately breathed life back into John Duncan's men. There was no recovery for Hereford, who lost what in effect was a six-pointer at Blackpool, the second game in a run which saw them collect only four points from six games.

It was just as well for Darlington, who were also showing signs of promotion jitters, picking up only five points from six games, while Bury's challenge for the championship faded as Chesterfield maintained their momentum to clinch it over the May Bank holiday weekend. Wrexham confirmed their move out of the bottom four with a 3-2 win at Bury, who then lost by the same score at Tranmere; but for the Shakers promotion was ample compensation.

There was still only a whisker separating the leading teams. On 9 March a Trevor Ross penalty gave Bury victory over Blackpool before 7,978 fans at Gigg Lane to put them three points above their victims, who were pushed down to fifth. On the same day Darlington saw off Halifax, who were reduced to eight men as Ces Podd and Alan Knill were sent off and goalkeeper Paddy Roche was carried off. The following Saturday Darlington briefly held a five-point lead, having won one of their backlog of fixtures in mid-week and winning their week-end game as well. Bury's match was postponed, and Hereford, Blackpool and Chesterfield all won.

That pattern did not last even a week as two crucial mid-week matches took place, Bury beating Darlington 1-0 at Gigg Lane and Chesterfield punching a hole in Hereford's armour by a similar scoreline at Edgar Street. On the Saturday Chesterfield reinforced their championship claims when they won 3-1 at Darlington to complete a bad week for the Quakers. None of their other rivals benefitted particularly from Darlington's defeat: Blackpool lost limply at Aldershot; Bury and Hereford had to settle for draws at Southend and Mansfield (where a penalty gave former England full-

Leading Scorers	League	FA Cup	Milk Cup	FRT*	Total
Clayton (Tranmere R.)	31	2	2	1	36
Clarke (Tranmere R.)	21	3	1	4	29
Adcock (Colchester Utd)	24	1	0	3	28
Madden (Bury)	22	1	1	1	25
Cammack (Scunthorpe Utd)	24	1	0	0	25
Phillips (Southend Utd)	20	3	0	0	23

*Freight Rover Trophy

FREIGHT ROVER TROPHY

First-named club is home team in 1st leg.

1st round Port Vale v Northampton Town 1-1, 1-2; Bolton Wanderers v Crewe Alexandra 3-2, 0-0; Burnley v Stockport County 5-1, 1-0; Bury v Chester 1-1, 2-1; Doncaster Rovers v York City 0-0, 0-2; Gillingham v Colchester United 2-2, 0-2; Halifax Town v Darlington 4-1, 0-7; Hull City v Mansfield 2-2, 1-2; Southend United v Millwall 0-2, 1-3; Plymouth Argyle v Bournemouth 2-1, 0-2; Newport County v Exeter City 3-1, 1-1; Orient v Aldershot 0-0, 1-0; Rochdale v Preston North End 2-2, 1-0; Rotherham United v Chesterfield 1-1, 0-1; Scunthorpe United v Bradford City 1-4, 1-2; Swansea City v Bristol Rovers 2-0, 0-0; Torquay United v Swindon Town 1-1, 0-0 (aet; Torquay won 4-3 on penalties); Wrexham v Wigan Athletic 2-2, 1-3; Blackpool v Tranmere Rovers 2-1, 1-4; Derby County v Walsall 1-0, 3-5; Hartlepool United v Lincoln City 2-1, 0-4; Hereford United v Bristol City 1-1, 0-1; Peterborough v Cambridge United 2-1, 0-2; Reading v Brentford 1-3, 0-2.

2nd round Bury 0 Wigan 1; Tranmere Rovers 2 Burnley 2 (aet; Tranmere won 5-4 on penalties); Rochdale 0 Bolton Wanderers 1; York City 1 Chesterfield 0; Bradford City 1 Mansfield Town 2; Bristol City 2 Port Vale 1; Bournemouth 2 Torquay United 1; Millwall 2 Orient 3; Brentford 1 Cambridge United; Walsall 1 Colchester United 0; Newport County 0 Swansea City 0 (aet; Swansea won 4-3 on penalties); Derby County 1 Lincoln City 3.

Quarter-finals Swansea City 0 Brentford 2; Bournemouth 2 Walsall 1; Orient 4 Millwall 2; Bristol City 1 Newport Cty 2; Wigan Ath. 3 Tranmere R. 1; York C. 2 Lincoln C. 3; Bolton W. 2 Darlington 1; Mansfield T. 1 Burnley 1 (aet, Mansfield won 5-3 on pens.).

Semi-finals Bournemouth 2 Brentford 3; Orient 1 Newport Cty 1 (aet, Newport won 4-2 on pens.); Lincoln C. 1 Wigan Ath. 3; Bolton W. 1 Mansfield T. 2).

Southern Final Brentford 6 Newport Cty 0
Northern Final Mansfield T. 1 Wigan Ath. 1 (aet; Wigan won 3-1 on pens.).
Final
Wembley (39,897)

Brentford (0) 1	Wigan Athletic (2) 3
Cooke	Newell, Kelly, Lowe

At the bottom Rochdale and Halifax Town, as in 1984, were involved in a last desperate bid to avoid applying for re-election. This time Rochdale succeeded; but Halifax, in spite of some bold late performances, could not quite escape, Bobby Moore's Southend United finishing safely above them on goal difference. The little West Yorkshire club joined Northampton Town, Torquay United and Stockport County to go cap-in-hand to ask for another chance.

Chesterfield eventually won promotion with points to spare. Here Bob Newton, the club's player of the year, scores the winner in the match at Southend.

Final Table

	P	W	D	L	F	A	W	D	L	F	A	Pts
		HOME					**AWAY**					
Chesterfield	46	16	6	1	40	13	10	7	6	24	22	91
Blackpool	46	15	7	1	42	15	9	7	7	31	24	86
Darlington	46	16	4	3	41	22	8	9	6	25	27	85
Bury	46	15	6	2	46	20	9	6	8	30	30	84
Hereford Utd	46	16	2	5	38	21	6	9	8	27	26	77
Tranmere R.	46	17	1	5	50	21	7	2	14	33	45	75
Colchester Utd	46	13	7	3	49	29	7	7	9	38	36	74
Swindon T.	46	16	4	3	42	21	5	5	13	20	37	72
Scunthorpe Utd	46	14	6	3	61	33	5	8	10	22	29	71
Crewe Alex.	46	10	7	6	32	28	8	5	10	33	41	66
Peterboro' Utd	46	11	7	5	29	21	5	7	11	25	32	62
Port Vale	46	11	8	4	39	24	3	10	10	22	35	60
Aldershot	46	11	6	6	33	20	6	2	15	23	43	59
Mansfield T.	46	10	8	5	25	15	3	10	10	16	23	57
Wrexham	46	10	6	7	39	27	5	3	15	28	43	54
Chester C.	46	11	3	9	35	30	4	6	13	25	42	54
Rochdale	46	8	7	9	33	30	5	7	11	22	39	53
Exeter C.	46	9	7	7	30	27	4	7	12	27	52	53
Hartlepool Utd	46	10	6	7	34	29	4	4	15	20	38	52
Southend Utd	46	8	8	7	30	34	5	3	15	28	49	50
Halifax T.	46	9	3	11	26	32	6	2	15	16	37	50
Stockport Cty	46	11	5	7	40	26	2	3	18	18	53	47
Northampton T.	46	10	1	12	32	32	4	4	15	21	42	47
Torquay Utd	46	5	11	7	18	24	4	3	16	20	39	41

SCOTLAND

Once again Aberdeen dominated the Scottish League with almost contemptuous ease, if anything winning it with even less challenge than they had the previous year and scoring a record number of points for the Premier Division. Rangers fell away after their Skol Cup victory had briefly promised a revival, and Dundee United failed to mount their expected challenge. Only Celtic offered any persistent threat.

Most worrying for Aberdeen's rivals was the way the loss of Gordon Strachan, Mark McGhee and Doug Rougvie from the 1984 championship team was shrugged aside. At the front Eric Black ensured that McGhee was not missed with a series of sparkling displays, ably supported by newcomer Mark McDougall. In midfield Billy Stark took over Strachan's mantle with panache, and scored even more regularly than had the red-headed Manchester United star. With Stuart McKimmie making great strides at full-back alongside new signing Tommy McQueen, Alex Ferguson's rebuilding was successful enough not to be noticed.

Although Aberdeen lived up to their reputation for clever, incisive and, above all, aggressive attacking play, their football was based on solid defensive work, with the strong spine of their trio of experienced internationals, goalkeeper Jim Leighton and centre-halves Alex McLeish and Willie Miller forming a formidable barrier.

Although Roy Aitken and the evergreen Danny McGrain ensured that Celtic, too, had invaluable experience at the back, their goals-against tally showed an important area of difference with Aberdeen. It was

a frustrating time for the Parkhead team, who must have believed that the addition of Maurice Johnston — Watford's goal-scoring sensation who had been homesick in England and had jumped at the chance of joining the club he had idolised as a boy — and Pierce O'Leary, David's younger brother, would enable them to close the gap on the Dons. If anything, it got wider, and their unhappy European experience against Rapid Vienna and the irritation of seeing Rangers lift the Skol Cup, did little to boost their morale until the intervention of Dundee United ensured that at least they did not have to face Aberdeen in the Scottish Cup Final again. Not the least galling thing for Celtic was that they held their own in the league matches with the Dons. But they could not equal Aberdeen's consistency, and silly points dropped to Dumbarton, Morton and Hibernian, teams in the Premier Division's basement, prevented their challenge from sticking.

If Celtic had problems, where did that leave the rest? Dundee United, who had as much talent as any team in the country and matched Manchester United stride for stride in two thrilling UEFA Cup matches, once again failed to sustain their attack on the league championship. Two Cup Finals provided some compensation, but their failure in the Skol final against Rangers once again raised question marks against either the application or the big-match temperament of the team. No-one could question their ability, and on their day they looked the best team in Scotland. Richard Gough, David Narey and Paul Hegarty were a stylish set of defenders in front of either Billy Thomson or the veteran Hamish McAlpine, who refused to allow the arrival of the Scotland number two goalkeeper to discountenance him.

The last of the big four, Rangers, had still less reason for satisfaction, even the presence of the Skol Cup on the Ibrox sideboard offering little consolation for another season in which the club made no impact on the leading positions. Not even Jock Wallace's fiery fundamentalism could inspire a limited team to pursue Aberdeen with any real hope, and questions were again asked whether the parsimony of the Ibrox board was the root cause. Certainly the departure of their captain and defensive rock John McClelland, who moved to Watford soon after the Skol victory in search of greater rewards, coincided with the team's decline from its brief promise of better things. Suggestions at the end of the season that their most exciting forward, Davie

Striker Eric Black was one of the Aberdeen stalwarts who made sure that the Dons' sale of three of their best players did not undermine the successful bid to retain the Premier Division championship. Here Black (left) fends off Celtic's Murdo McLeod in the League match at Parkhead.

Cooper, and the Swedish midfield player Roger Prytz, who had spent the year on monthly contracts, were both uncertaib to re-sign did little to encourage supporters, who over the years have seen a series of their heroes, from Jim Baxter to Jim Bett, leave Scotland's biggest club for more money elsewhere.

No-one, apart from the most diehard of Blues, would want to see a return to the days when Rangers totally dominated Scottish football. But a healthy, competitive Rangers would provide an important boost for the game, and not just in terms of attendances. For the Premier Division, far from making for more competitiveness, has simply gone the way of the old Division 1, with a Super League forming by default. When one of the four super leaguers is lagging, there is little competitiveness at the top. The objectives today of the 'middle-class' clubs – Dundee, Hibernian and Hearts – are, first, to avoid relegation and, second, to have a good enough run to qualify for Europe, with perhaps the odd cup upset thrown in. In these days of inflated expenses, saving discovery of oil (à la Aberdeen) or of an outstanding manager eager to stay and build a substantial club (à la Aberdeen and Dundee United), any higher ambitions are unrealistic.

In the end Hibernian, having flirted with relegation, escaped to safety, goalkeeper Alan Rough playing an important part and getting back into the Scotland party for the World Cup qualifying trip to Seville. Hearts, like their rivals, had their successes against the big four, but ultimately they had to be content to watch Dundee and St Mirren battle it out with Rangers for the prize of a UEFA Cup place.

For Dumbarton and part-timers Morton, even that limited ambition seemed like asking for the moon. In March, with Morton's fate already fixed beyond recall, their outstanding player Jim Duffy put things in perspective. Calling for sponsorship money to be used to enable pro-moted clubs to go 'full-time', Duffy recalled-: 'For one mid-week match this season I found myself finishing work at five o'clock, rushing home to get cleaned up, and then turning out to face Celtic for 90 minutes. What sort of preparation is that? What chance did we have of getting a result?'

Whether sponsorship money is the answer may be debatable, but Morton's story revealed that the problem is undeniable. With over six weeks of the season to go, a 2-7 thrashing by Celtic meant that their goals-against tally had already equalled the highest ever in the Premier Division's history (set by Motherwell in 1978/9). Dumbarton fared better, but even they could not establish a foothold.

Aberdeen led the league from the start, with Rangers on their heels initially. Inevitably Celtic were soon to show that they were the serious threat to the men from Pittodrie, and they stressed the point at the beginning of October, beating Aberdeen 2-1 to suggest that this year the race would be closer. That same month, however, their first chance of challenging the Dons went as they gave Morton's part-timers their most prized scalp, Morton coming back from a goal down to win 2-1. The result cost Celtic the leadership and seemed to suggest that their challenge could not yet be taken seriously.

As December arrived and Aberdeen turned the tables on Celtic with a 4-2 victory to take a five-point lead, that impression seemed confirmed. Christmas is not usually a significant footballing holiday in Scotland, but the Christmas and New Year period was to throw things into the balance again, as Dundee United made a charge to hint that they, too, intended to have a say in the destination of the championship. Faced with two matches against Aberdeen and one against Celtic in the 10-day period, United's holiday looked tough indeed. Instead it was to hold out enticing prospects. On 22 December, as the Old Firm match at Parkhead ended in a 1-1 draw, United's

St Mirren's Steve Clarke (left) disputes possession with Celtic's Paul McStay. The Buddies achieved a respectable fifth place in the Premier Division, equal on points with Rangers. Celtic, although comfortably second, finished seven points adrift of Aberdeen.

PREMIER DIVISION
League Table Before Christmas Matches 1984

	P	W	D	L	F	A	Pts
Aberdeen	19	15	2	2	42	12	32
Celtic	19	12	5	2	45	17	29
Rangers	19	8	9	2	22	10	25
Dundee United	19	9	4	6	34	22	22
St Mirren	19	8	2	9	23	32	18
Hearts	19	7	2	10	21	33	16
Dumbarton	19	4	6	9	20	25	31
Dundee	19	5	4	10	25	31	14
Hibernian	19	3	5	11	17	34	11
Morton	19	4	1	14	21	54	9

DIVISION 1
League Table Before Christmas Matches 1984

	P	W	D	L	F	A	Pts
Airdrie	20	11	4	5	37	24	26
Clydebank	20	10	6	4	32	21	26
Falkirk	21	11	2	8	47	42	24
Forfar Ath.	20	9	5	6	37	26	23
Hamilton Ac.	20	9	4	7	25	25	22
Motherwell	20	9	3	8	32	28	21
Clyde	20	7	7	6	32	29	21
Brechin C.	20	8	4	8	28	29	20
East Fife	20	5	8	7	30	29	18
Ayr Utd.	20	6	6	8	26	31	18
St Johnstone	20	7	3	10	33	37	17
Kilmarnock	20	6	4	10	19	37	16
Meadowbank Th.	21	4	7	10	28	36	15
Partick Th.	20	5	5	10	23	35	15

DIVISION 2
League Table Before Christmas Matches 1984

	P	W	D	L	F	A	Pts
Alloa Ath.	19	11	5	3	34	15	27
Montrose	19	12	3	4	26	20	27
Dunfermline	19	10	6	3	32	15	26
Cowdenbeath	19	8	4	7	35	25	20
Stranraer	18	9	2	7	31	27	20
Stenhousemuir	19	7	6	6	23	27	20
Raith R.	19	7	5	7	29	28	19
Stirling A.	19	5	8	6	29	23	18
Berwick R.	19	5	7	7	21	20	17
Queen of the South	19	5	6	8	25	29	16
Queen's Park	19	6	3	10	25	32	15
Albion R.	17	6	1	10	19	35	13
E. Stirling	18	2	8	8	19	29	12
Arbroath	19	4	4	11	16	39	12

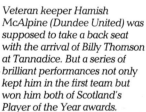

Veteran keeper Hamish McAlpine (Dundee United) was supposed to take a back seat with the arrival of Billy Thomson at Tannadice. But a series of brilliant performances not only kept him in the first team but won him both of Scotland's Player of the Year awards.

Richard Gough put a dent in Aberdeen's image by heading home an Eamonn Bannon cross for the only goal of the game. The combination repeated the performance to get the winners against Celtic and in the return with the Dons – and suddenly it

seemed the Premier title was up for grabs. Aberdeen's lead over Celtic had been cut to two points, and although United were still seven points adrift, in their current form few would bet against them catching up.

Such dreams lasted until the first Saturday in January, when the weather and United's inability to sustain a run combined to smile on Aberdeen. While the Dons were beating Hibs 2-0, Celtic's match with Morton was a weather victim and United proved their own worst enemies, going down 0-1 to St Mirren. The weather continued to smile on Pittodrie as the snow and ice made its presence felt more seriously elsewhere, so that by mid-February their lead over Celtic, who had three games in hand, had increased to nine points. Celtic then made their bid, and it looked a serious one. Morton were beaten 4-0 in a rearranged match, and on 23 February goals from Johnston and McStay gave them a 2-0 win over Aberdeen, cutting the gap to five points with two games in hand. It really seemed that a race was beginning in earnest. But Celtic had again flattered to decieve. Although an away draw with Dundee United the following week was an acceptable result, it allowed Aberdeen, who won, to increase their lead. Worse was to follow, as Celtic lost limply at home to Hibernian. The gap had widened again, this time irretrievably; and although Aberdeen had to wait unti 28 April, when a home draw with their closest rivals meant their championship was finally confirmed, it had seemed inevitable long before then.

If Aberdeen were the team of the season in the Premier Division, Motherwell were the Division 1 supremos, under Tommy McLean (brother of Dundee United's redoubtable Jim and of the less-fortunate Willie at Morton). McLean achieved a notable double, for the previous season he had led Morton to promotion before leaving the post for his brother. Motherwell began without fanfares, and at Christmas they were safely set in mid-table, six points behind leaders Airdrie and Clydebank. Airdrie, however, fell away and a fine second half to the season saw Motherwell clinch promotion – a goal from Andy Walker 15 minutes from time in their penultimate match against Brechin seeing them home. Clydebank made sure of promotion on the

Final Tables

PREMIER DIVISION

		HOME					AWAY					
	P	W	D	L	F	A	W	D	L	F	A	Pts
Aberdeen	36	13	4	1	49	13	14	1	3	40	13	59
Celtic	36	12	3	3	43	12	10	5	3	34	18	52
Dundee Utd	36	13	2	3	47	18	7	5	6	20	15	47
Rangers	36	7	6	5	21	14	6	6	6	26	24	38
St Mirren	36	10	2	6	29	24	7	2	9	22	32	38
Dundee	36	9	3	6	25	19	6	4	8	23	31	37
Hearts	36	6	3	9	21	26	7	2	9	26	38	31
Hibernian	36	5	4	9	23	30	5	3	10	15	31	27
Dumbarton	36	4	4	10	17	29	2	3	13	12	35	19
Morton	36	3	1	14	18	44	2	1	15	11	56	12

DIVISION 1

		HOME					AWAY					
	P	W	D	L	F	A	W	D	L	F	A	Pts
Motherwell	39	11	4	4	34	14	10	4	6	28	22	50
Clydebank	39	11	4	4	31	16	6	10	4	26	21	48
Falkirk	39	9	3	7	36	31	10	4	6	29	23	45
Hamilton A.	39	8	5	7	23	24	8	6	5	25	25	43
Airdrie	39	11	1	7	43	33	6	7	7	27	26	42
Forfar Ath.	39	9	7	4	27	18	5	6	8	27	31	41
Ayr Utd	39	9	6	5	31	25	6	3	10	26	27	39
Clyde	39	9	5	6	31	26	5	6	8	16	22	39
Brechin C.	39	7	5	8	25	28	7	4	8	24	29	37
East Fife	39	6	6	8	26	25	6	6	7	29	31	36
Partick Th.	39	8	5	6	28	22	5	4	11	22	33	35
Kilmarnock	39	8	8	4	23	23	4	2	13	19	38	34
Meadowbank Th.	39	5	5	9	25	33	6	5	9	25	33	32
St Johnstone	39	5	5	9	25	33	6	1	13	28	45	25

DIVISION 2

		HOME					AWAY					
	P	W	D	L	F	A	W	D	L	F	A	Pts
Montrose	39	11	5	3	29	21	11	4	5	28	19	53
Alloa Ath.	39	9	6	4	29	17	11	4	5	29	23	50
Dunfermline Ath.	39	7	9	4	34	20	10	6	3	27	16	49
Cowdenbeath	39	10	5	4	36	17	8	6	6	32	22	47
Stenhousemuir	39	9	6	5	27		6	9	4	18	18	45
Stirling A.	39	8	7	4	33	22	7	6	7	29	25	43
Raith R.	39	9	1	9	30	25	9	5	6	39	32	42
Queen of Sth.	39	6	7	7	27	25	4	7	8	15	31	34
Albion R.	39	7	2	11	27	39	6	6	7	22	33	34
Queen's Park	39	7	5	7	24	19	5	4	11	24	36	33
Stranraer	39	5	8	7	21	22	3	7	9	17	31	31
Berwick R.	39	5	7	7	18	20	3	5	12	18	29	28
Arbroath	39	6	5	9	22	28	3	2	14	13	38	25

Above *Maurice Johnston (ex-Watford) put in a series of brilliant early season performances for Celtic and Scotland.*

Below *Paul Sturrock (Dundee United) was again a key member of what was often the most exciting attacking force in Scottish football.*

same day, beating doomed St Johnstone. That first Saturday in May was to prove conclusive also for Meadowbank Thistle, whose home defeat by Hamilton, coupled with Kilmarnock's victory over Clyde, condemned them to relegation.

Montrose, who had held a slight advantage in a three-team scrap at the top of Division 2 for much of the season, had already made sure of replacing them, and an uninspiring 0-0 draw with Stenhousemuir earned them the championship on that same day. The battle for second place, however, still had a little life left in it as the two contenders, Alloa Athletic and Dunfermline Athletic, also drew 0-0, to leave Alloa with a point advantage but inferior goal difference.

With Alloa's final match away to Arbroath, while Dunfermline were at home to Berwick, the expectation was that Dunfermline would squeeze out the Wasps. They duly beat Berwick 2-1, but it did them no good as Alloa won 1-0 at Arbroath to claim the other Division 1 spot.

FA CUP

1st round
Bangor City v Tranmere Rovers 1-1, 0-7
Barry Town v Reading 1-2
Blackpool v Altrincham 0-1
Bradford City v Tow Law Town 7-2
Brentford v Bishop's Stortford 4-0
Bristol Rovers v King's Lynn 2-1
Buckingham v Orient 0-2
Burton Albion v Staines 2-0
Cambridge United v Peterboro' United 0-2
Dagenham v Swindon Town 0-0, 2-1 (aet)
Darlington v Chester City 3-2
Exeter City v Enfield 2-2, 0-3
Fisher Athletic v Bristol City 0-1
Frickley Athletic v Stalybridge Celtic 2-1
Gillingham v Windsor & Eton 2-1
Halifax Town v Goole Town 2-0
Hartlepool United v Derby County 2-1
Hereford United v Farnborough 3-0
Hull City v Bolton Wanderers 2-1
Kettering v AFC Bournemouth 0-0, 2-3
Lincoln City v Telford United 1-1, 1-2
Macclesfield v Port Vale 1-2
Mansfield Town v Rotherham United 2-1
Met. Police v Dartford 0-3
Newport County v Aldershot 1-1, 0-4
Northampton Town v VS Rugby 2-2, 1-0
Northwich Victoria v Crewe Alexandra 3-1
Nuneaton v Scunthorpe United 1-1, 1-2 (aet)
Penrith v Burnley 0-9
Plymouth Argyle v Barnet 3-0
Preston North End v Bury 4-3
Rochdale v Doncaster Rovers 1-2
Southend United v Colchester United 2-2, 2-3
  (aet)

The earlier rounds of the Cup were again illuminated by Telford United's capacity not merely to beat but often to outplay League clubs. Having already overcome Lincoln City, Preston North End, and Bradford City, they comfortably disposed of Darlington in a replay to reach the 5th round. Here David Mather scores Telford's first in the return match against the Quakers.

Stockport County v Walsall 1-2
Swansea City v Bognor Regis 1-1, 1-3
Torquay United v Yeovil 2-0
Weymouth v Millwall 0-3
Whitby Town v Chesterfield 1-3
Wrexham v Wigan Athletic 0-2
York City v Blue Star 2-0

No fewer than six non-league clubs eliminated League teams, Altrincham and Dagenham both winning away from home. Notable names scored the decisive goals for them: Mike Fagan, son of Liverpool's Joe, for Altrincham at Blackpool, and Les Whitton, brother of West Ham's Steve, for Dagenham in their replay at Swindon. Defeat was particularly embarrassing for Swansea, a Division 1 club two years previously, and Exeter City, who were outplayed by Enfield.

2nd round
Aldershot v Burton Albion 0-2
Altrincham v Doncaster Rovers 1-3
Bradford City v Mansfield Town 2-1
Brentford v Northampton Town 2-2, 0-0
  (abandoned after 26 mins) 2-0
Bristol City v Bristol Rovers 1-3
Burnley v Halifax Town 3-1
Colchester United v Gillingham 0-5
Dagenham v Peterboro' Utd 1-0
Darlington v Frickley 1-0
Dartford v AFC Bournemouth 1-1, 1-4
Hartlepool United v York City 0-2
Millwall v Enfield 1-0
Orient v Torquay United 3-0
Plymouth Argyle v Hereford United 0-0, 0-2
Port Vale v Scunthorpe United 4-1
Preston North End v Telford United 1-4
Reading v Bognor 6-2
Tranmere Rovers v Hull City 0-3
Walsall v Chesterfield 1-0
Wigan Athletic v Northwich Victoria 2-1

Further triumphs for Dagenham and Telford, plus an outstanding win away to Aldershot by Burton Albion, who were to make even bigger headlines in the next round. Winning 4-1 away to a famous Division 3 team emphasised just what an accomplished side Telford were. Peterboro' protested in vain that their tie at Dagenham finished five minutes early. There was a Bristol derby at this stage for the second season running. City, winners last year, finished well beaten.

3rd round
Barnsley v Reading 4-3
Birmingham City v Norwich City 0-0, 1-1 (aet)
  1-1 (aet) 1-0
Brighton v Hull City 1-0
Bristol Rovers v Ipswich Town 1-2
Burton Albion v Leicester City 1-6 (at Derby) 0-
  1 (at Coventry)

Giant Killings: League clubs knocked out by non-League opposition

Blackpool 0 Altrincham 1 (1st round)
Northwich V. 3 Crewe A. 1 (1st round)
Bognor 3 Swansea C. 1 (1st round rep.)
Enfield 3 Exeter C. 0 (1st round rep.)
Swindon T. 1 Dagenham 2 (1st round rep.)
Telford U. 2 Lincoln C. 1 (1st round rep.)
Aldershot 0 Burton Alb.2 (2nd round)
Dagenham 1 Peterboro' U. 0 (2nd round)
Preston N.E. 1 Telford U. 4 (2nd round)
Telford U.2 Bradford C.1 (3rd round)
Telford U.3 Darlington 0 (4th round rep.)

NOTE Telford went one better than in their 1983/4 Cup campaign, when they beat three League clubs to reach the 4th round.

Everton's Derek Mountfield soars between Luton Town's Steve Foster (headband) and Ricky Hill to score the winner in the Semi-final at Villa Park. Time after time, throughout the season, Mountfield scored match-saving or match-winning goals in both League and Cup games.

Carlisle United v Dagenham 1-0
Chelsea v Wigan Athletic 2-2, 5-0
Coventry City v Manchester City 2-1
Doncaster Rovers v Queen's Park Rangers 1-0
Fulham v Sheffield Wednesday 2-3
Gillingham v Cardiff City 2-1
Hereford United v Arsenal 1-1, 2-7
Leeds United v Everton 0-2
Liverpool v Aston Villa 3-0
Luton Town v Stoke City 1-1, 3-2
Manchester Utd v AFC Bournemouth 3-0
Middlesbrough v Darlington 0-0, 1-2
Millwall v Crystal Palace 1-1, 2-1
Notts County v Grimsby Town 2-2, 2-4
Nottingham Forest v Newcastle United 1-1, 3-1 (aet)
Oldham Athletic v Brentford 2-1
Orient v West Bromwich Albion 2-1
Portsmouth v Blackburn Rovers 0-0, 1-2
Shrewsbury Town v Oxford United 0-2
Southampton v Sunderland 4-0
Telford United v Bradford City 2-1
Tottenham Hotspur v Charlton Athletic 1-1, 2-1
Watford v Sheffield United 5-0
West Ham United v Port Vale 4-1
Wimbledon v Burnley 3-1
Wolverhampton Wanderers v Huddersfield Town 1-1, 1-3
York City v Walsall 3-0

Leicester City v Carlisle United 1-0
Liverpool v Tottenham Hotspur 1-0
Luton Town v Huddersfield Town 2-0
Manchester United v Coventry City 2-1
Nottingham Forest v Wimbledon 0-0, 0-1
Orient v Southampton 0-2
Oxford United v Blackburn Rovers 0-1
Sheffield Wednesday v Oldham Athletic 5-1
West Ham United v Norwich City 2-1
York City v Arsenal 1-0

The match between Burton and Division 1's Leicester was ordered to be replayed after Burton goalkeeper Paul Evans was hit by a nine-inch piece of wood. In the second match, behind closed doors at Coventry's ground, he was beaten only once. So Telford became the last non-league survivors again. QPR went out to Billy Bremner's Doncaster. Orient and Darlington (who had their biggest crowd for 25 years) were other giant-killers.

4th round
Barnsley v Brighton 2-1
Chelsea v Millwall 2-3
Darlington v Telford United 1-1, 0-3
Everton v Doncaster Rovers 2-0
Grimsby Town v Watford 1-3
Ipswich Town v Gillingham 3-2

York produced the shock of the season when Keith Houchen, late of Hartlepool and Orient, knocked out Arsenal with a last-minute penalty, awarded after Steve Williams had held his shirt. Tottenham lost the live-on-TV match to Ian Rush's early goal – their eleventh successive Anfield defeat—and another crucial penalty miss cost Chelsea dear against impressive Millwall. Only two of the 16 ties were drawn. In one replay Wimbledon manager Dave Bassett resumed his stranglehold on Brian Clough's team; and in the other Telford scored three splendid goals to earn a tie against the holders.

5th round
Blackburn Rovers v Manchester United 0-2
Everton v Telford United 3-0
Ipswich Town v Sheffield Wednesday 3-2
Luton Town v Watford 0-0, 2-2 (aet) 1-0
Millwall v Leicester City 2-0
Southampton v Barnsley 1-2
Wimbledon v West Ham United 1-1, 1-5
York City v Liverpool 1-1, 0-7

Although the last of the non-leaguers, Telford, went their gallant way in front of more than 47,000 at Goodison, there were deserved giant-killings by Barnsley, coming from a goal behind, at Southampton, and Millwall at home to Leicester. York played two contrasting games with Liverpool, scoring a late equaliser at home, then suffering devastation in the replay, and Wimbledon got the same treatment from West Ham, for whom Tony Cottee scored three. Luton eventually reversed the previous season's defeat by their greatest rivals Watford.

6th round
Barnsley v Liverpool 0-4
Everton v Ipswich Town 2-2, 1-0
Luton Town v Millwall 1-0
Manchester United v West Ham United 4-2

The holders Everton had luck on their side as they qualified for a record twentieth semi-final. At Goodison they equalised only after Ipswich defender Steve McCall was sent off, then won the replay with a bitterly disputed penalty (by Graeme Sharp) for handball against Russell Osman. Norman Whiteside and Ian Rush scored hat-tricks to put their teams on course for a semi-final collision. Barnsley offered disappointingly tame resistance to Liverpool, conceding the first two goals through defensive errors. Manchester United won an exciting tie against West Ham, who had considered asking for a postponement because of injuries and illness.

Sadly, the other tie will be remembered for some of the worst crowd disorders ever seen on a British ground. Millwall supporters, turning up in greater numbers than had been expected, invaded the pitch before, during and after a game decided by Brain Stein's first-half goal.

Semi-finals
Villa Park (45,289; £256,909)
Everton (0) 2   Luton Town (1) 1(aet)
   Mountfield, Sheedy   Hill
EVERTON Southall, Stevens, Van den Hauwe, Ratcliffe, Mountfield, Reid, Steven, Sharp, Gray, Bracewell, Sheedy
LUTON Sealey, Breacker, Thomas, Turner, Foster, Donaghy, Hill, Stein, Harford (Moss), Nwajiobi, Parker

Cup Crowds: biggest and smallest in each round

1st round
7,431 Hartlepool United v Derby County
1,202 Weymouth v Millwall
2nd round
19,367 Bristol City v Bristol Rovers
2,702 Orient v Torquay United
3rd round
36,877 Liverpool v Aston Villa
3,381 Wimbledon v Burnley
4th round
38,039 Manchester United v Coventry City
8,124 Telford United v Darlington
5th round
47,402 Everton v Telford United
13,485 York City v Liverpool
6th round
46,769 Manchester Utd v West Ham Utd
17,470 Luton Town v Millwall
Semi-finals
51,690 Liverpool v Manchester Utd
45,289 Everton v Luton Town

Having been apparently given the easy option in the draw, Everton made it look notably difficult and were lucky to gain the period of extra-time which they then went on to dominate. Luton, taking time off from their grim relegation battle, controlled the midfield even without Peter Nicholas and David Preece, both of whom were cup-tied. They took the lead when Ricky Hill drove a 20-yard shot in off the post and would have had a more substantial lead but for some excellent saves by Neville Southall.

Ten minutes from the end of normal time Everton were reduced to sending centre-half Derek Mountfield up front, where he earned the free-kick with which Kevin Sheedy defeated not only the defensive wall but Les Sealey, too. Extra-time found Luton struggling to hang on for a replay. They were denied even that when Mountfield got above Steve Foster and Hill to head in another Sheedy free-kick and book a second successive Cup Final appearance.

Goodison Park (51,690; £315,080)
Liverpool (0) 2   Manchester Utd (0) 2(aet)
   Walsh, Whelan Stapleton, Hughes
LIVERPOOL Grobbelaar, Neal, Beglin, Lawrenson, Hansen, Nicol, Dalglish (Gillespie), Whelan, Walsh, MacDonald, Wark
MAN UTD Bailey, Gidman, Albiston, Whiteside, McGrath, Hogg, Robson, Strachan, Hughes, Stapleton, Olsen

A semi-final which had looked as if it might run and run was eventually halted after three and a half hours of ferocious combat when Liverpool, having staged two spectacular late recoveries in the first match, were unable to manage another at Maine Road. The controversy over whether Mark Hughes' winning goal was fractionally offside should not obscure the fact that United thoroughly deserved their victory.

At Goodison they were within four minutes and then one minute off Wembley, only to be hauled back each time. Liverpool, trailing to the 69th minute goal, deflected in by Hughes from Robson's shot, which had enlivened the game after a desperately poor first half, forced extra-time when Ronnie Whelan repeated his 1983 Milk Cup Final goal, curling the ball delicately into the top corner. United recovered so well from what could have been a psychological trauma that Stapleton restored their lead in the first period of extra time. But with only 60 seconds left Rush produced an unusually powerful header from Dalglish's deep cross which Bailey could only push square, substitute Paul Walsh scrambling the ball in.

Four days later Rush's knee trouble forced him to miss the replay, an equally passionate occasion with a better first half,

in which Liverpool went ahead with McGrath's unfortunate headed own goal. They should immediately have doubled the lead, but Nicol pulled his shot wide. Again United responded splendidly, with Robson leading from the middle, surging forward to equalise with a 25-yard outswinger. Twelve minutes later came Hughes decisive goal, with Liverpool adamant that he was offside as he moved onto Strachan's through pass.

Final

Wembley (100,000; £1 million)
Manchester United (0) 1   Everton (0) 0 (aet)
   Whiteside
MANCHESTER UTD Bailey, Gidman, Albiston, (Duxbury), McGrath, Moran, Whiteside, Robson, Strachan, Hughes, Stapleton, Olsen
EVERTON Southall, Stevens, Van den Hauwe, Ratcliffe, Mountfield, Reid, Steven, Sharp, Gray, Bracewell, Sheedy

A disappointing final was trudging towards extra-time and probably a replay when a wholly unexpected intervention ensured that it would remain in both the memory and the record-books. McGrath's rare mistake put Reid briefly clear until he was abruptly halted by Kevin Moran's late challenge. A free-kick was clearly called for; a booking seemed reasonable. But a large majority of the watching millions must have been amazed to see referee Peter Willis sending off Moran, who had to be physically restrained by his team-mates and escorted in tears to the touchline – the first player ever to be dismissed in an FA Cup final.

United reacted magnificently, firmly rejecting the idea of shutting up shop in the hope of a replay, and pushing relentlessly forward to make the only real chances from then on. Whiteside missed one of them; then he cut in from the right, perpetrated a characteristically stiff-legged feint, which momentarily gave him a view of goal past Pat van den Hauwe, and curled a glorious left-footed shot around Southall and inside the far post. Everton, though they could point to Reid's early volley which was luckily deflected by Gidman's shin onto a post, were gracious enough to admit that United deserved victory; in truth they seemed jaded, lacking even the powerful self-belief that had put the skids under the confidence of so many sides in 1984/5. Four days later, after silly talk of official protests and even of handing back the Cup, United were placated when the FA's Challenge Cup committee decided to grant Moran the medal that had been withheld from him in the presentations at Wembley.

Final, Wembley. Main picture: Manchester United's Norman Whiteside (behind Pat van den Hauwe at centre, right) bends a perfectly judged left-foot shot beyond Neville Southall's reach to score the winner. Gordon Strachan is in the centre of picture; at right is Everton skipper Kevin Ratcliffe. Inset: Referee Peter Willis sends off hapless Kevin Moran, while team-mates (from left to right) Strachan, Bryan Robson, and Mark Hughes vainly intercede.

SCOTTISH FA CUP

1st round
Berwick Rangers v Albion Rovers 3-1
Dunfermline Athletic v East Stirling 1-3
Queen of the South v Arbroath 2-1
Stenhousemuir v Whitehall Welfare 2-1
Stranraer v Gala Fairydean 2-2, 1-0
Stirling Albion v Selkirk 20-0

The first round of the Scottish FA Cup is usually the opportunity for a non-league side to make a name for itself, but the amateurs of Selkirk could hardly have wished to do so in such a manner, suffering the heaviest defeat in British first-class football this century, going down 0-20.

2nd round
Alloa Athletic v East Stirlingshire 2-1
Berwick Rangers v Inverness Caledonians 1-1, 3-3(aet), 0-3
Cowdenbeath v Stirling Albion 2-1
Inverness Thistle v Spartans 1-1, 2-1
Keith v Brora Rangers 2-0
Queen of the South v Montrose 3-1
Queen's Park v Raith Rovers 0-0, 2-0
Stranraer v Stenhousemuir 0-0, 2-0

Those teams capable of settling their difference at the first time of asking on 5 January did themselves and everybody else a favour: the icy weather took hold at the beginning of the follow-ing week and protracted delays resulted. Stranraer and Stenhousemuir finally succeeded in getting their replay on 4 February. Pride of place was taken by Inverness Caledonians, who beat Berwick on their own ground in a second replay.

3rd round
Aberdeen v Aloa Athletic 5-0
Airdrie v Falkirk 0-3
Ayr United v Keith 3-1
Brechin City v East Fife 1-1, 4-0
Cowdenbeath v St Mirren 0-4
Dundee United v Hibernian 3-0
Forfar Atheletic v Clydebank 1-0
Hamilton Academical v Celtic 1-2
Heart of Midlothian v Inverness Caledonians 6-0
Inverness Thistle v Kilmarnock 3-0
Meadowbank Thistle v Partick Thistle 4-2
Morton v Rangers 3-3, 1-3
Motherwell v Dumbarton 4-0
Raith Roves v Clyde 2-2, 2-1
St Johnstone v Dundee 1-1, 1-2
Stranraer v Queen of the South 4-6

The most thrilling tie was one of only four to be played on the appointed date—but one of the last two to be settled. Part-timers Morton, the makeweights in the Premier Division, rose to the presence of Rangers and their fans at Capielow to trade blow for blow, coming back from 0-2 and 1-3 down before 12,012 excited spectators. There the dream ended, for Rangers proved too strong in the return at Ibrox. Stranraer found Queen of the South in no mood to mess about and trailed 1-4 at half-time.

4th round
Ayr United v St Mirren 0-1
Brechin City v Heart of Midlothian 1-1, 0-1
Forfar Athletic v Falkirk 2-1
Celtic v Inverness Thistle 6-0
Queen of the South v Dundee United 0-3
Raith Rovers v Aberdeen 1-2
Rangers v Dundee 0-1
Meadowbank Thistle v Motherwell 0-2

Biggest crowd of the round, 26,619, were at Ibrox to see Rangers go out to Dundee for the second season running, showing little resourcefulness as they attempted to come back against Jimmy Brown's ninth-minute goal. Two first half goals saw Aberdeen safely but unexcitingly past Raith, and Dundee United were too strong for Queen of the South. Hearts made heavy weather of Brechin, going through at the second attempt.

5th Round
Dundee v Celtic 1-1, 1-2
Hearts v Aberdeen 1-1, 0-1
Motherwell v Forfar Athletic 4-1
St Mirren v Dundee United 1-4

Stirling Albion put a record 20 goals past Selkirk in the 1st round. Here Stirling's David Thomson is about to score one of the seven he contributed.

The favourites came through, but both Celtic and Aberdeen needed home replays to beat their middle-of-the-table opponents. At Dens Park, before 21,301 fans, Mo Johnston gave Celtic the lead 20 minutes into the second half, but Brown, the scorer of the winner over Rangers, replied five minutes later. In the replay Dundee also equalised Celtic's opening strike rapidly, but when Johnston restored the led with 20 minutes remaining they could not come back a second time. At Tynecastle Aberdeen were behind for nearly half an hour, Eric Black saving them 12 minutes from time, and a single goal from Billy Stark proved enough in the replay.

Semi-finals
Hampden Park (30,536)
Celtic (1) 1   Motherwell (1) 1
  Burns   McAllister
CELTIC Bonner, Reid, McGrain, Aitken, O'Leary, McLeod, Provan, P. McStay, Johnston, Burns, McClair
MOTHERWELL Gardiner, McLeod, Murray, Doyle, Forbes, Boyd, Stewart, McAllister, Harrow, Mauchlen, Blair

Tynecastle Park (18,485)
Dundee United (0)   Aberdeen (0) 0
DUNDEE UTD McAlpine, Malpas, Holt, Gough, Hegarty, Narey, Bannon, Taylor, Kirkwood, Sturrock, Dodds
ABERDEEN Leighton, McKimmie, Cooper, Stark, McLeish, Miller, Black, Simpson, Hewitt, Bell, Cowan

Replays
Hampden Park (30,000)
Celtic (0) 3   Motherwell (0) 0
  Aitken,
  Johnston (2)
CELTIC Bonner, W. McStay, McGrain, Aitken, McAdam, McLeod, Provan, P. McStay, Johnston, Burns, McClair
MOTHERWELL Gardiner, McLeod, Murray, Doyle, Forbes, Boyle, Walker, McAllister, Harrow, Mauchlen, Blair

Tynecastle Park (10,771)
Dundee United (1) 2   Aberdeen (0) 1
  Sturrock, Beedie   Angus
DUNDEE UTD McAlpine, Malpas, Holt, Gough, Beedie, Narey, Bannon, Milne, Kirkwood, Sturrock, Dodds
ABERDEEN Leighton, McKimmie, Cooper, Stark, McLeish, Miller, Black, Simpson, Hewitt, Bell, Cowan (Angus)

In the end, Motherwell's fine run was halted, but it was not until the 73rd minute of the replay that Celtic finally breeched their defence with Aitken's goal. In the first match Celtic had been lucky to survive, a flashing shot from the dangerous Andy Harrow passing inches over the bar in the final minutes after Motherwell had had much the better of the game.

In the other semi-final Aberdeen's bid to win the Cup for the fourth consecutive year came to grief as Dundee United put up one of their best performances. United had been the better team in an error-riddled first match, Davie Dodds giving Alex McLeish and Willie Miller the run-around – but a goal just would not come. In the replay Paul Sturrock put United ahead after only five minutes, and Stuart Beedie ended the Dons' hopes with a second goal after 64 minutes.

Final
Hampden Park (60,346)
Celtic (0) 2   Dundee United (0) 1
  Provan,   Beedie
  McGarvey
CELTIC Bonner, W. McStay, McGrain, Aitken, McAdam, McLeod, Provan, P. McStay (O'Leary), Johnston, Burns (McClair), McGarvey
DUNDEE UTD McAlpine, Gough, Malpas, Beedie (Holt), Hegarty, Narey, Milne, Kirkwood, Sturrock, Dodds, Bannon

A magnificent recovery by Celtic ensured that the club at last had a trophy on the Parkhead sideboard after their recent toils in the shadow of Aberdeen. It left Dundee United in the sad position of beaten finalists in both of the season's cup competitions. The 100th Scottish FA Cup Final showed Celtic heading the list of winners with 27 successes – four more than Rangers.

United, however, took much of the credit in this match; they had looked the more accomplished side for most of the game, and fully deserved their 54th minute lead, brilliantly engineered by Dodds and well taken by Beedie. Then, as time seemed to be running out, a combination of Celtic passion from their supporters and their hero Roy Aitken (who had been sent off in the 1984 final) rallied the side. Aitken, abandoning his wholly defensive role, began to move forward, disrupting the previous dominance of David Narey and Paul Hegarty. With 14 minutes remaining Provan struck home a viciously bending free-kick. United hung on desperately but, with six minutes left, Aitken galloped down the right flank and crossed for McGarvey to head home powerfully.

Cup Final: Celtic celebrate their victory over Dundee United after a game they had looked set to lose until the final quarter of an hour.

MILK CUP

1st round

Aldershot v AFC Bournemouth 4-0, 1-0 (5-0)
Blackpool v Chester City 1-0, 3-0 (4-0)
Bolton Wanderers v Oldham Athletic 2-1, 4-4 (aet) (6-5)
Bradford City v Middlesbrough 2-0, 2-2 (4-2)
Brentford v Cambridge United 2-0, 0-1 (2-1)
Bristol City v Newport County 2-1, 3-0 (5-1)
Burnley v Crewe Alexandra 1-2, 3-0 (4-2)
Crystal Palace v Northampton Town 1-0, 0-0 (1-0)
Darlington v Rotherham United 1-2, 0-4 (1-6)
Derby County v Hartlepool United 5-1, 1-0 (6-1)
Doncaster Rovers v York City 2-3, 0-5 (2-8)
Exeter City v Cardiff City 1-0, 0-2 (1-2)
Gillingham v Colchester United 3-2, 2-0 (5-2)
Halifax Town v Chesterfield 1-1, 2-1 (3-2)
Hereford United v Oxford United 2-2, 3-5 (5-7)
Lincoln City v Hull City 0-2, 1-4 (1-6)
Orient v Southend United 2-1, 0-0 (2-1)
Plymouth Argyle v Torquay United 1-0, 1-0 (2-0)
Portsmouth v Wimbledon 3-0, 0-1 (3-1)
Port Vale v Bury 1-0, 1-2 (aet) (2-2: Port Vale won on away goal)
Reading v Millwall 1-1, 3-4 (4-5)
Scunthorpe United v Mansfield Town 0-1, 2-1 (2-2: Scunthorpe won on away goals)
Sheffield United v Peterboro' United 1-0, 2-2 (3-2)
Stockport County v Rochdale 3-1, 2-1 (5-2)
Swindon Town v Bristol Rovers 1-5, 1-0 (2-5)
Swansea City v Walsall 0-2, 1-3 (1-5)

Tranmere Rovers v Preston North End 2-3, 2-2 (aet) (4-5)
Wrexham v Wigan Athletic 0-4, 0-2 (0-6)

Teams expected to do well in Division 3 were among the goals. York City led the way with eight, John Byrne (soon to be sold to Queen's Park Rangers) scoring a hat-trick against Doncaster; Derby and Hull scored six, Millwall five (though they had to fight against Reading at the Den), and the two Bristol clubs cantered through, even though Rovers managed to lose their home leg against Swindon.

Kevin Wilson scored four of Derby's five at home to Hartlepool in front of the best crowd of the round (9,281), and Oxford, already making their mark in Division 2, had a hat-trickster in Billy Hamilton as Hereford fought bravely at the Manor Ground.

2nd round

Arsenal v Bristol Rovers 4-0, 1-1 (5-1)
Birmingham City v Plymouth Argyle 4-1, 1-0 (5-1)
Blackburn Rovers v Oxford United 1-1, 1-3, (2-4)
Brighton v Aldershot 3-1, 0-3 (aet) (3-4)
Bristol City v West Ham United 2-2, 1-6 (3-8)
Charlton Athletic v Notts County 0-1, 0-2 (0-3)
Chelsea v Millwall 3-1, 1-1 (4-2)
Fulham v Carlisle United 2-0, 2-1 (4-1)
Gillingham v Leeds United 1-2, 2-3 (3-5)
Grimsby Town v Barnsley 3-0, 1-1 (4-1)
Halifax Town v Tottenham Hotspur 1-5, 0-4 (1-9)
Ipswich Town v Derby County 4-2, 1-1 (5-3)
Leicester City v Brentford 4-2, 2-0 (6-2)
Manchester City v Blackpool 4-2, 3-1 (7-3)
Manchester United v Burnley 4-0, 3-0 (7-0)
Newcastle United v Bradford City 3-1, 1-0 (4-1)
Orient v Luton Town 1-4, 1-3 (2-7)
Portsmouth v Nottingham Forest 1-0, 0-3 (aet) (1-3)
Port Vale v Wolverhampton Wanderers 1-2, 0-0 (1-2)
Preston North End v Norwich City 3-3, 1-6 (4-9)
Scunthorpe United v Aston Villa 2-3, 1-3 (3-6)
Sheffield United v Everton 2-2, 0-4 (2-6)
Sheffield Wednesday v Huddersfield Town 3-0, 1-2 (4-2)
Shrewsbury Town v Bolton Wanderers 2-2, 1-2 (3-4)
Southampton v Hull City 3-2, 2-2 (5-4)
Stockport County v Liverpool 0-0, 0-2 (aet) (0-2)
Stoke City v Rotherham United 1-2, 1-1 (2-3)
Sunderland v Crystal Palace 2-1, 0-0 (2-1)
Walsall v Coventry City 1-2, 3-0 (4-2)
Watford v Cardiff City 3-1, 0-1 (4-2)
Wigan Athletic v West Bromwich Albion 0-0, 1-3 (1-3)

Semi-final, second leg: Chelsea, out to avenge a 0-2 beating in the first leg at Roker Park, found Sunderland (and especially old Stamford Bridge hand Clive Walker) in no mood to go quietly. The visitors' keeper Chris Turner, who had a tremendous Milk Cup campaign, here beats Chelsea's Doug Rougvie to a high cross.

York City v Queen's Park Rangers 2-4, 1-4 (3-8)

The holders Liverpool spent an embarrassing 187 minutes trying to score against Division 4's Stockport before Michael Robinson and Ronnie Whelan finally broke through in extra time at Anfield, Walsall, beaten by Liverpool in the semi-final the previous season, scored a stunning 3-0 win at Coventry after losing their home leg; and Stoke's wretched start to the season was compounded against Rotherham.

3rd round
Birmingham City v West Bromwich Albion 0-0, 1-3
Ipswich Town v Newcastle United 1-1, 2-1
Leeds United v Watford 0-4
Luton Town v Leicester City 3-1
Manchester City v West Ham United 0-0, 2-1
Manchester United v Everton 1-2
Norwich City v Aldershot 0-0, 4-0
Nottingham Forest v Sunderland 1-1, 0-1 (aet)
Notts County v Bolton Wanderers 6-1
Oxford United v Arsenal 3-2
Queen's Park Rangers v Aston Villa 1-0
Rotherham United v Grimsby Town 0-0, 1-6
Sheffield Wednesday v Fulham 3-2
Southampton v Wolverhampton Wanderers 2-2, 2-0
Tottenham Hotspur v Liverpool 1-0
Walsall v Chelsea 2-2, 0-3

After four years of success in the League Cup and then Milk Cup, Liverpool were finally beaten by a Clive Allen goal at White Hart Lane, keeper Bruce Grobbelaar being blamed for it by his manager. To add to Tottenham's joy, Arsenal went out in an exciting tie at Oxford and then West Ham unexpectedly lost at home to Manchester City, Steve Kinsey scoring the winner. Manchester United, looking to avenge a 0-5 thrashing at Goodison only four days earlier, got

another shock when John Gidman scored an own goal to put his old club through. Sunderland eventually squeezed past Nottingham Forest in the dourest tie of the round.

4th round
Chelsea v Manchester City 4-1
Everton v Grimsby Town 0-1
Ipswich Town v Oxford United 2-1
Norwich City v Notts County 3-0
Sheffield Wednesday v Luton Town 4-2
Southampton v Queen's Park Rangers 1-1, 0-0 (aet), 4-0
Sunderland v Tottenham Hotspur 0-0, 2-1
Watford v West Bromwich Albion 4-1

Home defeats for Everton and Spurs, Division 1's top two clubs, left the competition wide open. Paul Wilkinson's headed goal from a last-minute free-kick gave Grimsby a remarkable win at Goodison. Goalkeeper Chris Turner was Sunderland's hero, defying Tottenham at Roker Park and then saving Graham Roberts' second penalty in the replay. Kerry Dixon scored a hat-trick for the new favourites Chelsea, and Sheffield Wednesday's Andy Blair converted three penalties against Luton.

5th round
Chelsea v Sheffield Wednesday 1-1, 4-4 (aet), 2-1
Grimsby Town v Norwich City 0-1
Ipswich Town v Queen's Park Rangers 0-0, 2-1
Watford v Sunderland 0-1

Chelsea and Wednesday played out an epic tie which had run for almost five hours before Mickey Thomas headed the decisive goal; three exciting contests had each been watched by more than 36,000 people. In the second at Hillsbrough Chelsea went 0-3 down, then 4-3 up before conceding a penalty in the last minute which Mel Sterland converted.

Final: the winning goal. The cross from Norwich's John Deehan bounced off Mike Channon's legs into Asa Hartford's path – and his shot ricochetted off Sunderland defender Gordon Chisholm into the net! Seen here is the moment that the ball went from Channon to Hartford. From left: Terry Venison, Channon, Hartford, Chisholm, Gary Bennett.

Final: the penalty. Norwich's keeper Chris Woods is beaten by Clive Walker (immediately behind him), but the shot hits the foot of the post and rebounds clear.

The other quarter-finals were also settled by the odd goal – in Sunderland's case a very odd one as Clive Walker's shot flew in off a team-mate's back. Ipswich also failed to take their home advantage, but stood firm in the replay at Loftus Road after Simon Stainrod and their own Russell Osman had been sent off.

Semi-finals
Ipswich Town v Norwich City 1-0, 0-2 (1-2)
Sunderland v Chelsea 2-0, 3-2 (5-2)

Ipswich Town (1) 1   Norwich City (0) 0
   D'Avray   (27,404)
IPSWICH Cooper, Burley, Butcher, Cranston, McCall, Zondervan, Dozzell, Brennan, Putney, D'Avray, Gates
NORWICH Woods, Devine, Watson, Bruce, Van Wyk, Barham, Hartford, Mendham, Clayton, Channon, Deehan

Norwich City (1) 2   Ipswich Town (0) 0
   Deehan, Bruce   (23,545)

NORWICH Woods, Haylock, Van Wyk, Bruce, Mendham, Watson, Barham, Channon, Deehan, Hartford, Donowa
IPSWICH Cooper, Burley, McCall, Zondervan, Cranston, Butcher, Putney, Brennan, D'Avray (Sunderland), Dozzell, Gates

Norwich were fortunate not to concede more than Mich D'Avray's early goal at Portman Road: Romeo Zondervan's shot near the end was scraped off the line. A tight and fierce second leg saw John Deehan equalise and Steve Bruce (an outstanding prospect signed from Gillingham) head the winner in the 87th minute.

Sunderland (1) 2   Chelsea (0) 0
   West 2 (1 pen)   (32,440)
SUNDERLAND Turner, Venison, Pickering, Bennett, Chisholm, Elliott, Hodgson, Berry, West, Daniel, Walker
CHELSEA Niedzwiecki, Lee, Jones, Pates, McLaughlin (Jasper), Canoville, Nevin, Spackman, Dixon, Bumstead, Thomas

West to head another goal. More than 100 arrests were made – but the subsequent FA inquiry merely warned Chelsea, who were also told to fix their seats down more securely to stop them being used as missiles!

Final

At Wembley (100,000; £860,935)
Norwich City (0) 1   Sunderland (0) 0
    Chisholm (og)
NORWICH Woods, Haylock, Van Wyk, Bruce, Mendham, Watson, Barham, Channon, Deeham, Hartford, Donowa
SUNDERLAND Turner, Venison, Pickering, Bennett, Chisholm, Corner (Gayle), Daniel, Wallace, Hodgson, Berry, Walker

Like many Wembley matches, this was worth nothing like the amount paid to watch it – a disappointing final which turned on two incidents within the space of five minutes just after half-time. First David Corner, the young defender brought in to replace the suspended Sunderland captain Shaun Elliott, was caught in possession by John Deehan: his cross ran loose as Mike Channon challenged for it and Asa Hartford's shot was deflected in by poor Gordon Chisholm. As Sunderland retaliated Dennis Van Wyk clearly handled; but Walker's penalty clipped the outside of a post. (West, who had scored from the spot in the Semi-final, had been left out of the side; he joined Watford four days later.)

Apart from David Hodgson's dipping shot in the first 20 seconds, and Walker's run interrupted by a deliberate foul, Sunderland rarely looked like scoring and their supporters were as subdued as the team. Norwich contrived a number of fluent attacks and deserved a victory which would have taken them into Europe for the first time ever, veterans Mick Channon and Asa Hartford not only getting the better of a young defence but coaxing fine 90-minute performances from their own tired old legs.

Final: Norwich City's team celebrate the club's first major trophy – but within a few weeks they and fellow finalists Sunderland were relegated from Division 1; and Norwich will not even enjoy the rich pickings of European competition in the UEFA Cup.

Chelsea (1) 2   Sunderland (1) 3
    Speedie, Nevin   Walker 2, West
    (38,440)
CHELSEA Niedzwiecki, Jones, Rougvie, Pates, Jasper (Canoville), Bumstead, Nevin, Spackman, Dixon, Speedie, Thomas
SUNDERLAND Turner, Venison, Pickering, Bennett, Chisholm, Elliott, Hodgson, Berry, West, Daniel (Wallace), Walker

Two penalties given against young Chelsea substitute Dale Jasper after Joe McLaughlin dislocated his shoulder gave his team a great deal to do in the second leg. Colin West scored from the first and followed up after having his second kick saved.

When David Speedie halved the deficit early on at Stamford Bridge anything seemed possible but as Walker tormented his old club with two smart goals, the mood turned ugly. One fan attempted to assault Walker and others followed him onto the pitch; there was actually a policeman in the penalty area when Walker crossed for

SKOL CUP

1st round
Albion Rovers 2 Montrose 0
Dunfermline Athletic 4 Arbroath 0
East Stirling 1 Berwick Rangers 1 (aet: East
  Stirling won 5-3 on pens.)
Queen of the South 2 Queen's Park 1
Stirling Albion 2 Stenhousemuir 0
Stranraer 0 Cowdenbeath 3

Under yet another new format, as well as a new sponsor, the Skol Cup abandoned the experiment of playing mini-leagues in the middle of the competition, reverting to a straight knock-out. The decision to abolish home and away legs in the first two rounds ensured that there was a more dramatic element to the ties. The allied decision that replays would be eliminated from these stages of the competition by the use of penalty 'shoot-outs' was more controversial — Berwick becoming the first victims when their praiseworthy draw away to East Stirling was immediately nullified.

2nd round
Airdrie 3 Aberdeen 1
Ayr United 1 Motherwell 0
Cowdenbeath 3 Partick Thistle 0
Dundee 3 Hamilton Academical 0
Dundee United 5 Forfar Athletic 0
Dunfermline Athletic 2 Celtic 3
Heart of Midlothian 4 East Stirling 0
Hibernian 1 East Fife 0
Kilmarnock 1 Alloa Athletic 1 (aet: Kilmarnock
  won on pens.)
Meadowbank Thistle 2 Morton 1
Queen of the South 1 Dumbarton 2
Rangers 1 Falkirk 0
Raith Rovers 2 Clydebank 0
St Johnstone 2 Albion Rovers 1
St Mirren 1 Clyde 0 (aet)
Stirling Albion 1 Brechin City 4

Berwick's hard luck story was repeated by Alloa in the second round, when they, too, lost on penalties after doing the hard bit at Kilmarnock. But that story merited only a line compared to the sensation of the same night: Aberdeen's 1-3 defeat at Airdrie. The other big clubs made their expected progress with greater or lesser ease. Dundee, with United scoring five and their Dens Park neighbours three, took the greatest satisfaction of the big cities. Hearts, with a four-goal flourish, and Hibs rather less spectacularly kept Edinburgh's hopes high. Glasgow's big two had a harder task, an 84th-minute goal by Brian McClair putting Celtic through after they had trailed to Dunfermline, and Rangers showing little conviction as they squeezed past Falkirk at Ibrox by the slenderest margin.

3rd round
Airdrie 0 Celtic 4
Brechin City 2 St Johnstone 4
Cowdenbeath 2 St Mirren 0
Dumbarton 0 Dundee United 4
Dundee 1 Kilmarnock 1 (aet: Dundee won on
  pens.)
Heart of Midlothian 1 Ayr United 0
Hibernian 1 Meadowbank Thistle 2 (aet)
Rangers 4 Raith Rovers 0

12,000, the biggest crowd of the round, turned up to see if Airdrie could repeat their second round sensation — but it was the large group of Celtic fans at Broomfield Park who went away celebrating; Tommy Burns, Alan McInally and Peter Grant gave their side an unshakable advantage by the interval, Rangers also scored four in less-testing circumstances, as did Dundee United and St Johnstone. The giant-killing mantle passed once again into the safe hands of Meadowbank, who took Hibernian to extra time and emerged victorious after trailing 0-1 to the Premier Division side at Easter Road. Kilmar-

Final: Iain Ferguson repaid at a stroke most of the fee Rangers had paid Dundee for him in the close season by scoring the only goal of the match against the Dark Blues' Tannadice neighbours.

Rangers celebrate victory after the match.

nock were less fortunate, this time failing in the penalty shoot-out after an excellent draw at Dundee: the biter bit.

Quarter-finals
Cowdenbeath 1 Rangers 3
Dundee 0 Heart of Midlothian 1
Dundee United 2 Celtic 1 (aet)
Meadowbank Thistle 2 St Johnstone 1

After their heady victory over Hibernian, Meadowbank had been rewarded with a home tie against fellow Division 1 strugglers St Johnstone, and they made it count. Once again, though, they had to come from behind to do so. The titanic struggle of the round was at Tannadice Park, where 21,182 saw Dundee United finally overcome Celtic in extra time after Celtic had equalised with only eight minutes remaining. United's neighbours were less fortunate, Hearts confirming their impressive beginning to the season with victory at Dens Park. Rangers moved forward convincingly, Cowdenbeath at least having the consolation of a 9,925 crowd as they succumbed to three second-half goals.

Semi-finals
Heart of Midlothian v Dundee United 1-2, 1-3 (2-5)
Rangers v Meadowbank Thistle 4-0, 1-1 (5-1)

Ironically, after the previous rounds had produced games in which a second match would have been the best way of settling things, the two-leg semi-finals were both virtually decided in the first leg. Rangers put four past Meadowbank's goalkeeper Doug McNab to end that

romantic story; and two John Clark goals ensured that Dundee United won at Tynescastle to make the second leg almost a formality. So it proved, United winning with some comfort; Meadowbank at least took credit by holding their powerful visitors to a draw in their 'home' leg (actually at Tynecastle), and retired from the fray after another brave cup exploit.

Final
Hampden Park (44,000)
Rangers (1) 1   Dundee United (0) 0
    Ferguson
RANGERS McCloy, Dawson, McClelland, Fraser, Paterson, McPherson, Russell (Prytz), McCoist, Ferguson (Mitchell), Redford, Cooper
DUNDEE UNITED McAlpine, Holt (Clark), Malpas, Gough, Hegarty, Narey, Bannon, Milne (Beedie), Kirkwood, Sturrock, Dodds

Rangers' hoodoo over Dundee United continued, as Rangers won an undistinguished encounter 1-0 to leave United unsuccessful against the Glasgow team in three cup-final meetings in the 1980s. United did little to dispel the suspicion that they lacked the temperament for the big occasion, going down without ever displaying their known ability. For Rangers – at the time tucked in neatly behind the league leaders – it seemed to suggest that Jock Wallace's team were turning the corner, and it confirmed the value of their close-season £200,000 signing from Dundee, Iain Ferguson. The 21-year-old had found it difficult to integrate into his new team and had been dropped earlier in the season; but he repaid a large slice of the fee with his winner on the stroke of half-time.

EUROPEAN CUP

Holders: Liverpool
Seeded: Aberdeen, Benfica, Dinamo
 Bucharest, Feyenoord, FK Austria, IFK
 Gothenburg, Juventus, Liverpool, Stuttgart

1st round
Aberdeen (Scotland) v Dinamo Berlin (East
 Germany 2-1, 1-2 (aet), (3-3: Dinamo won on
 pens.)
Akranes (Iceland) v Beveren (Belgium) 2-2, 0-5
 (2-7)
Avenir Beggen (Luxembourg) v IFK
 Gothenburg (Sweden) 0-8, 0-9 (0-17)
Bordeaux (France) v Athletic Bilbao (Spain) 3-2,
 0-0 (3-2)
Dinamo Bucharest (Romania) v Omonia
 Nicosia (Cyprus) 4-1, 1-2 (5-3)
FK Austria (Austria) v Valletta (Malta) 4-0, 4-0
 (8-0)
Feyenoord (Holland) v Panathinaikos (Greece)
 0-0, 1-2 (1-2)
Grasshoppers (Switzerland) v Honved
 (Hungary) 3-1, 1-2 (4-3)
Ilves (Finland) v Juventus (Italy) 0-4, 1-2 (1-6)
Labinoti (Albania) v Lungby (Denmark) 0-3, 0-3
 (0-6)
Lech Poznan (Poland) v Liverpool (England) 0-1,
 0-4 (0-5)

Levsky Spartak (Bulgaria) v VFB Stuttgart
 (West Germany) 1-1, 2-2 (3-3: Levsky won on
 away goals)
Linfield (N. Ireland) v Shamrock Rovers
 (Ireland) 0-0, 1-1 (1-1: Linfield won on away
 goal)
Red Star Belgrade (Yugoslavia) v Benfica
 (Portugal) 3-2, 0-2 (3-4)
Trabzonspor (Turkey) v Dnepr (USSR) 1-0, 0-3
 (1-3)
Valerengen (Norway) v Sparta Prague
 (Czechoslovakia) 3-3, 0-2 (3-5)

Scottish champions Aberdeen failed on penalties in Berlin after two close games with Dinamo, cursing a late goal conceded in each leg. At Pittodrie Bernd Schulz halved their 2-0 lead: then after Ian Angus's equaliser in East Germany, a goal from Rainer Ernst with just five minutes to play took the tie into extra-time. That produced no more goals but a 4-5 defeat on penalties.

John Wark scored the only goal for Liverpool in Poland and a hat-trick at Anfield as the holders began their defence in impressive style. The two Irish teams were drawn against each other in a tie marred by crowd trouble. Linfield won it with David Jeffrey's away goal.

3rd round: Paul Walsh volleys home his second goal in the second leg against FK Austria; John Wark (centre) and Kevin MacDonald follow up. Walsh later missed his hat-trick by fluffing a penalty.

Elsewhere Feyenoord and Stuttgart joined Aberdeen as fallen seeds; Bernard Lacombe's goal gave the talented Frenchmen of Bordeaux a narrow first-leg win over Bilbao which they stubbornly held onto; and Gothenburg, UEFA Cup winners in 1982, fell short of Benfica's European Cup aggregate record of 18-0 by just one goal.

2nd round

Bordeaux v Dinamo Bucharest 1-0, 1-1 (aet) (2-1)
Dinamo Berlin v FK Austria 3-3, 1-2 (4-5)
IFK Gothenburg v Beveren 1-0, 1-2 (aet) (2-2
   Gothenburg won on away goal)
Juventus v Grasshoppers 2-0, 4-2 (6-2)
Levsky Spartak v Dnepr 3-1, 0-2, (3-3: Dnepr
   won on away goal)
Liverpool v Benfica 3-1, 0-1 (3-2)
Panathinaikos v Linfield 2-1, 3-3 (5-4)
Sparta Prague v Lyngby 0-0, 2-1 (2-1)

Ian Rush was Liverpool's hat-trickster this time, after Diamantino had equalised at Anfield. There were some uncomfortable moments in the Lisbon rain after Benfica got another goal back, both teams later being reduced to 10 men as Kenny Dalglish and Pietra were sent off. Linfield missed a glorious chance to beat the Greek champions, who they led 3-0 in the second leg before conceding three in 35 minutes. Bordeaux once again had Lacombe to thank for their winning goal in another close tie.

3rd round

FK Austria v Liverpool 1-1, 1-4 (2-5)
Bordeaux v Dnepr 1-1, 1-1 (aet) (2-2: Bordeaux
   won on pens.)
IFK Gothenburg v Panathinaikos 0-1, 2-2 (2-3)
Juventus v Sparta Prague 3-0, 0-1 (3-1)

FK Austria (1) 1	Liverpool (0) 1
Polster	Nicol
(20,000)	

FK AUSTRIA Koncilia, Dihanich, Obermayer, Tuermer, Degeorgi, Mustedanagic, Prohaska, Baumeister, Polster, Nyilasi, Steinkogler
LIVERPOOL Grobbelaar, Neal, Kennedy, Lawrenson, Hansen, Nicol, Whelan, MacDonald, Wark, Walsh, Rush

Liverpool (2) 4	FK Austria (0) 1
Walsh 2,	Prohaska
Nicol,	(32,761)
Obermayer (og)	

LIVERPOOL Grobbelaar, Neal, Kennedy, Lawrenson, Hansen, Nicol, Whelan, MacDonald, Wark, Walsh, Rush
FK AUSTRIA Koncilia, Dihanich, Obermayer, Degeorgi, Baumeister, Zore, Steinkogler, Prohaska, Polster, Nyilasi, Daxbacher

Liverpool again had a testing away leg and after Toni Polster scored his 19th goal in 17 games they needed Steve Nicol's first European goal near the end to avoid defeat. At Anfield it was more straightforward, though manager Joe

Fagan levelled charges of unprofessionalism after Paul Walsh, having scored two goals, was allowed to take a penalty instead of Phil Neal. It would have given Walsh his hat-trick – but he missed it.

Bordeaux (1) 1	Dnepr (1) 1
Lacombe	Liuti
(33,000)	
Dnepr (1) 1	Bordeaux (0) 1
Lysenko	Tusseau
(40,000)	

For the third successive round Bordeaux were unable to take real advantage of their home leg. Once again it was Lacombe's goal which gave them some hope for the away game, in which Thiery Tusseau snatched a second-half equaliser, then saw Leonard Specht and Fernando Chalana score from the spot to complete a 5-3 victory on penalties.

IFK Gothenburg (0) 0	Panathinaikos (1) 1
(40,026)	Saravokos (pen)
Panathinaikos (1) 2	IFK Gothenburg (1) 2
Dimopoulos,	Nilsson,
Saravokos,	Holmgren
(80,000)	

A brave effort by the Swedes in front of a large and passionate Athens audience was not enough to stop Panathinaikos, beaten finalists at Wembley in 1971, going into the semi-final. They were undone in the end by the penalty conceded in their own stadium.

Semi-final: Alain Giresse (Bordeaux) avoids a tackle by fellow French international Michel Platini (Juventus) in the second leg, when the French champions all but caught the Cup favourites after a naive first-leg performance in Turin.

Final: Zbigniev Boniek's tricky dribbling and prodigious acceleration caused problems to the Liverpool defence.

Juventus (1) 3   Sparta Prague (0) 0
   Tardelli, Rossi,
   Briaschi   (50,000)
Sparta (0) 1   Juventus (0) 0
   Berger (pen)   (38,000)

The Italian champions, though suffering their first defeat over 90 minutes in six legs, were never in danger of losing the handsome lead earned in Turin. It wasn't until much too late that Sparta pulled even one goal back; and, although unpredictable in the league, Juve continued to look impressive in Europe.

Semi-finals
Liverpool v Panathinaikos 4-0, 1-0 (5-0)
Juventus v Bordeaux 3-0, 0-2 (3-2)

Liverpool (1) 4   Panathinaikos (0) 0
   Wark, Rush 2,   (39,488)
   Beglin
LIVERPOOL Grobbelaar, Neal, Beglin, Lawrenson, Lee, Hansen, Dalglish, Whelan, Rush, MacDonald, Wark
PANATHINAIKOS Laftsis, Gerothodoros, Karoulias, Kyrastas, Zajec, Dontas, Saravakos, Lantoniou (Livathinos), Mavridis, Rocha, Dimopoulos (Kavouras)

Panathinaikos (0) 0   Liverpool (0) 1
   (60,000)   Lawrenson
PANATHINAIKOS Laftsis, Tarasis, Karoulias, Kyrastas, Zajec (Papavasiliou), Saravakos, Antoniou, Haralambides (Karavidas), Rocha, Dimopoulos
LIVERPOOL Grobbelaar, Neal, Beglin, Lawrenson, Nicol, Hansen, Dalglish, Whelan, Walsh (Johnston), Gillespie, Wark

Two exemplary displays took Liverpool into their fifth European Cup final, ensuring an English presence there for the eighth time in nine seasons. John Wark having put them ahead in the first half at Anfield, two goals straight after the interval by Rush left the Greeks hoping only for the consolation of an away goal. They were denied that by Grobbelaar and suffered a futher blow nine minutes from time when Irish full-back Jim Beglin marked his European debut by heading in Dalglish's free-kick.

With the visiting coach, Jacek Gmoch, theatrically raging about the referee and promising 'the game of my life' in Athens, Liverpool were uncomfortably aware that half a dozen of their players were only one booking away from missing the final through suspension. In the event it was a serene night on which Mark Lawrenson, playing in midfield, even added to the first leg lead with a well-taken goal on the hour; and referee Adolf Prokop's yellow card stayed in his pocket.

Juventus (1) 3   Bordeaux (0) 0
   Boniek, Briaschi,
   Platini   (67,000)
JUVENTUS Bondini, Favero, Cabrini, Bonini, Caricola, Scirea, Briaschi, Tardelli, Rossi, Platini, Boniek
BORDEAUX Dropsy, Rohr, Tusseau, Specht, Battiston, Girard (:Thouvenel), Tigana, Chalana, Lacombe, Giresse, Müller

Bordeaux (1)2   Juventus (0)0
   Müller,   (40,000)
   Battiston
BORDEAUX Dropsy, Thouvenal, Specht, Battiston, Tusseau, Girard, Rohr (Chalana), Tigana, Giresse, Lacombe, Müller
JUVENTUS Bodini, Favero, Caricola, Scirea, Cabrini, Bonini, Briaschi, Tardelli, Platini, Boniek (Pioli), Rossi (Prandelli)

Only a superb save in the last minute of the second leg by the Juventus goalkeeper Bodini spared his team the embarrassment of losing a three-goal lead. That had seemed a more than adequate margin to take to Bordeaux. But the 40,000 Frenchmen present who believed otherwise had their hopes fuelled after 24 minutes when Dieter Müller scored from Lacombe's cross. The Italian champions still looked reasonably happy until Batiston drove in a 30-yarder off a post with 11 minutes remaining. In a frantic finish Bodini had to thwart Tigana to earn Juventus their third European final in successive years.

Final

29 May '85: Heysel Stadium, Brussels (58,000)
Juventus (0)1   Liverpool (0)0
  Platini (pen)
JUVENTUS Tacconi, Favero, Cabrini, Bonini, Brio, Scirea, Briaschi (Prantelli), Tardelli, Rossi, (Vignola), Platini, Boniek.
LIVERPOOL Grobbelaar, Neal, Lawrenson (Gillespie), Hansen, Beglin, Nicol, Dalglish, Wark, Whelan, Walsh (Johnston), Rush.

The least important thing about the 1985 European Cup Final was the 90 minutes' football. By the time the players came on to the pitch, with some reluctance and an hour and a half late, 38 spectators were dead and the work of the murderous thugs posing as Liverpool fans had polluted television screens in 80 countries around the world. Had it not been for a fear that further violence would break out on the terraces, the game would have been called off — and, presumably, never played.

Within a few days the Football Association had withdrawn all English teams from European competitions for a year, a ban immediately trumped by UEFA who made it an indefinite one, while FIFA banned all international tours by English clubs. Simultaneous government and UEFA inquiries were left to try and piece together exactly how the mayhem began and how it might have been prevented. Liverpool officials criticised what they considered to be poor Belgian organization, an inadequate stadium, and what club chairman John Smith asserted to be the presence among the mob of cockney members of the National Front. Such criticisms met with scant sympathy abroad.

All that needs to be said about the game itself is that Platini's penalty (for an offence against Boniek committed comfortably outside the area) won it; that Platini's long pinpoint passes and Boniek's electrifying bursts through the centre of Liverpool's defence were the only sources of authentic quality in the match; and that, most important, further trouble was avoided. The macabre events overshadowed, but gave heightened poignancy to, Joe Fagan's resignation as manager, news of which had leaked out the previous night.

Final: Michel Platini beats Bruce Grobbelaar from the spot to score the winner. The fact that the penalty offence was committed well outside the area merely injected an element of farce into a match already totally devalued by the atrocious events of a couple of hours before.

EUROPEAN CUP-WINNERS' CUP

Holders: Juventus (competing this season in European Cup)

1st round

Apoel Nicosia (Cyprus) v Servette (Switzerland) 0-3, 1-3 (1-6)

Ballymena (N. Ireland) v Hamrun (Malta) 0-1, 1-2 (1-3)

Bayern Munich (W. Germany) v Moss (Norway) 4-1, 2-1 (6-2)

Dinamo Moscow (USSR) Hajduk Split (Yugoslavia) 1-0, 5-2 (6-2)

Inter Bratislava (Czechoslovakia) v Kuuysi Lahti (Finland) 2-1, 0-0 (2-1)

KB Copenhagen (Denmark) v Fortuna Sittard (Holland) 0-0, 0-3 (0-3)

Gent (Belgium) v Celtic (Scotland) 1-0, 0-3 (1-3)

Malmö (Sweden) v Dinamo Dresden (E. Germany) 2-0, 1-4 (3-4)

Metz (France) v Barcelona (Spain) 2-4, 4-1 (6-5)

Rapid Vienna (Austria) v Besiktas (Turkey) 4-1, 1-1 (5-2)

AS Roma (Italy) v Steaua Bucharest (Romania) 1-0, 0-0 (1-0)

Siofok Banyasz (Hungary) v Larisa (Greece) 1-1, 0-2 (1-3)

Trakia Plovdiv (Bulgaria) v Union Luxembourg 4-0, 1-1 (5-1)

University College Dublin (Ireland) v Everton (England) 0-0, 0-1 (0-1)

Wisla Krakow (Poland) v IB Vestmannaeyjar (Iceland) 4-2, 3-1 (7-3)

2nd round: Fourth Division Wrexham, having sensationally disposed of FC Porto, gave AS Roma a fight before going out. Here, in the second leg at Wrexham, Brazilian ace Paolo Falcão clears Roma's lines with keeper Franco Tancredi beaten.

Wrexham (Wales) v FC Porto (Portugal) 1-0, 3-4 (4-4: Wrexham won on away goals)

The first European sensation of the season was provided by French club Metz, who were 5-2 down at one stage during their second leg against Terry Venables' Barcelona – then scored four goals to silence the Nou Camp crowd and go through! Wrexham also achieved a remarkable triumph, beating the previous season's finalists Porto by the away goal which Barry Horne scored in the 88th minute of the second leg. Jim Steel's goal had won the home match, an impressive feat in itself.

Everton were almost on the wrong end of a similar performance by the students and part-time pros of University College: Graeme Sharp scored the only goal. Frank McGarvey's two helped Celtic past the Belgian Cup-holders. The best performance among the fancied teams was from Moscow Dinamo, winning 5-2 against Split, with a hat trick from Valeri Gassayev.

2nd round

Bayern Munich v Trakia Plovdiv 4-1, 0-2 (4-3)

Dinamo Dresden v Metz 3-1, 0-0 (3-1)

Dinamo Moscow v Hamrun 5-0, 1-0 (6-0)

Fortuna Sittard v Wisla Krakow 2-0, 1-2 (3-2)

Inter Bratislava v Everton 0-1, 0-3 (0-4)

Larisa v Servette 2-1, 1-0 (3-1)

Rapid Vienna v Celtic 3-1, 0-3 (replayed: 1-0) (4-1)

AS Roma v Wrexham 2-0, 1-0

Crowd trouble became an issue in British football again as Celtic were ordered to replay the second leg in which they had overturned Rapid's two-goal lead. The Austrians claimed that one of their players had been hit by a bottle thrown from the terraces. The atmosphere at 'neutral' Old Trafford for the replay was fearsomely hostile to Rapid, who nevertheless managed to break away for Peter Pacult to score the only goal immediately after Roy Aitken had hit the post at the other end. Although two Austrian players were attacked at the final whistle, Celtic escaped a European ban; but they were fined £17,000 and ordered to play their next European home game behind closed doors.

There was frustration, too, for Wrexham, struggling near the bottom of Division 4, when they went to Rome and lost to two dubious goals. Everton, beginning to assert themselves in the League, scored good wins over Bratislava, but Bayern Munich did not enjoy the last 40 minutes of their tie in Bulgaria, when one more goal conceded would have put them out.

3rd round
Bayern Munich v AS Roma 2-0, 2-1 (4-1)
Dinamo Dresden v Rapid Vienna 3-0, 0-5 (3-5)
Everton v Fortuna Sittard 3-0, 2-0 (5-0)
Larisa v Dinamo Moscow 0-0, 0-1 (0-1)

Everton (0) 3   Fortuna Sittard (0) 0
  Gray 3   (25,782)
EVERTON Southall, Stevens, Van den Hauwe,
Ratcliffe, Mountfield, Reid (Richardson),
Steven, Curran, Gray, Bracewell, Sheedy
FORTUNA Van Gerven, Maessen, Koevermans,
Schrijnemakers, Dekker, Suvrijn, Thijssen,
Hoyer, van Well, Holverda, Evers

Fortuna (0)   Everton (1) 2
  (20,000)   Sharp, Reid
FORTUNA Korver, Maessen, Boessen,
Koevermans, Hoyer, van Well, Philippen
(Reijners) Schrijnemakers, Dekker, (Evers),
Suvrijn, Thijssen
EVERTON Southall, Stevens, Van den Hauwe,
Ratcliffe, (Wakenshaw), Mountfield, Reid,
Steven, Curran, Sharp (Arnold), Harper,
Richardson

Andy Gray's splendid second-half hat-trick at
Goodison – his first for seven years – virtually
ensured Everton of a place in the semi-final. He
missed the second leg, along with Kevin Sheedy
and Paul Bracewell, but Peter Reid set up
Graeme Sharp for the first goal and then scored

the second himself. The little-known Fortuna,
with former Ipswich and Forest midfielder Frans
Thijssen in their side, were unable to disturb
Everton's smooth progress into the last four – the
first time they had got that far in nine European
campaigns.

Bayern Munich (1) 2   AS Roma (0) 0
  Augenthaler,   (50,000)
  Hoeness
AS Roma (0) 1   Bayern Munich (1) 2
  Nela   Matthäus (pen)
  (55,400)   Koegl

The Romans, having a poor season overall, left
themselves with too much to do after the first leg
and were in desperate trouble once Bayern's
captain Lothar Matthäus had converted a penalty in Rome, where the Italians eventually suffered the further indignity of a rare home defeat.

Dinamo Dresden (0) 3   Rapid Vienna (0) 0
  Trautmann, Minge,
  Kirsten   (36,000)
Rapid Vienna (3) 5   Dinamo Dresden (0) 0
  Pacult 2, Lainer,   (18,000)
  Panenka (pen),
  Krankl

Pacult, a scorer in both legs against Celtic, was
instrumental in a startling comeback by the
Austrian Cup-holders. Dinamo's lead had dis-

Semi-final: Bayern Munich's Michael Rummenigge beats Everton's Neville Southall to a high cross in a first-leg goalmouth incident. Looking on (from left) are Pat van den Hauwe, Derek Mountfield, Graeme Sharp, and Kevin Ratcliffe.

Final: Andy Gray volleys home Everton's first goal after Graeme Sharp has beaten Michael Konsel, Rapid Vienna's keeper, to a poorly directed back pass near the goal-line.

appeared by half-time, and when Hans Krankl scored the fifth the East Germans knew it was not their night.

Larisa (0) 0   Dinamo Moscow (0) 0
  (20,000)
Dinamo Moscow (0) 1   Larisa (0) 0
  Fomichev   (20,000)

Having achieved the result they wanted in Greece, Dinamo had to work hard for success in front of a modest crowd who clearly believed the result was a foregone conclusion.

Semi-finals
Bayern Munich v Everton 0-0, 1-3 (1-3)
Rapid Vienna v Dynamo Moscow 3-0, 1-1 (4-1)

Bayern Munich (0) 0   Everton (0) 0
  (67,000)
BAYERN Pfaff, Dremmler, Willmer, Eder, Augenthaler, Lerby, Pflügler, Mathäus, Hoeness, Rummenigge, Kögl
EVERTON Southall, Stevens, Van den Hauwe, Ratcliffe, Mountfield, Reid, Steven, Harper, Sharp, Bracewell, Richardson

Everton (0) 3   Bayern Munich (1) 1
  Sharp, Gray,   Hoeness
  Steven   (49,476)

EVERTON Southall, Stevens, Van den Hauwe, Ratcliffe, Mountfield, Reid, Steven, Sharp, Gray, Bracewell, Sheedy
BAYERN Pfaff, Dremmler, Willmer (Beierlorzer), Eder, Augenthaler, Lerby, Pfügler, Matthäus, Hoeness, Nachtweih, Kögl

Both teams went into this tie cherishing hopes of a domestic League and Cup double plus a European trophy. Bayern came off worse after leading on aggregate with only 17 minutes of the first half left by the away goal which Dieter Hoeness had stolen against the run of play. Sharp headed an equaliser (which was not enough on its own), then forced goalkeeper Jean-Marie Pfaff into a horrible error as they challenged for a long throw, leaving Gray to volley into an open net. A third goal, by Trevor Steven, ensured that Everton were no longer vulnerable to a late German retort.

In Munich, playing without Gray and Sheedy, they had given a most efficient performance, stifling the Germans so well that Kevin Richardson's goal-line clearance from Rummenigge was their only moment of anxiety.

Rapid Vienna (0) 3   Dinamo Moscow (1) 1
  Lainer, Krankl (pen),   Karatayev (pen)
  Hrstic   (20,000)
RAPID Konsel, Lainer, Gager, Pregesbauer

Final

15 May '85: Rotterdam (35,000)

Everton (0) 3   Rapid Vienna (0) 1
  Gray, Steven,   Krankl
  Sheedy

EVERTON Southall, Stevens, Van den Hauwe, Ratcliffe, Mountfield, Reid, Steven, Gray, Bracewell, Sheedy

RAPID Konsel, Lainer, Garger, Brauneder, Weber, Kienast, Kranjcar, Hrstic, Krankl, Weinhofer (Panenka), Pacult (Gross)

Final: Everton celebrate their comfortable victory in Rotterdam – just three days before they were to play in the FA Cup Final at Wembley.

(I Hrstic), Brauneder, Willfurth, Kranjcar, Panenka (Stadler), Krankl, Weinhofer, Pacult
DYNAMO Prudnikov, Silkin, Bulanov, Pozdnyakov, Novikov, Khapsalis (Borodyuk), Ataulin, Vasiliev (Pudishev), Karatayev, Stukashov, Gassayev

Dinamo Moscow (1) 1   Rapid Vienna (1) 1
  Pozdnyakov   Panenka
                      (55,000)
DINAMO Prudikov, Bulanov, Pozdnyakov, Ataulin, Karatayev, Vasiliev, Molodtsov (Pudishev), Stukashov, Khapsalis (Matyunin), Novikov, Golovnya
RAPID Konseil, Lainer, Weber, Brauneder, Kranjcar, Panenka (Hrstic), Gager, Krankl, Pacult (Willfurth), Brucic, Kienast

Rapid, a goal down at half-time in their home leg, completed a remarkable comeback to reach their first European final. Although Vasily Karatayev's penalty in Vienna put them under intense pressure, they recovered to score three times, including a penalty of their own by Hans Krankl. The tie was effectively decided four minutes into the second leg when their orchestrator, the veteran Czech Antonin Panenka, drilled in a fierce shot. Dinamo's equaliser on the night failed to produce the collapse which was the Russians' only hope.

Rapid proved less-effective opponents than the majority of Division 1 teams Everton had been brushing aside since Christmas, and never looked remotely like deflecting the Merseysiders from their attempted treble. It was one of the more one-sided finals, Everton producing a second-half performance which must have convinced any doubters among the Eurovision audience still unsure about the qualities of the city of Liverpool's other team. Neville Southall did not have a shot to save until the 82nd minute. When he was obliged to pick the ball out of his net two minutes later, having been rounded by the aging maestro Krankl, Everton's reaction was almost contemptuous, Sheedy immediately chipping in a third and decisive goal.

That they were unable to score before half-time was due to Michael Konsel's smart save from Sheedy; sweeper Herbert Weber's timely tidying-up; and the linesman's flag which signalled (wrongly according to TV replays) that Mountfield was offside as he headed back for Gray to 'score'. Gray eventually eased any nagging worries with a deft volley after Sharp picked up an inadequate back-pass, and Steven scored the second following a corner and more poor defensive work.

A great performance was manager Howard Kendall's verdict. If the celebrations were slightly muted, it was only because Wembley and Manchester United were just three days hence.

UEFA CUP

Holders: Tottenham Hotspur

1st round

AIK Stockholm (Sweden) v Dundee United (Scotland) 1-0, 0-3 (1-3)

Anderlecht (Belgium) v Werder Bremen (W. Germany) 1-0, 1-2 (aet) (2-2: Anderlecht won on away goal)

Bohemians Dublin (Ireland) v Rangers (Scotland) 3-2, 0-2 (3-4)

Bohemians Prague (Czechoslovakia) v Apollon (Cyprus) 6-1, 2-2 (8-3)

Cologne (W. Germany) v Pogon Szczecin (Poland) 2-1, 1-0 (3-1)

Dukla Bystrica (Czechoslovakia) v Borussia Mönchengladbach (W. Germany) 2-3, 1-4 (3-7)

Dinamo Minsk (USSR) v HJK Helsinki (Finland) 4-0, 60-0 (10-0)

Fenerbahce (Turkey) v Fiorentina (Italy) 0-1, 0-2 (0-3)

Glentoran (N. Ireland) v Standard Liège (Belgium) 1-1, 0-2 (1-3)

KR Reykjavik (Iceland) v Queen's Park Rangers (England) 0-3, 0-4 (0-7)

Lokomotiv Leipzig (E. Germany) v Lillestrom (Norway) 7-0, 0-3 (7-3);

Manchester United (England) v Rába ETO Györ (Hungary) 3-0, 2-2 (5-2)

Monaco (France) v CSKA Sofia (Bulgaria) 2-2, 1-2 (3-4)

Nottingham Forest (England) v Bruges (Belgium) 0-0, 0-1 (0-1)

OB Odense (Denmark) v Spartak Moscow (USSR) 1-5, 1-2 (2-7)

Olympiakos (Greece) v Neuchatel (Switzerland) 1-0, 2-2 (3-2)

Oester Växjö (Sweden) v Linzer ASK (Austria) 0-1, 0-1 (0-2)

Paris St-Germain (France) v Heart of Midlothian (Scotland) 4-0, 2-2 (6-2)

Rabat Ajax (Malta) v Partizan Belgrade (Yugoslavia) 0-2, 0-2 (0-4)

Real Betis (Spain) v Universitatea Craiova (Romania) 1-0, 0-1 (aet) (1-1: Craiova won on pens.)

Real Madrid (Spain) v SSW Innsbruck (Austria) 5-0, 0-2 (5-2)

Red Boys (Luxembourg) v Ajax Amsterdam (Holland) 0-0, 0-14 (0-14)

Sion (Switzerland) v Atlético Madrid (Spain) 1-0, 3-2 (4-2)

Sliven (Bulgaria) v Zeljeznicar (Yugoslavia) 1-0, 1-5 (2-5)

Southampton (England) v SV Hamburg (W. Germany) 0-0, 0-2 (0-2)

Sporting Braga (Portugal) v Tottenham Hotspur (England) 0-3, 0-6 (0-9)

Sporting Lisbon (Portugal) v Auxerre (France) 2-0, 2-2 (aet) (4-2)

Sportul (Romania) v Internazionale Milan (Italy) 1-0, 0-2 (1-2)

Valladolid (Spain) v Rijeka (Yugoslavia) 1-0, 1-4 (2-4)

Videoton (Hungary) v Dukla Prague (Czechoslovakia) 1-0, 0-0 (1-0)

Vorwärts (E. Germany) v PSV Eindhoven (Holland) 2-0, 0-3 (2-3)

Widzew Lódz (Poland) v Århus (Denmark) 2-0, 0-1 (2-1)

Although five English clubs competed (Spurs as holders), only three survived the initial round. Brian Clough's Forest went out to a late goal by Willy Wellens in Bruges and Southampton were well beaten in Hamburg. QPR, Manchester United and Spurs had more comfortable trips. Glasgow Rangers managed to lose their first leg in Dublin, amid predictable scenes of mayhem, and Hearts were no match for Paris St-Germain, while Dundee United left it until the second half of their second leg before seeing off AIK.

Ajax scored nine goals in 33 minutes of their second leg against Luxembourg's Red Boys, which made a nonsense of their failure to get even one in the away match; Anderlecht, last season's beaten finalists against Spurs, needed an own goal in Bremen to scrape through.

2nd round

Ajax Amsterdam v Bohemians Prague 1-0, 0-1 (aet) (1-1: Bohemians won on pens.)

Borussia Mönchengladbach v Widzew Lódz 3-2, 0-1 (aet) (3-3: Widzew on away goals)

Bruges v Tottenham Hotspur 2-1, 0-3 (2-4)

Fiorentina v Anderlecht 1-1, 2-6 (3-7)

SV Hamburg v CSK Sofia 4-0, 2-1 (6-1)

Inter Milan v Rangers 3-0, 1-3 (4-3)

Linzer ASK v Dundee United 1-2, 1-5 (2-7)

Lokomotiv Leipzig v Spartak Moscow 1-1, 0-2 (1-3)

1st round: Mark Falco scores Spurs' fifth goal in the 6-0 second-leg drubbing of Sporting Braga, from northern Portugal.

PSV Eindhoven v Manchester United 0-0, 0-1
(aet) (0-1)
Paris St-Germain v Videoton 2-4, 0-1 (2-5)
Queen's Park Rangers v Partizan Belgrade 6-2,
0-4 (6-6: Partizan won on away goals)
Rijeka v Real Madrid 3-1, 0-3 (3-4)
Sporting Lisbon v Dinamo Minsk 2-0, 0-2 (aet)
(2-2: Dynamo won on pens.)
Standard Liège v Cologne 0-2, 1-2 (1-4)
Universitatea Craiova v Olympiakos 1-0, 1-0
(2-0)
Zeljeznicar v Sion 2-1, 1-1 (3-2)

An eventful round for British clubs. In Bruges,
goalkeeper Birger Jensen's penalty put the holders Spurs 0-2 down with only 10 minutes to play.
One substitute, Glenn Hoddle, had already been
sent off; the other, Clive Allen, immediately
pulled a goal back. In the return Tottenham
scored three times in the first 35 minutes. London
rivals QPR battered Partizan 6-2 at Highbury
after being 1-2 behind, then collapsed in front of
a 60,000 Belgrade crowd and became the first
British club ever to lose a four-goal lead in
Europe. The repercussions rumbled on for some
time until manager Alan Mullery was sacked.

Manchester United needed an extra-time
penalty by Gordon Strachan to see off Eindhoven, while Rangers were outgunned by Inter
Milan, for whom Karl-Heinz Rummenigge and
Franco Causio scored important goals in the
second half of the first leg.

Anderlecht overwhelmed Claudio Gentile's
Fiorentina defence in an impressive second-leg
performance; Ajax and Borussia were notable, if
unlucky, casualties.

3rd round

Anderlecht v Real Madrid 3-0, 1-6 (4-6)
SV Hamburg v Inter Milan 2-1, 0-1 (2-2: Inter
won on away goal)
Manchester United v Dundee United 2-2, 3-2
(5-4)
Spartak Moscow v Cologne 1-0, 0-2 (1-2)
Tottenham Hotspur v Bohemians Prague 2-0,
1-1 (3-1)
Universitatea Craiova v Zeljeznicar 2-0, 0-4
(2-4)
Videoton v Partizan Belgrade 5-0, 0-2 (5-2)
Widzew Lódz v Dinamo Minsk 0-2, 1-0 (1-2)

Real staged one of the best comebacks of even
their distinguished European history to wipe out
Anderlecht, with new Spanish sensation Emilio
Butragueno scoring a hat-trick in front of a
near-capacity crowd. Manchester United did it
the hard way in their eventful all-British match,
Hamish McAlpine saving a Strachan penalty at
Old Trafford, then seeing Arnold Muhren's shot
deflected past him for the winner at Tannadice.

Rummenigge's away goal for Inter eventually
proved decisive after Liam Brady's penalty had
brought them level on aggregate against Hamburg in a tie watched by 141,000 over the two
legs. Partizan could not manage an even more
astonishing recovery than that against QPR.

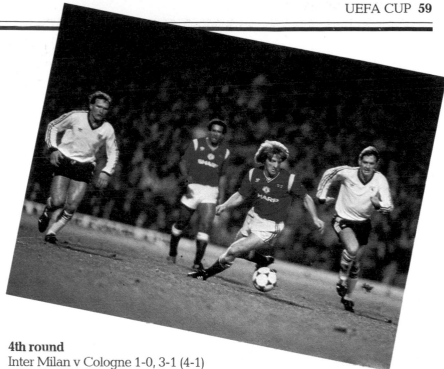

3rd round: Gordon Strachan on the attack in the first leg against Dundee United. In one of the best and most exciting ties of the competition, the Terrors, demonstrating Scottish attacking football at its most incisive, had the better of the Old Trafford tie – but could not complete their triumph in the return at Tannadice.

4th round
Inter Milan v Cologne 1-0, 3-1 (4-1)
Manchester United v Videoton 1-0, 0-1 (aet) (1-1:
Videoton won on pens.)
Tottenham Hotspur v Real Madrid 0-1, 0-0 (0-1)
Zeljeznicar v Dinamo Minsk 2-0, 1-1 (3-1)

Manchester United (0) 1   Videoton (0) 0
   Stapleton   (35,432)
MAN UTD Bailey, Gidman, Albiston, Duxbury,
McGrath, Hogg, Strachan, Whiteside, Hughes,
Stapleton, Olsen
VIDEOTON P. Disztl, Csuhay, Horvath, L. Disztl,
Vegh, Burcsa, Majer, Csongradi (Vaszil,
Borsanyi), Szabo, Vadasz, Palkovics

Videoton (1) 1   Manchester United (0) 0
   Wittman   (25,000)
VIDEOTON P. Disztl, Borsanyi, L. Disztl, Horvath,
Vegh, Burcsa, Vaszil (Gomori), Wittman, Palko-
vics, Szabo, Vadasz
MAN UTD Bailey, Gidman, Albiston, Duxbury,
McGrath, Hogg, Strachan, Whiteside, Staple-
ton, Robson (Olsen), Hughes

The penalty lottery which had brought European trophies to Liverpool and Tottenham the
previous season went against United as Frank
Stapleton shot over the bar and Mark Hughes
had his kick saved. The Hungarian league
leaders had been fortunate to leave Old Trafford
only one goal behind, Stapleton scoring on the
hour, but they equalised after 15 minutes at
home. Although United, with Bryan Robson
starting a game for the first time in two months,
dominated much of the play, they failed to take
their chances.

Tottenham Hotspur (0) 0   Real Madrid (1) 1
   (39,914)   Perryman (og)
TOTTENHAM Clemence, Stevens, Hughton,
Hazard, Miller (Dick), Perryman, Chiedozie
(Brooke), Falco, Galvin, Hoddle, Crooks
REAL Miguel Angel, Chendo, Sanchis, Stielike,
Salguero, Camacho, Gallego, Angel, Michel,
Butragueno (Juanito), Valdano (Santillana)

Real Madrid (0) 0   Tottenham Hotspur (0) 0
  (92,000)
REAL Miguel Angel, Chendo, Camacho,
Salguero, Sanchis, Angel, Pineda (San Jose),
Michel, Butragueno (Lozano), Gallego, Valdano
TOTTENHAM Clemence, Thomas, Hughton,
Roberts, Miller, Perryman, Hazard, Falco,
Galvin (Dick), Hoddle, Crooks (Brooke)

Having lost a home leg for the first time in 43
European ties, the holders faced an uphill task in
front of 92,000 at the Bernabeu stadium. Real
played unexpectedly well in London, scoring
early on when Butragueno went past Paul Miller
and saw his cross bounce in off Steve Perryman's
knee. Spurs might have lost that game more
heavily. In Madrid they had a goal by Mark Falco
unluckily disallowed and as their frustration
increased Perryman was sent off for a high, late
tackle to stop Jorge Valdano breaking clear.
Falco squandered a late chance to take the tie
into extra-time – and for the first time in five
UEFA Cup campaigns Tottenham had failed to
reach the semi-finals.

Inter Milan (0) 1   Cologne (0) 0
  Causio   (80,000)
Cologne (0) 1   Inter Milan (1) 3
  Bein   Marini, Rummenigge 2
  (59,000)

Inter looked to be in trouble when defender
Ricardo Ferri was sent off after only ten minutes
of the second leg. They immediately brought on
defender Bihi for Causio and within five minutes
Marini scored a crucial away goal. After Bein's
equaliser on the night, Rummenigge rounded
off a brilliant team performance with two more.
Inter had made hard work of the first leg in
Brady's absence, his deputy Causio managing
the only score.

4th round: Karl-Heinz Rummenigge (AC Milan, behind post) turns after scoring from the spot – his second goal of the match against his colleague in West Germany's national team, Cologne's goalkeeper Harald Schumacher.

Zeljeznicar (0) 2   Dinamo Minsk (0) 0
  Samardizja,   (22,000)
  Bazdarevic
Dinamo Minsk (1) 1   Zeljeznicar (1) 1
  Kisten   Bahtic
  (28,000)

The Yugoslavs were given a useful first leg lead
when Bazdarevic ran from the halfway line to
score a fine individual goal. Kisten equalised
early in Minsk, but Bahtic's effort only eight
minutes later effectively decided matters.

Semi-finals
Inter Milan v Real Madrid 2-0, 0-3 (2-3)
Videoton v Zeljeznicar 3-1, 1-2 (4-3)

Inter Milan (1) 2   Real Madrid (0) 0
  Brady (pen),   (80,000)
  Altobelli
INTER Zenga, Bergomi, Mandorini, Pasinato
(Corso), Marini, Baresi, Cucchi, Sabato,
Altobelli, Brady, Rummenigge
REAL MADRID Miguel Angel, Chendo (San
Jose), Camacho, Salguero, Sanchis, Isidro,
Vazquez (Juanito), Gallego, Butragueno,
Lozano, Valdano

Real Madrid (2) 3   Inter (0) 0
  Santillana 2,   (110,000)
  Michel
REAL MADRID Miguel Angel, Chendo,
Camacho, Stielike, Salguero (Fraile, Juanito),
San Jose, Pineda, Michel, Santillana, Gallego,
Valdano
INTER Zenga, Bergomi (Pasinato, Causio),
Mandorini, Baresi, Collovati, Bibni, Cucchi,
Sabato, Altobelli, Brady, Rummenigge

Inter appealed unsuccessfully against their
dramatic dismissal on the grounds that Giuseppe Bergomi, who had to be carried off, had been
hit by a marble thrown from the crowd. A UEFA
committee ruled that there was no evidence to
show that he had been hit.
    That incident occurred at a crucial stage, Real
having cut their deficit to 2-1 with an early goal
by Carlos Santillana. Within 10 minutes Santillana scored again, this time from San Jose's
centre, and with 110,000 wildly excited fans
sensing some glory after all at the end of a
miserable domestic season, Michel Gonzalez hit
a 20 yard shot past Walter Zenga for the winner.
Brady's penalty in Milan, followed by a goal from
Alessandro Altobelli, had convinced the Italian
crowd that Inter would get through.

Videoton (2) 3   Zeljeznicar (1) 1
  Burcsa, Disztl,   Skoro
  Vadasz   (30,000)
VIDEOTON P. Disztil, Vegh, L. Disztl, Csuhay,
Horvath, Burcsa, Wittman, Vadasz, Gyenti
(Borsanyi), Szabo, Palkovics (Vaszil)
ZELJEZNICAR Skrba, Komsic, Capljic,
Sabandadovic, Cilic, Skoro, Bazdarevic, Balic,
Mihailovic, Samardzija

Final: Carlos Santillana, Real Madrid's captain, scores the Spaniards' second goal against Videoton, after a superbly created move, in the first leg in Hungary.

Zeljeznicar (1) 2   Videoton (0) 1
    Bahtic, Curic   Csuhay
      (37,000)
ZELJEZNICAR Skrba, Berjan, Baljic, Sabanadovic, Capljic, Komsic, Bahtic, Curic (Cilic), Bazdarevic, Samardzija
VIDEOTON P. Disztl, Csuhay, Horvath (Novath), L. Disztl, Vegh, Burcsa, Borsanyi, Wittman, Szabo, Vadesz, Pakkovics

Manchester United's conquerors stole victory again, this time when defender Csuhay popped up to score just three minutes from the end of a fluctuating second leg. The Yugoslavs' away goal in the first leg left the second well balanced and it swung their way with a goal in each half by Bahtic and Curic before Csuhay's dramatic late intervention.

Final
Székesféhervar: 8 May '85 (30,000)
Videoton (0)0   Real Madrid (1)3
             Michel, Santillana,
             Juanito
VIDEOTON P. Disztl, Csuhay, Horvath, L. Disztl, Vegh, Burcsa, Wittmann, Vadasz (Gyenti), Novath, Palkovics, Borsanyi.
REAL Miguel Angel, Chendo, Camacho, Stielike, Sanchis, San Jose, Butragueno (Juanito), Michel, Santillana (Salguero), Gallego, Valdano.

Madrid: 22 May '85 (110,000)
Real Madrid (0) 0   Videoton (0) 1
             Majer
REAL Miguel Angel, Chendo, Camacho, Stielike, Sanchis, San Jose, Butragueno, Michel, Santillana, Gallego, Valdano (Juanito)
VIDEOTON P. Disztl, Csuhay, Horvath, L. Disztl, Vegh, Burcsa, Majer, Csongradi (Wittmann), Szabo, Vadasz, Novath (Palkovics).

The winning of Real's first European trophy for 19 years hit a slightly anti-climatic note with a rare home defeat by foreign opposition in the second leg; but with the hard part done well in Hungary, the Spanish fans did not seem to mind too much. Their three-goal lead could have been even larger, Butragueno missing an open goal in between the chances taken by Michel (32 minutes), Santillana (76 – a superbly constructed goal) and Juanito (88). In Madrid Real even squandered a penalty, Peter Disztl saving Valdano's weak kick, then going on to make a series of fine saves. Four minutes from time, with the celebrations well underway, winger Lajos Majer, one of three Videoton players absent from the first leg, scored with a powerful 20-yarder.

EUROPEAN SUPER CUP

Turin (55,000)
Juventus (1) 2   Liverpool (0) 0
    Boniek 2
JUVENTUS Bodini, Favero, Cabrini, Bonini, Brio, Scirea, Briaschi, Tardelli, Rossi, Platini, Boniek
LIVERPOOL Grobbelaar, Neal, Kennedy, Lawrenson (Gillespie), Nicol, Hansen, Walsh, Whelan, Rush, MacDonald, Wark

Juventus, making full use of their home advantage in poor conditons, deserved to win what turned out to be a preview of the European Cup final, though Liverpool were furious about a number of offside decisions against them. Zbigniew Boniek had a lob cleared off the line by Phil Neal and scored twice, the second sealing the match 12 minutes from time.

While many would argue that this competition is simply a nuisance in an over-crowded calendar, UEFA have decided that it will continue, but as a compulsory single match between the winners of the European Cup and the Cup-Winners' Cup, played on neutral ground in Monaco.

EUROPEAN CLUB SOCCER

Spain

No British expatriate could have enjoyed more success than Terry Venables, crowning his first year as coach at Barcelona by taking the rich Catalan club to their first Spanish championship since the heyday of Johan Cruyff 11 years ago. Venables had not been a unanimous choice to succeed Argentina's much more famous César Luis Menotti. In fact, when it came to taking a decision, Barcelona's two senior vice-presidents had cast their votes in favour of the Swiss-German Helmut Benthaus, who had just won the West German title with VFB Stuttgart. But chairman Nuñez had been more impressed with Venables and carried the other directors with him; he would not regret his choice.

As Venables arrived, Barcelona were selling the controversial maestro Diego Maradona to Napoli for £5 million. They immediately spent one fifth of that fee on Scotland's Steve Archibald from Tottenham – and, again, would not be disappointed. Many of the Barcelona players were suspicious of Venables, fearing that they would be expected to play what they regarded as typically British 'up-and-under' football.

All those suspicions and doubts were dispelled in the most dramatic fashion when Barcelona won their first league match – away to deadly rivals Real Madrid. From that point they never looked back, leading all the way to the finish and ending up 10 points clear of runners-up Atlético Madrid. Archibald, after a slow start, was Barcelona's top scorer with 15 of the club's 69 goals in 34 games. The Scot finished third overall in the Division 1 scoring charts, four goals behind Hugo Sanchez, Atlético Madrid's Mexican, and two behind Real Madrid's Argentinian, Jorge Valdano.

At the other end of the table Malaga, Elche and Murcia were relegated. But the most publicised slide was that of Real Madrid, who finished fifth – their lowest placing in eight years. That was too much for the fans to bear. They protested long and loud, forcing the early retirement of president Luis De Carlos and the dismissal of coach Amancio. Both men had the last laugh, however, when caretaker manager Luis Molowny took Madrid to success in the UEFA Cup. Their achievement in becoming the first Spanish club to win the trophy was notable for some remarkable victories along the way over Anderlecht of Belgium, Tottenham, and Internazionale of Milan. If Barcelona had produced new stars in Juan Carlos Rojo and Francisco Clos and Ramon Caldere, Madrid discovered their own brilliant newcomers in striker Emilio Butragueno and midfielder Michel.

Italy

The most refreshing thing about the Italian league season was the way little Verona did a 'Nottingham Forest', capturing the championship from under the noses of the big guns.

Verona had invested modestly in the summer of 1984 in the West German defender Hans-Peter Briegel and the Danish striker Preben Elkjaer. They had also acted shrewdly on the Italian market to sign Juventus cast-offs Pietro Fanna and Giuseppe Galderisi – both of whom played well enough to win places in the national side. And so, while the likes of Juventus, Internazionale, AC Milan, Roma, and the improving Sampdoria of Genoa all took vital points off each other, Verona coach Osvaldo Bagnoli steered a sensible, stealthy course through to the top of the table.

No-one believed that Verona could stand the pace. But their first-match victory over Napoli, in which Briegel not only contributed a vital goal but played Diego Maradona out of the game, should have served as warning. And in terms of consistency – which is what league competition is all about – Verona could not be faulted eventually winning the title comfortably.

Inter had signed West German Karl-Heinz Rummenigge and Irishman Liam Brady for the new season, but they ultimately paid the penalty for a slow start while these star newcomers were settling in; champions Juventus suffered through the poor form first of goalkeeper Stefano Tacconi and then of Paolo Rossi up front; Roma took far too long to adjust to the tactical changes introduced by new coach Sven-Goran Eriksson, and they were handicapped by the long absence

Terry Venables, appointed coach of Barcelona against some local opposition, had a triumphant first season, taking the club to their first championship for 11 seasons.

of Brazilian midfield general Paolo Falcão.

The British imports did well, restoring a reputation questioned after the disappointing spells in Italy experienced by Joe Jordan and Luther Blissett. Trevor Francis and Scotland's Graeme Souness took Sampdoria back into European competition for the first time in more than 20 years, and Mark Hateley set off like a rocket at AC Milan until he was both injured and then embroiled in a contract dispute in mid-season. Much of the credit for Hateley's success was due to Milan's wisdom in signing Ray Wilkins at the same time to provide the bullets for the former Portsmouth spearhead to fire.

Diego Maradona took a little while to settle down at his new club. But Napoli weren't complaining: his presence brought average home attendances of more than 70,000, and the 3-1 win over Inter produced record league receipts of a staggering £550,000. And Maradona's authentic genius ultimately shone brightly enough for him to play a key role in Argentina's qualification for the World Cup finals in 1986.

West Germany

West German teams had an unhappy time of it in European competition, but a revival of interest in the Bundesliga was inspired by the fresh air breathed into the national team by its new manager, the great Franz Beckenbauer. His warning that 'we don't want any "fat cats" here,' appeared to have a startling effect in restoring professional values.

At no club was this more noticeable than Beckenbauer's old stamping-ground, Bayern Munich. They were unimpressive in defeat against Everton in the semi-finals of the Cup-Winners' Cup. But in the league they shrugged off a string of injury problems to hold off a top-of-the-table challenge from a Werder Bremen inspired by the goals of Rudi Völler.

When Bayern sold Rummenigge to Inter of Italy, few fans saw them as title favourites. In the event, the use of that £3 million fee to buy Rolf Wohlfarth for the attack and, in particular, Lothar Matthäus for midfield more than made up for his loss. Rummenigge's younger brother Michael also proved his quality as a forward well worth a place in Beckenbauer's World Cup squad. The only domestic blemish for Bayern was in being beaten 1-2 by Bayer Uerdingen in the Cup Final when the double appeared well within reach – particularly after they had taken the lead through Dieter Hoeness in the eighth minute.

The pre-season promise of SV Hamburg remained unfulfilled. Later in the season, injury would force the premature retirement of defender Holger Hieronymus; and coach Ernst Happel suspended defenders Manni Kaltz and Jurgen Groh. But their failings were as nothing compared with those of Eintracht Braunschweig (Brunswick). The club spent heavily on a losing legal battle to try to adopt the name of their brewer sponsors and, almost unnoticed in the fuss, lost game after game, ultimately to crash into Division 2.

Holland

Dutch football, at both club and international levels, is going through something of a fallow period – at least compared with the glories of the 1970s. In the 1984/5 season there was as much interest in events off the field as on – especially at Ajax, who continued their domination in Holland. They contrived to give their rivals PSV Eindhoven and Feyenoord some hope with a players' revolt towards the end of the season. Coach Aad de Mos returned from a week's absence through illness to drop star striker Marco Van Basten and veteran Belgian defender Walter Meeuws. This provoked an angry team meeting at which the players passed a vote of no confidence in de Mos and informed the directors – who duly gave de Mos his marching orders. The players then returned to the formality of wrapping up the league title. In the Cup, outsiders Utrecht were surprise winners.

Belgium

Anderlecht collected their 18th championship with a style and dash which made nonsense of their 1-6 UEFA Cup thrashing in mid-season by Real Madrid. They conceded only 26 goals in 34 games and finished 11 points clear of Club Brugge, thanks to a record total of 100 goals. Top scorer for the champions was Belgian international Alex Czerniatynski with 21 goals. But for a lean spell in mid-season, when he was dropped by coach Paul Van Himst – such is the pressure on places at Anderlecht – he would surely have won the overall league scoring race. Instead that triumph fell to Ronny Martens, himself a former Anderlecht player, who scored 22 goals for Gent.

The Cup Final produced a dramatic finish to a game which was otherwise overshadowed by the Heysel stadium disaster only four days earlier. Cercle Bruges led Beveren 1-0 until Paul Courant equalised with a last-kick penalty in injury time. There were no more goals and so, after extra time, the match went to penalties, which Cercle won 5-4.

Above Lothar Matthäus, a midfielder bought by Bayern Munich with part of the huge fee received for the sale of Karl-Heinz Rummenigge, proved one of the great successes of the season in the Bundesliga and figures in manager Franz Beckenbauer's plans for the national squad.

Below Giuseppe Galderisi, a Juventus cast-off, dramatically revived his career with surprise championship winners Verona, and was rewarded with a well-deserved place in Italy's national squad.

Fernando Gomes (FC Porto) scored a phenomenal 39 League goals during the season, so regaining the Golden Boot award as Europe's top marksman.

France

Bordeaux retained their championship title despite being without France midfielder Alain Girese and Portugal's Fernando Chalana for important chunks of the season because of injuries. Indeed Chalana, signed after his success in the 1984 European Championship, was hurt in a pre-season friendly and did not play a competitive match until the spring. Jean Tigana completes a midfield creative triumvirate which, when it has settled down, could become the most dangerous in European club football.

Biggest overall disappointment was the failure of the twin-pronged Paris challenge in Division 1. Paris Saint-Germain, tipped for the title, struggled out of the relegation zone eventually, and also reached the final of the cup, losing to Monaco (1984's losing finalists); but the reconstituted Racing Club were demoted.

Portugal

FC Porto suffered an early-season humiliation at the hands of Division 4's Wrexham in the Cup-Winners' Cup. But after that they never looked back, losing only one of their 30 league games and finishing eight points clear of John Toshack's Sporting Lisbon. At least Porto could claim one European success: skipper Fernando Gomes scored 39 goals to regain the Golden Boot awarded to Europe's top league goalscorer.

It is indicative of the demand for success in Portugal that Sporting's comparative failure – only runners-up! – led to the resignation of Toshack two weeks before the end of the season. Neighbours Benfica were also caught in the critical crossfire for finishing in a 'disastrous' third place – 12 points behind Porto. Long before the end of the season they had arranged to replace Hungarian coach Pal Csernai with Southampton's assistant manager, John Mortimore. They eventually salvaged some pride by beating Porto in the final of the Cup.

Eastern Europe

The cult of superstardom which goes hand in hand with professional football in western Europe has always been frowned upon in the Soviet Union. Several players from champions Zenit Leningrad were formally reprimanded early in the 1985 season for 'lacking professional discipline'; and in a further disciplinary crackdown, the national team's midfielder Khoren Oganessian, from Ararat Erevan, was suspended for an indefinite period. Heavy drinking was blamed by the official press for the relegation of Pakhatakor Tashkent from Division 1. Former internationals Mustafa Belyalov and Nuritdin Amriyev – known as Taskent's George Best – were dismissed and transferred.

Hungarian football continued to attract trouble: cup finalists Tatabanya were involved in a match-fixing scandal which followed hard on the heels of what the authorities had hoped was the last of a series of trials of more than 200 officials, players and fans accused of 'bending' games to cash in on the Pools. In Yugoslavia Red Star Belgrade emerged from their recent doldrums to win the Cup; and in Bulgaria league scoring rates increased for the first time in years after a decision that no points would be awarded to teams involved in goal-less draws. Romania saw a 100,000 attendance in Bucharest for a double-header involving title challengers Dinamo and Steaua; and there was a welcome revival in Poland for Gornik Zabrze who remain – thanks to their 1970 Cup-Winners' Cup run – the only Polish team ever to have reached a European club final.

Elsewhere ...

In Greece, controversy on and off the field surrounded Athenian club Panathinaikos's attempt to defend their league title. Argentinian midfielder Juan Ramon Rocha was sentenced to 14 months in jail in mid-season for forging Greek nationality and immigration papers. His sentence was suspended pending appeal, while Panathinaikos went on to the Champions' Cup semi-finals; and it was eventually quashed and replaced by a conditional discharge. Greek fans remained as excitable as ever: 16 were seriously hurt and six were arrested after a 1-4 defeat away to Larisa.

In Turkey, former West German national team manager Jupp Derwall just about saved his job when his club Galatasaray won the Cup, even though the league title was carried off by their deadly rivals in Istanbul, Fenerbahce, on goal difference from Besiktas. At least Galatasaray had the satisfaction of knowing that they beat Fenerbahce in the Cup quarter-finals. Fenerbahce's success in the league was hard-earned, considering that they were without Turkey's star forward, Selcuk, for most of the season.

In Sweden, IFK Gothenburg maintained their domination with their third successive league crown; in Denmark, Vejle – despite losing star forward Allan Simonsen, who had broken his leg in the European Championship finals in June – regained the league title for the first time in six years.

HONOURS

Country	Titles	Footballer of the Year
Albania	League: 17 Nëntori Cup: Flamurtari 2, Partizani 1	
Austria	League: FK Austria Cup: Rapid Vienna 3, FK Austria 3 (Rapid won 6-5 on pens.)	Herbert Prohaska (FK Austria)
Belgium	League: Anderlecht Cup: Cercle Bruges 1 Beveren 1 (Bruges won 5-4 on pens.)	Enzo Scifo (Anderlecht)
Bulgaria:	League: Trakia Plovdiv Cup: CSKA 2, Levsky Spartak 1 (result revoked)	Plamen Nikolov (Levsky)
Cyprus	League: Omonia Nicosia Cup: AEL 1, EPA 0	
Czechoslovakia	League: Sparta Prague Cup: Dukla Prague 3, Košice 2	
Denmark	League: Vejle Cup: Lyngby 2, KB Copenhagen 1	Preben Elkjaer (Verona)
East Germany	League: Dinamo Berlin Cup: Dinamo Dresden 3, Dinamo Berlin 2	Hans-Jürgen Dörner (Dresden)
Finland	League: Kuusysi Lahti Cup: Haka 1, Lahden Reipas 0	Olli Huttunen (Haka)
France	League: Bordeaux Cup: Monaco 1, Paris St-Germain 0	
Greece	League: PAOK Salonika Cup: Larisa 4, PAOK 1	
Holland	League: Ajax Amsterdam Cup: Utrecht 1, Helmond Sport 0	
Hungary	League: Honved Cup: Honved 5, Tatabanya 0	
Iceland	League: IA Akranes Cup: IA Akranes 2, Fram 1	Bjarni Sigurdsson (Akranes)
Italy	League: Verona Cup: Sampdoria 3, AC Milan 1 (on agg.)	
Luxembourg	League: Jeunesse d'Esch Cup: Red Boys 1, Jeunesse d'Esch 0	
Malta	League: Rabat Ajax Cup: Zurrieq 2, Valletta 1 (rep.)	
Norway	League: Valerengen Cup: Fredrikstad 3, Viking 2 (replay)	Per Egil Ahlsen (Fredrikstad)
Poland	League: Gornik Zabrze Cup: Widzew Lodz 0, GKS 0 (Widzew 3-1 on pens.)	Miroslav Okonski (Lech Poznan)
Portugal	League: FC Porto Cup: Benfica 3, FC Porto 1	
Romania	League: Steaua Bucharest Cup: Steaua 2, Craiova 0	Silviu Lung (Un. Craiova)
Spain	League: Barcelona Cup: Atlético Madrid 2, Athletic Bilbao 1	
Sweden	League: IFK Gothenburg Cup: Malmö FF 1, Landskrona 0	Sven Dahlqvist (AIK)
Switzerland	League: Servette Geneva Cup: Aarau 1, Neuchatel Xamax 0	Heinz Hermann (Grasshoppers), Rolf Osterwalder (Aarau)
Turkey	League: Fenerbahce Cup: Galatasaray bt Trabzonspor 2-1, 0-0	
USSR	League: Zenit Leningrad Cup: Dynamo Moscow 2, Zenit 0	Gennadi Litovchenko (Dnepr)
West Germany	League: Bayern Munich Cup: Bayer Uerdingen 2, Bayern Munich 1	Harald Schumacher (Cologne)
Yugoslavia	League: Sarajevo Cup: Red Star Belgrade bt Dinamo Zagreb 2-1, 1-1	Velimir Zajec (Panathinaikos)

Enzo Scifo, Anderlecht's wonderfully gifted midfielder, deservedly won Belgium's Player of the Year award.

INTERNATIONAL SEASON

ENGLAND

After the experiments of the previous year Robson returned to the nucleus of the team which he had inherited for the friendly against East Germany in September. And although England did not play badly, their depressingly familiar inability to penetrate tight defences was again exposed. The rumbling disaffection on the terraces from the smallest-ever Wembley crowd for an international against foreign opposition was reaching a crescendo when Bryan Robson's brilliant goal won the match eight minutes from the end.

That goal was to prove a turning point, although initially it did not save Bobby Robson from criticism, as admirers of Hateley, who had been transferred to Milan on the strength of his performance against Brazil, demanded his inclusion. The suspicion was that Robson, for reasons difficult to determine and impossible to justify, still preferred Paul Mariner to Hateley for the opening Group 3 match of the World Cup qualifying campaign against Finland at Wembley in October.

Then fate took a hand. Mariner, who would certainly have played, and Trevor Francis, who might have done, were injured and Hateley was included. His performance seemed to end any question about the England centre-forward berth, barring injuries, for the foreseeable future and gave the Wembley crowd a new hero as he tore the Finnish defence apart with his power and speed. Hateley's second goal (England's third) just after half-time was a brilliant individual effort; Kenny Sansom scored his first goal for his country; England left the field to a standing ovation – and Bobby Robson compared Hateley to Nat Lofthouse and Tommy Taylor.

That analysis did not appeal to those critics who want to see English football adopting European styles, and they asserted – with some justice – that Hateley's experience with AC Milan had made him a better, more subtle and sophisticated player. Hateley, however, suffered a severe injury before England's next match – a World Cup qualifying game against Turkey in Istanbul a month later – and Robson turned to Peter Withe as his replacement. That, and Viv Anderson for Mike Duxbury (who had been injured against Finland), were the only changes, and the virtues of an almost unchanged team and the effect of confidence from one good win were to be seen as England fired a warning around Europe that a powerful side was being formed. Finland had looked a bad side on the night; Turkey unquestionably were a terrible one. Yet to beat anybody 8-0 away from home is a stunning performance, and England ran riot after imposing their aggressive physical presence on a shaky home team.

Qualification looked certain as three points were gathered from the two most difficult away matches in Group 3 – against Northern Ireland and Romania. Windsor Park, Belfast, does not have the same intimidating effect on England (who have not lost there for 58 years) as it does on continental sides; but even England could hardly relish their visit in February 1985. And as it turned out they had to compete fiercely, and at times desperately, in a game played at breakneck speed. Luck was on England's side, however, the crossbar stopping a Jimmy Quinn header with Peter Shilton beaten, before Hateley, who had been provided with few opportunities by his relentlessly harried midfield, fastened powerfully onto a long ball to give England their victory.

So England, even without Robson (injured) and Mark Wright (omitted for disciplinary reasons), had achieved what they had set out to do. Their record of played three, won three, with a goal difference of 14-0, seemed to place them beyond criticism, but the Belfast performance had not pleased everybody.

After a desultory friendly with the Republic of Ireland at Wembley, in which Hateley's touch let him down in front of goal before (more worryingly) he limped off and Lineker took the chance to score on a promising debut, the trip to Bucharest brought a satisfactory, if somewhat fortunate draw. Shilton, abetted by Terry Butcher, Anderson and Sansom, often brilliantly resisted all that was thrown at him for another clean sheet. Yet if

England v. Finland: Mark Hateley bursts through the Finnish defence to score his second (and England's third) goal. Hateley was the star of a fine team performance at Wembley. But England would find the Finns in a very different mood in the return at Helsinki.

the result was satisfactory, the performance, apart from that of the defence, was disappointing. Surprisingly Robson and his team escaped with less criticism than from the more commendable performance in Belfast. With Woodcock and Hateley both injured, Robson recalled the old partnership of Mariner and Francis, whose ineffectiveness was thrown into sharp relief by the brilliance of the Romanian forwards Hagi and Camataru.

Popular approval was to fade as quickly as it had come, when in the last two matches of the season England's players began to look jaded after the nine months slog. A 1-1 draw thanks to a Hateley equaliser in Finland, against a much better organised Finland team than the one at Wembley, thrilled no-one, even though it was another step towards qualification. When on the following Saturday the side lost a dreadfully tedious game at Hampden Park (England's first defeat there since 1976), criticism mounted furiously. One popular newspaper insisted 'Robson Must Go!' on its front page; and as the team set off for its altitude-acclimatization tour of Mexico Robson could have been forgiven if he had twinges of déjà vu.

SCOTLAND

Group 7, like Group 3, had two British teams; but with only four countries in the group, the runners-up would qualify only if they beat the winners of the Oceania/Israel group. And with Spain, the early favourites, in the same group, it looked as if Scotland and Wales might be battling for one place. Scotland, however, harboured few doubts about their qualification in the early stages. Iceland, the fourth team in the group, offered little resistance at Hampden Park, where a brace from Paul McStay and one from his former Celtic colleague Charlie Nicholas got the Scots off to a flying start. Yugoslavia having been beaten 6-1 in an early-season friendly, the Iceland game confirmed Scots in the belief that their team would take some stopping – a belief that received powerful reinforcement when Spain visited Hampden in November.

With Wales in the toils, not only chauvinistic Scots regarded this match as being between the two candidates for first place, and Scotland's claims looked irresistible as Spain were swept aside. Mo Johnston celebrated his recent return to Celtic with a brace of headed goals before the interval, and although the Bilbao centre-half Andoni Goicoechea pulled one back after half-time, Kenny Dalglish restored the two-goal margin with a strike spectacular even by his standards to equal Dennis Law's Scottish record of 50 goals.

All seemed set fair for Mexico, and not even defeat in the next match, the return with Spain in Seville, caused many doubts. In spite of the hostile crowd, who pelted Jim Leighton continuously with oranges and more dangerous missiles, Scotland looked the better team for most of the first half, before going down to a headed goal from Francisco Clos.

Turkey v. England: the Turks were victims of an English goal avalanche in the match at Istanbul, beginning with this one – the first of Bryan Robson's three.

Four weeks later the bubbling Scottish confidence was deflated when Wales came to Hampden, clamped down tight on the Scottish attack and midfield while at the other end the young Welsh bull and the deadly Welsh matador, Mark Hughes and Ian Rush, first unsettled and then devastated the linchpins of Jock Stein's (and Aberdeen's) defence, Alex McLeish and Willie Miller, Rush putting away the first-half winner. Indeed, none of the Scots seemed able to break out of the Welsh stranglehold. David Phillips did such a fine job in midfield that Graeme Souness's frustration eventually showed in a disgusting foul on Peter Nicholas. Without Souness's subtly probing passes from midfield, the attack, so fluent in previous games, stuttered badly; Johnston saw one chance go begging and the other thwarted by a magnificent save by Neville Southall three minutes from time. For the rest, with Joey Jones revelling in his new position as centre-half, Scotland's attacks finally dwindled away, and the team left the field to hoots of derision from the fans.

The last week of May, however, restored a little pride to the squad and gave a boost to their World Cup hopes. Pride was achieved when a splendid Richard Gough goal was enough to beat England at Hampden Park (the game had been switched from Wembley after Government pressure on the English FA). The following Tuesday gave less cause for pride as a scuffling performance brought a lucky win in Iceland, thanks to a Jim Bett goal four minutes from time against an Iceland team which had their Sheffield Wednesday star Sigi Jonsson carried off after a fierce Souness tackle and which also missed a penalty. The win, though, was crucial: it meant that Scotland could go to Cardiff in September knowing that a draw would be enough.

NORTHERN IRELAND

Fixture arrangements meant that after the disastrous beginning to their World Cup campaign in Finland in May 1984, Northern Ireland were given the opportunity to pick up the pieces at Windsor Park, Belfast, playing all four of their home matches in .Group 3 during the 1984/5 season.

The results were better than they might have feared, but failure to get at least a richly deserved point out of the game with England left their fate still in the balance as they prepared for trips to Turkey, Romania, and Wembley in the autumn and early winter of 1985. With the Irish, of course, you never can tell. Billy Bingham, their vastly experienced and clever manager, admits that their fluctuating away form baffles him.

Much will depend on the availability of Pat Jennings, who set a new record for British and Irish players when he made his 110th appearance against Turkey in May. No-one who saw the evergreen 40-year-old goalkeeper last season could doubt that he is still in the first rank of his profession, but Arsenal's surprising decision not to offer one of the best-loved players of recent years a new contract made Jennings think very carefully about his future, with retirement uppermost in his mind.

If there is no new goalkeeping star on the horizon at the moment, last season confirmed that in Norman Whiteside Northern Ireland have the best attacking player in Ireland, north or south, to emerge since George Best, and a player likely to have a greater impact on the international stage than was ever allowed to Best. With seven goals from 21 internationals, the boy from East Belfast seems certain to overtake the current Irish scoring record held by his team-mate Gerry Armstrong, even if Armstrong still has time to increase his current figure of 11.

He has shown the ability not just to score goals but to score the vital ones. He did so during the World Cup matches, getting the crucial second goal to put Ireland in the lead against Romania, and scoring both when Turkey put up surprisingly strong resistance in the final international of the 1984/5 season. Yet goals are only a part of his contribution: his competitiveness, leadership, and awareness of his colleagues all stand out in his play.

Whiteside's impact was essential, for Bingham was not once able to field his strongest team. Fortunately he was without Sammy McIlroy only for the match with Romania (which he regarded with reason as the main threat for the runners-up spot behind England). In the end Romania went the way of most continental visitors to Belfast, but they provided a difficult obstacle. As Ireland stuttered it took an own goal to open the way, and when Romania immediately equalised, thanks to a rare mistake by Jennings, the prospects looked ominous. In the second half Northern Ireland moved up a gear, Whiteside and Martin O'Neill giving them a more comfortable lead; but in the last quarter Romania played their best football of the match, pulling one goal back, and at the end the Irish were pleased to hear the final whistle.

Hamilton was the only absentee against Finland, who came to Belfast believing that they could claim the runners-up spot, in spite of their 0-5 thrashing at Wembley. That belief was reinforced as Ireland again began badly, Mika Lipponen giving his country the lead. John O'Neill equalised minutes before half-time, and Gerry Armstrong equalled the Irish scoring record from the penalty spot when Whiteside was wrestled to the ground during a spell of intense Irish pressure.

By the time England arrived in February, Martin O'Neill had joined Hamilton on the injured list. In his absence Sammy McIlroy captained the team and dominated midfield but the old jinx worked again, England getting a desperately lucky win. England's failure to repeat the result in Bucharest did Ireland no favours, and Ireland entertained Turkey that evening knowing that a win was imperative, a large margin of victory desirable. Without Armstrong as well as Hamilton and Martin O'Neill, a decisive win was beyond them as Turkey proved a much better side than they had been earlier in the season. Whiteside rose to the occasion to end their resistance with two headed goals, but he also collected his second booking of the group matches (the one for leaving the pitch against Romania being rubbed out), and ominously would miss the return match in September.

WALES

If the England team's transformation was swift, that of Mike England's team was even swifter. Twice in recent times – in the 1982 World Cup and the 1984 European Championship – they had seen qualification snatched from their grasp at the last. And 1983/4 had ended on a low note with a toothless performance in a friendly in Israel in June, to angry criticism from their usually protective manager. The refrain was picked up in September as the new season began, when Iceland beat them 1-0 in Reykjavik in the first of their World Cup qualifying matches. Without the injured Ian Rush, Wales had never threatened against the weakest team in the group, and it seemed that their aspirations were ended before they realised the tournament

Scotland v. Spain: in their finest performance for years in a game of any significance, the Scots beat Spain at Hampden Park more easily than the score suggested. Here Maurice Johnston scores his and Scotland's second, beating defenders Andoni Goicoechea (5) and Santiago Urquiaga (2) and putting in a fierce header.

had begun. A trip to Seville a month later only underlined the feeling, as Spain won as convincingly as the 3-0 scoreline suggests.

The return match with Iceland at Cardiff in November brought their first points, but there was little comfort to be derived from the 2-1 win. True, Ian Rush had returned and, with the Everton duo of goalkeeper Southall and central defender Kevin Ratcliffe, gave Wales the strong spine down the centre of the team which many managers feel is the basis for success. But Rush was still searching unavailingly for his first World Cup goal (indeed, for his normal Liverpool form). Hughes scored the winner and was clearly developing promisingly. Ratcliffe, astonishingly fast, showed himself to be a world-class central defender.

It was not a lot on which to build. In particular, Mike England was searching desperately for a partner for Ratcliffe; and for a friendly match with Norway he experimented with Robbie James in that unfamiliar positon. The experiment was not a success, and that game, too, did little to suggest that Wales were about to make a major impact, Norway drawing 1-1 in spite of being without their best players.

The corner was about to be turned, however, with devastating effect. A month later, at Hampden Park, Hughes, who during the season had undergone a remarkable transformation from novice to one of the most effective strikers in the Football League, now brought his thrillingly muscular talent to bear in the service of his country in stunning partnership with Rush. Joey Jones had been drafted in to fill the problem positon at centre-half, and with Ratcliffe and Southall formed a barrier the Scots beat against in vain. The goal that won the game perfectly illustrated the destructive talents of the two strikers: Hughes at once outmanoeuvred and overpowered McLeish for a high ball, and Rush instantaneously despatched the knock-down in a blur past Leighton.

There were other successes: Peter Nicholas, whose move to Luton Town had revived his career; David Phillips, whose improvement over the course of the season with Manchester City had been remarkable; and Mickey Thomas, enjoying his part in Chelsea's successful return to Division 1. These three were forming an increasingly effective midfield.

Suddenly Group 7 seemed to have been turned upside down. And if that conclusion needed confirmation, it was received at Wrexham a month later as Spain were comprehensively dismissed 3-0. Hughes and Rush fired a warning that Wales now possessed one of the most lethal striking partnerships in Europe. Rush scored two goals, the first a tap-in after a mix up in the Spanish defence, the second when he was put through brilliantly by his partner. Hughes scored the other, and memorable it was, launching into a scissors-kick to volley the shoulder-high ball home as a corner was half-cleared to him. Pat van den Hauwe, a somewhat improbable Welshmen – he had opted for the principal-

ity when Belgium informed him he would have to do National Service if he wished to play for the land of his father – had an almost undisturbed debut in the unusual positon of centre-half as deputy for the suspended Joey Jones. Both will be available to give Scotland an unfriendly welcome in September; so, the Scots will note quakingly, will Hughes and Rush.

ENGLAND: INTERNATIONAL SEASON
WORLD CUP QUALIFYING GROUP 3

Wembley: 14 October '84
England (2) 5   Finland (0) 0
  Hateley 2, Woodcock,
  Robson, Sansom
ENGLAND Shilton, Duxbury (Stevens), Sansom, Williams, Wright, Butcher, Robson (Chamberlain), Wilkins, Hateley, Woodcock, Barnes
FINLAND Huttunen, Pekonen, Kymalainen, Lahtinen, Petaja, Haaskivi (Turunen), Houtsonen, Ukkonen, Ikalainen, Rautiainen, Valvee (Hjelm)

Istanbul: 14 November '84
Turkey (0) 0   England (3) 8
                Robson 3, Woodcock 2,
                Barnes 2, Anderson
TURKEY Yasar, Ismail, Yusuf, Kemal, Cem, Rasit, Mujdat, Ridvan, Ahmet, Ilyas (Tuncay), Erdal
ENGLAND Shilton, Anderson, Sansom, Williams (Stevens), Wright, Butcher, Robson, Wilkins, Withe, Woodcock (Francis), Barnes

Belfast: 27 February '85 – see Northern Ireland results section

Bucharest: 1 May '85
Romania (0) 0   England (0) 0
ROMANIA Lung, Negrila, Iorgulescu (Iovan), Stefanescu, Ungureanu, Rednic, Hagi, Coras (Lakatus), Boloni, Klein, Camataru
ENGLAND Shilton, Anderson, Sansom, Steven, Wright, Butcher, Robson, Wilkins, Mariner (Lineker), Francis, Barnes (Waddle)

Helsinki: 22 May '85
Finland (1)1   England (0)1
  Rantanen   Hateley
FINLAND Huttunen: Lahtinen (Petaja), Kymalainen, Ikalainen, Nieminen, Turunen, Houtsonen, Ukkonen (Hjelm), Lipponen, Rautiainen, Rantanen
ENGLAND Shilton, Anderson, Sansom, Steven (Waddle), Fenwick, Butcher, Robson, Wilkins, Hateley, Francis, Barnes

The table at mid-June read:

	P	W	D	L	F	A	Pts
England	5	3	2	0	15	1	8
N. Ireland	5	3	0	2	7	5	6
Finland	6	2	2	2	6	10	6
Romania	4	1	2	1	6	4	4
Turkey	4	0	0	4	1	15	0

Amid the ups and downs of England's performances over the past few seasons, Terry Butcher has quietly established himself as the best central defender in the national squad – and arguably is now one of the best in Europe.

Romania v. England: in this crucial tie, England somewhat luckily escaped with a draw. Most of the creative football was played by the Romanians, whose winger Hagi (seen here with Kenny Sansom) delighted in testing England's defence almost to breaking point.

Remaining fixtures: 28 August, Romania v. Finland; 11 September, Turkey v. Northern Ireland, England v. Romania; 25 September, Finland v. Turkey; 16 October, Romania v. Northern Ireland, England v. Turkey; 14 November, Turkey v. Romania.

OTHER MATCHES: 1984/5

Friendlies

Wembley: 12 September '84
England (0) 1   East Germany (0) 0
  Robson
ENGLAND Shilton, Duxbury, Sansom, Williams, Wright, Butcher, Robson, Wilkins, Mariner (Hateley), Woodcock (Francis), Barnes
E. GERMANY Muller, Kreer, Doerner, Stahmann, Zoeztsche, Liebers, Troppa, Ernst (Raab), Steinbach, Streich (Richter), Minge.

Wembley: 26 March '85
England (1) 2   Republic of Ireland (0) 1
  Steven,   Brady
  Lineker
ENGLAND Bailey, Anderson, Sansom, Steven, Wright, Butcher, Robson (Hoddle), Wilkins, Lineker, Hateley (Davenport), Waddle
IRELAND Bonner, Hughton, Beglin, Lawrenson, McCarthy, Brady, Whelan, Waddock, O'Keefe (Byrne), Stapleton, McGrath (O'Leary)

Sir Stanley Rous Cup

Hampden Park: 25 May '85
Scotland (0) 1   England (0) 0
  Gough
SCOTLAND Leighton, Gough, Malpas, Aitken, McLeish, Miller, Strachan (McLeod), Souness, Archibald, Bett, Speedie
ENGLAND Shilton, Anderson, Sansom, Hoddle (Lineker), Fenwick, Butcher, Robson, Wilkins, Hateley, Francis, Barnes (Waddle)

Mexican Tour

Azteca Stadium: 6 June '85
Italy (0) 2   England (0) 1
  Bagni,   Hateley
  Altobelli
  (pen.)
ITALY Galli (Tancredi), Bergomi, Vierchowod, Baresi, Collovati (Cabrini), Tricella, Conti (Fanna), Bagni, Galderisi (Tardelli), Di Gennaro, Altobelli
ENGLAND Shilton, Stevens, Sansom, Steven (Hoddle), Wright, Butcher, Robson, Wilkins, Hateley, Francis (Lineker), Waddle (Barnes)

Azteca Stadium: 9 June '85
Mexico (1) 1   England (0) 0
  Flores
MEXICO Larios, Trejo, Quirarte, Cruz, Amador, Muñoz, España (de los Cobos), Aguirre, Negrete, Boy (Hermosillo), Flores (Dominguez)
ENGLAND Bailey, Anderson, Sansom, Hoddle (Reid), Fenwick, Watson, Robson, Wilkins (Dixon), Hateley, Francis, Barnes (Waddle)

Azteca Stadium: 12 June '85
England (1) 3   West Germany (0) 0
  Robson,
  Dixon 2
ENGLAND Shilton, Stevens, Sansom, Hoddle, Wright, Butcher, Robson (Bracewell), Reid, Dixon, Lineker (Barnes), Waddle
W. GERMANY Schumacher, Berthold, Brehme, Jakobs, Herget, Augenthaler, Littbarski (Wass), Matthäus (Thon), Mill, Magath, Rahn

United States Match

Los Angeles: 16 June '85
United States (0) 0   England (2) 5
                       Dixon 2, Lineker 2,
                       Steven
USA Mausser (Harris), van der Beck, Windischmann, Canter (Brady), Caliajiuri, Radwanski (Synder), Crow, Kerr (Hooker), Perez, Davis, Murray (Ladouceur)
ENGLAND Woods, Anderson, Sansom (Watson), Hoddle (Steven), Fenwick, Butcher, Robson (Reid), Bracewell, Dixon, Lineker, Waddle (Barnes)

SCOTLAND: INTERNATIONAL SEASON
WORLD CUP QUALIFYING GROUP 7

Hampden Park: 17 October '84
Scotland (2) 3   Iceland (0) 0
  McStay 2, Nicholas
SCOTLAND Leighton, Nicol, Albiston, Souness, McLeish, Miller, Dalglish (Nicholas), McStay, Johnston, Bett, Cooper
ICELAND Sigurdsson, Thrainsson, Edvaldsson, Bergs, Margeirsson, Jonsson, Gudlaugsson, LGudjohnsen, Betursson, Sigurvinsson, Sveinsson

Hampden Park: 14 November '84
Scotland (2) 3   Spain (0) 1
  Johnston 2,   Goicoechea
  Dalglish
SCOTLAND Leighton, Nicol, Albiston, Souness, McLeish, Miller, Dalglish, McStay, Johnston, Bett, Cooper
SPAIN Arconada, Urquiaga, Camacho, Maceda, Goicoechea, Gordillo, Señor, Victor, Santillana, Urtubi (Carrasco), Rincon (Butragueno)

Seville: 27 February '85
Spain (0) 1   Scotland (0) 0
  Clos
SPAIN Arconada, Gerardo, Maceda, Goicoechea, Camacho, Señor, Roberto, Gallego (Julio Alberto), Gordillo, Clos, Butragueno
SCOTLAND Leighton, Gough, Albiston, Souness, McLeish, Miller, Archibald (Nicholas), McStay, Johnston, Bett, Cooper

Hampden Park: 27 March '85
Scotland (0) 0   Wales (1) 1
                  Rush
SCOTLAND Leighton, Nicol, Albiston (Hansen), Souness, McLeish, Miller, Dalglish, McStay

(C. Nicholas), Johnston, Bett, Cooper
WALES Southall, Slatter, Jackett, Ratcliffe,
Jones, Phillips, James, P. Nicholas, Rush,
Thomas, Hughes

OTHER MATCHES 1984/5
Hampden Park: 12 September '84
Scotland (3) 6   Yugoslavia (1) 1
   Cooper, Souness,   Vokrri
   Dalglish, Sturrock,
   Johnston, Nicholas
SCOTLAND Leighton, Nicol, Albiston, Souness,
McLeish, Miller, Dalglish, Wark, Johnston, Bett
(Sturrock), Cooper (Nicholas)
YUGOSLAVIA Pantelic (Stojic), Miljus, Baljic,
Jessic, Matijevic (Jozic), Radanovic, Bahtic,
Georgijevski, Vokrri (Pancev), Siskovic,
Batrovic.

Reykjavik: 28 May '85
Iceland (0) 0   Scotland (0) 1
                   Bett
ICELAND Gudmundsson, Thrainsson, Sigi
Jonsson, Bergs, Petursson, Saevar Jonsson,
Gudlaugsson, Edvaldsson, Thordasson
(Grelarsson), Thorbjornsson, Sveinsson
SCOTLAND Leighton, Gough, Malpas, Aitken,
McLeish, Miller, Strachan, Souness, Gray
(Archibald), Bett, Sharp

NORTHERN IRELAND: INTERNATIONAL SEASON

WORLD CUP QUALIFYING GROUP 3
Pori: 27 May '84
Finland (0) 1   Northern Ireland (0) 0
   Valvee
FINLAND Huttunen, Pekonen, Kymalainen,
Ikalainen, Petaja, Turunen, Houtsonen,
Ukkonen, Rantanen, Rautiainen, Valvee
N. IRELAND Jennings, Nicholl, McElhinney,
McClelland, Donaghy, M.O'Neill, McIlroy
(Worthington), Armstrong (Cochrane),
Hamilton, Whiteside, Stewart

Belfast: 12 September '84
Northern Ireland (1) 3   Romania (1) 2
   Iorgulescu (og),   Hagi, Geolgau
   Whiteside,
   O'Neill
N. IRELAND Jennings, Nicholl, Donaghy,
McClelland, McElhinney, M.O'Neill,
Armstrong, McCreery, Hamilton, Whiteside,
Stewart
ROMANIA Lung, Rednic, Stefanescu,
Iorgulescu, Ungureanu, Ticleanu (Movila),
Andone, Klein, Irimescu (Geolgau), Augustin,
Hagi

Belfast: 14 November '84
Northern Ireland (1) 2   Finland (1) 1
   J.O'Neill,   Lipponen
   Armstrong (pen)
N. IRELAND Jennings, Nicholl, Donaghy, J.
O'Neill, McClelland, M. O'Neill, Armstrong,
McIlroy, Quinn, Whiteside, Stewart

FINLAND Huttunen, Pekonen, Kymalainen,
Lahtinen, Ikalainen, Turunen, Europeus,
Ukkonen, Houtsonen, Hjelm, Lipponen

Belfast: 27 February '85
Northern Ireland (0) 0   England (0) 1
                            Hateley
N. IRELAND Jennings, Nicholl, Donaghy, J.
O'Neill, McClelland, Ramsey, Armstrong,
McIlroy, Whiteside, Quinn, Stewart
ENGLAND Shilton, Anderson, Sansom, Steven,
Martin, Butcher, Stevens, Wilkins, Hateley,
Woodcock, Barnes

Belfast: 1 May '85
Northern Ireland (1) 2   Turkey (0) 0
   Whiteside 2
N.IRELAND Jennings, Nicholl, Donaghy,
J. O'Neill, McClelland, Ramsey, Brotherston,
McIlroy, Quinn, Whiteside, Stewart
TURKEY Erhan, Rasit, Abdulkerim, Semih,
O. Hasan, Yusuf, Ismail, Metin, Ilyas, Mujdat,
K. Hasan

OTHER MATCHES: 1984/5
Belfast: 16 October '84
Northern Ireland (3) 3   Israel (0) 0
   Whiteside,
   Quinn,
   Doherty
N.IRELAND Dunlop, Ramsey, Worthington,
J. O'Neill, McClelland, Cleary, Penney,
Doherty, Quinn, Whiteside (McGaughey),
Stewart (Brotherston)
ISRAEL Ginzburg, Shirazy, Pizanty, Ekhoys,
Cohen, Barda, Urmley, Turk, Landau, Maman,
Ohana.

Palma de Mallorca: 27 March '85
Spain (0) 0   Northern Ireland (0) 0
SPAIN Arconada, Gerardo, Julio Alberto,
Goicoechea, Maceda, Gordillo, Señor, Roberto,
Clos (Rincon), Gallego (Victor), Butragueno
(Rojo)
N.IRELAND Jennings, Nicholl, Donaghy,
McClelland, J. O'Neill, Ramsey, Quinn,
Armstrong (McCreery), Hamilton, Whiteside
(Worthington), Stewart

Wales v. Spain: in the home tie at Wrexham, Wales devastated the Spaniards with three goals — one a gift, the other two of the highest quality. This is the third: Mark Hughes' fulminating volley at chest height — a goal fit to grace the World Cup Finals.

WALES: INTERNATIONAL SEASON

WORLD CUP QUALIFYING GROUP 7
Reykjavik: 12 September '84
Iceland (0) 1   Wales (0) 0
  Bergs
ICELAND Sigurdsson, Thraisson, Sveinsson,
Bergs, Jonsson, Sigurvinsson, Edvaldsson,
Thorbjornsson, Gudlaugsson, Petursson,
Gratarsson
WALES Southall, Slatter, Hopkins, Ratcliffe,
G. Davies (Charles), Jackett, Thomas,
A. Davies, James, Hughes

Seville: 17 October '84
Spain (1) 3   Wales (0) 0
  Rincon, Carrasco,
  Butragueno
SPAIN Arconada, Goicoechea, Maceda,
Camacho, Señor, Victor, Francisco (Roberton),
Gordillo, Carrasco, Butragueno, Rincon
WALES Southall, Slatter, Charles, Ratcliffe,
Jackett, Phillips, James, Nicholas, Thomas
(Vaughan), Hughes, Curtis

Cardiff: 14 November '84
Wales (1) 2   Iceland (0) 1
  Thomas,   Petursson
  Hughes
WALES Southall, Slatter, Charles (Hopkins),
Ratcliffe, Jackett, Phillips, James, A. Davies,
Thomas, Hughes, Rush
ICELAND Sigurdson, Sigurdur Jonsson, Bergs,
Gratarsson (Eidsson), Savaer Jonsson,
Edvaldsson, Gudjohnsen, Petursson,
Margeirsson (Gislasson), Thorbjornsson,
Sveinsson

Hampden Park: 27 March '85 – *see Scotland
results section*

Wrexham: 30 April '85
Wales (1) 3   Spain (0) 0
  Rush 2, Hughes
WALES Southall, Slatter, Jackett, Ratcliffe, van
den Hauwe, Phillips, James, Nicholas,
Thomas, Rush, Hughes
SPAIN Arconada, Gerardo, Julio Alberto,
Maceda, Goicoechea, Gordillo, Rincon,
Liceranzu, Victor, Gallego (Caldere), Rojo

*Mexico City's Azteca Stadium,
venue for the Final of the World
Cup in 1986.*

1986 WORLD CUP PREVIEW

The choice of Mexico, with its problems not only of heat but of altitude, has loaded the dice against the European teams: it would be a considerable surprise if the winners were not South or Central American. Yet with Brazil and Argentina having only just begun their qualifying group matches at the time of writing, the strength of either is difficult to assess. Brazil, who lost to Chile (unsuccessful in the one South American group completed earlier) a week before their first qualifying match, typically changed their manager at the last moment – re-appointing Tele Santana in place of Evaristo. Brazil, who now seem likely to include their foreign superstars, will almost certainly be among the favourites. Argentina will be less powerful than at home, but should be better than in Spain; in particular, Diego Maradona seems to have rediscovered his appetite for the game. Uruguay, who sneaked past Chile in South America Group 2, have quite impressed some observers; they are strong and technically gifted but perhaps lack flair – though their new super-star Enzo Francescoli is capable of winning matches on his own.

Interest too will centre on which footballing country in the Third World emerges to make the sort of impression that Cameroon and Algeria made in Spain in 1982. Among the African qualifiers Zambia, who beat Cameroon in the second round, Algeria, Nigeria, Morocco and Tunisia could yield teams to create a major stir.

Europe, however, will inevitably pose the major threat to South America, with West Germany or England, if their qualifications can be assumed, the most likely candidates along with Italy, and perhaps France, if they can emerge from what had become one of the tightest groups at the time of going to press.

EUROPEAN GROUPS
Group 1
The group would be decided when Poland entertained Belgium on 11 September; it seemed likely that the always reliable Poles would go through as group winners. That would leave Belgium, as runners up in a four-team group, to play off against Holland, runners up in Group 5. Poland have a good record in World Cup final rounds, but unless the draw is favourable in Mexico it is difficult to see them repeating their third placings of 1974 and 1982.

	P	W	D	L	F	A	Pts
Poland	5	3	1	1	10	6	7
Belgium	5	3	1	1	7	3	7
Albania	5	1	1	4	5	8	3
Greece	5	1	1	4	4	9	3

Group 2
West Germany can not officially book their hotels in Mexico yet, but their 5-1 slaughter of Czechoslovakia in Prague in May was a telling indication that under Franz Beckenbauer the

major European football power of the past two decades was back on course. By the end of June they had qualified in all but name, and they looked the most likely finalists of all the European sides. Who would go to Mexico with them was still an open question. Sweden, having lost at home to Portugal in their first match, won the return in Lisbon to keep their own chances high. Second spot seemed between these two.

	P	W	D	L	F	A	Pts
West Germany	5	5	0	0	18	4	10
Sweden	5	3	0	2	9	4	6
Portugal	5	3	0	2	8	7	6
Czechoslovakia	5	1	1	3	6	9	3
Malta	6	0	1	5	3	20	1

Remaining matches: 25 September Sweden v. West Germany, Czechoslovakia v. Portugal; 12 October, Portugal v. Malta, 16 October, Czechoslovakia v. Sweden, West Germany v. Portugal; 17 November, West Germany v. Czechoslovakia, Malta v. Sweden.

Group 3: *see England report*

Group 4

The most convoluted group of all; two qualifiers. France, the European Champions – with Michel Platini, Jean Tigana, Alain Giresse, and the rest of the squad, they are the most exhilarating team in Europe on their day – should get through. They have the advantage of a home match (with Yugoslavia) to wrap up their programme on 16 November. But neither Yugoslavia, who have shown some signs of harnessing their enviable individual talents into a team, nor (especially) the formidable Bulgars can be treated lightly. By mid-June Bulgaria were leading not only on points but also on goal difference, and they seemed the likeliest to qualify with France.

	P	W	D	L	F	A	Pts
Bulgaria	6	4	1	1	9	2	9
Yugoslavia	6	3	2	1	6	4	8
France	5	3	1	1	7	2	7
East Germany	5	2	0	3	10	7	4
Luxembourg	6	0	0	6	1	18	0

Remaining fixtures: 11 September, East Germany v. France; 25 September, Luxembourg v. Bulgaria; 28 September, Yugoslavia v. East Germany; 30 October, France v Luxembourg; 16 November, France v Yugoslavia; E. Germany v Bulgaria.

Group 5

Hungary's progress to qualification was smooth enough for observers to conclude that, after years in the doldrums, a good Magyer side was developing again. Whether that will be enough to make them serious contenders in Mexico is more doubtful; and that doubt seemed to be confirmed when Holland – who were a far cry from the great Dutch sides of recent years –

Young fans at Denmark's fine victory against the USSR at Copenhagen. The Danes were the classiest team in Group 6 – but in summer 1985 each of the four other teams in the group still had a chance of joining them in Mexico.

snatched the runners-up spot on goal difference from Austria with a 1-0 win in Hungary in the final match. Holland would now play off against the runners-up from Group 1 (Belgium or Poland). The final table read:

	P	W	D	L	F	A	Pts
Hungary	6	5	0	1	12	4	10
Holland	6	3	1	2	11	5	7
Austria	6	3	1	2	9	8	7
Cyprus	6	0	0	6	3	18	0

Group 6

Possibly the hardest group of all, it seemed to prove far too much for a disorganised Republic of Ireland side, who failed to build on a brilliant opening match in which they beat the USSR in Dublin. That was followed by a lamentable 0-1 defeat at the hands of outsiders Norway and a collapse against the impressive Denmark team. A home draw with Norway, which led to renewed calls for the dismissal of manager Eoin Hand, made their chances of qualifying almost disappear. Denmark, with the impressive Morten Olsen dictating things from the back and some silky attacking players, looked favourites to win the group. Switzerland, who began well, and the USSR, with some outstanding players but a questionable away record, seemed to be the Danes' likeliest challengers. But anything could still happen – and Ireland certainly did their fading hopes a favour by a decisive home victory against Switzerland in June.

	P	W	D	L	F	A	Pts
Denmark	4	3	0	1	8	3	6
Ireland	5	2	1	2	4	4	5
Switzerland	5	2	1	2	4	9	5
USSR	5	1	2	2	9	8	4
Norway	5	1	2	2	2	3	4

Remaining fixtures: 11 September, Switzerland v. Ireland; 25 September, USSR v. Denmark; 9 October, Denmark v. Switzerland; 16 October, Norway v Denmark, USSR v. Ireland; 30 October, USSR v Norway; 13 November, Switzerland v. Norway, Ireland v. Denmark.

Group 7: *see Scotland report*

SOUTH AMERICA

Enzo Francescoli, the latest superstar in South American football, should figure prominently for Uruguay in the World Cup finals. How long before one of the top Spanish or Italian clubs lures him to Europe?

Enzo Francescoli is a name known to few European football fans – yet. But in the next couple of years he could be acclaimed as the greatest player in the world.

Francescoli, a 23-year-old Uruguayan, dominated South American football in 1984. A slim, immensely skilful player and very quick on the turn, he is one of the best things to have happened to Uruguayan and Argentinian football for several years.

He was the undoubted star of Uruguay's 1983 victory in the Campeonato Sudamericano de Fútbol, the nations' championship. But he plays his football in Argentina for the famous old River Plate club, for whom he was top scorer with 24 goals – including two which beat Unión Santa Fe in the last game of the season. Despite Francescoli's personal triumph, River Plate finished in mid-table. They are, in fact, only just emerging from a long period of economic crisis. Their chances of a brighter future rest heavily on Francescoli, whose displays for both River and his country in a series of warm-up matches before the world Cup qualifiers earned him the South American Footballer of the Year accolade.

Francescoli finished in front of two Argentinian stars. Runner-up was international goalkeeper Ubaldo Fillol, by then playing for Brazilian club Flamengo; third was Ricardo Enrique Bochini, the guiding light behind the double success of Independiente, who finished 1984 not only as winners of the Copa de los Libertadores, the continental club championship, for a record seventh time, but also as world club champions thanks to their defeat of Liverpool in the Toyota Cup match in Tokyo.

In the South American final Independiente dethroned the reigning world and continental champions, Gremio of Brazil. Yet Independiente concentrated so much on this prize that they finished out of the frame in Argentina, where the national club championship was won by little Argentinos Juniors – the club that earned fame (and fortune) thanks to the multi-million-dollar sale of Diego Maradona.

It was, in fact, a very good year for the little clubs. In Uruguay, Central Español, promoted only last season, won the league title – only the fourth club in 70 years to break the stranglehold exerted by the two giants, Peñarol and Nacional.

In Brazil, however, the minnows were put firmly in their place. Fluminense and former world club champions Santos (Pelé's old club) won the Río and São Paulo titles respectively. Fluminense thus completed a double: they had also won the national cup. It was generally agreed to be a rather unexciting year in Brazilian football, with stars like Zico, Cerezo, Socrates, Falcâo, Junior and others making their fortunes in Europe.

Continental Survey

Outside the big three countries – Brazil, Argentina and Uruguay – there were the usual excitements and scandals on and off the pitch.

In *Bolivia* Blooming club of Santa Cruz de la Sierra won the championship for the first time in their 38-year history. In a play-off they beat champions Bolívar – who boast the best-paid footballer in the country in Erwin Romero, a midfielder, who is alleged to command the princely sum of £100 a week.

In *Chile* the game was thrown into confusion when the FA president Antonio Martinez was arrested on bank-fraud charges; and the situation of the FA became even more desperate when court officials seized the association's office equipment to meet the back-pay claim of a former player of debt-ridden Universidad de Chile. The title went to their age-old rivals, Universidad Catolica, whose brightest star was Jorge Aravena – nicknamed the Mortar because of the ferocity of his shooting.

In *Ecuador* the army club, Nacional, won the championship – to nobody's surprise since they and their influential fans appeared to regard football as merely another form of warfare. When one Nacional match turned into a pitched battle between the players, a senior army colonel arrested the football federation's official observer and ordered all press cameras to be seized and smashed so as to ruin the films and destroy the evidence.

In *Paraguay*, in one of the most complex of South American league championships, the six-year reign of former continental and world club champions Olímpia was at last broken. The new champions were Guarani of Asunción, managed by former international centre-forward Cayetano Re – who was immediately lured away by the national federation to rebuild Paraguay's team for the 1986 World Cup qualifying matches. As for unfashionable Guarani, they had been the first Paraguayan champions, back in 1906, and played in the first-ever official football match in that country – against Olímpia!

In *Peru* former World Cup boss Marcos Calderón took unfashionable Sport Boys, from the port of Callao, to the domestic title. But it was the famous old club Alianza of Lima (for whom World Cup star Teófilo Cubillas plays) who grabbed most headlines. The bad news was the worst-ever first division crowd in Lima – just 526 to see Alianza's game against struggling Octavio Espinoza. The good news was Alianza's 11-0 win over Sport Pilsen – a record for the Peruvian first division.

In *Venezuela*, where football remains second in popularity to baseball, Táchira won the championship; while in *Colombia* America Cali landed the title for the third year in a row.

FOOTBALLER OF THE YEAR

Chosen by the Football Writers' Association
1 Neville Southall (Everton)
2 Peter Reid (Everton)
3 Mark Hughes (Manchester United)

In January 1983, after 40 games in Division 1, former dustman Neville Southall found himself on loan to Port Vale and wondering where, if anywhere, his career was heading. True, Everton had considered him worth paying Bury £150,000 for; but that was 18 months earlier, at a time when their transfer dealings were not exactly a model of financial prudence – and the Division 4 was Division 4, whether at Vale Park or Gigg Lane.

He was not, however, destined to stay for long at that level. Manager Howard Kendall, who had authorised the cheque to Bury, and then almost immediately spent even more on his old Blackburn goalkeeper Jim Arnold, insists that Southall was a prized possession, merely gaining experience in the Football League rather than the Central League.

That experience was put to such good use by both men that last spring the nation's footballer writers decided he was a worthy successor to the likes of Matthews, Finney, Blanchflower, Moore, Best and Dalglish as Footballer of the Year – only the fourth goalkeeper, after Bert Trautmann (1956), Gordon Banks (1972) and Pat Jennings (1973), to win the award.

It was understandable that they should be looking for candidates through blue-tinted glasses. Claims could be made, and votes cast, for Reid and Ratcliffe in particular. So they were: Evertonians collected more than 60 per cent of all nominations. But Southall's timing was perfect. As the snow-bound season came out of hibernation and football journalists' thoughts turned to their annual poll, he produced a series of performances impossible to overlook.

In what turned out to be the most decisive week of the championship race there were superlative saves from Kevin Bond at Southampton and Mark Falco at Tottenham – earning his team six points instead of two. In the FA Cup Semi-final at Villa Park he made half a dozen notable stops to prevent Luton upsetting the odds. Three days later, with some of his defenders possibly resting on their laurels, four more outstanding saves at home to West Bromwich Albion ensured a flattering win and a four-point lead at the top. Add to that a clean sheet away to Bayern Munich in the European Cup-Winners' Cup Semi-final and seldom can any footballer have done a better month's work.

For Kendall he is 'the best in the business'; for Peter Reid, runner-up to him in this poll, even less ambiguously 'the best in the world'. For the rest of us he remains a splendid example of the late developer (not establishing himself in Division 1 until the age of 25) who, having endured the hard life, genuinely appreciates his privileges. Like Ian Rush, he is an unpretentious North Walian who even declines to wear the gaudy modern goalkeeper's jerseys, preferring to buy and tend his own. When you've been a bin-man, high fashion doesn't count for much.

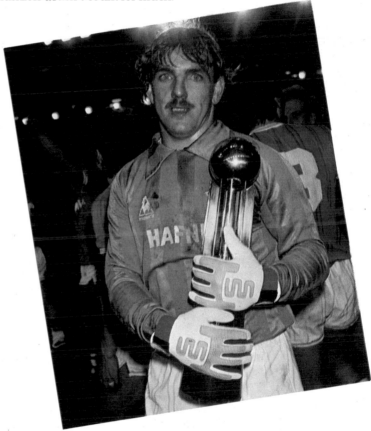

PFA Player of the Year 1984/5
(chosen by the Professional Footballers' Association)
1. Peter Reid (Everton)
2. Bryan Robson (Manchester United)
3. Mark Lawrenson (Liverpool)
Special Merit Award for Services to Football: Ron Greenwood

The selection of Peter Reid as Player of the Year for 1984 came as a surprise to some. Unsung and perhaps even unnoticed by many supporters and critics, he was nevertheless a linchpin of an Everton side that in the course of an astonishingly successful calendar year lost only five League games, made three separate trips to Wembley

Neville Southall, Everton and Wales goalkeeper, with the League Championship trophy he helped to bring to Goodison. A popular choice as Footballer of the Year, he and Peter Shilton ran neck and neck in most people's arguments about the best keeper in Europe.

Play-maker, gap-plugger, morale-booster and general work-horse, Peter Reid is one of those super-competent jacks-of-all-trades that are an essential element of all the great club sides. His all-round gifts were successfully translated into the international arena when he was awarded his first England cap at the end of the season.

warming triumph over the old adversary, injury. As Reid himself says, 'It makes success all the sweeter'. After playing a leading role when his first club, Bolton Wanderers, won the Division 2 championship in 1978, he suffered the first of a whole series of injuries, and for four successive seasons he missed more games than he played.

Those were unhappy days when the late Jim Edrich, Bolton's physiotherapist, did more than anyone to keep Reid going and keep him hoping. Once he got fit, the chance came to join Arsenal and, later, Wolves. Both moves fell through, however, and he was a 26-year-old who had failed to translate potential into achievement when Howard Kendall paid a modest £60,000 to bring him to his native Merseyside.

That was December 1982, and after only seven games Reid was injured again and missed the rest of the season. Twelve months later Everton and Kendall were at their lowest ebb, but Reid, in his quiet, unspectacular way, held the team together, collecting the ball from his defenders, giving it in turn to his trusted midfield henchmen or sending Sharp or Heath forward.

Another year and a bit, and as the 1985 season approached its climax the Spurs manager Peter Shreeves, finally conceding that Everton were the championship favourites, picked Reid out to deny suggestion that they were a team with no stars. 'Peter Reid is a star,' he said, 'But a star who conforms to the team pattern. He controls the ball, he uses it and his passing is superb'.

The man himself is typically down-beat about this belated recognition. 'I'm lucky with the players I have around me. And the team's great turn-around has mainly been a matter of confidence, just confidence in our own ability. We've got a strong squad, and when players have come in they're not well-known but they've done a good job'.

As for manager Kendall, what does he feel he got for his £60,000? 'The kind of player who can make things happen. Makes openings and has excellent defensive qualities ... and works like a Trojan'.

All in all, not a bad investment.

(winning twice), and finally shook off the feelings of inferiority engendered for too long by Merseyside's other team.

Neither Reid's style nor his physical presence are calculated to impress. In the days when he weighed in 160lb, his 5ft 7in frame looked positively dumpy; even today, when he is almost a stone lighter, he is never going to be mistaken for, say, team-mate Trevor Steven. Thick-set and greying, he looks more than his 29 years, and the slightly hunched style and ungainly run mark him as a stayer rather than a sprinter.

An unflattering picture; and when his fellow-professionals looked the Division 1 up and down to find the year's most distinguished contributor, this George Smiley of a footballer was the man their thoughts turned to most often. He became the first non-international to win the PFA award.

Many of them were doubtless attracted to his

PFA YOUNG PLAYER OF THE YEAR

MARK HUGHES (MANCHESTER UNITED)

There was never much doubt that Mark Hughes, Manchester United's 21-year-old Welsh forward, would win the Young Player of the Year award, for his impact in his first full season was breathtaking. He burst into the limelight at the very start of the season, keeping Alan Brazil (Ron Atkinson's latest expensive signing) out of the side with a series of dazzling performances. It was not merely that he scored 25 goals for his club, impressive as that total is: just as important was their quality, for they included a high proportion of spectacular efforts that stamped Hughes as a player of exceptional ability as well as strength.

Few will forget the glorious volley which flew past Luis Arconada when Spain played Wales in a World Cup qualifier at Wrexham in April 1985. That goal required courage as well as high skill, for it was taken with coolness while defenders' boots lunged desperately to get it away. Almost as thrilling was a trio of volleys – two of which counted, the third crashing off the woodwork – when Hughes, showing a nice sense of timing, claimed a hat-trick against Aston Villa the day before the award was officially announced. It is often said that today's football lacks players with a flair and skill of past giants, but it is doubtful whether the watching Bobby Charlton (now a United director) ever struck the ball consistently better than Hughes did that afternoon. Add his dribbling skill and his eye for the killing pass, and it is clear that Hughes is well on the way to becoming a player to stand with the great forwards of Manchester United's past.

Hughes not only scores superb goals: he has the knack of scoring vital ones, including the winner in the FA Cup Semi-final replay against Liverpool, when he ran on to Strachan's beautifully weighted forward pass, with the Liverpool defence at his heels, to beat Grobbelaar with a perfectly placed low shot. Shooting and dribbling ability are not the young Welshman's only assets. He is also good and brave in the air for someone of his height, and, as his powerful thighs suggest, he is formidably strong in the tackle, as befits a player who went to Old Trafford initially as a midfield player. Indeed physical contact is an important part of the quiet, intelligent Hughes' approach, and defenders are left in no doubt that they will know they have been in a game when they are facing him. 'I like to get my tackles in early in the game', he says

with relish. He certainly let the Spanish defence know he was around very early in the Wrexham game; and the way he battled with Scotland's Alex McLeish to lay on the chance for Ian Rush which gave Wales their vital World Cup qualifier win at Hampden Park was a classic example of his competitiveness and strength. He is already talked about as a £1m player; if he can repeat the form of 1984/5 he will soon be regarded as beyond price.

Mark Hughes' authentic star quality resides in his strength, his courage and, above all, in his priceless ability to score truly vital goals, often of a thrilling virtuosity.

MANAGERS OF THE YEAR

HOWARD KENDALL (EVERTON)

Merseyside had won virtually everything available on the domestic scene in the 1983/4 season, and Howard Kendall's choice as Manager of the Year for 1984/5 was both a forgone conclusion and perhaps the most popular of all the awards.

It is almost impossible to believe now that Kendall – with victories in the League Championship, European Cup-Winners' Cup, FA Cup (1984) and two other final appearances in 15 months under his belt – was thought to be fighting for his managerial life only three months before the success story began. In January 1984 Everton had sunk to 18th in Division 1, and gates at Goodison had fallen as low as 13,000 – a figure

that included quite a number of supporters who were handing out leaflets demanding the dismissal of their young manager, who had been a member of the famous 1970 league-championship midfield with Alan Ball and Colin Harvey.

Everton's chairman Philip Carter, however, was unimpressed with the demonstrations and was unwavering in support of his manager. And by then, although the demonstrating fans did not realise it, the corner had already been turned. On 18 January a back pass by Oxford United's Kevin Brock let in Adrian Heath for a late equaliser in Everton's 5th-round Milk Cup tie at Oxford. From then onwards Everton did not look back, going on to reach the first of two Wembley Cup finals that year. Kendall, in fact, had already

Howard Kendall, talented, uncompromising but fair as a midfielder in his playing days at Goodison (see page 93) has brought all these qualities to his managerial career. His success is such that, for 1984/5, he had no serious rival as the Football League Manager of the Year.

assembled the team which made such an impact in 1984/5; the final touches had appeared in November 1983 with the signing of striker Andy Gray and the promotion of Kendall's former midfield partner Harvey to first-team coach.

Kendall, who had returned to Goodison after taking Blackburn Rovers into Division 2, has deserved his success. He refused to be deflected by the criticism, and he has responded to success in the same level-headed, determined manner. His teams, like him as a player, display total commitment and also a good deal of skill. Andy Gray, Peter Reid, Paul Bracewell, Trevor Steven – all Kendall signings – and most others in the squad bring flair, competitiveness, and a daunting self-belief to his side. That the quiet north-easterner – in 1964 the youngest player to play in a Cup Final, when he was with Preston North End – was never to gain an England cap is one of football's anomalies; and Everton's sudden descent into mediocrity after their league championship in 1970 left Kendall sadly short of medals. He seems bound to make up for those gaps as a manager.

Among the other candidates for the managers of the year awards, the claims of Jim Smith (Oxford United) for the Division 2 slot could scarcely be ignored. Many old soccer hands had thought that, however total the club's dominance of Division 3 might have been in the 1983/4 season, United could find themselves out of their depth in Division 2. As it turned out, Smith's side not only won the divisional championship but proved mature enough on numerous occasions, and in spite of the long absence of their key striker Billy Hamilton, to regain their

---

Divisional Managers of the Year

Division 2 Jim Smith (Oxford United)
Division 3 Trevor Cherry (Bradford City)
Division 4 John Duncan (Chesterfield)

---

momentum after sticky spells. There is, perhaps, better reason to cast doubt on their prospects in Division 1, especially after the departure of Smith to take over at Queen's Park Rangers.

The managerial awards for the two lowest divisions went to distinguished former players who look set to prosper in their new careers. At Valley Parade, Bradford City's Trevor Cherry, the former Leeds United and England defender, has formed a fruitful partnership with Terry Yorath, once an inspirational captain of Wales. And the promotion of Chesterfield from Division 4 was a nice reward for John Duncan after his experiences as manager at Scunthorpe United.

TOMMY McLEAN (MOTHERWELL)

Last year's winner Alex Ferguson, whose Aberdeen team withstood the loss of Strachan, McGee and Rougvie to emerge without challenge as champions; Celtics's Davie Hay, who took a major trophy back to Parkhead at last; the oldest member of the McLean clan, Jim, whose Dundee United side reached two finals – all made powerful bids for the Scottish Brewers' Managerial Personality of the Year award. Yet few would quarrel with the eventual decision to give it to the youngest managerial McLean, Tommy, who has made such a stunning impact in less than two seasons in charge of Motherwell. Tommy was noted as a clever, thoughtful player during his career with Kilmarnock and Rangers, and it was no surprise when he joined John Greig's staff at Ibrox, where his former colleague had taken over as manager. But, that being the way things happen in football, Tommy's fate was bound with Greig's, and when the expected successes at Ibrox were not forthcoming, both he and Greig left the club they had served so well in November 1983. McLean has not looked back. He almost immediately went to Morton – as part-time manager of a part-time team – and took the Greenock club to the Division 1 championship that year after less than a full season in charge. Morton replaced Motherwell, a bigger club with bigger resources, in the Premier Division – but Tommy stayed in Division 1 to take over at Fir Park. He met with considerable success at once: Motherwell won the championship to regain their place in the top flight at the first time of asking; and they also had an excellent Scottish FA Cup run, reaching the semi-final. There they fell to Celtic, but the Parkhead giants needed a replay to get through, and might well have lost to Motherwell in the first game. If confirmation was still needed that there is a McLean on the horizon who could threaten his eldest brother's position as one of the two outstanding managers in the country, those semi-final performances provided it. Tommy McLean's shrewd appraisal of the opposition and clever tactical planning marked him down as a manager of exceptional promise. In the not too distant future Alex Ferguson and Jim McLean may have to look to their laurels.

NON-LEAGUE

Wealdstone and Telford United could both fairly lay claim to any 'Non-League Team of the Season' award. The latter's exploits in the FA Cup (which exceeded even their magnificent efforts of the season before) are chronicled elsewhere, while Wealdstone became the first team in non-league soccer history to achieve the unique double of Gola League title and FA Trophy in the same season. Not to be outdone were Halesowen Town. They too achieved a remarkable double, in their case success in the FA Vase to go with their championship of the West Midlands League. Had Everton won the FA Cup, they would have been only the third side of the season to achieve a 'double'!

With the 1983/4 Gola League champions Maidstone going through something of a transition period under their new ex-Barnet manager Barry Fry, Wealdstone took the title, while, for the second season running, Nuneaton gained the runners-up spot. Bath City were the Gola League's candidates for election to the Football League; but at the Football League's Annual General Meeting in June they canvassed only eight votes; as usual, the four clubs seeking re-election were all successful.

A further blow to the aspirations of the Gola League to be regarded as a genuine 'Fifth Division' came when the Football League also rejected the suggestion of an annual play-off between the bottom club in Division 4 and the Gola League champions for a Football League place.

Further down the non-league scale, the strength of the game at this level was consolidated by the expansion of the Servowarm Isthmian League into four divisions. Sutton United, winners of the Hitachi Cup in 1983/4, took the Premier Division title while Worthing, runners-up to Harrow Borough in the previous campaign, once more had to be satisfied with the bridesmaid's role. New sponsors are backing the Isthmian League next season: with Servowarm bowing out, car giants General Motors take over. They have christened their new offspring the Vauxhall-Opel Isthmian League.

THE CUPS

FA Trophy
Winners Wealdstone
Runners-up Boston Utd
FA Vase
Winners Halesowen Town
Runners-up Fleetwood Town
Bob Lord Trophy
Winners Runcorn
Runners-up Maidstone Utd
Bill Dellow Cup
Winners Fisher Athletic
Runners-Up Cheltenham Town

Hitachi Cup
Winners Wycombe Wanderers
Runners-up Farnborough Town

THE LEAGUE

Gola League
Winners Wealdstone
Runners-up Nuneaton Borough
Northern Premier League
Winners Stafford Rangers
Runners-up Macclesfield Town
Southern League Premier Division
Winners Cheltenham Town
Runners-up Kings Lynn
Southern League Midland Division
Winners Dudley Town
Runners-up Aylesbury Utd
Southern League Southern Division
Winners Basingstoke Town
Runners-up Gosport Borough
Servowarm Isthmian League Premier Division
Winners Sutton Utd
Runners-up Worthing
Servowarm Isthmian League Division 1
Winners Farnborough Town
Runners-up Kingstonian
Servowarm Isthmian League Division 2 North
Winners Leyton-Wingate
Runners-up Finchley
Servowarm Isthmian League Division 2 South
Winners Grays Athletic
Runners-up Uxbridge

FA Trophy: Boston United keeper Kevin Blackwell saves the 20th-minute penalty from Wealdstone's Dennis Byatt (4). Looking on are Wealdstone's Lee Holmes (8) and Brian Greenaway (7), and Boston's Ian Ladd (5).

CLUB
DIRECTORY

Right *Len Walker (Aldershot), who made a club-record 450 League appearances in 1964-76.*

Preceding two pages *The Kop at Anfield, Liverpool.*

Below *Diminutive baggy-trousered Alex James was an elusive, deadly striker when Herbert Chapman brought him to Highbury from Preston North End in 1929. For Arsenal he evolved into possibly the greatest British midfielder of the inter-war years, master-minding four League titles and two Cup triumphs in seven seasons.*

ALDERSHOT

Chairman R.J. Driver
Team Manager Len Walker until November 1984; Ron Harris from November 1984
Asst Manager/1st team coach Ian Gillard
Captain Ian Macdonald
Year formed 1926
Ground address Recreation Ground, High St, Aldershot, Hants GU11 1TW
Telephone 0252 20211
Present ground capacity 16,000
Record crowd 19,138 v. Carlisle United, FA Cup, 4th round replay, 28 January 1970
Nickname 'The Shots'

1984/5 Record
League 13th, Div 4
FA Cup Lost to Burton Albion, 2nd rnd, 0-3
Milk Cup Lost to Norwich City, 3rd rnd rep., 0-4

Historical Highlights
League Best position – 8th in Div 3, 1974. Div 3, 1973-6; Div 3(S) 1932-58; Div 4 1958-73, 1976-
FA Cup Best – 5th round, 1933, 1979
League/Milk Cup Never past 3rd rnd
Top Scorer John Dungworth: 26 (1978/9)

ARSENAL

Chairman P.D. Hill-Wood
Team Manager Don Howe
1st team coach Terry Burton
Captain Kenny Sansom from August 1985
Year formed 1886
Previous names Royal Arsenal, 1886-91; Woolwich Arsenal, 1891-1914

Ground address Arsenal Stadium, Highbury, London N5
Telephone 01-226 0304
Present ground capacity 60,000
Record crowd 73,295 v. Sunderland, Division 1, 9 March 1935
Nickname 'The Gunners'
Sponsor JVC

1984/5 Record
League 7th, Div 1
FA Cup Lost to York C., 4th rnd, 0-1
Milk Cup Lost to Oxford United, 3rd round, 2-3

Historical Highlights
League Div 1 Champions 1931, 1933, 1934, 1935, 1938, 1953, 1971; runners-up 1926, 1932, 1973. Div 1, 1904-13, 1919-; Div 2, 1893-1904, 1913-19
FA Cup Winners 1930, 1936, 1950, 1971, 1979; runners-up 1927, 1932, 1952, 1972, 1978, 1980
League/Milk Cup Runners-up 1968, 1969
Europe European Cup 1972; European Cup-Winners' Cup 1980 (runners-up); Fairs Cup 1964, 1970 (winners), 1971; UEFA Cup 1979, 1982, 1983
Top Scorer Ted Drake: 42 (1934/5)

ASTON VILLA

Chairman H.D. Ellis
Team Manager Tony Barton until June 1984; Graham Turner from July 1984
Asst Manager/1st team coach Bill Shorthouse
Captain Allan Evans
Year formed 1878
Ground address Villa Park, Trinity Road, Birmingham B6 6HE
Telephone 021 327 6604
Present ground capacity 48,000
Record crowd 76,588 v. Derby County, FA Cup, qtr final, 2 March 1946
Nickname 'The Villans'
Sponsor Mita Copiers

1984/5 Record
League 10th, Div 1
FA Cup Lost to Liverpool, 3rd rnd, 0-3
Milk Cup Lost to Queen's Park Rangers, 3rd rnd, 0-1

Historical Highlights
League Div 1 champions 1894, 1896, 1897, 1899, 1900, 1910, 1981. Div 1, 1888-1936, 1938-59, 1960-7, 1975-; Div 2, 1936-8, 1959-60, 1967-70, 1972-5; Div 3, 1970-2
FA Cup Winners 1887, 1895, 1897, 1905, 1913, 1920, 1957; runners-up 1892, 1924
League/Milk Cup Winners 1962, 1975, 1977; runners-up 1963, 1971

Europe European Cup 1982 (winners), 1983; UEFA Cup 1976, 1978; World Club Championship 1982; European Super Cup 1982 (winners).
Top Scorer 'Pongo' Waring: 49 (1930/1)

BARNSLEY

Chairman G. Buckle, LLB
Team Manager Bobby Collins until June 1985; then Allan Clarke
Asst Manager/1st team coach Eric Winstanley
Captain Joe Joyce
Year formed 1887
Ground address Oakwell Ground, Grove St, Barnsley, Sth Yorks S71 1ET
Telephone 0226 295353
Present ground capacity 35,554
Record crowd 40,255 v. Stoke City, FA Cup, 5th round, 15 February 1936
Nickname 'The Tykes' or 'The Reds'
Sponsor Hayselden & Sons

1984/5 Record
League 11th, Div 2
FA Cup Lost to Liverpool, 6th rnd, 0-4
Milk Cup Lost to Grimsby T., 2nd rnd, 1-4 on agg.

Historical Highlights
League Best position – 3rd in Div 2, 1915, 1922. Div 2, 1898-1932, 1934-8, 1946-53, 1955-9, 1981-; Div 3, 1959-65, 1968-72, 1979-81; Div 3(N), 1932-4, 1938-9, 1953-5; Div 4, 1965-8, 1972-9
FA Cup Winners 1912; runners-up 1910

League/Milk Cup 5th rnd 1982
Top Scorer Cecil McCormack: 33 (1950/1)

BIRMINGHAM CITY

Chairman C.K. Coombs
Team Manager Ron Saunders
Asst Manager/1st team coach Keith Leonard
Captain Billy Wright
Year formed 1875
Previous names Small Heath Alliance 1875-78; Small Heath 1888-1905
Ground address St Andrew's, Birmingham B9 4NH
Telephone 021 772 0101/2689
Present ground capacity 44,500
Record crowd 66,844 v. Everton, FA Cup, 5th round, 11 February 1939
Nickname 'The Blues'
Sponsor Ansell's Brewery

1984/5 Record
League 2nd, Div 2: promoted
FA Cup Lost to Norwich, 3d rnd rep., 0-1
Milk Cup Lost to W. Brom, 3rd rnd rep., 1-3

Historical Highlights
League Best position – 6th in Div 1, 1956. Div 1, 1894-6, 1901-2, 1903-8, 1921-39, 1948-50, 1955-65, 1972-9, 1980-4; Div 2, 1892-4, 1896-1901, 1902-3, 1908-21, 1946-8, 1950-5, 1965-72, 1979-80, 1984-5
FA Cup Runners-up 1931, 1956
League/Milk Cup Winners 1963
Europe Fairs Cup 1958, 1960 (runners-up), 1961 (runners-up), 1962
Top Scorer Walter Abbott: 33 (1898/9)

Above *Aston Villa's Gordon Cowans (left) and skipper Allan Evans celebrate their European Cup triumph over Bayern Munich in May 1982 – the sixth win in succession by a British club.*

Below *Trevor Francis was only 16 when he became a star striker at Birmingham City. He was the subject of the first British £1 million transfer fee when Brian Clough brought him to Nottingham Forest in February 1979.*

Above *Nat Lofthouse (Bolton Wanderers), a great England centre forward of the 1950s in the Dixie Dean and Tommy Lawton mould – big, strong and a superb header of the ball.*

BLACKBURN ROVERS

Chairman W. Fox
Team Manager Bobby Saxton
Asst Manager/1st team coach
  Jim Furnell & Tony Parkes
Captain Derek Fazackerley
Year formed 1875 from
  Blackburn Grammar School
  O.B. Football Club
Ground address Ewood Park, Blackburn
Telephone 0254 55432
Present ground capacity 23,400
Record crowd 61,783 v. Bolton Wanderers,
  FA Cup, qtr final, 2 March 1929
Nickname 'The Blue & Whites'
Sponsor ICI

1984/5 Record
League 5th, Div 2
FA Cup Lost to Manchester Utd, 5th rnd, 0-2
Milk Cup Lost to Oxford Utd, 2nd rnd, 2-4

Milk Cup Lost to Ipswich Town, 2nd round,
  4-6 on agg.

Historical Highlights
League Div 1 champions 1912, 1914. Div 1,
  1888-1936, 1946-7, 1957-66; Div 2, 1936-9,
  1947-57, 1966-71, 1975-9, 1980-; Div 3,
  1971-5, 1979-80
FA Cup Winners 1884, 1885, 1886, 1890, 1891,
  1928; runners-up 1882, 1960
League/Milk Cup Semi-final 1962
Top Scorer Ted Harper: 43 (1925/6)

BLACKPOOL

Chairman K. Chadwick, LLB
Team Manager Sam Ellis
Asst Manager/1st team coach
  Jack Chapman
Captain Steve Hetzke
Year formed 1887
Previous names Blackpool St
  John's Club, 1887-99; South
  Shore combined with
  Blackpool in 1899
Ground address Bloomfield Road, Blackpool
Telephone 0253 404331
Present ground capacity 18,000
Record crowd 39,118 v. Manchester United,
  Division 1, 19 April 1952
Nickname 'The Seasiders'
Sponsor F.H. Brown & Co

1984/5 Record
League 2nd, Div 4: promoted
FA Cup Lost to Altrincham, 1st rnd, 0-1
Milk Cup Lost to Manchester City, 2nd rnd,
  3-7 on agg.

Historical Highlights
League Best position – Div 1 runners-up 1956.
  Div 1, 1930-3, 1937-67, 1970-1; Div 2, 1896-9,
  1900-30, 1933-7, 1967-70, 1971-8; Div 3,
  1978-81; Div 4, 1981-
FA Cup Winners 1953; runners-up 1948
League/Milk Cup Semi-final 1962
Europe Anglo-Italian Cup 1971 (winners),
  1972 (runners-up)
Top Scorer Jimmy Hampson: 45 (1929/30)

Right *Bournemouth's Division 3 team that reached the quarter-finals of the FA Cup in 1957.*

BOLTON WANDERERS

Chairman T. Edge
Team Manager John McGovern to January 1985; Charlie Wright from January 1985
Asst Manager/1st team coach Charlie Wright to Jan 1985
Captain Brian Borrows
Year formed 1874 as Christchurch Football Club, until 1877
Ground address Burnden Park, Manchester Road, Bolton BL3 2QR
Telephone 0204 389200
Present ground capacity 43,000
Record crowd 69,912 v. Manchester City, FA Cup, 5th round, 18 February 1933
Nickname 'The Trotters'
Sponsor: H. B. Electronics

1984/5 Record
League 17th, Div 3
FA Cup Lost to Hull C., 1st rnd, 1-2
Milk Cup Lost to Notts C., 3rd rnd, 1-6

Historical Highlights
League Best position – 3rd in Div 1, 1892, 1921, 1925. Div 1, 1888-9, 1900-3, 1905-8, 1909-10, 1911-33, 1935-64, 1978-80; Div 2, 1889-1900, 1903-5, 1908-9, 1910-11, 1933-5, 1964-71, 1973-8, 1980-3; Div 3, 1971-3, 1983-
FA Cup Winners 1923, 1926, 1929, 1958; runners-up 1894, 1904, 1953
League/Milk Cup Semi-final 1967
Top Scorer Joe Smith: 38 (1920/1)

AFC BOURNEMOUTH

Chairman Rodney J. C. Barton
Team Manager Harry Redknapp
Asst Manager/1st team coach Stuart Morgan
Captain Roger Brown
Year formed 1899
Previous names Boscombe FC, 1899-1923; Bournemouth & Boscombe Ath., 1923-71
Ground address Dean Court Ground, Bournemouth, Dorset BH7 7AH
Telephone 0202 35381
Present ground capacity 19,175
Record crowd 28,799 v. Manchester United, FA Cup, qtr final, 2 March 1957
Nickname 'The Cherries'
Sponsor Coopers of Wessex

1984/5 Record
League 10th, Div 3
FA Cup Lost to Man. Utd, 3rd rnd, 0-3
Milk Cup Lost to Aldershot, 1st rnd, 0-5 on agg.

Historical Highlights
League Best position – 3rd in Div 3, 1962, 1972. Div 3, 1948-70, 1971-5, 1982-; Div 3 (5), 1923-48; Div 4, 1970-1, 1975-82
FA Cup 6th rnd, 1957
League/Milk Cup 4th rnd, 1962, 1964, 1971
Associate Members' Cup Winners 1984
Top Scorer Ted Macdougall: 42 (1970/1)

BRADFORD CITY

Chairman Stafford Heginbotham
Team Manager Trevor Cherry
Asst Manager/1st team coach Terry Yorath
Captain Peter Jackson
Year formed 1903
Ground address Valley Parade Ground, Bradford BD8 7DY
Telephone 0274 306062
Present ground capacity 16,000
Record crowd 39,146 v Burnley, FA Cup, 4th round, 11 March 1911
Nickname 'The Bantams'
Sponsor Bradford Mythbreakers

1984/5 Record
League Champions, Div 3: promoted
FA Cup Lost to Telford Utd, 3rd rnd, 1-2
Milk Cup Lost to Newcastle United, 2nd rnd, 1-4 on agg.

Historical Highlights
League Best position – 5th in Div 1, 1911. Div 1, 1908-22; Div 2, 1903-8, 1922-7, 1929-37; Div 3, 1937-61, 1969-72, 1977-8, 1982-5; Div 3(N), 1927-9; Div 4, 1961-9, 1972-7, 1978-82
FA Cup Winners 1911
League/Milk Cup 5th rnd 1965
Top Scorer David Layne: 34 (1961/2)

Bradford City had their best-ever year in 1911, coming fifth in Division 1 and, as the picture shows, winning the FA Cup, beating Newcastle United 1-0 in a replay.

Above *Dai Hopkins, 1930s stalwart for Brentford. His 12 caps (for Wales) remain a record for the club.*

Below *Peter Ward, a devastating striker for Brighton in the mid-1970s, holds the club's record for League goals – 32 in 1976/7.*

BRENTFORD

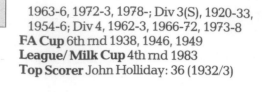

Chairman M.M. Lange
Team Manager Frank McLintock
Asst Manager/1st team coach Frank Blunstone until February 1984; John Docherty from February 1984
Captain Terry Hurlock
Year formed 1889
Ground address Griffin Park, Braemar Road, Middx, TW8 ONT
Telephone 01-847 2511
Present ground capacity 37,000
Record crowd 39,626 v. Preston North End, FA Cup, qtr final, 5 March 1938
Nickname 'The Bees'
Sponsor KLM Airlines

1984/5 Record
League 13th, Div 3
FA Cup Lost to Oldham Ath, 3rd rnd, 1-2
Milk Cup Lost to Leicester C.,, 2nd rnd, 0-6 on agg.
Freight Rover Trophy Finalists: lost to Wigan Ath, 1-3

Historical Highlights
League Best position – 5th in Div 1, 1936. Div 1, 1935-47; Div 2, 1933-5, 1947-54; Div 3, 1963-6, 1972-3, 1978-; Div 3(S), 1920-33, 1954-6; Div 4, 1962-3, 1966-72, 1973-8
FA Cup 6th rnd 1938, 1946, 1949
League/Milk Cup 4th rnd 1983
Top Scorer John Holliday: 36 (1932/3)

BRIGHTON & HOVE ALBION

Chairman M.K. Bamber
Team Manager Chris Cattlin
Reserve team youth coach/chief scout George Petchey & George Aitken
Captain Danny Wilson
Year formed 1900 as Brighton & Hove Rangers
Ground address Goldstone Ground, Old Shoreham Rd, Hove, Sussex BN3 7DE
Telephone 0273 739535
Present ground capacity 28,600
Record crowd 36,747 v. Fulham, Division 2, 27 December 1958
Nickname 'The Seagulls'
Sponsor Phoenix Breweries

1984/5 Record
League 6th, Div 2
FA Cup Lost to Barnsley, 4th rnd, 1-2
Milk Cup Lost to Aldershot, 2nd rnd, 3-4 on agg.

Historical Highlights
League Best position – 16th in Div 1, 1980. Div 1, 1979-83; Div 2, 1958-62, 1972-3, 1977-9, 1983-; Div 3, 1962-3, 1965-72, 1973-7; Div 3(S), 1920-58
FA Cup Runners-up 1983
League/Milk Cup 5th rnd 1979
Top Scorer Peter Ward: 32 (1976/7)

BRISTOL CITY

Chairman D. Williams
Team Manager Terry Cooper
Asst Manager/1st team coach Clive Middlemass
Captain Bob Hutchinson
Year formed 1894 as Bristol South End; as Bristol City from 1897
Ground address Ashton Gate, Bristol, BS3 2EJ
Telephone 0272 632812
Present ground capacity 30,868
Record crowd 43,335 v. Preston North End, FA Cup, 5th round, 16 February 1935
Nickname 'The Robins'
Sponsor Hire-Rite Ltd

1984/5 Record
League 5th, Div 3
FA Cup Lost to Bristol Rovers, 2nd rnd, 1-3
Milk Cup Lost to West Ham United, 2nd rnd, 3-8 on agg.

Historical Highlights
League Best position – Div 1 runners-up 1907.
Div 1, 1906-11, 1976-80; Div 2, 1901-6 1911-22, 1923-4, 1927-32, 1955-60, 1965-76, 1980-1; Div 3, 1960-5, 1981-2; Div 3(S), 1922-3, 1924-7, 1932-55; Div 4, 1982-4
FA Cup Runners-up 1909
League/Milk Cup Semi-final 1971
Anglo-Scottish Cup Winners 1978
Top Scorer Don Clark: 36 (1946/7)

BRISTOL ROVERS

Chairman Martin R. Flook
Team Manager David Williams
Asst Manager/1st team coach
 Wayne Jones
Captain Brian Williams
Year formed 1883
Ground address Bristol
 Stadium, Eastville,
 Bristol BS5 6NN
Telephone 0272 573687
Present ground capacity 12,500
Record crowd 38, 472 v. Preston North End, FA
 Cup, 4th round, 30 January 1960
Nickname 'The Pirates'
Sponsor Toshiba UK

1984/5 Record
League 6th, Div 3
FA Cup Lost to Ipswich T., 3rd rnd, 1-2
Milk Cup Lost to Arsenal, 2nd rnd, 1-5 on agg.

Historical Highlights
League Best position – 6th in Div 2 1956, 1959.
 Div 2, 1953-62, 1974-81; Div 3, 1962-74, 1981-; Div 3(S), 1920-53
FA Cup 6th rnd 1952, 1958
League/Milk Cup 5th rnd 1971, 1972
Top Scorer Geoff Bradford: 33 (1952/3)

BURNLEY

Chairman J. E. Jackson
Team Manager John Benson
 until May 1985; Martin
 Buchan from June 1985
Asst Manager/1st team coach
 John Benson & John Sainty
 until August 1984
Captain Derek Scott
Year formed 1881 as Burnley
 Rovers, until 1882
Ground address Turf Moor,
 Brunshaw Road, Burnley BB10 4BX

Telephone 0282 27777/38021
Present ground capacity 23,000
Record crowd 54,775 v. Huddersfield Town,
 FA Cup, 3rd round, 23 February 1924
Nickname 'The Clarets'
Sponsor Multi-Part

1984/5 Record
League 21st, Div 3: relegated
FA Cup Lost to Wimbledon, 3rd rnd, 1-3
Milk Cup Lost to Man. Utd., 2nd rnd, 0-7 agg.

Historical Highlights
League Div 1 champions 1921, 1960;
 runners-up 1920, 1962. Div 1, 1888-97,
 1898-1900, 1913-30, 1947-71, 1973-6; Div 2,
 1897-8, 1900-13, 1930-47, 1971-3, 1976-80,
 1982-3; Div 3, 1980-2, 1983-
FA Cup Winners 1914; runners-up 1947, 1962
League/Milk Cup Semi-final 1961, 1969
Anglo-Scottish Cup Winners 1979
Europe European Cup 1961; Fairs Cup 1967
Top Scorer George Beel: 35 (1927/8)

Above *John Atyeo (Bristol City) holds the club record with 315 goals in 1951-66.*

Below *Jimmy McIlroy, brilliant orchestrator of Burnley and Northern Ireland teams of the 1950s and 1960s.*

Above Bury's FA Cup-winning side of 1903, when they thrashed Derby County 6-0 – the biggest winning margin in the competition's history.

Below Cardiff City's FA Cup-winning side of 1927 which beat hot favourites Arsenal 1-0 – the only time the Cup has left England.

BURY

Chairman T. Robinson
Team Manager Jim Iley until February 1984; then Martin Dobson
Asst Manager/1st team coach Wilf McGuinness
Captain Joe Jakub
Year formed 1885
Ground address Gigg Lane, Bury, Lancashire BL9 9HR
Telephone 061 764 4881/2
Present ground capacaity 22,500
Record crowd 35,000 v. Bolton Wanderers, FA Cup, 3rd round, 9 January 1960
Nickname 'The Shakers'
Sponsor Spraybreakers

1984/5 Record
League 4th, Div 4: promoted
FA Cup Lost to Preston North End, 1st round, 3-4
Milk Cup Lost to Port Vale, 1st rnd, 2-2 on away goals

Historical Highlights
League Best position – 4th in Div 1 1926. Div 1, 1895-1912, 1924-9; Div 2, 1894-5, 1912-24, 1929-57, 1961-7, 1968-9; Div 3, 1957-61, 1967-8, 1969-71, 1974-80; Div 4, 1971-4, 1980-5
FA Cup Winners 1900, 1903
League/Milk Cup Semi-final 1963
Top Scorer Craig Madden: 35 (1981/2)

CAMBRIDGE UNITED

Chairman D. A. Ruston
Team Manager John Ryan until February 1985; Ken Shellito from February 1985
Asst Manager/1st team coach Malcolm Webster
Captain Steven Spriggs
Year formed 1919 as Abbey United, until 1949
Ground address Abbey Stadium, Newmarket Road, Cambridge
Telephone 0223 241237
Present ground capacity 12,000
Record crowd 14,000 v. Chelsea (friendly), 1 May 1970
Nickname 'United'
Sponsor Spraymates

1984/5 Record
League 24th, Div 3: relegated
FA Cup Lost to Peterboro Utd, 1st rnd, 0-2
Milk Cup Lost to Brentford, 1st rnd, 1-2 on agg.

Historical Highlights
League Best position – 8th in Div 2, 1980. Div 2, 1978-84; Div 3, 1973-4, 1977-8, 1984-5; Div 4, 1970-3, 1974-7
FA Cup 4th rnd 1980
League/Milk Cup 4th rnd 1981
Top Scorer Alan Biley: 21 (1977/8)

CARDIFF CITY

Chairman J. Leonard
Team Manager Alan Durban
Asst Manager/1st team coach Jimmy Mullen
Captain Jake King
Year formed 1899 as Riverside, until 1910
Ground address Ninian Park, Sloper Road, Cardiff CF1 8SX
Telephone 0222 398636/7/8
Present ground capacity 42,500
Record crowd 61,566, Wales v. England, 14 October 1961
Nickname 'The Bluebirds'
Sponsor Merthyr Motor Auctions

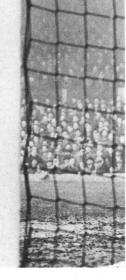

Left *Goalkeeper Sam Bartram, Charlton Athletic's most popular and longest-serving player: 583 games in 1934-56.*

1984/5 Record
League 21st, Div 2: relegated
FA Cup Lost to Gillingham,
   3rd rnd, 1-2
Milk Cup Lost to Watford, 2nd round, 2-4
   on agg.

Historical Highlights
League Best position – Div 1 runners-up 1924.
   Div 1, 1921-9, 1952-7, 1960-2; Div 2, 1920-1,
   1929-31, 1947-52, 1957-60, 1962-75, 1976-82,
   1983-5; Div 3, 1975-6, 1982-3; Div 3(S),
   1931-47
FA Cup Winners 1927; runners-up 1925
League/Milk Cup Semi-final 1966
Europe European Cup-Winners' Cup (as
   Welsh Cup winners) 1965, 1966, 1968, 1969,
   1970, 1971, 1972, 1974, 1975, 1977, 1978
Top Scorer Stan Richards: 31 (1946/7)

CARLISLE UNITED

Below *Allan Simonsen, brilliant Danish international winger, was bought by Charlton from Barcelona and spent a few not very satisfying months at the Valley in 1982/3.*

Chairman H. A. Jenkins
Team Manager Bob Stokoe
Asst Manager/1st team coach
   Tommy Craig
Captain Jack Ashurst
Year formed 1904
Ground address Brunton Park,
   Carlisle CA1 1LL
Telephone 0228 26237
Present ground capacity 16,000 (increasing for
   1985/6 season)
Record crowd 27,500 v. Birmingham, FA Cup,
   3rd rnd, 5 January 1957; v. Middlesbrough,
   FA Cup, 5th rnd, 7 February 1970
Nickname 'The Cumbrians'
Sponsor McEwen Younger Breweries

1984/5 Record
League 16th, Div 2
FA Cup Lost to Leicester C., 4th rnd, 0-1

Milk Cup Lost to Fulham, 2nd round, 1-4

Historical Highlights
League Best position – 22nd in Div 1, 1975.
   Div 1, 1974-5; Div 2, 1965-74, 1975-7, 1982-;
   Div 3(N), 1928-58; Div 4, 1958-62, 1963-4
FA Cup 6th rnd 1975
League/Milk Cup Semi-final 1969
Top Scorer Jimmy McConnell: 42 (1928/9)

CHARLTON ATHLETIC

Chairman M. Hulyer
Team manager Lennie
   Lawrence
Asst Manager/1st team coach
   Eddie May
Captain Mark Hazelwood
Year formed 1905
Ground address The Valley,
   Floyd Road, Charlton,
   London SE7 8AW
Telephone 01-853 0444
Present ground capacity 20,000
Record crowd 75,031 v. Aston Villa, FA Cup,
   5th round, 12 February 1938
Nickname 'The Haddicks', 'The Robins', or
   'The Valiants'
Sponsors Woolwich Building Society

1984/5
League 17th, Div 2
FA Cup Lost to Spurs, 3rd rnd rep., 1-2
Milk Cup Lost to Notts County, 2nd rnd,
   0-3 on agg.

Historical Highlights
League Div 1 runners-up, 1937. Div 1, 1936-57;
   Div 2, 1929-33, 1935-6, 1957-72, 1975-80,
   1981-; Div 3, 1972-5, 1980-1; Div 3 (S), 1921-9,
   1933-5
FA Cup Winners 1947; runners-up 1946
League/Milk Cup 4th rnd 1963, 1965, 1979
Top Scorer Ralph Allen: 32 (1934/5)

Above *One of Chelsea's favourite sons in the 1970s, Charlie Cooke, brilliant as a winger or in midfield for club and Scotland, ended his career in the NASL.*

Below *Gary Talbot, Chester City's top aggregate scorer, with 83 goals in 1963-70.*

CHELSEA

Chairman K. W. Bates
Team Manager John Neal to June 1985; John Hollins from June 1985
Asst Manager/1st teach coach Ian McNeill
Captain Colin Pates
Year formed 1905
Ground address Stamford Bridge, Fulham Road, London SWT 1HB
Telephone 01-385 5546
Present ground capacity 45,000
Record crowd 82,905 v. Arsenal, Division 1, 12 October 1935
Nickname 'The Blues'
Sponsor Gulf Air

1984/5 Record
League 6th, Div 1
FA Cup Lost to Millwall, 4th rnd, 2-3
Milk Cup Lost to Sunderland, Semi-final, 2-5 on agg.

Historical Highlights
League Div 1 champions 1955. Div 1, 1907-10, 1912-14, 1930-62, 1963-75, 1977-9; 1984-; Div 2, 1905-7, 1910-12, 1924-30, 1962-3, 1975-7, 1979-84
FA Cup Winners 1970; runners-up 1915, 1967

League/Milk Cup Winners 1965; runners-up 1972
Europe European Cup-Winners' Cup 1971 (winners), 1972; Fairs Cup 1960, 1966, 1969
Top Scorer Jimmy Greaves: 41 (1960/1)

CHESTER CITY

Chairman E. Barnes
Team Manager John McGrath to December 1984, then Michael Speight
Asst Manager/1st team coach Cliff Sear
Captain Andrew Holden
Year formed 1884
Ground address The Stadium, Sealand Road, Chester CH1 4LW
Telephone 0244 371376
Present ground capacity 19,500
Record crowd 20,500 v. Chelsea, FA Cup, 3rd round replay, 16 January 1952
Nickname 'The Seals'
Sponsor Lucas Engineering (Chester)

1984/5
League 16th, Div 4
FA Cup Lost to Darlington, 1st rnd, 2-3
Milk Cup Lost to Blackpool, 1st rnd, 0-4 on agg.

Historical Highlights
League Best position – 5th in Div 3, 1978. Div 3, 1975-82; Div 3(N), 1932-58; Div 4, 1958-75, 1982-
FA Cup 5th rnd 1977, 1980
League/Milk Cup Semi-final 1975
Top Scorer Dick Yates: 36 (1946/7)

CHESTERFIELD

Chairman B. W. Hubbard
Team Manger John Duncan
Asst Manager/1st team coach Kevin Randall
Captain Steve Baines
Year formed 1866
Ground address Recreation Ground Chesterfield
Telephone 0246 209765
Present ground capacity 19,750
Record crowd 30,968 v. Newcastle United, Division 2, 7 April 1939
Nickname 'The Blues' or 'The Spireites'
Sponsor Coalite

1984/5 Record
League Champions, Div 4: promoted
FA Cup Lost to Walsall, 2nd rnd, 0-1
Milk Cup Lost to Halifax Town, 1st rnd, 2-3 on agg.

Historical Highlights

League Best position – 4th in Div 2, 1947. Div 2, 1899, 1931-3, 1936-51; Div 3, 1958-61, 1970-83; Div 3(N), 1921-31, 1933-6, 1951-8; Div 4, 1961-70, 1983-4
FA Cup 5th rnd 1933, 1938, 1950
League/Milk Cup 4th rnd 1965
Anglo-Scottish Cup Winners 1981
Top Scorer Jimmy Cookson: 44 (1925/6)

COLCHESTER UNITED

Chairman M. J. Cadman
Team Manager Cyril Lea
Asst Manager/1st team coach Stewart Houston
Captain Ian Phillips
Year formed 1873
Ground address Layer Road Ground, Colchester, Essex C02 7JJ
Telephone 0206 574042
Present ground capacity 15,000
Record crowd 19,072 v. Reading, FA Cup, 1st round, 27 November 1948
Nickname 'The U's'
Sponsor Royal London Mutual Insurance

1984/5 Record

League 7th, Div 4
FA Cup Lost to Gillingham, 2nd rnd, 0-5
Milk Cup Lost to Gillingham, 1st rnd, 2-5 on agg.

Historical Highlights

League Best position – 5th in Div 3, 1980. Div 3, 1958-61, 1962-5, 1966-8, 1974-6, 1977-81; Div 3(S), 1950-8; Div 4, 1961-2, 1965-6, 1968-74, 1976-7, 1981-
FA Cup 6th rnd 1971
League/Milk Cup 5th rnd 1975
Top Scorer Bobby Hunt: 37 (1961/2)

COVENTRY CITY

Chairman J. W. Jamieson
Team Manager Bobby Gould to December 1984; then Don Mackay
Asst Manager/1st team coach Mike Taylor
Captain Trevor Peake
Year formed 1883 as Singers Football Club, until 1898
Ground address Highfield Road Stadium, King Richard St, Coventry CV2 4FW
Telephone 0203 57171
Present ground capacity 22,000
Record crowd 51,456 v. Wolverhampton Wanderers, Division 2, 29 April 1967
Nickname 'The Skyblues'
Sponsor Glazepta

1984/5 Record

League 18th, Div 1
FA Cup Lost to Man. Utd, 4th rnd, 1-2
Milk Cup Lost to Walsall, 2nd rnd, 2-4 on agg.

Historical Highlights

League Best position – 6th in Div 1, 1970. Div 1, 1967-; Div 2, 1919-25, 1936-52, 1964-7; Div 3, 1959-64; Div 3(N), 1925-6; Div 3 (S) 1926-36, 1952-8; Div 4, 1958-9
FA Cup 6th rnd 1963, 1973, 1982
League/ Milk Cup Semi-final 1981
Europe Fairs Cup 1971
Top Scorer Clarrie Bourton: 49 (1931/2)

CREWE ALEXANDRA

Chairman N. Rowlinson
Team Manager/1st Team Coach Dario Gradi
Captain Bob Scott
Year formed 1877
Ground Address Gresty Road, Crewe CW2 64B
Telephone 0270 213014
Present ground capacity 17,000
Record crowd 20,000 v. Tottenham Hotspur, FA Cup, 4th round, 30 January 1960
Nickname 'The Railwaymen'
Sponsor County Glass

1984/5 Record

League 10th, Div 4
FA Cup Lost to Northwich Victoria, 1st rnd, 1-3
Milk Cup Lost to Burnley, 1st rnd, 2-4 on agg.

Historical Highlights

League Best position – 10th in Div 2, 1893. Div 2, 1892-6, Div 3, 1963-4, 1968-9; Div 3(N), 1921-58; Div 4, 1958-9, 1964-8, 1969-
FA Cup Semi-final 1888
League/Milk Cup Never past 3rd rnd
Top Scorer Terry Harkin: 34 (1964/5)

Above *David Blakey holds Chesterfield's record for most League appearances: 613 in 1948-67.*

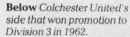

Below *Colchester United's side that won promotion to Division 3 in 1962.*

Johnny Byrne, a Crystal Palace favourite of the early 1960s, was awarded an England cap in 1961, when Palace were in Division 3. An often brilliantly elusive forward, he later moved to West Ham, scoring in the League Cup Final of 1966.

DARLINGTON

Chairman K. W. Warne
Team Manager Cyril Knowles
1st team coach John Craggs
Captain David McLean
Year formed 1883
Ground address Feethams Ground, Darlington, County Durham DL1 5JB
Telephone 0325 465097/467712
Present ground capacity 20,000
Record crowd 21,023 v. Bolton Wanderers, League Cup, 3rd round, 14 November 1960
Nickname 'The Quakers'
Sponsor McEwen's Breweries

1984/5 Record
League 3rd, Div 4: promoted
FA Cup Lost to Telford Utd, 4th rnd rep., 0-3
Milk Cup Lost to Rotherham Utd, 1st rnd, 1-6 on agg.

Historical Highlights
League Best position – 15th in Div 2, 1926. Div 2, 1925-7; Div 3(N), 1921-5, 1927-58- Div 4, 1958-66, 1967-
FA Cup 5th rnd 1958
League/Milk Cup Never past 3rd rnd
Top Scorer David Brown: 39 (1924/5)

CRYSTAL PALACE

Chairman R. G. Noades
Team Manager Steve Coppell from June 1984
Asst Manager/1st team coach Harry Cripps to May 1984; Ian Evans from June 1984
Captain Jim Cannon
Year formed 1905
Ground address Selhurst Park, London SE25 6PU
Telephone 01-653 4462
Present ground capacity 38,500
Record crowd 51,482 v. Burnley, Division 2, 11 May 1979
Nickname 'The Eagles'
Sponsor Red Rose (South Suburban Co-operative Society)

1984/5 Record
League 15th, Div 2
FA Cup Lost to Millwall, 3rd rnd rep., 1-2
Milk Cup Lost to Sunderland, 2nd rnd, 1-2 on agg.

Historical Highlights
League Best position – 13th in Div 1, 1980. Div 1, 1969-73, 1979-81; Div 2, 1921-5, 1964-9, 1973-4, 1977-9, 1981; Div 3, 1961-4, 1974-7; Div 4, 1958-61
FA Cup Semi-final 1976
League/Milk Cup 5th rnd 1969, 1971
Top Scorer Peter Simpson: 46 (1930/1)

DERBY COUNTY

Chairman J. N. Kirkland BSc, C.Eng., M.I.C.E.
Team Manager Arthur Cox
Asst Manager/1st team coach Roy McFarland
Captain Steve Powell
Ground address Baseball Ground, Shaftesbury Crescent, Derby DE3 8NB
Telephone 0332 40105
Present ground capacity 33,000
Record crowd 41,826 v. Tottenham Hotspur, Division 1, 20 September 1969
Nickname 'The Rams'
Sponsor Bass Worthington

1984/5 Record
League 7th, Div 3
FA Cup Lost to Hartlepool Utd, 1st rnd, 1-2
Milk Cup Lost to Ipswich, 2nd rnd, 3-5 on agg.

Historical Highlights
League Div 1 winners 1972, 1975; runners-up 1896, 1930, 1936. Div 1, 1888-1907, 1912-14, 1915-21, 1926-53, 1969-80; Div 2, 1907-12, 1914-15, 1921-26, 1953-5, 1957-69, 1980-; Div 3(N), 1955-7
FA Cup Winners 1946
League/Milk Cup Semi-final 1968

Europe European Cup 1973, 1976; UEFA Cup 1975, 1977

Top Scorers 37: Jack Bowers (1930/1), Ray Straw (1956/7)

DONCASTER ROVERS

Chairman I. M. Jones
Team manager Billy Bremner
Asst Manager/1st team coach Dave Bentley
Captain Ian Snodin
Year formed 1879
Ground address Belle Vue Ground, Doncaster DN4 5HT
Telephone 0302 539441
Present ground capacity 21, 150
Record crowd 37,149 v. Hull City, Division 3(N), 2 October 1948
Nickname 'The Rovers'
Sponsor Pilkington Glass

1984/5 Record
League 14th, Div 3
FA Cup Lost to Leicester C., 4th rnd, 0-1
Milk Cup Lost to York City, 1st rnd, 2-8 on agg.

Historical Highlights
League Best position – 7th in Div 2, 1902. Div 2, 1901-3, 1935-7, 1947-8, 1950-8; Div 3, 1958-9, 1966-7, 1969-71, 1981-3; Div 3(N), 1923-35, 1937-47, 1948-50; Div 4, 1959-66, 1967-9, 1971-81, 1983-4
FA Cup 5th rnd 1952, 1954, 1955, 1956
League/Milk Cup 5th rnd 1976
Top Scorer Clarrie Jordan: 42 (1946/7)

EVERTON

Chairman P. D. Carter, CBE
Team Manager Howard Kendall
Asst Manager/1st team coach Colin Harvey
Captain Kevin Ratcliffe
Year formed 1878 as St Domingo's Sunday School Club, until 1879
Ground address Goodison Park, Liverpool L4 4EL
Telephone 051 521 2020
Present ground capacity 53,419
Record crowd 78,299 v. Liverpool, Division 1, 18 September 1948
Nickname 'The Toffees'
Sponsor NEC

1984/5 Record
League Champions, Div 1
FA Cup Finalists: lost to Man. Utd 0-1 (aet)
Milk Cup Lost to Grimsby, 4th rnd, 0-1
European Cup-Winners' Cup Winners: beat Rapid Vienna 3-1

Historical Highlights
League Div 1 winners in 1891, 1915, 1928, 1932, 1939, 1963, 1970; runners-up 1890, 1895, 1902, 1905, 1909, 1912. Div 1, 1888-1930, 1931-51, 1954-; Div 2, 1930-1, 1951-4
FA Cup Winners 1906, 1933, 1966, 1984; runners-up 1893, 1897, 1907, 1968
League/Milk Cup Runners-up 1976, 1984
Europe European Cup 1964, 1971; European Cup-Winners' Cup 1967; Fairs Cup 1963, 1965; UEFA Cup 1976, 1979, 1980
Top Scorer 'Dixie' Dean: 60 (1927/8)

Above Clarrie Jordan (Doncaster Rovers), who broke his club's record with 42 League goals in 1946/7, which also made him top scorer in the Football League that season.

Below For all too briefly at the end of the 1960s Everton had the finest midfield trio in England. Two of them are seen here: Alan Ball (left), whose infectious zest and inexhaustible stamina brought him many goals, and Howard Kendall, a skilful and fiercely competitive ball-winner. The third, least durable, but perhaps most creative member of the trio was Colin Harvey, now coach at Goodison under Kendall.

EXETER CITY

Chairman W. C. Hill
Team Manager Colin
Appleton from May 1985
Asst Manager/1st team coach
Malcolm Musgrove
Captain Jim McNichol
Year formed 1904
Ground address St James's
Park, Exeter EX4 6PX
Telephone 0392 54073
Present ground capacity 17,500
Record crowd 20,984 v. Sunderland, FA Cup,
qtr final replay, 4 March 1931
Nickname 'The Grecians'
Sponsor LCD Advertising

1984/5 Record
League 18th, Div 4
FA Cup Lost to Enfield, 1st rnd, 0-3
Milk Cup Lost to Cardiff, 1st rnd, 1-2 on agg.

Historical Highlights
League Best position – 8th in Div 3, 1980. Div 3,
1964-6, 1977-84; Div 3(S), 1920-58; Div 4,
1958-64, 1966-77
FA Cup 6th rnd 1931
League/Milk Cup Never beyond 3rd rnd
Top Scorer Fred Whitlow: 34 (1932/3)

Johnny Haynes, midfield organiser for Fulham and England, was a master of superlatively accurate long passes. He made a record 598 appearances for Fulham in 1952/70, scoring 159 goals, and gained 56 international caps.

FULHAM

Chairman E. Clay
Team Manager Ray Harford
Asst Manager/1st team coach
Ray Harford to April 1984;
Terry Mancini from May
1984 to June 1985
Captain Ray Lewington
Year formed 1879
Ground address Craven Cottage,
Stevenage Road, Fulham, London
SW6 6HH
Telephone 01-736 6561/2/3
Present ground capacity 20,000
Record crowd 49,335 v. Millwall, Division 2,
8 October 1938
Nickname 'The Cottagers'
Sponsor William Younger

1984/5 Record
League 9th, Div 2
FA Cup Lost to Sheffield Wednesday, 3rd rnd,
2-3
Milk Cup Lost to Sheffield Wednesday, 3rd
rnd, 2-3

Historical Highlights
League Best position – 10th in Div 1, 1960. Div
1, 1949-52, 1959-68; Div 2, 1907-28, 1932-49,
1952-9, 1968-9, 1971-80, 1982-; Div 3,
1969-71, 1980-2; Div 3(S), 1928-32
FA Cup Runners-up 1975
League/Milk Cup 5th rnd 1968, 1971
Top Scorer Frank Newton: 42 (1931/2)

GILLINGHAM

Chairman Charles L. Cox
Team Manager Keith Peacock
Asst Manager/1st team coach
Paul Taylor & Ted Buxton
Captain Dave Mehmet
Year formed 1893 as New
Brompton, until 1913
Ground address Priestfield
Stadium, Gillingham, Kent
ME7 4DD
Telephone 0634 51854
Present ground capacity 22,000
Record crowd 23,002 v. Queens Park Rangers,
FA Cup, 3rd round, 10 January 1948
Nickname 'The Gills'
Sponsor Zanussi

1984/5 Record
League 4th, Div 3
FA Cup Lost to Ipswich, 3rd rnd, 2-3
Milk Cup Lost to Leeds Utd, 2nd rnd, 3-5 on
agg.

Historical Highlights
League Best position – 4th in Div 3, 1979. Div 3,

1964-71, 1974-; Div 3(S), 1920-38, 1950-8; Div 4, 1958-64, 1971-4; non-league 1938-50
FA Cup 5th rnd 1970
League/Milk Cup never beyond 3rd rnd
Top Scorers 32: Ernie Morgan (1945/5), Brian Yeo (1973/4)

1951-6; Div 4, 1968-72, 1977-9
FA Cup Semi-finals 1936, 1939
League/Milk Cup 5th rnd 1980
Top Scorer Pat Glover: 42 (1933/4)

GRIMSBY TOWN

Chairman R.K. Middleton
Team Manager David Booth
Asst Manager/1st team coach Chris Nicholl to July 1985
Captain Kevin Moore
Year formed 1878 as Grimsby Pelham, until 1879
Ground address Blundell Park, Cleethorpes, Sth Humberside DN35 7PY
Telephone 0472 697111
Present ground capacity 22,146
Record crowd 31,657 v. Wolves, FA Cup, 5th round, 20 February 1937
Nickname 'The Mariners'
Sponsor NISA

1984/5 Record
League 10th, Div 2
FA Cup Lost to Watford, 4th rnd, 1-3
Milk Cup Lost to Norwich C., 5th rnd, 0-1

Historical Highlights
League Best position – 5th in Div 1, 1935. Div 1, 1901-3, 1929-32, 1934-48; Div 2, 1892-1901, 1903-10, 1911-20, 1926-9, 1932-4, 1948-51, 1956-9, 1962-4, 1980-; Div 3, 1920-1, 1959-62, 1964-8, 1972-7, 1979-80; Divs 3(N), 1921-6,

HALIFAX TOWN

Chairman J. Turner
Team Manager Mickey Bullock to October 1984; Billy Ayres appointed Player-Manager, November 1984
Captain Alan Little
Year formed 1911
Ground address Shay Ground, Halifax HX1 2YS
Telephone 0422 53423
Present ground capacity 16,500
Record crowd 36,885 v. Tottenham Hotspur, FA Cup, 5th round, 14 February 1953
Nickname 'The Shaymen'
Sponsor Madeleys

1984/5 Record
League 21st, Div 4: re-elected
FA Cup Lost to Burnley, 2nd rnd, 1-3
Milk Cup Lost to Tottenham H., 2nd rnd, 1-9 on agg.

Historical Highlights
League Best position – 3rd in Div 3, 1971. Div 3, 1958-63, 1969-76; Div 3(N), 1921-58; Div 4, 1963-9, 1976-
FA Cup 5th rnd 1933, 1953
League/Milk Cup Never beyond 3rd rnd
Top Scorer Albert Valentine: 34 (1934/5)

Huddersfield Town's FA Cup-winning team of 1922. Middle row, from left: J.W. Wood, C. Slade, A. Mutch, Tom Wilson (capt.), W. Watson, Sam Wadsworth. Front row, from left: Herbert Chapman (manager), G. Richardson, F. Mann., E. Islip, Clem Stephenson, Billy Smith (whose penalty beat Preston in the Final), J. Chaplin (trainer). Probably the finest English side of the 1920s, especially after they acquired the brilliant 'Wembley Wizard' Alec Jackson, Huddersfield won the League three years in succession (1924-6) and were runners-up in the following two seasons. Manager Herbert Chapman was to take Arsenal to even greater glory in the 1930s.

HARTLEPOOL UNITED

Chairman J. V. Barker
Team Manager Bill Horner
Asst Manager/1st team coach Ray Kennedy and George Smith until June 1984;
Captain Tony Smith
Year formed 1908 (West Hartlepool & Old Hartlepool combined)
Ground address Victoria Ground, Clarence Road, Hartlepool, Cleveland
Telephone 0429 72584
Present ground capacity 18,000
Record crowd 17,426 v. Manchester United, FA Cup, 3rd round, 5 January 1957
Nickname 'The Dockers' or 'The Pool'
Sponsor J.W. Cameron

1984/5 Record
League 19th, Div 4
FA Cup Lost to York C., 2nd rnd. 0-2
Milk Cup Lost to Derby Cty, 1st rnd, 1-6 on agg.

Historical Highlights
League Best position – 22nd in Div 3, 1969. Div 3, 1968-9; Div 3(N), 1921-58; Div 4, 1958-68, 1969-
FA Cup 4th rnd 1955, 1978
League/Milk Cup Never past 3rd round
Top Scorer Bill Robinson: 28 (1927/8)

HEREFORD UNITED

Chairman P. S. Hill, FRICS
Team Manager John Newman
Asst Manager/1st team coach Alan Ashman & Peter Isaac
Captain Tony Larkin
Year formed 1924

Ground address Edgar St, Hereford HR4 9JU
Telephone 0432 276666
Present ground capacity 17,500
Record crowd 18,114 v. Sheffield Wednesday, FA Cup, 3rd round, 4 January 1958
Nickname 'United'
Sponsor Weston Cider

1984/5 Record
League 5th, Div 4
FA Cup Lost to Arsenal, 3rd rnd rep., 2-7
Milk Cup Lost to Oxford Utd, 1st rnd, 5-7 on agg.

Historical Highlights
League Best position – 22nd in Div 2, 1977. Div 2, 1976-7; Div 3, 1973-6, 1977-8; Div 4, 1972-3, 1978-
FA Cup 4th rnd 1972, 1977, 1982
League/Milk Cup Never beyond 3rd round
Top Scorer 'Dixie' McNeil: 35 (1975/6)

HUDDERSFIELD TOWN

Chairman K. S. Longbottom
Team Manager Mick Buxton
Asst Manager/1st team coach John Haseleen
Captain Dave Sutton
Year formed 1908
Ground address Leeds Road, Huddersfield, W. Yorkshire HD1 6PE
Telephone 0484 20335/6
Present ground capacity 48,000
Record crowd 67,037 v. Arsenal, FA Cup, qtr final, 27 February 1932
Nickname 'The Terriers'
Sponsor Daihatsu

1984/5 Record
League 13th, Div 2
FA Cup Lost to Luton T., 4th rnd, 0-2
Milk Cup Lost to Sheff. Wed, 2nd rnd, 2-4 on
  agg.

Historical Highlights
League Division 1 champions 1924, 1925, 1926;
  runners-up 1927, 1928, 1934. Div 1, 1920-52,
  1953-6, 1970-2; Div 2, 1910-20, 1952-3,
  1956-70, 1972-3, 1983-; Div 3, 1973-5, 1980-3
FA Cup Winners 1922; runners-up 1920, 1928,
  1930, 1938
League/Milk Cup Semi-final 1978
Top Scorers 35: Sam Taylor (1919/20), George
Brown (1925/6)

HULL CITY

Chairman Donald Robinson
Team Manager Brian Horton
Asst Manager/1st team coach
  Chris Chilton
Captain Gareth Roberts
Year formed 1904
Ground address Boothferry
  Park, Hull, Humberside
  HU4 64U
Telephone 0482 51119
Present ground capacity 42,000
Record crowd 55,019 v. Manchester United,
  FA Cup, qtr final, 26 February 1949
Nickname 'The Tigers'
Sponsor Arrow Air

1984/5 Record
League 3rd, Div 3: promoted
FA Cup Lost to Brighton, 3rd rnd, 0-1
Milk Cup Lost to Southampton, 2nd rnd, 4-5
  on agg.

Historical Highlights
League Best position – 3rd in Div 2, 1919. Div
  2, 1905-30, 1933-6, 1949-56, 1959-60,
  1966-78; Div 3, 1958-9, 1960-6, 1978-81,
  1983-; Div 3(N), 1930-3, 1936-49, 1956-8; Div
  4, 1981-3
FA Cup Semi-final 1930
League/Milk Cup 4th rnd 1974, 1976, 1978
Associate Members' Cup Runners-up 1984
Top Scorer Bill McNaughton: 39 (1932/3)

IPSWICH TOWN

Chairman P. M. Cobbold
Team Manager Bobby
  Ferguson
Asst Manager/1st team coach
  Charlie Woods
Captain Terry Butcher
Year formed 1887
Ground address Portman
  Road, Ipswich, Suffolk IP1 2DA
Telephone 0473 219211
Present ground capacity 37,000
Record crowd 38,010 v. Leeds United, FA Cup,
  qtr final, 8 March 1975
Nickname 'The Blues' or 'Town'
Sponsor Pioneer

1984/5 Record
League 17th, Div 1
FA Cup Lost to Everton, 5th rnd rep., 0-1
Milk Cup Lost to Norwich C., Semi-finals, 1-2

Historical Highlights
League Div 1 winners 1962; runners-up 1981,
  1982. Div 1, 1962-4, 1968-; Div 2, 1954-5,
  1957-61, 1964-8; Div 3(S), 1938-54, 1955-7
FA Cup Winners 1978
League/Milk Cup Semi-final 1982
Europe European Cup 1963; European Cup-
  Winners' Cup 1979; UEFA Cup 1974, 1975,
  1976, 1978, 1980, 1981 (winners), 1982, 1983
Top Scorer Ted Phillips: 41 (1956/7)

Above Centre-half and player-manager Terry Neill (Hull City) in a League match against Orient in 1970. He later moved to Arsenal as manager after a spell of running the Northern Ireland side and then Tottenham Hotspur. As a player he gained 60 caps for Northern Ireland (a number exceeded only by Pat Jennings).

Left Two Ipswich Town stalwarts, George Burley and Terry Butcher, sandwich Tottenham's Gary Stevens in a 1983/4 League match; Graham Roberts (Tottenham) is at right. For more than two decades Ipswich have enjoyed a level of success in League and Cup out of all proportion to their modest size and resources.

LEEDS UNITED

Chairman L. Silver, OBE
Team Manager Eddie Gray, MBE
Asst Manager/1st team coach Jimmy Lumsden
Captain Mervyn Day
Year formed 1904 as Leeds City; disbanded by FA order; Leeds United formed in 1919
Ground address Elland Road, Leeds LS11 OES
Telephone 0532 716037
Present ground capacity 43,900
Record crowd 57,892 v. Sunderland, FA Cup, 5th round replay, 15 March 1967
Nickname 'The Peacocks'
Sponsor WGK

1984/5 Record
League 7th, Div 2
FA Cup Lost to Everton, 3rd rnd, 0-2
Milk Cup Lost to Watford, 3rd rnd, 0-4

Historical Highlights
League Div 1 champions 1969, 1974; runners-up 1965, 1966, 1972. Div 1, 1924-7, 1928-31, 1932-47, 1956-60, 19684-82; Div 2, 1920-4, 1927-8, 1931-2, 1947-56, 1960-4, 1981-
FA Cup Winners 1972; runners-up 1965, 1970, 1973
League/Milk Cup Winners 1968
Europe European Cup 1970, 1975 (runners-up); European Cup-Winners' Cup 1973 (runners-up); Fairs Cup 1966, 1967 (runners-up), 1968 (winners), 1969, 1971 (winners); UEFA Cup 1972, 1974, 1980
Top Scorer John Charles: 42 (1953/4)

LEICESTER CITY

Chairman T. W. Shipman
Team Manager Gordon Milne
Asst Manager/1st team coach Gerry Summers
Captain John O'Neill
Year formed 1884 as Leicester Fosse, until 1919
Ground address City Stadium, Filbert St, Leicester LE2 7FL
Telephone 0533 555000
Present ground capacity 32,000
Record crowd 47,298 v. Tottenham Hotspur, FA Cup, 5th round, 18 February 1938
Nickname 'The Filberts' or 'The Foxes'
Sponsor Ind Coope

1984/5 Record
League 15th, Div 1
FA Cup Lost to Millwall, 5th rnd, 0-2
Milk Cup Lost to Luton Town, 3rd rnd, 1-3

Historical Highlights
League Best position – 2nd in Div 1, 1929. Div 1, 1908-9, 1925-35, 1937-9, 1954-5, 1957-69, 1971-8, 1980-1, 1983-; Div 2, 1894-1908, 1909-25, 1935-7, 1946-54, 1955-7, 1969-71, 1978-80, 1981-3
FA Cup Runners-up 1949, 1961, 1963, 1969
League/Milk Cup Winners 1964; runners-up 1965
Europe European Cup-Winners' Cup 1962
Top Scorer Arthur Rowley: 44 (1956/7)

LINCOLN CITY

Chairman D. W. Houlston
Team Manager Colin Murphy until June 1985; John Pickering from July 1985
Asst Manager/1st team coach John Pickering to July 1985
Captain Gordon Simmonite
Year formed 1883
Ground address Sincil Bank, Lincoln LN5 8LD
Telephone 0522 22224

Below *Don Revie, a great inside forward for Manchester City and England in the 1950s, built Leeds United into the most powerful side in the country in the late 1960s.*

Bottom *Leeds United's most influential players of this era were their midfielders, the inspirational and abrasive Billy Bremner (left) and the elegantly inventive Johnny Giles, captains respectively of Scotland and the Republic of Ireland.*

Present ground capacity 16,225
Record crowd 23,196 v Derby County, League
  Cup, 4th round, 15 November 1967
Nickname 'The Red Imps'
Sponsor Fossitt & Thorne

1984/5 Record
League 19th, Div 3
FA Cup Lost to Telford Utd, 1st rnd, 1-2
Milk Cup Lost to Hull C., 1st rnd, 1-6 on agg.

Historical Highlights
League Best position – 5th in Div 2, 1902. Div 2,
  1892-1908, 1909-11, 1912-20, 1932-4, 1948-9,
  1952-61; Div 3, 1961-2, 1976-9, 1981-; Div
  3(N), 1921-32, 1934-48, 1949-52; Div 4,
  1962-76, 1979-81
FA Cup 4th rnd 1954, 1961, 1976
League/Milk Cup 4th rnd 1968
Top Scorer Allan Hall: 42 (1931/2)

LIVERPOOL

Chairman J. W. Smith, CBE, JP
Team Manager Joe Fagan
  until June 1985; Kenny
  Dalglish (as Player-Manager)
  from June 1985
Asst Manager/1st team coach
  Ronnie Moran
Captain Phil Neal
Year formed 1892
Ground address Anfield Road,
  Liverpool L4 0TH
Telephone 051 263 2361
Present ground capacity 46,000
Record crowd 61,905 v. Wolverhampton
  Wanderers, FA Cup, 2 February 1952
Nickname 'The Reds' or 'The Pool'
Sponsor: Crown Paints

1984/5 Record
League 2nd, Div 1
FA Cup Lost to Manchester Utd., Semi-final
  rep., 1-2
Milk Cup Lost to Tottenham, 3rd rnd, 0-1
European Cup Finalists: lost to Juventus, 0-1

Historical Highlights
League Div 1 champions 1901, 1906, 1922,
  1923, 1947, 1964, 1966, 1973, 1976, 1977,
  1979, 1980, 1982, 1983; runners-up 1899,
  1910, 1969, 1974, 1975, 1978
FA Cup Winners 1965, 1974; runners-up 1914,
  1950, 1971, 1977
League/Milk Cup Winners in 1981, 1982,
  1983, 1984; runners-up 1978
Europe European Cup 1965, 1967, 1974, 1977
  (winners), 1978 (winners), 1979, 1980, 1981,
  1982, 1983, 1984 (winners); European Cup-
  Winners' Cup 1966 (runners-up), 1972, 1975;
  Fairs Cup 1958, 1969, 1970, 1971; UEFA Cup
  1973 (winners), 1976 (winners)
Top Scorer Roger Hunt: 41 (1961/2)

LUTON TOWN

Chairman D. Mortimer
Team Manager David Pleat
Asst Manager/1st team coach
  Trevor Hartley
Captain Steve Foster from
  December 1984
Year formed 1885
Ground address 70-2
  Kenilworth Road, Luton,
  Bedfordshire LU1 1DH
Telephone 0582 411622
Present ground capacity 22,601
Record crowd 30,069 v. Blackpool, FA Cup,
  qtr final replay, 4 March 1959
Nickname 'The Hatters'
Sponsor Bedford Trucks

1984/5 Record
League 13th, Div 1
FA Cup Lost to Everton, Semi-final, 1-2
Milk Cup Lost to Sheffield Wednesday, 4th
  rnd, 2-4

Historical Highlights
League Best position – 8th in Div 1, 1958. Div 1,
  1955-60, 1974-5, 1982-; Div 2, 1897-1900,
  1937-55, 1960-3, 1970-4, 1975-82; Div 3, 1920,
  1963-5, 1968-70; Div 3(S) 1921-37; Div 4,
  1965-8
FA Cup Runners-up 1959
League/Milk Cup 5th rnd 1979
Top Scorer Joe Payne: 55 (1936/7)

Above *Liverpool's Bill
Shankly receiving a Bell's
Manager of the Month
award. A Merseyside
legend, Shankly initiated
the irresistible rise of
Liverpool in the early 1970s.*

Below *Joe Payne (Luton
Town), who scored a
League-record 10 goals
against Bristol Rovers in
April 1936. The following
season he topped the
League list with 55 goals.*

MANCHESTER CITY

Chairman P. J. Swales
Team Manager Billy McNeill
Asst Manager/1st team coach
  Jimmy Frizzell
Captain Paul Power
Year formed 1887 as Ardwick
  Football Club, until 1895
Ground address Maine Road,
  Moss Side, Manchester
  M14 7WN
Telephone 061 226 1191/2
Present ground capacity 52,500
Record crowd 84,569 v. Stoke City, FA Cup,
  qtr final, 3 March 1934 (record attendance for
  any British match outside London and
  Glasgow)
Nickname 'The Citizens'
Sponsor Phillips

1984/5 Record
League 3rd, Div 2: promoted
FA Cup Lost to Coventry City, 3rd round, 1-2
Milk Cup Lost to Chelsea, 4th rnd, 1-4

Historical Highlights
League Div 1 champions 1937, 1968;
  runners-up 1904, 1921, 1977. Div 1,
  1899-1902, 1903-9, 1910-26, 1928-38,
  1947-50, 1951-63, 1966-83; Div 1894-9,
  1902-3, 1909-10, 1926-8, 1938-47, 1950-1,
  1963-6, 1983-
FA Cup Winners 1904, 1934, 1956, 1969;
  runners-up 1926, 1933, 1955, 1981
League/Milk Cup Winners 1970, 1976;
  runners-up 1974
Europe European Cup 1969; European
  Cup-Winners' Cup 1970 (winners), 1971;
  UEFA Cup 1973, 1977, 1978, 1979
Top Scorer Tom Johnson: 38 (1928-9)

MANCHESTER UNITED

Chairman C. M. Edwards
Team Manager Ron Atkinson
Asst Manager/1st team coach
  Mick Brown
Captain Bryan Robson
Year formed 1878 as Newton
  Heath, until 1902
Ground address Old Trafford,
  Manchester M16 0RA
Telephone 061 872 1661/2
Present ground capacity 58,504
Record crowd 70,504 v. Aston Villa, Division 1,
  27 December 1920
Ground record 76,962, Wolverhampton
  Wanderers v. Grimsby Town (FA Cup,
  semi-final, 25 March 1939)
Nickname 'The Red Devils'
Sponsor Sharp Electronics

1984/5 Record
League 4th, Div 1
FA Cup Winners: beat Everton 1-0 (aet)
Milk Cup Lost to Everton, 3rd rnd, 1-2

Historical Highlights
League Div 1 champions 1908, 1911, 1952,
  1956, 1957, 1965, 1967; runners-up 1947,
  1948, 1949, 1951, 1959, 1964, 1968, 1980. Div
  1, 1906-22; 1925-31, 1936-7, 1938-74, 1975-;
  Div 2, 1894-1906, 1922-5, 1931-6, 1937-8,
  1974-5
FA Cup Winners 1909, 1948, 1963, 1977, 1983;
  runners up 1957, 1958, 1976, 1979
League/Milk Cup Runners-up 1983
Europe European Cup 1957, 1958, 1966, 1968
  (winners), 1969; European Cup-Winners'
  Cup 1964, 1978; Fairs Cup 1965; UEFA Cup
  1977, 1981, 1983, 1984
Top Scorer Denis Viollet: 32 (1959-60)

Below Malcolm Allison, a superlative coach, had his finest managerial spell with Manchester City in partnership with Joe Mercer in the late 1960s.

Bottom One of the most exciting and deadly strikers to emerge in Britain since World War II, Denis Law came to Manchester City from Huddersfield Town in March 1960. The following year he became the first British £100,000 player when City sold him to Torino, and in 1962 Manchester United brought him back to England. In 1958 he had become the youngest player to appear for Scotland, gaining the first of his 55 caps at the age of 18 years and 256 days.

MANSFIELD TOWN

Chairman R. C. Hartley
Team Manager Ian Greaves
Asst Manager/1st team coach
  John Jarman
Captain George Foster
Year formed 1891 as
  Mansfield Wesleyans, until
  1905
Ground address Field Mill
  Ground, Quarry Lane,
  Mansfield, Notts
  NG18 5DA
Telephone 0623 23567
Present ground capacity 23,500
Record crowd 24,467 v. Nottingham Forest, FA
  Cup, 3rd round, 10 January 1963
Nickname 'The Stags'
Sponsor Evinson's Garage

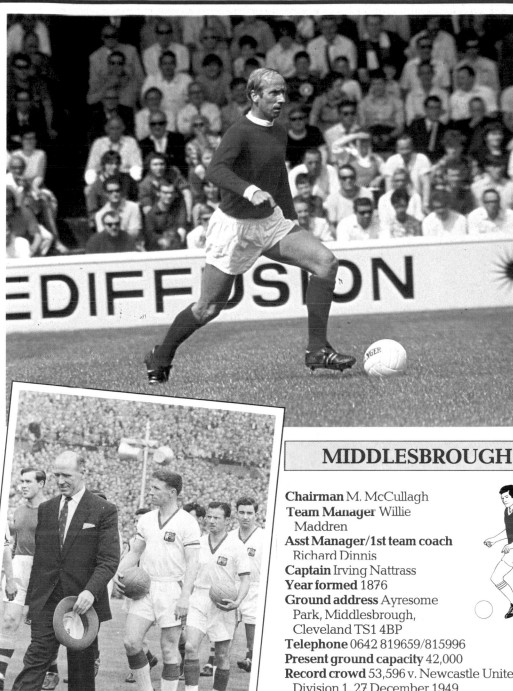

Left, above *Bobby Charlton (Manchester United), one of the greatest forwards in Europe since the last war, shot with fearsome power with either foot. He played 106 times for England, scoring 49 goals, and in 606 appearances for United in 1956-73 he scored a record 198 goals. He was made a director of his old club in 1984.*

Left, below *Manchester United's Matt Busby leads his team out at Wembley for the 1957 Cup Final against Aston Villa. The following February eight of his players died in the Munich air crash, yet within a decade Busby developed a team good enough to win the League championship and European Cup.*

MIDDLESBROUGH

Chairman M. McCullagh
Team Manager Willie Maddren
Asst Manager/1st team coach Richard Dinnis
Captain Irving Nattrass
Year formed 1876
Ground address Ayresome Park, Middlesbrough, Cleveland TS1 4BP
Telephone 0642 819659/815996
Present ground capacity 42,000
Record crowd 53,596 v. Newcastle United, Division 1, 27 December 1949
Nickname 'The Boro'
Sponsor Cameron's Ales

Below *Brian Clough (Middlesbrough) was one of the deadliest marksmen in the League in the late 1950s, scoring 121 goals in three seasons from August 1957. His playing career cut short by knee injuries, he then carved out even greater success as a manager, most notably with Derby County and Nottingham Forest.*

1984/5 Record
League 19th, Div 2
FA Cup Lost to Darlington, 3rd round replay, 1-2
Milk Cup Lost to Bradford C., 1st rnd, 2-4 on agg.

Historical Highlights
League Best position – 4th in Div 1, 1914. Div 1, 1902-24, 1927-8, 1929-54, 1974-82; Div 2, 1899-1902, 1924-7, 1928-9, 1954-66, 1967-74, 1982-; Div 3, 1966-7
FA Cup 6th rnd 1936, 1947, 1970, 1975, 1977, 1978, 1981
League/Milk Cup Semi-final 1976
Anglo-Scottish Cup Winners 1976
Top Scorer George Camsell: 59 (1926-7)

1984/5 Record
League 14th, Div 4
FA Cup Lost to Bradford City, 2nd round, 1-2
Milk Cup Lost to Scunthorpe Utd, 1st rnd, 2-2 on away goals

Historical Highlights
League Best position – 21st in Div 2, 1978. Div 2, 1977-8; Div 3, 1958-60, 1963-72, 1978-80; Div 3(S), 1931-2, 1937-47; Div 3(N), 1932-7, 1947-58; Div 4, 1960-3, 1972-5, 1980-
FA Cup 6th rnd 1969
League/Milk Cup 5th rnd 1976
Top Scorer Ted Harston: 55 (1936-7)

Above *Millwall stalwart Derek Possee, who holds the club's aggregate scoring record – 79 goals in 1967/73.*

Below *A folk hero on Tyneside, Jackie Milburn gained three FA Cup-winner's medals with Newcastle United, his first one (in 1951) after he had scored in every round. As a striker he was best known for his thunderous left-foot shot: here, however, in the 1955 Final against Manchester City, he scores with his head after just 45 seconds – the fastest-ever goal in a Wembley Final.*

MILLWALL

Chairman Alan A. Thorne
Team Manager George Graham
Asst Manager/1st team coach Theo Foley
Captain Les Briley
Year formed 1885
Ground address The Den, Cold Blow Lane, New Cross, London SE14 5RH
Telephone 01-639 3143/4
Present ground capacity 32,000
Record crowd 48,672 v. Derby County, FA Cup, 5th round, 20 February 1937
Nickname 'The Lions'
Sponsor London Dockland Development Corporation

1984/5 Record
League 2nd, Div 3: promoted
FA Cup Lost to Luton T., 6th rnd, 0-1
Milk Cup Lost to Chelsea, 2nd rnd, 2-4 on agg.

Historical Highlights
League Best position – 3rd in Div 2, 1972. Div 2, 1928-34, 1938-48, 1966-75, 1976-9; Div 3, 1962-4, 1965-6, 1975-6, 1979-; Div 3(S),

1920-8, 1934-8, 1948-58; Div 4, 1958-62, 1964-5
FA Cup Semi-final 1900, 1903, 1937
League/Milk Cup 5th rnd 1974, 1977
Top Scorer Dick Parker: 37 (1926/7)

NEWCASTLE UNITED

Chairman S. Seymour
Team Manager Jack Charlton until August 1985
Asst Manager/1st team coach Willie McFaul
Captain Glen Roeder
Year formed 1882 as Newcastle East End, until 1892
Ground address St James's Park, Newcastle-upon-Tyne, Tyne & Wear NE1 4ST
Telephone 0632 328361
Present ground capacity 37,718
Record crowd 68,386 v. Chelsea, Division 1, 3 September 1930
Nickname 'The Magpies'
Sponsor Newcastle Breweries Ltd

1984/5 Record
League 14th, Div 1
FA Cup Lost to Nottingham Forest, 3rd rnd rep., 1-3
Milk Cup Lost to Ipswich Town, 3rd rnd rep., 1-2

Historical Highlights
League Div 1 champions 1905, 1907, 1909, 1927. Div 1, 1898-1934, 1948-61, 1965-78, 1984-; Div 2, 1893-8, 1934-48, 1961-5, 1978-84
FA Cup Winners 1910, 1924, 1932, 1951, 1952, 1955; runners-up 1905, 1908, 1911, 1974
League/Milk Cup Runners-up 1976
Europe Fairs Cup 1969 (winners), 1970, 1971; UEFA Cup 1977, 1978; Anglo-Italian Cup 1973 (winners)
Top Scorer Hughie Gallacher: 36 (1926/7)

NEWPORT COUNTY

Chairman R. A. Ford
Team Manager Colin Addison
  to May 1985; then Bobby
  Smith
Asst Manager/1st team coach
  David Williams
Captain Terry Boyle
Year formed 1912
Ground address Somerton
  Park, Newport, Gwent,
  Monmouthshire NPT OHZ
Telephone 0633 277543/277472/277271
Present ground capacity 18,000
Record crowd 24,268 v. Cardiff City, Division
  3(S), 16 October 1937
Nickname 'The Ironsides'
Sponsor *South Wales Argus*

1984/5 Record
League 18th, Div 3
FA Cup Lost to Aldershot, 1st rnd, 0-4
Milk Cup Lost to Bristol C., 1st rnd, 1-5 on agg.

Historial Highlights
League Best position – 22nd in Div 2, 1947. Div
  2, 1946-7; Div 3, 1920-1, 1958-62, 1980-; Div
  3(S), 1921-31, 1932-9, 1947-58; Div 4, 1962-80
League Best position – 22nd in Div 2, 1947.
FA Cup 5th rnd, 1949
League/Milk Cup Never past 3rd rnd
Europe European Cup-Winners' Cup 1981
Top Scorer Tudor Martin: 34 (1929/30)

NORTHAMPTON TOWN

Chairman N. J. Ronson
Team Manager Tony Barton
  to April 1985; then Graham
  Kerr
Asst Manager/1st team coach
  Richie Norman
Captain Billy Jeffrey
Year formed 1897
Ground address County
  Ground, Abington Avenue,
  Northampton NN1 4PS
Telephone 0604 31553
Present ground capacity 17,000
Record crowd 24,523 v. Fulham, Division 1,
  23 April 1966
Nickname 'The Cobblers'
Sponsor Expanding Northampton

1984/5 Record
League 23rd, Div 4: re-elected
FA Cup Lost to Brentford, 2nd rnd, 0-2
Milk Cup Lost to Crystal Pal., 1st rnd, 0-1 on
  agg.

Historical Highlights
League Best position – 21st in Div 1, 1966. Div
1, 1965-6; Div 2, 1963-5, 1966-7; Div 3,
1920-1, 1961-3, 1967-8, 1976-7; Div 3(S)
1921-58; Div 4, 1958-61, 1968-76, 1977-
FA Cup 5th rnd 1934, 1950, 1970
League/Milk Cup 5th rnd 1965, 1967
Top Scorer Cliff Holton: 36 (1961/2)

NORWICH CITY

Chairman Sir Arthur South, JP
Team Manager Ken Brown
Asst Manager/1st team coach
  Mel Machin
Captain Dave Watson
Year formed 1905
Ground address Carrow Road,
  Norwich, Norfolk NR1 1JE
Telephone 0603 612131
Present ground capacity 29,000
Record crowd 43,984 v. Leicester City, FA
  Cup, qtr final, 30 March 1963
Nickname 'The Canaries'
Sponsor Poll & Witney Windows

1984/5 Record
League 20th, Div 1: relegated
FA Cup Lost to West Ham United, 4th rnd,
  1-2
Milk Cup Winners: beat Sunderland, 1-0

Historical Highlights
League Best position – 10th in Div 1, 1976. Div
  1, 1972-4, 1975-81, 1982-; Div 2, 1934-9,
  1960-72, 1974-5, 1981-2; Div 3, 1920-1,
  1946-60; Div 3(S), 1921-34
FA Cup Semi-final 1959
League/Milk Cup Winners 1962
Top Scorer Ralph Hunt: 31 (1955/6)

Above *Cliff Holton holds
the Northampton Town
record for League goals in a
season: 36 in 1961/2. He
also holds a similar record
for Watford, for whom he
scored 42 goals in 1959/60,
including hat-tricks on two
consecutive days in April.*

Below *Mick Channon, a
swift and deadly striker for
Southampton and England
in the 1970s, has lately
exchanged some of his
speed for greater guile in his
seasons with Norwich City.*

Above Leslie Bradd holds the scoring record for Notts County: 125 goals in 1967-78.

Below Peter Shilton, currently the best goalkeeper in Britain and, possibly, in the world, was elected PFA Player of the Year in 1978 when with Nottingham Forest. He is now with Southampton, where he had been largely responsible for making the defence one of the tightest in the League.

NOTTINGHAM FOREST

Chairman M. Roworth
Team Manager Brian Clough
Asst Manager/1st team coach Ronnie Fenton
Captain Ian Bowyer
Year formed 1865
Ground address City Ground, Pavilion Road, West Bridgeford, Nottingham NG2 5FJ.
Telephone 0602 822202
Present ground capacity 35,000
Record crowd 49,945 v. Manchester United, Division 1, 28 October 1967
Nickname 'The Reds'
Sponsor Skol Lager

1984/5 Record
League 9th, Div 1.
FA Cup Lost to Wimbledon, 4th round replay, 0-1
Milk Cup Lost to Sunderland, 3rd round replay, 0-1

Historical Highlights
League Div 1 champions 1978; runners-up 1967, 1979. Div 1, 1892-1906 1907-11, 1922-5, 1957-72, 1977-; Div 2, 1906-7, 1911-22, 1925-49, 1951-7, 1972-7; Div 3(S), 1951-7
FA Cup Winners 1898, 1959
League/Milk Cup Winners 1978, 1979; runners-up 1980
Anglo-Scottish Cup Winners 1977

Europe European Cup 1979 (winners), 1980 (winners), 1981; UEFA Cup 1984; European Super Cup 1980 (winners), 1981; World Club Championship 1981
Top Scorer Wally Ardron: 36 (1950/1)

NOTTS COUNTY

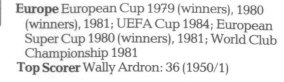

Chairman J. J. Dunnett MA, MP
Team Manager Larry Lloyd until October 1984, then Richie Barker to April 1985
Asst Manager/1st team coach Dave Watson
Captain Steve Sims
Year formed 1862 (oldest club in League)
Ground address County Ground, Meadow Lane, Nottingham NG2 3HJ
Telephone 0602 861155
Present ground capacity 23,680
Record crowd 47,310 v. York City, FA Cup, qtr final, 12 March 1955
Nickname 'The Magpies'
Sponsors Home Breweries and KLG Glass

1984/5 Record
League 20th, Div 2: relegated
FA Cup Lost to Grimsby Town, 3rd rnd replay, 2-4
Milk Cup Lost to Norwich C., 4th rnd, 0-3

Historical Highlights
League Best position – 3rd in Div 1, 1891, 1901. Div 1, 1888-93, 1897-1913, 1914-20, 1923-6, 1981-4; Div 2, 1893-7, 1913-14, 1920-3, 1926-30, 1931-5, 1950-8, 1973-81; Div 3, 1958-9, 1960-4, 1971-3; Div 4, 1959-60.
FA Cup Winners 1894; runners-up 1891
League/Milk Cup 5th rnd 1964, 1973, 1976

OLDHAM ATHLETIC

Chairman I. H Stott
Team Manager Joe Royle
Asst Manager/1st team coach Billy Urmson
Captain Darren McDonough
Year formed 1894 as Pine Villa, until 1899
Ground address Boundary Park, Furtherwood Road, Oldham, Greater Manchester, OL1 2PA
Telephone 061 624 4972
Present ground capacity 26,324
Record crowd 47,671 v. Sheffield Wednesday, FA Cup, 4th round, 25 January 1930
Nickname 'The Latics'
Sponsor Lees Brewery

1984/5 Record
League 14th, Div 2
FA Cup Lost to Sheffield Wednesday, 4th rnd, 1-5
Milk Cup Lost to Bolton Wanderers, 1st rnd, 5-6 on agg.

Historical Highlights
League Best position 2nd in Div 1, 1915. Div 1, 1910-23; Div 2, 1907-10, 1923-35, 1953-4, 1974-; Div 3, 1963-9, 1971-4; Div 3(N), 1935-53, 1954-8; Div 4, 1958-63, 1969-71
FA Cup Semi-final 1913
League/Milk Cup Never past 3rd rnd
Top Scorer Tommy Davis: 33 (1936/7)

ORIENT

Chairman N. Ovendon
Team Manager/1st team coach Frank Clark
Captain Tommy Cunningham
Year formed 1881, as Glyn Cricket & Football Club; 1886-88 as Eagle F.C; 1888-98 as Orient F.C; 1898-1946 as Clapton Orient; 1946-66 as Leyton Orient
Ground address Leyton Stadium, Brisbane Road, Leyton, London E10 5NE
Telephone 01-539 2223/4
Present ground capacity 26,500
Record crowd 34,345 v. West Ham United, FA Cup, 4th round, 25 January 1964
Nickname 'The O's'

1984/5 Record
League 22nd, Div 3: relegated
FA Cup Lost to Southampton, 4th rnd, 0-2
Milk Cup Lost to Luton Town, 2nd rnd, 2-7 on agg.

Historical Highlights
League Best position – 22nd in Div 1, 1963. Div 1, 1962-3; Div 2, 1905-29, 1956-62, 1963-6, 1970-82; Div 3, 1966-70, 1982-; Div 3(S), 1929-56
FA Cup Semi-final 1978
League/Milk Cup 5th rnd 1963
Top Scorer Tommy Johnston: 35 (1957/8)

OXFORD UNITED

Chairman Robert Maxwell, MC
Team Manager Jim Smith to June 1985
Asst Manager/1st team coach Ray Graydon to June 1985
Captain Malcolm Shotton
Year formed 1896 as Headington United, until 25 June 1960
Ground address Manor Ground, Headington, Oxford OX3 7RS
Telephone 0865 61503
Present ground capacity 17,350
Record crowd 22,730 v. Preston North End, FA Cup, qtr final, 29 February 1964
Nickname 'The U's'
Sponsor British Printing & Communications Corp.

1984/5 Record
League Champions, Div 2: promoted
FA Cup Lost to Blackburn R., 4th rnd, 0-1
Milk Cup Lost to Ipswich T., 4th rnd, 1-2

Historical Highlights
League Best position – 1st in Div 2, 1985. Div 2, 1968-76, 1984-5; Div 3, 1965-8, 1976-84; Div 4, 1962-5
FA Cup 6th rnd, 1964
League/Milk Cup 5th rnd, 1970, 1984
Top Scorer John Aldridge: 30 (1984/5)

Left Oldham Athletic's side that won the Division 3 championship in 1973/4.

Left Laurie Cunningham, first of a growing number of gifted black forwards to play for England, began his career at Orient. After a stint at West Bromwich he was transferred to Real Madrid, where his career has been plagued by injury.

PETERBOROUGH UNITED

Chairman W. O'Neill Wilde
Team Manager John Wile
Asst Manager/1st team coach Bill Harvey
Captain Trevor Quow
Year formed 1923 as Peterbrough & Fletton United, until 1934
Ground address London Road Ground, Peterborough PE2 8AL
Telephone 0733 63947
Present ground capacity 28,000
Record crowd 30,096 v. Swansea Town, FA Cup, 5th round, 20 February 1965
Nickname 'The Posh'
Sponsor Sodastream

1984/5 Record
League 11th, Div 4
FA Cup Lost to Dagenham, 2nd rnd, 0-1
Milk Cup Lost to Sheffield Utd, 1st rnd, 2-3 on agg.

Historical Highlights
League Best position — 4th in Div 3, 1978. Div 3, 1961-8, 1974-9; Div 4, 1960-1, 1968-74, 1979-
FA Cup 6th rnd 1965
League/Milk Cup Semi-final 1966
Top Scorer Terry Bly: 52 (1960/1)

Right Jimmy Dickinson, uncompromising Portsmouth half-back, holds the club's record for League appearances (764 in 1946-65) and also of caps (48 for England). He died in 1983.

Above Plymouth Argyle's 1929/30 side that won promotion to Division 2 for the first time.

PLYMOUTH ARGYLE

Chairman S. W. Dawe
Team Manager John Hore to October 1984, then Dave Smith
Asst Manager/1st team coach Martin Harvey
Captain Gerry McElhinney
Year formed 1886 as Argyle Athletic, until 1903
Ground address Home Park,
Plymouth, Devon PL2 3DQ
Telephone 0752 52561/2/3
Present ground capacity 38,000
Record crowd 43,596 v. Aston Villa, Division 2, 10 October 1936
Nickname 'The Pilgrims'
Sponsor Ivor Jones

1984/5 Record
League 15th, Div 3
FA Cup Lost to Hereford Utd, 2nd rnd rep., 0-2
Milk Cup Lost to Birmingham C., 2nd rnd, 1-5

Historical Highlights
League Best position — 4th in Div 2, 1932, 1953. Div 2, 1930-50, 1952-6, 1959-68, 1975-7; Div 3, 1958-9, 1968-75, 1977-; Div 3(S), 1920-30, 1950-2, 1956-8
FA Cup Semi-final 1984
League/Milk Cup Semi-final 1965, 1974
Top Scorer Jack Cock: 32 (1925/6)

PORTSMOUTH

Chairman B. J. Deacon
Team Manager Alan Ball
Captain Mick Kennedy
Year formed 1898
Ground address Fratton Park, Frogmore Road, Portsmouth PO4 8RA
Telephone 0705 731204/5
Present ground capacity 36,000
Record crowd 51,385 v. Derby County, FA Cup, qtr final, 26 February 1949
Nickname 'Pompey'

1984/5 Record
League 4th, Div 2
FA Cup Lost to Blackburn Rovers, 3rd rnd rep., 1-2
Milk Cup Lost to Nottm Forest, 2nd rnd, 1-3 on agg.

Historical Highlights

League Div 1 champions 1949, 1950. Div 1, 1927-59; Div 2, 1924-7, 1959-61, 1962-76, 1983-; Div 3, 1920-1, 1961-2, 1976-8, 1980-3; Div 3(S), 1921-4; Div 4, 1978-80
FA Cup Winners 1939; runners-up 1929, 1934
League/Milk Cup 5th rnd 1961
Top Scorer Bill Haines: 40 (1926/7)

PORT VALE

Chairman J. D. Lloyd
Team Manager John Rudge
Asst Manager/1st team coach
  Colin Dobson
Captain Barry Siddall
Year formed 1876
Ground address Vale Park, Burslem, Stoke-on-Trent, Staffs ST6 1AW
Telephone 0782 814134
Present ground capacity 35,000
Record crowd 50,000 v. Aston Villa, FA Cup, 5th round, 20 February 1960
Nickname 'The Valiants'
Sponsor Potteries Motor Traction Company

1984/5 Record

League 12th, Div 4
FA Cup Lost to West Ham United, 3rd rnd, 1-4
Milk Cup Lost to Wolverhampton W., 2nd rnd, 1-2 on agg.

Historical Highlights

League Best position – 5th in Div 2, 1931. Div 2 1892-6, 1898-1907, 1919-29, 1930-6, 1954-7; Div 3, 1959-65, 1970-8, 1980-4; Div 3(N), 1929-30, 1936-8, 1952-4; Div 3(S), 1938-52, 1957-8; Div 4, 1958-9, 1965-70, 1978-83, 1984-
FA Cup Semi-final 1954
League/Milk Cup Never past 2nd rnd
Top Scorer Wilf Kirkham: 38 (1926/7)

PRESTON NORTH END

Chairman Keith W. Leeming
Team Manager Alan Kelly until February 1985; Tommy Booth from March 1985
Asst Manager/1st team coach
  Brian Kidd
Captain Jonathan Clark
Year formed 1881
Ground address Deepdale, Preston PR1 6RU
Telephone 0772 795919
Present ground capacity 25,000
Record crowd 42,684 v. Arsenal, Division 1, 23 April 1938

Nickname 'The Lilywhites' or 'North End'
Sponsor Lombard Insurance

1984/5 Record

League 23rd, Div 3: relegated
FA Cup Lost to Telford United, 2nd round, 1-4
Milk Cup Lost to Norwich C., 2nd rnd, 4-9 on agg.

Historical Highlights

League Div 1 champions 1889, 1890; runners-up 1891, 1892, 1893, 1906, 1953, 1958. Div 1, 1888-1901, 1904-12, 1913-4, 1919-25, 1934-49, 1951-61; Div 2, 1901-4, 1912-3, 1914-5, 1925-34, 1949-51, 1961-70, 1971-4, 1978-81; Div 3, 1970-1, 1974-8, 1981-
FA Cup Winners 1889, 1938; runners up 1888, 1922, 1937, 1954, 1964
League/Milk Cup 4th rnd 1963, 1966, 1972, 1981
Top Scorer Ted Harper: 37 (1932/3)

Tom Finney, the Flying Plumber, was a one-club player, joining Preston North End as an amateur in 1937 and making 569 appearances for them before his retirement in 1960. The greatest goal-scoring winger of his day, he made 76 appearances for England (mainly as outside-left), scoring 18 times in his first 24 games; his 187 League goals for Preston remain a club record.

Above *Ronnie Blackman, prolific goal-scorer for Reading, claims the club's League record for a season (39 goals in 1951-2) and career total (156 in 1947-54).*

Below *Rodney Marsh was one of the great entertainers of English football during his heyday at Queen's Park Rangers in the 1960s. In 1972 he left to begin a none too happy spell at Manchester City, and later finished his career as a star in the NASL.*

QUEEN'S PARK RANGERS

Chairman J. A. Gregory
Team Manager Alan Mullery to December 1984; Frank Sibley from December 1984 to June 1985; then Jim Smith
Asst Manager/1st team coach Bobby Campbell until June 1985
Captain Terry Fenwick
Year formed 1885 as St Jude's until 1887
Ground address Rangers Stadium, South Africa Road, London W12 7PA

Telephone 01 743 0262/3/4/5
Present ground capacity 27,000
Record crowd 35,353 v. Leeds United, Division 1, 27 April 1974
Nickname 'Rangers' or 'The R's'
Sponsor Guinness

1984/5 Record
League 19th, Div 1
FA Cup Lost to Doncaster R., 3rd rnd, 0-1
Milk Cup Lost to Ipswich, 5th rnd rep., 1-2

Historical Highlights
League Best position – 2nd in Div 1, 1976. Div 1, 1968-9, 1973-9, 1983-; Div 2, 1948-52, 1967-8, 1969-73, 1979-83; Div 3, 1958-67; Div 3(S), 1920-48, 1952-8
FA Cup Runners-up 1982
League/Milk Cup Winners 1967
Europe UEFA Cup 1977
Top Scorer George Goddard: 37 (1929/30)

READING

Chairman Roger Smee
Team Manager Ian Branfoot
Asst Manager/1st team coach Stuart Henderson
Captain Martin Hicks
Year formed 1871
Ground address Elm Park, Norfolk Road, Reading, Berks RG3 2EF
Telephone 0734 507878/9
Present ground capacity 27,000
Record crowd 33,042 v. Brentford, FA Cup, 5th round, 19 February 1927
Nickname 'The Royals'
Sponsor Courage Breweries

1984/5 Record
League 9th, Div 3
FA Cup Lost to Barnsley, 3rd rnd, 3-4
Milk Cup Lost to Millwall, 1st round, 4-5 on agg.

Historical Highlights
League Best position – 14th in Div 2, 1927. Div 2, 1926-31; Div 3, 1920-1, 1958-71, 1976-7, 1979-83; Div 3(S), 1921-6, 1931-58; Div 4, 1971-6, 1977-9, 1983-4
FA Cup Semi-final 1927
League/Milk Cup 4th rnd 1965, 1966, 1978
Top Scorer Ronnie Blackman: 39 (1951/2)

ROCHDALE

Chairman D. F. Kilpatrick
Team Manager Vic Halom
Captain Joe Cooke
Year formed 1907
Ground address Spotland, Sandy Lane, Rochdale
Telephone 0706 44648/9
Present ground capacity 28,000
Record crowd 24,231 v Notts County, FA Cup, 2nd round 10 December 1949
Nickname 'The Dale'
Sponsor All-in-One Garden Centre

1984/5 Record
League 17th, Div 4
FA Cup Lost to Doncaster Rovers, 1st round, 1-2
Milk Cup Lost to Stockport Cty, 1st rnd, 2-5 on agg.

Historical Highlights
League Best position – 9th in Div 3, 1970. Div 3, 1958-9, 1969-74; Div 3(N), 1921-58; Div 4, 1959-60, 1974-
FA Cup 4th rnd 1971
League/Milk Cup Runners-up 1962
Top Scorer Albert Whitehurst: 44 (1926/7)

ROTHERHAM UNITED

Chairman M. McGarry
Team Manager George Kerr until May 1985; Norman Hunter from June 1985
Asst Manager/1st team coach Barry Claxton & Phil Henson
Captain Mike Pickering
Year formed 1884 as Thornhill United, until 1905; 1905-1924 as Rotherham County; amalgamated with Rotherham Town in 1925 to form Rotherham United
Ground address Millmoor Ground, Rotherham, South Yorks
Telephone 0709 562434
Present ground capacity 19,000
Nickname 'The Merry Millers'
Sponsor Patrick (UK) Ltd

1984/5 Record
League 12th, Div 3
FA Cup Lost to Mansfield Town, 1st round, 1-2
Milk Cup Lost to Grimsby Town, 3rd rnd rep., 1-6

Historical Highlights
League Best Position – 3rd in Div 2, 1955. Div 2, 1893-6, 1919-23, 1951-68, 1981-3; Div 3, 1968-73, 1975-81, Div 4, 1973-5
FA Cup 5th rnd 1953, 1968
League/Milk Cup Runners-up 1961
Top Scorer Wally Ardron: 38 (1946/7)

SCUNTHORPE UNITED

Chairman D. J. Wraith
Team Manager Allan Clarke until August 1984; then Frank Barlow until August 1984
Asst Manager/1st team coach Frank Barlow
Captain John Green
Year formed 1904; Amalgamated with Lindsay United in 1910, known as Scunthorpe & Lindsay United until 1958
Ground address Old Show Ground, Scunthorpe, Sth Humberside DN15 7RH
Telephone 0724 848077
Present ground capacity 25,000
Record crowd 23,935 v. Portsmouth, FA Cup, 4th round, 30 January 1954
Nickname 'The Iron'
Sponsor Scunthorpe E.Z.

1984/5 Record
League 9th, Div 4

FA Cup Lost to Port Vale, 2nd rnd, 1-4
Milk Cup Lost to Aston Villa, 2nd rnd, 3-6 on agg.

Historical Highlights
League Best position – 4th in Div 2, 1962. Div 2, 1958-64; Div 3, 1964-84, 1972-3, 1983-; Div 3(N), 1950-8; Div 4, 1968-72, 1973-83
FA Cup 5th rnd 1958, 1970
League/Milk Cup never past 3rd rnd
Top Scorer Barry Thomas: 31 (1961/2)

Below *Barry Thomas, Scunthorpe United's goals-in-a-season record holder, with 31 in 1961/2.*

SHEFFIELD UNITED

Chairman R. J. Brealey
Team Manager Ian Porterfield
Asst Manager/1st team coach John McSeveney
Captain Colin Morris
Year formed 1889
Ground address Brammall Lane, Sheffield S2 4SU
Telephone 0742 738955/6/7
Present ground capacity 49,000
Record crowd 68,287 v. Leeds United, FA Cup, 5th round, 15 February 1936
Nickname 'The Blades'
Sponsor Simonds

1984/5 Record
League 18th, Div 2
FA Cup Lost to Watford, 3rd rnd, 0-5
Milk Cup Lost to Everton, 2nd round, 2-6 on agg.

Historical Highlights
League Div 1 winners in 1898; runners-up 1897, 1900. Div 1, 1893-1934, 1946-9, 1953-6, 1961-8, 1971-6; Div 2, 1892-3, 1934-9, 1949-53, 1956-61, 1968-71, 1976-9; Div 3, 1979-81, 1983-4; Div 4, 1981-2
FA Cup Winners in 1899, 1902, 1915, 1925; runners-up 1901, 1936
League/Milk Cup 5th rnd, 1962, 1967, 1972
Top Scorer Jimmy Dunne: 41 (1930/1)

Below *Joe Shaw, Sheffield United's long-service record holder, with 629 League appearances in 1948-66.*

Above *Arthur Rowley scored a record 38 goals for Shrewsbury Town in 1958/9; for Leicester City he had notched 39 in 1952/3 and 44 in 1956/7. He had a Football League career record of 434 goals in 619 matches.*

Below *Derek Dooley, rumbustious centre-forward for Sheffield Wednesday, topped the League with 46 goals in 1951/2. His tragically brief career was ended in February 1953 by a leg amputation following a fracture in a match against Preston.*

SHEFFIELD WEDNESDAY

Chairman H. E. McGee
Team Manager Howard Wilkinson
Asst Manager/1st team coach Peter Eustace
Captain Mick Lyons
Year formed 1867
Ground address Hillsborough, Sheffield S6 1SW
Telephone 0742 343123
Present ground capacity 50,174
Record crowd 72,841 v. Manchester City, FA Cup, 5th round, 17 February 1934
Nickname 'The Owls'
Sponsor MHS

1984/5 Record

League 8th, Div 1
FA Cup Lost to Ipswich T., 5th rnd, 2-3
Milk Cup Lost to Chelsea, 5th rnd rep., 1-2

Historical Highlights

League Div 1 champions 1903, 1904, 1929, 1930; runners-up 1961. Div 1, 1892-9, 1900-20, 1926-37, 1950-1, 1952-5, 1956-8, 1959-70, 1984-; Div 2, 1899-1900, 1920-6, 1937-50, 1951-2, 1955-6, 1958-9, 1970-5, 1980-4; Div 3, 1975-80
FA Cup Winners 1896, 1907, 1935; runners-up 1890, 1966
League/Milk Cup 5th rnd 1983
Europe Fairs Cup: 1962, 1964

Top Scorer Derek Dooley: 46 (1951/2)

SHREWSBURY TOWN

Chairman H. S. Yates
Team Manager Phil Bates
Captain Ross Maclaren
Year formed 1886
Ground address Gay Meadow, Shrewsbury, Shropshire SY2 6AB
Telephone 0743 60111
Present ground capacity 16,000
Record crowd 18,917 v. Walsall, Division 3, 26 April 1961
Nickname 'Town'
Sponsor Link 51

1984/5 Record

League 8th, Div 2
FA Cup Lost to Oxford Utd, 2nd rnd, 0-2
Milk Cup Lost to Bolton W., 2nd rnd, 3-4 on agg.

Historical Highlights

League Best position – 8th in Div 2, 1985. Div 2, 1979-; Div 3, 1959-74, 1975-9; Div 3(N), 1950-1; Div 3(S), 1951-8; Div 4, 1958-9
FA Cup 6th rnd 1979, 1982
League/Milk Cup Semi-final 1961
Top Scorer Arthur Rowley: 38 (1958/9)

SOUTHAMPTON

Chairman A. A. Woodford
Team Manager Lawrie McMenemy until June 1985; Chris Nicholl from July 1985
Asst Manager/1st team coach John Mortimore (until May 1985) and Lew Chatterley (until June 1985)
Captain Nick Holmes
Year formed 1885 as Southampton St Mary's
Ground address The Dell, Milton Road, Southampton, Hants SO9 4XX
Telephone 0703 39445/39633
Present ground capacity 25,000
Record crowd 31,044 v. Manchester United, Division 1, 8 October 1969
Nickname 'The Saints'
Sponsor Draper Tools

1984/5 Record

League 5th, Div 1
FA Cup Lost to Barnsley, 5th rnd, 1-2
Milk Cup Lost to Queen's Park Rangers, 4th rnd rep., 0-4

Historical Highlights

League Best position – 2nd in Div 1, 1984. Div 1, 1966-74, 1978-; Div 2, 1922-53, 1960-6 1974-8; Div 3, 1958-60; Div 3(S), 1920-2, 1953-8

FA Cup Winners 1976; runners-up 1900, 1902
League/Milk Cup Runners-up 1979
Europe European Cup-Winners' Cup 1977;
Fairs Cup 1970; UEFA Cup 1972, 1982, 1983,
1984
Top Scorer Derek Reeves: 39 (1959/60)

SOUTHEND UNITED

Chairman Andrew
  McHutchon
Team Manager Bobby Moore
Asst Manager/1st team coach
  Harry Cripps
Captain Mickey Stead
Year formed 1906
Ground address Roots Hall
  Ground, Victoria Ave,
  Southend-on-Sea, Essex
Telephone 0702 340707
Present ground capacity 32,000
Record crowd 31,033, v. Liverpool, FA Cup,
  3rd round, 10 January 1979
Nickname 'The Shrimpers'
Sponsor Motorplan

1984/5 Record
League 20th, Div 4
FA Cup Lost to Colchester Utd, 1st rnd, 2-3
Milk Cup Lost to Orient, 1st rnd, 1-2 on agg.

Historical Highlights
League Best position – 7th in Div 3, 1982. Div 3,
  1920-1, 1958-66, 1972-6, 1978-80, 1981-4; Div
  3(S), 1921-58; Div 4, 1966-72, 1976-8, 1980-1
FA Cup 5th rnd 1926, 1952, 1976
League/Milk Cup Never past 3rd rnd
Top Scorers 31: Jim Shankly (1928/9), Sammy
  McCrory (1957/8)

STOCKPORT COUNTY

Chairman A. N. Kirk
**Team Manager/1st team
  coach** Eric Webster
Captain Tommy Sword
Year formed 1883 as Heaton
  Norris Rovers; 1888-90
  Heaton Norris; 1890
  Stockport County.
Ground address Edgeley Park,
  Hardcastle Road, Stockport,
  Cheshire SK3 9DD
Telephone 061 480 8888
Present ground capacity 16,500
Record crowd 27,833 v. Liverpool, FA Cup, 5th
  round, 11 February 1950
Nickname 'The Hatters'
Sponsor Langdale Services

1984/5 Record
League 22nd, Div 4: re-elected

FA Cup Lost to Walsall, 1st rnd, 1-2
Milk Cup Lost to Liverpool, 2nd rnd, 0-2 on
  agg.

Historical Highlights
League Best position – 12th in Div 2, 1914. Div
  2, 1900-4, 1905-21, 1922-6, 1937-8; Div 3,
  1958-9, 1967-70; Div 3(N), 1921-2, 1926-37,
  1938-58; Div 4, 1959-67, 1970-
FA Cup 5th rnd 1935, 1950
League/Milk Cup 4th rnd 1973
Top Scorer Alf Lythgoe: 46 (1933/4)

STOKE CITY

Chairman Frank Edwards
Team Manager Bill Asprey to
  April 1985; Tony Lacey to
  June 1985; then Mick Mills
Asst Manager/1st team coach
  Tony Lacey until April 1985
Captain Sammy McIlroy
Year formed 1863
Ground address Victoria
  Ground, Stoke-on-Trent, Staffs
  ST4 4EG
Telephone 0782 413511
Present ground capacity 35,000
Record crowd 51,380 v. Arsenal, Division 1,
  29 March 1937
Nickname 'The Potters'
Sponsor Ricoh
1984/5 Record
League 22nd, Div 1: relegated
FA Cup Lost to Luton Town, 3rd rnd rep., 2-3
Milk Cup Lost to Rotherham Utd, 2nd rnd, 2-3
  on agg.

Historical Highlights
League Best position – 4th in Div 1, 1936, 1947.
  Div 1, 1888-90, 1891-1907, 1922-3, 1933-53,
  1963-77, 1979-; Div 2, 1907-8, 1919-22,
  1923-6, 1927-33, 1953-63, 1977-9; Div 3(N),
  1926-7
FA Cup Semi-finals 1899, 1971, 1972
League/Milk Cup Winners 1972
Europe UEFA Cup 1973, 1975
Top Scorer Freddie Steele: 33 (1936/7)

*Above Stockport County's
side that beat Halifax Town
13-0 in January 1934. This,
with Newcastle's similar
trouncing of Newport
County in October 1946, is
the highest score without
reply in a Football League
match.*

*Below Gordon Banks
(Stoke City), the greatest
goalkeeper of his day,
earned 73 caps for England
in 1963-72. He started his
career with Leicester City
(where his understudy was
the young Peter Shilton),
and ended it with Fort
Lauderdale Strikers in the
North American league.*

Above *Len Shackleton, the idol of Roker Park, came to Sunderland in February 1948 from Newcastle United, for whom he had scored six goals on his League début. His prodigious skills were too individualistic for some tastes, including the England selectors' – he won only a handful of representative honours.*

Below *John Charles (Swansea City), perhaps the greatest-ever Welsh footballer, played with equal distinction at centre-forward and centre-half. He spent much of his career with Leeds United and, from 1957, with Juventus. He made his international début against Ireland in 1950 when only 18 years 71 days old.*

SUNDERLAND

Chairman T. Cowie
Team Manager Len Ashurst until May 1985; Lawrie McMenemy from July 1985
Asst Manager/1st team coach Frank Burrowes until June 1985; Lew Chatterley from July 1985
Captain Sean Elliott
Year formed 1879 as Sunderland & District Teachers AFC: as Sunderland from 1881
Ground address Roker Park, Grantham Rd., Roker, Tyne & Wear SR6 9SW
Telephone 0783 40332
Present ground capacity 37,683
Record crowd 75,118 v. Derby County, FA Cup, qtr final replay, 8 March 1933
Nickname 'The Rokerites'
Sponsor Cowie's

1984/5 Record
League 21st, Div 1: relegated
FA Cup Lost to Southampton, 3rd round, 0-4
Milk Cup Finalists: lost to Norwich City, 0-1

Historical Highlights
League Div 1 champions 1892, 1893, 1895, 1902, 1913, 1936; runners-up 1894, 1898, 1901, 1923, 1935. Div 1, 1890-1958, 1964-70, 1976-7, 1980-; Div 2, 1958-64, 1970-6, 1977-80
FA Cup Winners 1937, 1973; runners-up 1913
League/Milk Cup Semifinals 1963
Europe European Cup-Winners' Cup 1974
Top Scorer David Halliday: 43 (1928/9)

SWANSEA CITY

Chairman D. J. Sharpe
Team Manager Colin Appleton until December 1984; John Bond from January 1985
Asst Manager/1st team coach Fred Davies
Captain Nigel Stevenson
Year formed 1900 as Swansea Town, until February 1970
Ground address Vetch Field, Swansea, Glamorgan SA1 3SU
Telephone 0792 474114
Present ground capacity 26,237
Record crowd 32,796 v. Arsenal, FA Cup, 4th round, 17 February 1968
Nickname 'The Swans'
Sponsor DP Ltd

1984/5 Record
League 20th, Div 3
FA Cup Lost to Bognor Regis, 1st rnd, 1-3
Milk Cup Lost to Walsall, 1st rnd, 1-5 on agg.

Historical Highlights
League Best position – 6th in Div 1, 1982. Div 1, 1981-3; Div 2, 1925-47, 1949-65, 1979-81, 1983-4; Div 3, 1920-1, 1965-7, 1970-3, 1978-9; Div 3(S), 1921-5, 1947-9; Div 4, 1967-70, 1973-8
FA Cup Semi-finals 1926, 1964
League/Milk Cup 4th rnd 1965, 1977
Europe European Cup-Winners' Cup 1962, 1967, 1982, 1983
Top Scorer Cyril Pearce: 35 (1931/2)

SWINDON TOWN

Chairman N. W. Earle
Team Manager Lou Macari
Asst Manager/1st team coach John Trollope
Captain Andy Rowland
Year formed 1881
Ground address County Ground, Swindon, Wiltshire SWF1 2ED
Telephone 0793 22118
Present ground capacity 28,000
Record crowd 32,000 v. Arsenal, FA Cup, 3rd round, 15 January 1972
Nickname 'The Robins'
Sponsor Lowndes Lambert

1984/5 Record
League 8th, Div 4
FA Cup Lost to Dagenham, 1st rnd, 1-2
Milk Cup Lost to Bristol Rovers, 1st rnd, 2-5 on agg.

Historical Highlights
League Best position – 5th in Div 2, 1970. Div 2, 1963-5, 1969-74; Div 3, 1920-1, 1958-63, 1965-9, 1974-82; Div 3 (S), 1921-58; Div 4, 1982-
FA Cup Semi-finals 1910, 1912
League/Milk Cup Winners 1969
Europe Anglo-Italian Cup 1970 (winners)
Top Scorer Harry Morris: 47 (1926/7)

TORQUAY UNITED

Chairman L. W. Cope from March 1984
Team Manager David Webb
Asst Manager/1st team coach Alan Slough until January 1984; Eddie Kelly from January 1984
Captain John Impey
Year formed 1898 as Torquay

Town, until 1921
Ground address Plainmoor Ground, Torquay, Devon TQ1 3PS
Telephone 0803 38666/7
Present ground capacity 17,500
Record crowd 21,908 v. Huddersfield Town, FA Cup, 4th round, 29 January 1955
Nickname 'The Gulls'
Sponsor Leisure Industries

1984/5 Record

League 24th, Div 4: re-elected
FA Cup Lost to Orient, 2nd rnd, 0-3
Milk Cup Lost to Plymouth A., 1st rnd, 0-2 on agg.

Historical Highlights

League Best position – 4th in Div 3, 1968. Div 3, 1960-2, 1966-72; Div 3(S), 1927-58; LDiv 4, 1958-60, 1962-6, 1972-
FA Cup 4th rnd 1949, 1955, 1971, 1983
League/Milk Cup Never past 3rd rnd
Top Scorer Sammy Collins: 40 (1955/6)

TOTTENHAM HOTSPUR

Chairman D. A. Alexiou
Team Manager Keith Burkinshaw until June 1984; Peter Shreeves from July 1984
Asst Manager/1st team coach John Pratt
Captain Steve Perryman
Year formed 1882 as Hotspur Football Club, until 1885
Ground address White Hart Lane, 748 High Rd, Tottenham, London N17
Telephone 01-801 3411
Present ground capacity 49,000
Record crowd 75,038 v. Sunderland, FA Cup, qtr final, 5 March 1938
Nickname 'Spurs'

Sponsor Holsten Lager

1984/5 Record

League 3rd, Div 1
FA Cup Lost to Liverpool, 4th rnd, 0-1
Milk Cup Lost to Sunderland, 4th round replay, 1-2

Historical Highlights

League Div 1 champions 1951, and 1961; runners-up 1922, 1952, 1957, 1963
FA Cup 1901, 1921, 1961, 1962, 1967, 1981, 1982 (equal record number of wins)
League/Milk Cup Winners 1971, 1973; runners-up 1982
Europe European Cup 1962; European Cup-Winners' Cup 1963 (winners), 1964, 1968, 1982, 1983; UEFA Cup 1972 (winners), 1973, 1974 (runners-up), 1984 (winners), 1985
Top Scorer Jimmy Greaves: 37 (1962/3)

Below *Jimmy Greaves (Tottenham), one of the deadliest finishers in post-war British football, scored 357 League goals for Chelsea, Spurs and (briefly) West Ham, and 44 in 57 appearances for England. He was only 31 when he retired in 1971.*

Bottom *Tottenham's players, staff, and board in 1961, when Spurs became the first Football League club this century to achieve the League and Cup double. Captain Danny Blanchflower is fifth from left in the middle row.*

Right *John Barnes (Watford), a winger with the ability to conjure spectacular goals out of nothing, seems destined to become one of the finest England players of the mid-1980s.*

TRANMERE ROVERS

Chairman G. A. Gould
Team Manager Bryan Hamilton until February 1985; Frank Worthington (as Player-Manager) from July 1985
Asst Manager/1st team coach Ray Matthias
Captain John Williams
Year formed 1883
Ground address Prenton Park, Prenton Rd West, Birkenhead L42 9PN
Telephone 051 608 3677/4194
Present ground capacity 18,000
Record crowd 24,424 v. Stoke City, FA Cup, 4th round, 5 February 1972
Nickname 'The Rovers'
Sponser Hugh Foulerton Cutlery

1984/5 Record
League 6th, Div 4
FA Cup Lost to Hull C., 2nd rnd, 0-3
Milk Cup Lost to Preston, 1st rnd, 4-5 on agg.

Historical Highlights
League Best position – 22nd in Div 2, 1939. Div 2, 1938-9; Div 3, 1958-61, 1967-75, 1976-9; Div 3(N), 1921-38, 1946-58; Div 4, 1961-7, 1975-6, 1979
FA Cup 5th rnd 1968
League/Milk Cup 4th rnd 1962, 1982
Top Scorer John Clayton: 36 (1984/5)

Above *Mark Rees (7), an accomplished forward for Walsall, one of the most attractive footballing sides of Division 3 in the 1983/4 season. The club ran Liverpool close in the Milk Cup semi-final, after having comfortably disposed of Arsenal in a previous round.*

WALSALL

Chairman K. E. Wheldon
Team Manager Alan Buckley
Asst Manager/1st team coach Gary Pendry
Captain Peter Hart
Year formed 1877 as Walsall Swifts; 1888 amalgamated with Walsall Town to become Walsall Town Swifts until 1895

Ground address Fellows Park, Walsall, West Midlands WS2 9DB
Telephone 0922 22791
Present ground capacity 24,100
Nickname 'The Saddlers'
Sponsor Deeley Castings

1984/5 Record
League 11th, Div 3
FA Cup Lost to York C., 3rd rnd, 0-3
Milk Cup Lost to Chelsea, 3rd round replay, 0-3

Historical Highlights
League Best postion – 6th in Div 2 in 1899. Div 2, 1892-5, 1896-1901, 1961-3; Div 3, 1960-1, 1963-79, 1980-; Div 3(N), 1921-7, 1931-6; Div 3(S), 1927-31, 1936-58; Div 4, 1958-60, 1979-80
FA Cup 5th rnd 1939, 1975, 1978
League/Milk Cup 4th rnd 1967
Top Scorer Gilbert Alsop: 40 (1933/4, 1934/5)

WATFORD

Chairman Elton John
Team Manager Graham Taylor
Asst Manager/1st team coach John Ward
Captain Wilf Rostron
Year formed 1891 as West Herts, until 1898
Ground address Vicarage Road Stadium, Watford, Herts WD1 8ER
Telephone 0923 49747/8/9

Ground address The Hawthorns, West
  Bromwich, West Midlands B71 4LF
Telephone 021 525 8888
Present ground capacity 38,600
Record crowd 64,815 v. Arsenal, FA Cup, qtr
  final, 6 March 1937
Nickname 'The Baggies', 'The Throstles',
Sponsor West Midlands Health Authority

1984/5 Record
League 12th, Div 1
FA Cup Lost to Orient, 3rd rnd, 1-2
Milk Cup Lost to Watford, 4th rnd, 1-4

Historical Highlights
League Div 1 champions 1920; runners-up
  1925, 1954. Div 1, 1888-1901, 1902-4,
  1911-27, 1931-8, 1949-73, 1976-; Div 2,
  1901-2, 1904-11, 1927-31, 1938-49, 1973-6
FA Cup Winners 1888, 1892, 1931, 1954, 1968;
  runners-up 1886, 1887, 1895, 1912, 1935
League/Milk Cup Winners 1966
Europe European Cup-Winners' Cup 1969;
  Fairs Cup 1967; UEFA Cup 1979, 1980, 1982
Top Scorer William Richardson: 39 (1935/6)

Above *Cyrille Regis, West
Bromwich Albion's strong
and skilful striker (left), was
slow to get back to top form
after injury deprived him of
a place in England's 1982
World Cup squad. He now
plays for Coventry City.*

Present ground capacity 28,500
Record crowd 34,099 v Manchester United, FA
  Cup, 4th round, 3 February 1969
Nickname 'The Hornets'
Sponsor Iveco

1984/5 Record
League 11th, Div 1
FA Cup Lost to Luton Town, 5th round replay,
  0-1
Milk Cup Lost to Sunderland, 5th round,
  0-1

Historical Highlights
League Best position – Div 1 runners-up 1983.
  Div 1, 1982-; Div 2, 1969-72, 1979-82; Div 3,
  1920-1, 1960-9, 1972-5, 1978-9; Div 3(S),
  1928-58; Div 4, 1958-60, 1976-8
FA Cup Runners-up 1984
League/Milk Cup Semi-final 1979
Europe UEFA Cup 1984
Top Scorer Cliff Holton: 42 (1959/60)

WEST BROMWICH ALBION

Chairman J. S. Lucas
Team Manager Johnny Giles
  from February 1984
Asst Manager/1st team coach
  Norman Hunter (until June
  1985) and Nobby Stiles
Captain Alastair Robertson
Year formed 1879 as West
  Bromwich Strollers,
  until 1881

WEST HAM UNITED

Chairman L. C. Cearns
Manager/1st team coach
  John Lyall
Captain Alvin Martin
Year formed 1900
Ground address Boleyn
  Ground, Green St, Upton
  Park, London E13
Nickname 'The Hammers', 'The Irons'
Sponsor Avco Trust
Telephone 01-472 2740
Present ground capacity
  35,500
Record crowd 42,322 v.
  Tottenham Hotspur, Division 1,
  17 October 1970

1984/5 Record
League 16th, Div 1
FA Cup Lost to Manchester United, 5th
  round replay, 2-4
Milk Cup Lost to Manchester C., 3rd rnd rep,
  1-2

Historical Highlights
League Best position – 6th in Div 1, 1927, 1959,
  1973. Div 1, 1923-32, 1958-78, 1981-; Div 2,
  1919-23, 1932-58, 1978-81
FA Cup Winners in 1964, 1975, 1980;
  runners-up 1923
League/Milk Cup Runners-up 1966, 1981
Europe European Cup-Winners' Cup 1965
  (winners), 1966, 1976 (runners-up), 1981
Top Scorer Vic Watson: 41 (1929/30)

Below *Great club servant
and captain, West Ham's
fiercely competitive Billy
Bonds helped to put iron
into his team's defence.*

Above *Glyn Hodges (Wimbledon) combines a sharp appetite for goals with his creative midfield work.*

Below *Billy Wright (Wolverhampton Wanderers), England half-back and captain in the 1950s, made a (then) record 105 international appearances, and he holds Wolves' club record of 491 games in 1946-59.*

WIGAN ATHLETIC

Chairman B. Heathcote
Team Manager Bryan Hamilton
Asst Manager Roy Tunks
Captain Colin Methven
Year formed 1932
Ground address Springfield Park, Wigan, Lancs
Telephone 0942 44433
Present ground capacity 30,000
Record crowd 27,500 v. Hereford United, FA Cup, 2nd round, 12 December 1953
Nickname 'The Latics'
Sponsor Heinz

1984/5 Record
League 16th, Div 3
FA Cup Lost to Chelsea, 3rd rnd rep., 0-5
Milk Cup Lost to WBA, 2nd rnd, 1-3 on agg
Freight Rover Trophy Winners

Historical Highlights
League Best position – 18th in Div 3, 1983. Div 3, 1982-; Div 4, 1978-82
FA Cup 4th rnd 1980
League/Milk Cup 4th rnd 1982
Top Scorer Les Bradd: 19 (1981/2)

WIMBLEDON

Chairman S. G. Reeds
Team Manager Dave Bassett
Asst Manager/1st team coach Allan Gillett
Captain Alan Cork
Year formed 1889 as Wimbledon Old Centrals, until 1905
Ground address Plough Lane Ground, Durnsford Rd, London SW19
Telephone 01-946 6311
Present ground capacity 15,000
Record crowd 18,000 v. HMS Victory, FA Amateur Cup, 3rd round, 23 February 1935
Nickname 'The Dons'
Sponsor John Lelliott

1984/5 Record
League 12th, Div 2
FA Cup Lost to West Ham, 5th rnd, 1-5
Milk Cup Lost to Portsmouth, 1st rnd, 1-3 on agg.

Historical Highlights
League Best position – 2nd, Div 3, 1984. Div 3, 1979-80, 1981-2, 1983-4; Div 4, 1977-9, 1980-1, 1982-3
FA Cup 4th rnd 1975, 1981
League/Milk Cup 4th rnd 1980
Top scorer Alan Cork: 28 (1983/84)

WOLVERHAMPTON WANDERERS

Chairman Derek Dougan
Team Manager Tommy Docherty until July 1985
Ass Manager/1st team coach Mike Docherty
Captain Peter Zelem
Year formed 1876 as St Luke's School Blakenhall; 1880 amalgamated with The Wanderers
Ground address Molineux Ground, Waterloo Road, Wolverhampton WV1 4QR
Telephone 0902 712181
Present ground capacity 39,000
Record crowd 61,315 v. Liverpool, FA Cup, 5th round, 11 February 1939
Nickname 'Wolves'
Sponsor Tatungs

1984/5 Record
League 22nd, Div 2: relegated
FA Cup Lost to Huddersfield T., 3rd rnd rep. 1-3
Milk Cup Lost to Southampton, 3rd rnd rep., 0-2

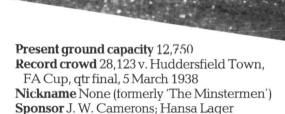

Historical Highlights

League Div 1 champions 1954, 1958, 1959;
runners-up 1938, 1939, 1950, 1955, 1960. Div
1, 1888-1906, 1932-65, 1967-76, 1977-82,
1983-4; Div 2, 1906-23, 1924-32, 1965-7,
1976-7, 1982-3; Div 3(N), 1923-4
FA Cup Winners 1893, 1908, 1949, 1960;
runners-up 1889, 1896, 1921, 1939
League/Milk Cup Winners 1974, 1980
Europe European Cup 1959, 1960; European
Cu-Winners' Cup 1961; UEFA Cup 1972
(runners-up), 1974, 1975, 1981
Top Scorer Dennis Westcott: 37 (1946/7)

WREXHAM

Chairman F. J. Tomlinson
Team Manager Dixie McNeill
from March 1985
Asst Manager/1st team coach
George Showell
Captain Steve Charles
Year formed 1873
Ground address Racecourse
Ground, Mold Road, Wrexham, Clwyd
Telephone 0978 262129
Present ground capacity 28,500
Record crowd 34,445 v. Manchester United, FA
Cup, 4th round, 26 January 1957
Nickname 'The Robins'
Sponsor Crossville Motor Services

1984/5 Record

League 15th, Div 4
FA Cup Lost to Wigan Ath., 1st rnd, 0-2
Milk Cup Lost to Wigan, 1st rnd, 0-5 on agg.
European Cup-Winners' Cup Lost to AS
Roma, 2nd rnd, 0-3 on agg.

Historical Highlights

League Best position – 15th in Div 2, 1979. Div
2, 1978-82; Div 3, 1958-60, 1962-4, 1970-8,
1982-3; Div 3(N), 1921-58; Div 4, 1960-2,
1964-70, 1983-
FA Cup 6th rnd, 1974, 1978
League/Milk Cup 5th rnd 1962, 1978
Europe European Cup-Winners' Cup
(qualifying as winners of Welsh Cup) 1973,
1976, 1979, 1980
Top Scorer Tom Bamford: 44 (1933/4)

YORK CITY

Chairman M. D. B. Sinclair
Team Manager Denis Smith
Asst Manager/1st team coach
Viv Busby
Captain Sean Haselgrave
Year formed 1922
Ground address Bootham
Crescent, York YO3 7AQ
Telephone 0904 24447

Present ground capacity 12,750
Record crowd 28,123 v. Huddersfield Town,
FA Cup, qtr final, 5 March 1938
Nickname None (formerly 'The Minstermen')
Sponsor J. W. Camerons; Hansa Lager

1984/5 Record

League 8th, Div 3
FA Cup Lost to Liverpool, 5th round replay,
0-7
Milk Cup Lost to Queen's Park Rangers, 2nd
rnd, 3-8 on agg.

Historical Highlights

League Best position – 15th in Div 2, 1975. Div
2, 1974-6; Div 3, 1959-60, 1965-6, 1971-4,
1976-7, 1984; Div 3 (N), 1929-58; Div 4, 1958-9,
1960-5, 1966-71, 1977-84
FA Cup Semi-finals 1955
League/Milk Cup 5th rnd 1962
Top Scorers 31: Bill Fenton (1951/2), Alf
Bottom (1955/6)

*Above Arfon Griffiths
(Wrexham, left) scores the
winning goal for Wales
against Austria in the 1968
European Championship
qualifying round. Griffiths
made a record 592
appearances for Wrexham
in 1959-79.*

*Left Roger Jones, York
City's goalkeeper, was
acquired on a free-transfer
during the 1982/3 campaign.
He proved the bargain of
the Division 4 season, and in
1983/4 was voted a member
of the Divisional Team of
the Season, along with
clubmates McPhail, Byrne
and Walwyn.*

Aberdeen celebrate victory in the European Cup-Winners' Cup Final against Real Madrid in May 1983. They went on to beat European Cup-holders SV Hamburg to take the European Super Cup. The Dons set the pace in Scottish football in the first half of the 1980s.

ABERDEEN

Chairman Richard Donald
Team Manager Alex Ferguson
Asst Manager/1st team coach
  Willie Garner
Captain Willie Miller
Year formed 1903
Ground address Pittodrie
  Stadium, Aberdeen, Grampian
  AB2 1QH
Telephone 0224 632329
Present ground capacity 24,000
Record crowd 45,061 v. Hearts, Scottish Cup,
  4th round, 13 March 1954
Nickname 'The Dons'

1984/5 Record
League Champions, Premier Division
Scottish FA Cup Lost to Dundee Utd, Semi-
  finals, 1-2
Skol Cup Lost to Airdrie, 2nd round, 1-3
European Cup Lost to Dinamo Berlin, 2nd rnd,
  3-3 (on pens.)

Historical Highlights
League Premier Division champions 1980,
  1984; runners-up 1978, 1981, 1982; Div 1
  champions 1955; runners-up 1911, 1937,
  1956, 1971, 1972
Scottish FA Cup Winners 1947, 1970, 1982,
  1983, 1984; runners-up 1937, 1953, 1954,
  1959, 1967, 1978
League Cup Winners 1946, 1956, 1977;
  runners-up 1947, 1979, 1980
Europe European Cup 1981, 1985; European
  Cup-Winners' Cup 1968, 1970, 1979, 1983
  (winners), 1984; UEFA Cup 1972, 1973, 1974,
  1978, 1980, 1982; Super Cup 1983 (winners)
Top Scorer Benny Yorston: 38 (1929-30)

AIRDRIE

Chairman James Ferguson
Team Manager Ally McCleod
Asst Manager/1st team coach
  Willie Reid & Bobby Morrison
Captain Jamie Fairley
Year formed 1878
Ground address Broomfield
  Park, Airdrie, Strathclyde
  ML6 9LJ
Telephone 023 64 62067
Present ground capacity 20,000
Record crowd 24,000 v. Hearts, Scottish Cup,
  4th round, 8 March 1952
Nickname 'The Diamonds', 'The Waysiders'
Sponsor Dalzeil

1984/5 Record
League 5th, Div 1
Scottish FA Cup Lost to Falkirk, 3rd round,
  0-3
Skol Cup Lost to Celtic, 3rd rnd, 0-4

Historical Highlights
League Best position – 7th in Premier Div,
  1981. Premier Div 1981-2; Div 1, 1904-36,
  1948-9, 1952-4, 1956-65, 1967-73, 1975-80,
  1982-; Div 2, 1895-1903, 1937-47, 1949-50,
  1955-6, 1966-7, 1974-5
Scottish Cup Winners 1924; runners-up 1975
Top Scorer H. G. Yarnall: 45 (1916-7)

ALBION ROVERS

Chairman Thomas Fagan
Team Manager Joe Baker
Asst Manager/1st teach coach
  Jim Wilson & Jim McCusker
Captain Tony Gallagher
Year formed 1882
Ground address Cliftonhill
  Park, Coatbridge, Strathclyde
  M15 9XX
Telephone 0236 32350
Present ground capacity 10,000
Record crowd 27,381 v. Rangers, Scottish Cup,
  2nd round, 18 February 1936
Nickname 'The Wee Rovers'

1984/5 Record
League 8th, Div 2
Scottish FA Cup Lost to Berwick R., 1st rnd,
  1-3
Skol Cup Lost to St Johnstone, 2nd round,
  1-2

Historical Highlights
Best position – 11th in Div 1, 1922. Div 1,
  1920-3, 1934-7, 1938-9, 1948-9; Div 2,
  1904-15, 1923-34, 1937-8, 1946-8, 1949-
Scottish Cup Runners-up 1920
Top Scorer Jim Renwick: 41 (1932-3)

ALLOA ATHLETIC

Chairman Ronald Todd
Team Manager Alec Thompson
Asst Manager/1st team coach Alec Turnbull
Captain Kenny Thompson
Year formed 1883
Ground address Recreation Ground, Alloa, Clackmannanshire, Central
Telephone 0259 722695
Present ground capacity 9,000
Record crowd 13,000 v. Dunfermline Athletic, Scottish Cup, 3rd round replay, 26 February 1939
Nickname 'The Wasps'

1984/5 Record
League 2nd, Div 2: promoted
Scottish FA Cup Lost to Aberdeen, 3rd round, 0-5
Skol Cup Lost to Kilmarnock, 2nd rnd, 2-2 (on pens.)

Historical Highlights
League Best position – 6th in Div 1, 1983. Div 1, 1922-3, 1977-8, 1983-; Div 2, 1921-2, 1924-77, 1978-82
Scottish Cup Quarter-final 1939, 1961
Top Scorer 'Wee' Willie Crilley: 49 (1931-2)

ARBROATH

Chairman Ian Stirling
Team Manager Jimmy Bone
Asst Manager/1st team coach John Young
Captain Tony Hill
Year formed 1878
Ground address Gayfield Park, Arbroath, Tayside DD11 12B
Telephone 0241 72157
Present ground capacity 10,000
Record crowd 13,510 v. Rangers, Scottish Cup, 3rd round, 23 February 1952
Nickname 'The Red Lichties'
Sponsor Smokey's Disco

1984/5 Record
League 14th, Div 2
Scottish FA Cup Lost to Queen of South, 1st rnd, 1-2
Skol Cup Lost to Dunfermline Athletic, 1st rnd, 0-4

Historical Highlights
League Best position – 5th in Div 1, 1976. Div 1, 1936-9, 1960, 1969, 1973-80; Div 2, 1922-35, 1947-59, 1961-8, 1970-2, 1981-

Scottish Cup Semi-final 1974
Top Scorer Dave Easson: 45 (1958-9)

AYR UNITED

Chairman Andrew Charters
Team Manager George Caldwell
1st team coach David Wells
Captain Mark Shanks
Year formed 1910
Ground address Somerset Park, Ayr, Strathclyde KA8 9NB
Telephone 0292 263435
Present ground capacity 18,500
Record crowd 25,225 v. Rangers, Division 1, 13 September 1969
Nickname 'The Honest Men'
Sponsor Barr Construction

1984/5 Record
League 7th, Div 1
Scottish FA Cup Lost to St Mirren, 4th rnd, 0-1
Skol Cup Lost to Hearts, 3rd rnd, 0-1

Historical Highlights
League Best position – 6th in Premier Div, 1976. Premier Div, 1976-8; Div 1, 1914-25, 1929-36, 1938-9, 1957, 1960-1, 1967, 1970-5, 1979-; Div 2, 1899-1913, 1926-8, 1937, 1947-56, 1958-9, 1962-6, 1968-9
Scottish Cup Semi-final 1973
Top Scorer Jimmy Smith: 66 (1927-8) – record for English and Scottish Leagues

Billy Pirie, one of Arbroath's best postwar strikers, was transferred to Aberdeen for a record fee in 1974. Failing to settle there, he moved to Dundee, with whom he was the top League striker in 1976/7 (36 goals) and 1977/8 (35).

BERWICK RANGERS

Chairman Alex MacNabb
Team Manager Eric Tait
Asst Manager/1st team coach
  Ian Smith
Captain David Steadman
Year formed 1881
Ground address Shielfield
  Park, Berwick-on-Tweed,
  Northumberland T15 2EF
Telephone 0289 307424
Present ground capacity 10,673
Record crowd 13,365 v. Rangers, Scottish Cup,
  1st round, 28 January 1967
Nickname 'The Borderers'
Sponsor Polychrome

1984/5 Record
League 13th, Div 2
Scottish FA Cup Lost to Inverness Cal., 2nd
  rnd rep., 0-3
Skol Cup Lost to E. Stirling, 1st rnd, 1-1 (pens.)

Historical Highlights
League Best position — 12th in Div 1, 1980. Div
  1, 1980-1; Div 2, 1956-79, 1982-
Scottish Cup Quarter-final 1980
Top Scorer Ken Bowron: 38 (1963-4, 1968-9)

Eric Tait, Player/Manager of Berwick Rangers, has been with the club since 1970. By the end of 1983/4 he had played over 470 games for the Borderers, scoring 101 goals.

BRECHIN CITY

Chairman David Will
Team Manager Iain Fleming
Asst Manager John Richie
Captain John May
Year formed 1906
Ground address Glebe Park,
  Brechin, Tayside DD9 6BJ
Telephone 035 62 2856
Present ground capacity 7,500
Record crowd 8,123 v. Aberdeen, Scottish
  Cup, 3rd round, 3 February 1973

1984/5 Record
League 9th, Div 1
Scottish FA Cup Lost to Hearts, 4th rnd, 0-1
Skol Cup Lost to St Johnstone, 3rd rnd, 2-4

Historical Highlights
League Div 2 champions 1983. Div 1, 1983-;
  Div 2, 1930-9, 1955-83
Scottish Cup 6th rnd 1956
Top Scorer Willie McIntosh: 26 (1959-60)

CELTIC

Chairman Desmond White
Team Manager David Hay
Asst Manager/1st team coach
  1983/4 Frank Connor
Captain Danny McGrain
Year formed 1888
Ground address Celtic Park,
  Parkhead, Glasgow G40 3RE
Telephone 041 554 2710
Present ground capacity 67,500
Record crowd 92,000 v. Rangers, Division 1,
  1 January 1938
Nickname 'The Bhoys'
Sponsor C. R. Smith

1984/5 Record
League 2nd, Premier Division
Scottish FA Cup Winners
Skol Cup Lost to Dundee Utd, Qtr-finals, 1-2
European Cup-Winners' Cup Lost to Rapid
  Vienna, 2nd rnd, 1-4 on agg.

Historical Highlights
League Premier Div champions 1977, 1979;
  1981, 1982; runners-up 1976, 1980, 1984; Div 1
Champions 1893, 1894, 1896, 1898, 1898, 1905,
1906, 1907, 1908, 1909, 1910, 1914, 1915, 1916,
1917, 1919, 1922, 1926, 1936, 1938, 1954, 1966,
1967, 1968, 1969, 1970, 1971, 1972, 1973, 1974;
runners-up 1892, 1895, 1900, 1901, 1902, 1912,
1913, 1918, 1920, 1921, 1928, 1929, 1931, 1935,
1939, 1955. Premier Div, 1976-; Div 1,
1891-1975
Scottish Cup Winners 1892, 1899, 1900, 1904,
1907, 1908, 1911, 1912, 1914, 1923, 1925, 1927,
1931, 1933, 1937, 1951, 1954, 1965, 1967, 1969,

1971, 1972, 1974, 1975, 1977, 1980; runners-up
1889, 1893, 1894, 1901, 1902, 1909, 1926, 1928,
1955, 1956, 1961, 1963, 1966, 1970, 1984
League Cup Winners 1957, 1958, 1966, 1967,
1968, 1969, 1970, 1975, 1983; runners-up 1965,
1971, 1972, 1973, 1974, 1976, 1977, 1978, 1984
Europe European Cup 1967 (winners), 1968,
1969, 1970 (runners-up), 1971, 1972, 1973,
1974, 1975, 1978, 1980, 1982, 1983; European
Cup-Winners' Cup 1964, 1966, 1976, 1981;
Fairs Cup 1963, 1965; UEFA Cup 1977
Top Scorer Jimmy McGrory: 50 (1935-6)

CLYDE

Chairman Ian Patterson
Team Manager Craig Brown,
BA, DPE
Asst Manager/1st team coach
Robert Thorburn
Captain John McVeigh
Year formed 1878
Ground address Shawfield
Stadium, Shawfield Park,
Glasgow C5 0AN
Telephone 041 647 6329
Present ground capacity 25,000
Record crowd 52,000 v. Rangers, Division 1,
21 November 1908
Nickname 'The Bully Wee'
Sponsor Solrite

1984/5 Record
League 8th, Div 1
Scottish FA Cup Lost to Raith, 3rd rnd rep., 1-2
Skol Cup Lost to St Mirren, 2nd rnd, 0-1

Historical Highlights
League Best position – 3rd in Div 1, 1909, 1912,
1967. Div 1, 1892-3, 1895-1900, 1907-1924,
1927-51, 1953-6, 1958-61, 1963, 1965-72,
1974-6, 1979-80, 1983-; Div 2, 1894, 1901-6,
1925-6, 1952, 1957, 1962, 1964, 1973, 1977-8,
1981-2
Scottish Cup Winners 1939, 1955, 1958;
runners-up 1910, 1912, 1949
Top Scorer Bill Boyd: 32 (1932-3)

CLYDEBANK

Chairman Charles Steadman
Team Manager/Coach Sam
Henderson
Captain Jim Fallon
Year formed 1965
Ground address Kilbowie
Park, Clydebank, Strathclyde
Telephone 041 952 2887
Present ground capacity 9,950
Record crowd 14,900 v. Hibs,
Scottish Cup, 1st rnd, 10 Feb. 1965
Nickname 'The Bankies'

1984/5 Record
League 2nd, Div 1: promoted
Scottish FA Cup Lost to Forfar Athletic,
3rd rnd, 0-1
Skol Cup Lost to Raith R., 2nd rnd, 0-2

Historical Highlights
League Best position – 10th in Premier Div,
1978. Premier Div, 1978; Div 1, 1977, 1979-;
Div 2, 1965-76
Scottish Cup Quarter-final 1981
Top Scorer Blair Miller: 28 (1978-9)

*Jock Stein, the most
successful manager in
British football since the
war, led Celtic to nine
consecutive Scottish
League titles in 1965-74 and
in 1966/7 the club won
every competition they
entered – the League, the
Scottish Cup, the Scottish
League Cup, and the
European Cup.*

COWDENBEATH

Chairman Eric Mitchell
Asst Manager/1st team coach
John Clark
Captain Ronnie Scott
Year formed 1881
Ground address Central Park,
Cowdenbeath, Fife KY4 9NP
Telephone 0383 511205
Present ground capacity 10,000
Record crowd 25,596 v. Rangers, League Cup,
qtr final, 21 September 1949
Nickname 'Cowden'
Sponsor TC Oil Tools

1984/5 Record
League 4th, Div 2
Scottish FA Cup Lost to Motherwell, 3rd rnd,
0-4
Skol Cup Lost to Rangers, Qtr-finals, 1-3

Historical Highlights
League Best position – 5th in Div 1, 1925. Div 1,
1925-34, 1971; Div 2, 1906-24, 1935- 70, 1972-
Scottish Cup Quarter-final 1931
Top Scorer Willie Devlin: 40 (1925-6)

DUMBARTON

Chairman R. Robertson
Team Manager Davie Wilson
from March 1984
Asst Manager/1st team coach
Derek Whiteford
Captain Tommy Coyle
Year formed 1872 as Dumbarton
Athletic
Ground address Boghead Park,
Dumbarton, Strathclyde
G82 2JA
Telephone 0389 62569
Present ground capacity 18,000
Record crowd 18,000 v. Raith Rovers, Scottish
Cup, qtr final, 2 March 1957
Nickname 'The Sons'
Sponsor Spallsports

1984/5 Record
League 9th, Premier Division: relegated
Scottish FA Cup Lost to Motherwell, 3rd rnd,
0-4
Skol Cup Lost to Dundee Utd, 3rd rnd, 0-4

Historical Highlights
League Div 1 joint champions (with Rangers)
1891; Div 1 champions 1892. Div 1, 1891-6,
1914-22, 1973-; Div 2, 1897, 1907-13, 1923-54,
1956-72
Scottish Cup Winners 1883; runners-up 1881,
1882, 1887, 1891, 1897
Top Scorer Kenny Wilson: 38 (1971-2)

John Duncan joined Dundee in 1966 and had become one of the most stylish strikers in Scotland when he was lured South to join Tottenham Hotspur in 1974. He never settled there, often being asked to play out of position, and his career went into a steady decline. A paltry, single cap – for the Scottish League against the Football League in 1973, when he scored both goals in a 2-2 draw – did scant justice to his talent. Now he manages Chesterfield.

DUNDEE

Chairman Ian Gellatly
Team Manager Archie Knox
Asst Manager/1st team coach
John Scott
Captain John McCormack
Year formed 1893
Ground address Dens Park,
Dundee, Tayside DD1 1RQ
Telephone 0382 826104
Present ground capacity 22,381
Record crowd 43,024 v. Rangers, Scottish Cup,
2nd round, 7 February 1953
Nickname 'The Dark Blues of the Dee'

1984/5 Record
League 6th, Premier Division
Scottish FA Cup Lost to Celtic, 5th round replay,
1-2
Skol Cup Lost to Heart of Midlothian,
Qtr-finals, 0-1

Historical Highlights
League Div 1 champions 1962; runners-up
1903, 1907, 1909, 1949. Premier Div 1976,
1980, 1982-; Div 1, 1894-1917, 1920-38,
1948-75, 1977-9, 1981; Div 2, 1939, 1947
Scottish Cup Winners 1910; runners-up 1925,
1952, 1964
League Cup Winners 1952, 1953, 1974;
runners-up 1968, 1981
Europe UEFA Cup 1974
Top Scorer Dave Halliday: 38 (1923-4)

DUNDEE UNITED

Chairman J. Johnstone-Grant
Team Manager Jim McLean
Asst Manager/1st team coach
Walter Smith & Gordon
Wallace
Captain Paul Hegerty
Year formed 1909 as Dundee
Hibernians, until 1923
Ground address Tannadice
Park, Dundee, Tayside DD3 7JW
Telephone 0382 826289
Present ground capacity 22,250
Record crowd 28,000 v. Barcelona, Fairs Cup,
2nd round, 16 November 1966
Nickname 'The Terrors'

1984/5 Record
League 3rd, Premier Division
Scottish FA Cup Finalists: lost to Celtic, 1-2
Skol Cup Finalists: lost to Rangers, 0-1

Historical Highlights
League Premier Div champions 1983. Premier
Div, 1976-; Div 1, 1926-7, 1930, 1932,
1962-75; Div 2, 1911-22, 1924-5, 1928-9, 1931,
1933-60

Scottish FA Cup Runners-up 1974, 1981
League Cup Winners 1980, 1981; runners-up 1982, 1984
Europe European Cup 1984 (semi-final); UEFA Cup 1980, 1981

DUNFERMLINE ATHLETIC

Chairman J. Watters
Team Manager Jim Leishman
Captain Bobby Robertson
Year formed 1885
Ground address East End Park, Dunfermline, Fife
Telephone 0383 724295
Present ground capacity 27,500
Record crowd 27,816 v. Celtic, Division 1, 30 April 1968
Nickname 'The Pars'

1984/5 Record
League 3rd, Div 2
Scottish FA Cup Lost to East Stirling, 1st rnd, 1-3
Skol Cup Lost to Celtic, 2nd rnd, 2-3

Historical Highlights
League Best position – 3rd in Div 1, 1965, 1969. Div 1, 1927-8, 1935-7, 1956-7, 1959-72, 1974-6, 1980-3; Div 2, 1922-6, 1929-34, 1938-55, 1958, 1973, 1977-9, 1983-
Scottish Cup Winners 1961, 1968; runners-up 1965
League Cup Runners-up 1950
Top Scorer Bobby Skinner: 53 (1925-6)

EAST FIFE

Paul Sturrock, a key figure in Dundee United's successful campaigns of the 1980s, has yet to achieve a regular place in Scotland's presently unsettled national side.

Chairman James Baxter
Team Manager David Clarke
Asst Manager/1st team coach Michael Marshall
Captain Graham Hutt
Year formed 1903
Ground address Bayview Park, Methil, Fife KY8 3AG
Telephone 0333 26323
Present ground capacity 15,000
Record crowd 22,515 v. Raith Rovers, Division 1, 2 January 1950
Nickname 'The Fifers'
Sponsor Lander Alarms

1984/5 Record
League 10th, Div 1
Scottish FA Cup Lost to Brechin City, 3rd round replay, 0-4
Skol Cup Lost to Hibernian, 2nd round, 0-1

Historical Highlights
League Best position – 3rd in Div 1, 1952, 1953. Div 1, 1931, 1949-58, 1972-4, 1976-8; Div 2, 1922-30, 1932-48, 1959-71, 1975, 1979-
Scottish Cup Winners 1938, runners-up 1927, 1950
League Cup Winners 1948, 1950, 1954
Top Scorer Henry Morris: 41 (1947-8)

EAST STIRLING

Chairman John Turnbull
Team Manager/1st team coach Davie Whiteford
Captain Jim Meakin
Year formed 1881
Ground address Firs Park, Falkirk, Central FK2 7AY
Telephone 0324 23583
Ground capacity 12,000
Record crowd 11,500 v. Hibernian, Scottish Cup, 10 February 1969
Nickname 'The Shire'
Sponsor Sun Life of Canada

1984/5 Record
League 12th, Div 2
Scottish FA Cup Lost to Alloa Ath., 2nd rnd, 1-2
Skol Cup Lost to Heart of Midlothian, 2nd rnd, 0-4

Historical Highlights
League Best position – 11th in Div 1, 1981. Div 1, 1933, 1964, 1981-2; Div 2, 1902-15, 1922-3, 1925-32, 1934-9, 1956-63, 1965-80, 1983-
Scottish Cup Quarter-final 1981
Top Scorer Malcolm Morrison: 36 (1938-9)

John Brown, of Hamilton Academical, on 2 August 1980 became the only full-back in British football to score a hat-trick in which none of the goals was a penalty. The occasion was a Division 1 match against Berwick Rangers, the Accies winning 9-1 at Douglas Park; the result equalled the Borderers' biggest-ever defeat.

FALKIRK

Chairman Edward Moffat
Team Manager Billy Lamont
  from March 1984
Asst Manager/1st team coach
  Billy Simpson
Year formed 1876
Ground address Brockville Park,
  Falkirk Central
Telephone 0324 24121
Present ground capacity 22,550
Record crowd 23,100 v. Celtic, Scottish Cup,
  3rd round, 21 February 1953
Nickname 'The Bairns'
Sponsor Coasters Arena

1984/5 Record
League 3rd, Div 1
Scottish FA Cup Lost to Forfar Ath., 4th rnd,
  1-2
Skol Cup Lost to Rangers, 2nd rnd, 0-1

Historical Highlights
League Best position – runners-up in Div 1,
  1908, 1910. Div 1, 1906-35, 1937-51, 1953-9,
  1962-9, 1971-4, 1976-7, 1981-; Div 2, 1903-5,
  1936, 1952, 1960-1, 1970, 1975, 1978-80
Scottish Cup Winners 1913, 1957
League Cup Runners-up 1948
Top Scorer Evelyn Morrison: 43 (1928-9)

FORFAR ATHLETIC

Chairman Sam Smith
Team Manager Doug Houston
Asst Manager/1st team coach
  Henry Hall
Captain Ian McPhee
Year formed 1884
Ground address Station Park,
  Forfar, Tayside DD8 1DA
Telephone 0307 63576/62817
Present ground capacity 9,300
Record crowd 10,780 v Rangers, Scottish Cup
  2nd round, 2 February 1970
Nickname 'The Sky Blues'
Sponsor Ramsey Ladders

1984/5 Record
League 6th, Div 1
Scottish FA Cup Lost to Motherwell, Qtr-finals,
  1-4
Skol Cup Lost to Dundee United., 2nd round,
  0-5

Historical Highlights
League Best position – 6th in Div 1, 1985. Div 2,
  1922-5, 1927-39, 1950-84
Scottish Cup Semi-final 1982
League Cup Semi-final 1978
Top Scorer David Kilgour: 45 (1929-30)

HAMILTON ACADEMICAL

Chairman Jan Stepek
Team Manager John Lambie
Asst Manager/1st team coach
  Jim Dempsey
Captain Alex Hamill
Year formed 1875
Ground address Douglas Park,
  Hamilton, Strathclyde
  ML3 0DF
Telephone Hamilton (0698) 286103
Present ground capacity 14,065
Record crowd 28,690 v Hearts, Scottish Cup
  3rd round, 3 March 1937
Nickname 'The Accies'
Sponsor Trust Motors

1984/5 Record
League 4th, Div 1
Scottish FA Cup Lost to Celtic, 3rd rnd, 1-2
Skol Cup Lost to Dundee, 2nd rnd, 0-3

Historical Highlights
League Best position – 4th in Div 1, 1935. Div 1,
  1907-47, 1954, 1966, 1976-; Div 2, 1899-1906,
  1948-53, 1955-65, 1967-75
Scottish Cup Runners-up 1911, 1935
Top Scorer David Wilson: 34 (1936-7)

HEART OF MIDLOTHIAN

Chairman A. W. Mercer
Team Manager Alex
  MacDonald
Asst Manager/1st team coach
  Walter Borthwick
Captain Walter Kidd
Year formed 1874
Ground address Tynecastle
  Park, Gorgie Road,
  Edinburgh EH1 2NL
Telephone 031 337 6132
Present ground capacity 27,900
Record crowd 53,496 v Rangers, Scottish Cup
  3rd round, 13 February 1932
Nickname 'Jam Tarts'
Sponsor Renault

1984/5 Record
League 7th, Premier Division
Scottish FA Cup Lost to Aberdeen, 5th rnd
  rep., 0-1
Skol Cup Lost to Dundee Utd., Semi-finals, 1-2

Historical Highlights
League Div 1 champions 1895, 1897, 1958,
  1960; runners-up 1894, 1899, 1904, 1906,
  1915, 1938, 1954, 1957, 1959, 1965. Premier
  Div 1976-7, 1979, 1981, 1983-; Div 1, 1891-

1975, 1978, 1980, 1982
Scottish Cup Winners 1891, 1896, 1901, 1906, 1956; runners-up 1903, 1907, 1968, 1976
League Cup Winners 1955, 1959, 1960, 1963; runners-up 1962
Top Scorer Barney Battles: 44 (1930-1)

HIBERNIAN

Chairman Kenneth Waugh
Team Manager John Blackley
Asst Manager/1st team coach Tommy Craig
Captain Gordon Rae
Year formed 1875
Ground address Easter Road Stadium, Edinburgh EH7 5QG
Telephone 031 661 2159
Present ground capacity 29,464
Record crowd 66,840 v Hearts, Division 1, 2 January 1950
Nickname 'Hi-Bees' or 'Hibs'

1984/5 Record
League 8th, Premier Division
Scottish FA Cup Lost to Dundee Utd, 3rd rnd, 0-3
Skol Cup Lost to Meadowbank Th., 3rd rnd, 1-2 (aet)

Historical Highlights
League Div 1 champions 1903, 1948, 1951, 1952; runners-up 1897, 1947, 1950, 1953, 1974. Premier Div, 1976-80, 1982-; Div 1, 1896-1931, 1934-75, 1981; Div 2, 1894-5, 1932-3
Scottish Cup Winners 1887, 1902; runners-up 1896, 1914, 1923, 1924, 1947, 1958, 1972, 1979
League Cup Winners 1973; runners-up 1951, 1969, 1975
Europe UEFA Cup 1973
Top Scorer Joe Baker: 42 (1959-60)

KILMARNOCK

Chairman T. M. Laughlan, OBE
Team Manager Eddie Morrison
Asst Manager/1st team coach Bill Munro
Captain Alan Robertson
Year formed 1869
Ground address Rugby Park, Kilmarnock, Strathclyde KA1 2DP
Telephone 0563 25184
Present ground capacity 18,500
Record crowd 34,246 v Rangers, League Cup Section Match, 17 August 1963
Nickname 'Killie'
Sponsor A. T. Mays Travel

1984/5 Record
League 12th, Div 1
Scottish FA Cup Lost to Inverness Th., 3rd rnd, 0-3
Skol Cup Lost to Dundee, 3rd rnd, 2-3 (pens.)

Historical Highlights
League Div 1 champions 1965; runners-up 1960, 1961, 1963, 1964, 1976, 1979, 1982. Premier Div 1977, 1980-1; Div 1, 1900-47, 1955-73, 1976, 1978-9, 1982-; Div 2, 1948-54, 1974-5
Scottish Cup Winners 1920, 1929; runners-up 1898, 1932, 1938, 1957, 1960
League Cup Runners-up 1953, 1961, 1963
Top Scorer Peerie Cunningham: 35 (1927-8)

MEADOWBANK THISTLE

Chairman J. P. Blacklaw
Team Manager Terry Christie
Asst Managers Lawrie Glasson & Tom McLaren
Captain Jim Stewart
Year formed 1943 as Ferranti Thistle, until 1974
Ground address Meadowbank Stadium, Edinburgh EH7 6AE
Telephone 031 337 2442 (extn 3666)
Present ground capacity 16,000
Record crowd 4,000 v Albion Rovers, Scottish Cup, 9 August 1974
Nickname 'Thistle'
Sponsor Ferranti

1984/5 Record
League 13th, Div 1
Scottish FA Cup Lost to Mo'well, 4th rnd, 0-2
Skol Cup Lost to Rangers, Semi-final, 1-5

Historical Highlights
League Best position – in Div 1, 1984. Div 1, 1983-; Div 2, 1975-83
Scottish Cup 4th round 1978, 1979, 1982
Top Scorer John Jobson: 17 (1979-80)

Above Jimmy Wardhaugh is Hearts' record scorer with 206 goals in 1946-59, and he topped Division 1 in 1955/6 (28 goals) and 1957/8 (28).

Below Joe Baker, of Hibernian, was top League scorer in 1959/60 with 42 goals. An English international, he later enjoyed a successful spell with Arsenal.

MONTROSE

Chairman William Johnstone
Team Manager Ian Stewart
 from January 1984
Captain Raymond Charles
Year formed 1879
Ground address Links Park,
 Montrose, Tayside
 DD10 8QD
Telephone 0674 73200
Present ground capacity 9,000
Record crowd 8,983 v. Dundee, Scottish Cup,
 3rd round 17 March 1973
Nickname 'The Gable Endies'

1984/5 Record

League Champions, Div 2: promoted
Scottish FA Cup Lost to Queen of the South,
 2nd rnd, 1-3
Skol Cup Lost to Albion Rovers, 1st round,
 0-2

Historical Highlights

League Best position – 3rd in Div 1, 1976. Div 1,
 1976-9; Div 2, 1930-9, 1956-75, 1980-5
Scottish Cup Quarter-final 1948, 1973, 1976

MORTON

Chairman H. M. Currie
Team Manager Willy McLean
 until May 1985
Asst Manager/1st team coach
 Jim Fleeting until May 1985
Captain Alec McAneskie
Year formed 1874
Ground address Capielow
 Park, Greenock, Strathclyde
 PA15 2TY
Telephone 0475 25594
Present ground capacity 16,400
Record crowd 23,500 v. Celtic, Division 1, 1922
Nickname 'The Ton'

1984/5 Record
League 10th, Premier Division: relegated
Scottish FA Cup Lost to Rangers, 3rd rnd rep.,
 1-3
Skol Cup Lost to Meadowbank Th., 2nd rnd,
 1-2

Historical Highlights
League Best position – 6th in Premier Div 1980.
 Premier Div, 1979-83; Div 1, 1901-27, 1930-3,
 1938, 1947-9, 1951-2, 1965-6, 1968-78,
 1983-4; Div 2, 1894-1900, 1928-9, 1934-7,
 1939, 1950, 1953-64, 1967
Scottish FA Cup Winners 1922; runners-up
 1948
League Cup Runners-up 1964
Europe Fairs Cup 1969
Top Scorer Allan McGraw: 41 (1963-4)

MOTHERWELL

Chairman W. Dickie
Team Manager Tommy
 McLean
Asst Manager/1st team coach
 Tom Forsyth
Captain Alistair Mauchlen
Year formed 1885 as Wee Alpha,
 until 1886
Ground address Fir Park,
 Motherwell, Strathclyde ML1 2QN
Telephone 0698 61437
Present ground capacity 22,600
Record Crowd 35, 632 v. Rangers, Scottish
 Cup, 4th round replay, 12 March 1952
Nickname 'The Well'
Sponsor The Ian Skelly Centre

1984/5 Record

League Champions, Div 1: promoted
Scottish FA Cup Lost to Celtic, Semi-final rep.,
 0-3
Skol Cup Lost to Ayr United, 2nd round,
 0-1

Historical Highlights

League Div 1 champions 1932; runners-up
 1927, 1930, 1933, 1934, Premier Div 1976-9,
 1983; Div 1, 1904-53, 1955-68, 1970-5, 1980-
 2, 1984-5; Div 2, 1954, 1969
Scottish Cup Winners 1952; runners-up 1931,
 1933, 1939, 1951
League Cup Winners 1951: runners-up 1955
Top Scorer Willie McFadyen: 52 (1931-2)

PARTICK THISTLE

Chairman P. Shand
Team Manager Benny Rooney
Asst Manager/1st team coach
 Donald McKinnon
Captain Joe Carson
Year formed 1876
Ground address Firhill Park,
 Glasgow, G20 5AL
Telephone 041 946 2673
Present ground capacity 21,500
Record Crowd 49,838 v. Rangers, Division 1,
 18 Febuary 1922
Nickname 'The Jags'
Sponsor Morton's Rolls

1984/5 Record
League 11th, Div 1
Scottish FA Cup Lost to Meadowbank Th., 3rd
 rnd, 2-4
Skol Cup Lost to Cowdenbeath, 2nd rnd, 0-3

Historical Highlights
League Best position – 5th in Premier Div,
 1977. Premier Div, 1977-83; Div 1, 1898-9,
 1901, 1903-70, 1972-6, 1983-; Div 2, 1894-7,
 1900, 1971

Joe Harper began his career at Capielow Park, but found his greatest fame when Morton sold him to Aberdeen, for whom he scored in their Scottish Cup Final victory over Celtic in 1970. He topped the League chart in 1971/2 with 33 goals. He spent a brief, unsatisfactory spell with Everton in the 1970s before returning to Aberdeen.

Scottish Cup Winners 1921; runners-up 1930
League Cup Winners 1972; runners-up 1954, 1957, 1959
Europe Fairs Cup 1964; UEFA Cup 1974
Top Scorer Alec Hair: 41 (1926-7)

QUEEN OF THE SOUTH

Chairman William Harkness CBE
Team Manager/1st team coach Robert Clark
Captain Graeme Robertson
Year formed 1919
Ground address Palmerston Park, Terregles St, Dumfries, Dumfries & Galloway DG2 9BA
Telephone 0387 54853
Present ground capacity 20,000
Record crowd 24,250 v. Hearts, Scottish Cup 3rd round, 23 February 1952
Nickname 'The Queens'
Sponsor Elopark

1984/5 Record
League 11th, Div 2
Scottish FA Cup Lost to Dundee Utd, 4th rnd, 0-3
Skol Cup Lost to Dumbarton, 2nd rnd, 1-2

Historical Highlights
League Best position – 4th in Div 1, 1934. Div 1, 1934-50, 1952-9, 1963-4, 1976-9, 1982-3; Div 2, 1926-33, 1951, 1960-2, 1965-75, 1980-1, 1983-
Scottish Cup Semi-final 1950
Top Scorer Jimmy Gray: 33 (1927-8)

QUEEN'S PARK

President Thomas Barr
Team Manager/coach 1983/4 Edward Hunter
Captain James Nicholson
Year formed 1867 (oldest club in Scottish League)
Ground address Hampden Park, Glasgow G42 2BA
Telephone 041 632 1275
Present ground capacity 78,800 by end of 1983/4 season
Record crowd 97,000 v. Rangers, Scottish Cup, 2nd round, 18 February 1933; ground record, 149,547, Scotland v. England, 17 April 1937 (record British gate)
Nickname 'The Spiders'

1984/5 Record
League 9th, Div 2
Scottish FA Cup Lost to Raith R., 2nd rnd rep., 0-1
Skol Cup Lost to Queen of South, 1st rnd, 1-2

Historical Highlights
League Best position – 5th in Div 1, 1929. Div 1, 1901-22, 1924-48, 1957-8, 1982-3; Div 2, 1923, 1949-56, 1959-81, 1983-
Scottish Cup Winners 1874, 1875, 1876, 1880, 1881, 1882, 1884, 1886, 1889, 1893; runners-up 1892, 1900
FA Cup Runners-up 1884, 1885
Top Scorer Peter Buchan: 32 (1962-3)

RAITH ROVERS

Chairman J. Urquhart
Team Manager Robert Wilson
1st team coach Dick Campbell
Captain Donald Urquhart
Year formed 1883
Ground address Starks Park, Pratt St, Kirkcaldy, Fife KY1 1SA
Telephone 0592 263514
Present ground capacity 22,000
Record crowd 31,306 v. Hearts, Scottish Cup, 2nd round, 7 February 1953
Nickname None
Sponsor Bukta Sports

1984/5 Record
League 7th, Div 2
Scottish FA Cup Lost to Aberdeen, 4th rnd, 1-2
Skol Cup Lost to Rangers, 3rd rnd, 0-4

Historical Highlights
League Best position – 3rd in Div 1, 1922, Div 1, 1911-17, 1920-26, 1928-9, 1939, 1950-63, 1968-70, 1977, 1979-84; Div 2, 1903-10, 1927, 1930-8, 1947-9, 1964-7, 1971-6, 1978
Scottish Cup Runners-up 1913
League Cup Runners-up 1949
Top Scorer Norman Haywood: 39 (1937-8)

Above *Alex Forsyth (left) was bought by Partick Thistle from Arsenal as a junior in 1968 and made his name (and international reputation) with them before moving to Manchester United in 1973.*

Below *Raith Rovers have been one of the great nurseries of Scottish football talent, starting with the immortal Alex James in the 1920s. Post-war, their greatest discovery was the wayward genius Jim Baxter (seen here) whose all-too-brief career peaked brilliantly after he joined Rangers in 1961.*

RANGERS

Chairman John Paton
Team Manager Jock Wallace
Asst Manager/1st team coach
  Alex Totten
Captain Campbell Fraser
Year formed 1873
Ground address Ibrox Stadium,
  Glasgow
Telephone 041 427 0159
Present ground capacity 44,000
Record crowd 118,567 v. Celtic, Division 1,
  2 January 1939
Nickname 'Gers' or 'The Blues'

1984/5 Record
League 4th, Premier Division
Scottish FA Cup Lost to Dundee, 4th round,
  0-1
Skol Cup Winners: beat Dundee United,
  2-1
UEFA Cup Lost to Inter Milan, 2nd rnd, 3-4

Historical Highlights
League Premier Div Champions 1976, 1978;
  runners-up 1977, 1979; Div 1 joint champions
  1891; Div 1 champions 1899, 1900, 1901,
  1902, 1911, 1912, 1913, 1918, 1920, 1921,
  1923, 1924, 1925, 1927, 1928, 1929, 1930,
  1931, 1933, 1934, 1935, 1937, 1939, 1947,
  1949, 1950, 1953, 1956, 1957, 1959, 1961,
  1963, 1964, 1975; runners-up 1893, 1896,
  1898, 1905, 1914, 1916, 1919, 1922, 1932,
  1936, 1948, 1951, 1952, 1958, 1962, 1966,
  1967, 1968, 1969, 1970, 1973
Scottish Cup Winners 1894, 1897, 1898, 1903,
  1928, 1930, 1932, 1934, 1935, 1936, 1948,
  1949, 1950, 1953, 1960, 1962, 1963, 1964,
  1966, 1973, 1976, 1978, 1979, 1981;
  runners-up 1877, 1879, 1899, 1904, 1905,
  1909, 1921, 1922, 1929, 1969, 1971, 1977,
  1980, 1982
League Cup Winners 1947, 1949, 1961, 1962,
1964, 1965, 1971, 1976, 1978, 1979, 1982, 1984;
  runners-up 1952, 1958, 1966, 1967, 1983
Europe European Cup 1957, 1958, 1960, 1962,
  1964, 1965, 1976, 1977, 1979; European
  Cup-Winners' Cup 1961 (runners-up), 1963,
  1967 (runners-up), 1970, 1972 (winners),
  1974, 1978, 1980, 1982; Fairs Cup 1968, 1969,
  1971; UEFA Cup 1983
Top Scorer Sam English: 44 (1931-2)

Davie Cooper, one of the best of Rangers' current crop of stars, is in the great Scottish tradition of goal-scoring wingers who beat defenders as much by guile as by speed.

ST JOHNSTONE

Chairman Alec Lamond
Team Manager Alec Rennie
Asst Manager/1st team coach
  Dennis Lawson
Captain Drew Rutherford
Year formed 1884
Ground address Muirton Park,
  Perth, Tayside PH1 5AP
Telephone 0738 26961
Present ground capacity 24,950
Record crowd 29,972 v. Dundee, Scottish Cup,
  2nd round, 10 February 1952
Nickname 'The Saints'

1984/5 Record
League 14th, Div 1: relegated
Scottish FA Cup Lost to Dundee, 3rd rnd rep.,
  1-2
Skol Cup Lost to Meadowbank Th., Qtr-finals,
  1-2

Historical Highlights
League Best position – 10th in Premier Div,
  1976. Premier Div, 1976, 1983-4; Div 1,
  1925-30, 1933-9, 1961-2, 1964-75, 1977-82,
  1984-5; Div 2, 1912-5, 1922-4, 1931-2, 1947-
  60, 1963
Scottish Cup Semi-final 1934, 1968
League Cup Runners-up 1970
Top Scorer Jimmy Benson: 36 (1931-2)

ST MIRREN

Chairman J. W. Craig
Team Manager Alex Miller
Asst Manager/1st team coach
  Martin Ferguson & Drew
  Jarvey
Captain Tony Fitzpatrick
Year formed 1876
Ground address St Mirren Park,
  Love Street, Paisley, Strathclyde
  PA3 2EJ
Telephone 041 889 2558/
  840 1337
Present ground capacity 25,800
Record crowd 47,428 v. Celtic, Scottish Cup,
  4th round, 7 March 1925
Nickname 'The Buddies'
Sponsor Graham's Buses

1984/5 Record
League 5th, Premier Division
Scottish FA Cup Lost to Dundee Utd., Qtr-
finals, 1-4
Skol Cup Lost to Cowdenbeath, 3rd rnd, 0-2

Historical Highlights
League Best position — 3rd in Premier Div 1980.
Premier Div, 1978-; Div 1, 1891-1935,
1937-67, 1969-71, 1976-77; Div 2, 1936, 1968,
1972-5
Scottish Cup Winners 1926, 1959; runners-up
1908, 1934, 1962
League Cup Runners-up 1956
Top Scorer 'Dunky' Walker: 45 (1921-2)

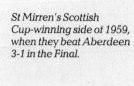

St Mirren's Scottish Cup-winning side of 1959, when they beat Aberdeen 3-1 in the Final.

STENHOUSEMUIR

Chairman J. Cook
Team Manager Jim Black
Asst Manager/1st team coach
Tommy Murray
Captain Harry Erwin
Year formed 1884
Ground address Ochilview
Park, Lambert,
Stenhousemuir, Central
FK5 4QL
Telephone 0324 562992
Present ground capacity 10,450
Record crowd 12,500 v. East Fife, Scottish Cup,
4th round, 11 March 1950
Nickname 'The Warriors'
Sponsor Hogan Sports

1984/5 Record
League 6th, Div 2
Scottish FA Cup Lost to Stanraer, 2nd rnd, 0-2
Skol Cup Lost to Stirling Alb., 1st rnd, 0-2

Historical Highlights
League Best position — 3rd in Div 2, 1959, 1961,
Div 2, 1922-
Scottish Cup Quarter-final 1933, 1949, 1950,
1956
Top Scorers 31: Evelyn Morrison (1927-8),
Robert Murray (1936-7)

STIRLING ALBION

Chairman Peter Gardiner
Team Manager Alex Smith
Asst Manager/1st team coach
George Peebles
Captain James Shirra
Year formed 1945
Ground address Annfield
Park, Stirling, Central
S7K 83D
Telephone 0786 3584
Present ground capacity 20,000
Record crowd 26,400 v. Celtic, Scottish Cup,

4th round, 14 March 1959
Nickname 'The Albion'

1984/5 Record
League 5th, Div 2
Scottish FA Cup Lost to Cowdenbeath, 2nd
rnd, 1-2
Skol Cup Lost to Brechin C., 2nd rnd, 1-4

Historical Highlights
League Best position — 5th in Div 1, 1978. Div 1,
1950, 1952, 1954-6, 1959-60, 1962, 1966-8,
1978-81; Div 2, 1948-9, 1951, 1953, 1957-8,
1961, 1963-5, 1969-77, 1982-
Scottish Cup Qtr-final 1950, 1959, 1962, 1965
Top Scorer Joe Hughes: 29 (1969-70)

STRANRAER

Chairman William Fullerton
Team Manager Dave Sneddon
Asst Manager/1st team coach
John Taylor
Captain Danny MacDonald
Year formed 1870
Ground address Stair Park,
London Rd, Stranraer,
Dumfries & Galloway
Telephone 0776 3271
Present ground capacity 5,500
Record crowd 6,500 v. Rangers, Scottish Cup,
1st round, 24 January 1948
Nickname 'The Blues'

1984/5 Record
League 10th, Div 2
Scottish FA Cup Lost to Queen of the South,
3rd rnd, 4-6
Skol Cup Lost to Cowdenbeath, 1st rnd, 0-3

Historical Highlights
League Best position — 4th in Div 2, 1961, 1977.
Div 2, 1956-
Scottish Cup 5th rnd 1957
Top Scorer Derek Frye: 27 (1977-8)

PAST & PRESENT

FOOTBALL LEAGUE
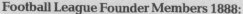

Alf Common, who in February 1905 featured in the first £1,000 transfer fee when he joined Middlesbrough from Sunderland. Three years before he had been the subject of the first £500 fee when Sunderland signed him from Sheffield United.

Preceding two pages:
Blackburn Rovers FA Cup-winning side 1884.

Below *Preston North End's team of 1888/9, which won the Cup and League double and went the entire season without losing a game.*

The formation of the Football League in 1888 was a direct result of the legalisation of professionalism in 1885. The guiding light behind the setting-up of the League was a Scot, William McGregor. He realised that the wages of professionals could be met only if the clubs had a regular income, and that the best way to raise such income was not from the County Cup competitions, challenge matches, and friendlies that had hitherto provided the football fare, but from a league competition, spread over several months, that would sustain the interest of spectators and so guarantee the all-important regular income.

Twelve clubs agreed to join the Football League, all of them from the English north and midlands (the south was still very much in the hold of the amateur sides which had dominated the early days of the FA Cup competition). The first League Championship in 1888/9 was won by Preston North End, who were undefeated that season, with Aston Villa runners-up. In 1890 Stoke, who had finished bottom of the League in both previous seasons, dropped out; they were replaced by Sunderland, who won the Championship in the following season, when the League was expanded to 14 clubs with the return of Stoke and the election of Darwen (who finished bottom in their first year).

Such was the success and popularity of the League that in 1892 it was expanded to 16 clubs by the election of The Wednesday and Newton Heath, while a second division of 12 clubs was formed. At the end of the 1892/3 season a series of 'Test Matches' was played between the three bottom sides in Division 1 and the three top sides of Division 2 to determine promotion and relegation. This system remained in force until the beginning of the 1898/9 season, when automatic promotion and relegation with 'two up, two

down' was adopted. In that season, each division was expanded to 18 clubs.

Of the 36 clubs now engaged in regular League competition, only Woolwich Arsenal were from the south. They were the first southern side to embrace professionalism and had been admitted to Division 2 in 1893. With a change of location from south-east London to the north of the capital, and the dropping of 'Woolwich' from their name, the side was destined to become the first outside the north-midlands axis to win the Division 1 title. (That success was still many years in the future, however, for the early years were not kind to the south, despite a steady increase in the number of London clubs entering the League.)

In the first eight years of Division 1 Aston Villa won the championship five times, before first The Wednesday and later Newcastle rose to brief prominence. In 1905 history was made by the first £1,000 transfer, which took Alf Common from Sunderland to Middlesbrough – proof, if such were needed, that the game was now becoming as much a business as a sport.

By the time competition was suspended for the duration of World War I, each of the two divisions comprised 20 clubs, of which just five – Arsenal, Chelsea, Clapton Orient, Fulham, and Tottenham – were from London; only one other, Bristol City, was outside the north or midlands. The position was to change dramatically, however, when competition resumed with the 1919/20 season.

Reorganisation proceeded at a great pace after the war. When competition re-started there were 22 clubs in each division. For the following season a third division of a further 22 clubs came into being, while by the start of the 1921/2 season, the reorganisation had been completed: there were now 22 clubs each in Divisions 1 and 2; 20 in a new Division 3 (North);

and 22 in a new Division 3 (South). This structure was to endure for more than 30 years.

The last piece of fine tuning to the game concerned a change to the offside law made at the start of the 1925/6 season. Previously, the law had stated that a player was offside if, when he received the ball, there were three opponents or less between himself and the goal-line. This in turn had led to the perfecting of an offside 'trap' by a Newcastle defender called Bill McCracken, which involved him and his fellow-defenders moving swiftly upfield at opportune moments and so placing attackers in an offside position. As a result, goals became scarce. Now, the changed law required that only two men or less had to be between an attacker and the goal-line. The result: more goals, particularly in the 1927/8 season, when Everton's 'Dixie' Dean scored 60 times in League games – a record that still stands and is now unlikely ever to be broken.

Despite the major expansion of the League and the offside law change, the Division 1 title continued to elude southern clubs, although Tottenham Hotspur became the first London side to win a divisional title when they amassed a then-record 70 points to win the Division 2 championship in 1919/20.

Huddersfield Town underlined the north's superiority with a hat-trick of Division 1 championship wins between 1924 and 1926 – the first ever recorded. Huddersfield's manager at that time was Herbert Chapman, who was then lured south to take over at Arsenal, where he developed the tactical 'WM Formation', a sort of '3-4-3' based on a 'stopper' (purely defensive) centre-half called Herbie Roberts, around whom a team of quite remarkable talents evolved. In 1928, Chapman paid the first £10,000 transfer fee to bring David Jack from Bolton. Jack was one of seven England internationals in the Arsenal side, which also included Welsh international Bob John and the incomparable Scot Alex James, a member of the 'Wee Blue Devils' side which had annihilated England 5-1 at Wembley in 1928.

With such a side, Arsenal won the Division 1 championship four times in five years, including a hat-trick between 1933 and 1935, and were runners-up in the year Everton managed to break their monopoly. They also achieved one other (largely unremarked) feat: their champ-

ionship win in 1931 was the first by a southern side – a long overdue success.

Following Arsenal's domination of the Thirties, the late Forties (1948/9, 1949/50) belonged briefly to Portsmouth, before the emergence of two outstanding sides in the Fifties – Stan Cullis's Wolverhampton Wanderers and Manchester United's 'Busby Babes'. United, managed by Matt Busby, won the Division 1 title in 1956 and

William 'Dixie' Dean, England centre-forward, scored 60 goals in League games for Everton in 1927/8. His record – which still stands in the English League – beat by one George Camsell's tally for Middlesbrough in Division 2 in 1926/7, but it was eclipsed by Jimmy Smith's 66 for Ayr United in Scotland's Division 2 in 1927/8.

Right *Duncan Edwards (Manchester United) a few months before his death in February 1958. England's youngest-ever international, he played left-half against Scotland in April 1955 when he was exactly 18½ years old. His loss to both club and country was incalculable.*

Below *The ability of Leeds United, the top English side of the late 1960s, to steamroller their opponents belied the individual flair of many of their players. Here, in a 1969 league match, white-shirted Hunter (at right), Giles and Reaney try to close down Manchester United's Best (then the greatest tormentor of defences in Europe), supported by right-winger Morgan.*

1957 and seemed poised to become every bit as dominant a force as Arsenal had been 20-odd years before. Then, while returning from a European Cup game in Yugoslavia in February 1958, their plane crashed on take-off at Munich airport and eight players died. Although it's invidious to select individuals from that distinguished casualty list, the name of Duncan Edwards cannot be ignored. Although only 21 when he died, Edwards was by then an established England international with 18 caps. He had made his debut for United when 16; a year later he was in the England Under-23 side; and at the age of 18½ he became the youngest player to appear for the full England side. A wing-half of strength and skill, he seemed certain to become one of the game's all-time 'greats'.

Wolves followed in the path of that young

Liverpool's Terry McDermott, Ray Kennedy, Tommy Smith and (behind him) Phil Neal celebrate winning the 1976/7 League title. In the nine seasons from 1975/6 the Merseysiders' monopoly of the League has been broken only by Nottingham Forest (1977/8) and Aston Villa (1980/1).

Goals: Teams

The highest number of goals scored in a League season is 134 in 46 games by Peterborough United (including 52 by striker Terry Bly) in winning the Division 4 championship in 1960/1. The highest number of goals scored over 42 games is 128, shared by Bradford City in winning the Division 3 (North) championship in 1928/9, and Aston Villa in finishing Division 1 runners-up in 1930/1. The Division 1 champions in 1930/1 were Arsenal, who scored 127 goals – the highest total by Division 1 winners.

United side, a team of power and purpose but without the poise or creative spark of United. Though they dominated the domestic game in the late Fifties, their ventures into Europe exposed their shortcomings. It was left to the Tottenham Hospur side of the early Sixties to become the first club this century to win the League and Cup 'double' in 1960/1, before going on in the following season to become the first British side to win a major European trophy.

After Tottenham's League win, followed by unlikely success for unfashionable (and newly promoted) Ipswich, the Sixties pendulum once again swung north, with two championships for a rebuilt Manchester United, one for their great rivals, City, and two wins apiece for Liverpool and Everton.

The 'nearly' side, however, was Leeds, a side fashioned by Don Revie, which lost only two games in winning the 1968/9 championship. In the late Sixties and early Seventies they were the dominant force in English football and yet had precious little in the way of trophies to show

for their efforts. Almost always the League's bridesmaids – they were runners-up five times from 1964/5 to 1971/2 – Leeds collected their second title in 1973/4; but by then, another star had risen on the other side of the Pennines.

The Seventies had opened with little hint of what was to come. Arsenal emulated their neighbours Spurs with the century's second League and Cup double, before the abrasive but inspirational Brian Clough notched up his first success with Derby County in 1971/2. Then Liverpool won the title, then Leeds, then Derby again, before Liverpool began to exercise the kind of stranglehold on the Division 1 championship not seen before or since. Up to the end of the 1983/4 season, they had won the title seven times in nine years, a record of phenomenal consistency achieved first under the late Bill Shankly and latterly under Bob Paisley and Joe Fagan. Players have come and gone, but the

Points

Before the introduction of three points for a win (instead of two) from the start of the 1980/1 season, the highest number of points scored in a 42-game season was 72 by Doncaster Rovers in winning the Division 3 (North) championship in 1946/7. Had the current scoring system been in operation then, their record of 33 wins and 6 draws would have given them 105 points. Under the new system, the highest number of points scored is 98 in 46 games by Wimbledon in winning the Division 4 championship in 1982/3. The highest number of points scored over 42 games is 88 by Luton Town in winning the Division 2 championship in 1981/2.

Right *Soberly dressed club chairman Elton John with Watford's squad at the start of the 1983/4 season. In four seasons from 1978 the club climbed from Division 4 to Division 1. Watford's pool of gifted home-grown youngsters and experienced older players has been greatly strengthened by manager Graham Taylor's astute excursions into the transfer market.*

FOOTBALL LEAGUE CHAMPIONS

	Division 1	Division 2	Division 3 (N)	Division 3 (S)
1888/9	Preston North End			
1889/90	Preston North End			
1890/1	Everton			
1891/2	Sunderland			
1892/3	Sunderland	Small Heath		
1893/4	Aston Villa	Liverpool		
1894/5	Sunderland	Bury		
1895/6	Aston Villa	Liverpool		
1896/7	Aston Villa	Notts County		
1897/8	Sheffield Utd	Burnley		
1898/9	Aston Villa	Manchester City		
1899/1900	Aston Villa	The Wednesday		
1900/1	Liverpool	Grimsby Town		
1901/2	Sunderland	West Bromwich Alb.		
1902/3	The Wednesday	Manchester City		
1903/4	The Wednesday	Preston North End		
1904/5	Newcastle Utd	Liverpool		
1905/6	Liverpool	Bristol City		
1906/7	Newcastle Utd	Nottingham Forest		
1907/8	Manchester Utd	Bradford City		
1908/9	Newcastle Utd	Bolton Wanderers		
1909/10	Aston Villa	Manchester City		
1910/1	Manchester Utd	West Bromwich Alb.		
1911/2	Blackburn Rovers	Derby County		
1912/3	Sunderland	Preston North End		
1913/4	Blackburn Rovers	Notts County		
1914/5	Everton	Derby County		
1915-1919	*No competition*			
1919/20	West Bromwich Alb.	Tottenham Hotspur		
1920/1	Burnley	Birmingham City		
1921/2	Liverpool	Nottingham Forest	Stockport County	Crystal Palace
1922/3	Liverpool	Notts County	Nelson	Southampton
1923/4	Huddersfield Town	Leeds Utd	Wolverhampton Wndrs	Bristol City
1924/5	Huddersfield Town	Leicester City	Darlington	Portsmouth
1925/6	Huddersfield Town	Sheffield Weds.	Grimsby Town	Swansea Town
1926/7	Newcastle Utd	Middlesbrough	Stoke City	Reading
1927/8	Everton	Manchester City	Bradford Park Avenue	Bristol City
1928/9	Sheffield Weds.	Middlesbrough	Bradford City	Millwall
1929/30	Sheffield Weds.	Blackpool	Port Vale	Charlton Athletic
1930/1	Arsenal	Everton	Chesterfield	Plymouth Argyle
1931/2	Everton	Wolverhampton Wndrs	Lincoln City	Notts County
1932/3	Arsenal	Stoke City	Hull City	Fulham
1933/4	Arsenal	Grimsby Town	Barnsley	Brentford
				Norwich City

style remains the same – that of a football juggernaut, endlessly adaptable, with the character that separates a truly great team from a merely good one. With their system of bringing players carefully into first team football now so finely honed, there seems no reason why Liverpool cannot continue in their present vein for years – a daunting prospect for the other 21 sides in Division 1.

Despite the temptation to end a review, however brief, of the League's history with one of its most outstanding sides, two notable present-day achievements cannot go unnoticed. In 1977/8 Watford won the Division 4 championship, while Swansea City, who came third, also gained promotion. The following season Watford and Swansea finished second and third respectively in Division 3 and again won promotion. In 1979/80 Swansea were 12th in Division 2, while Watford finished 18th. In 1980/1 Swansea won promotion to the top flight, and in 1981/2 Watford followed suit to complete a remarkable run of success by those two clubs. For Swansea, however, there was a sad end to the story, for they were back in Division 2 after just two seasons. But Watford caught Division 1 by surprise, being runners-up to Liverpool in 1982/3. There can be few people in England, whether soccer followers or not, who are unaware that pop star Elton John is Watford's chairman. It's pleasing to reflect that, even in the modern game, beset as it is with all manner of problems both on and off the field, the most unlikely dream – like that of a pop singer leading his boyhood favourites from obscurity to glory – can still come true.

	Division 1	Division 2	Division 3 (N)	Division 3 (S)
1934/5	Arsenal	Brentford	Doncaster Rovers	Charlton Athletic
1935/6	Sunderland	Manchester Utd	Chesterfield	Coventry City
1936/7	Manchester City	Leicester City	Stockport County	Luton Town
1937/8	Arsenal	Aston Villa	Tranmere Rovers	Millwall
1938/9	Everton	Blackburn Rovers	Barnsley	Newport County
1939-1946	*No competition*			
1946/7	Liverpool	Manchester City	Doncaster Rovers	Cardiff City
1947/8	Arsenal	Birmingham City	Lincoln City	Queen's Park Rangers
1948/9	Portsmouth	Fulham	Hull City	Swansea Town
1949/50	Portsmouth	Tottenham Hotspur	Doncaster Rovers	Notts County
1950/1	Tottenham Hotspur	Preston North LEnd	Rotherham Utd	Nottingham Forest
1951/2	Manchester Utd	Sheffield Weds.	Lincoln City	Plymouth Argyle
1952/3	Arsenal	Sheffield Utd	Oldham Athletic	Bristol Rovers
1953/4	Wolverhampton Wndrs	Leicester City	Port Vale	Ipswich Town
1954/5	Chelsea	Birmingham City	Barnsley	Bristol City
1955/6	Manchester Utd	Sheffield Weds.	Grimsby Town	Leyton Orient
1956/7	Manchester Utd	Leicester City	Derby County	Ipswich Town
1957/8	Wolverhampton Wndrs	West Ham Utd	Scunthorpe Utd	Brighton & Hove Albion
	Division 1	**Division 2**	**Division 3**	**Division 4**
1958/9	Wolverhampton Wndrs.	Sheffield Weds.	Plymouth Argyle	Port Vale
1959/60	Burnley	Aston Villa	Southampton	Walsall
1960/1	Tottenham Hotspur	Ipswich Town	Bury	Peterborough Utd
1961/2	Ipswich Town	Liverpool	Portsmouth	Millwall
1962/3	Everton	Stoke City	Northampton Town	Brentford
1963/4	Liverpool	Leeds Utd	Coventry City	Gillingham
1964/5	Manchester Utd	Newcastle Utd	Carlisle Utd	Brighton & Hove Albion
1965/6	Liverpool	Manchester City	Hull City	Doncaster Rovers
1966/7	Manchester Utd	Coventry City	Queen's Park Rangers	Stockport County
1967/8	Manchester City	Ipswich Town	Oxford Utd	Luton Town
1968/9	Leeds Utd	Derby County	Watford	Doncaster Rovers
1969/70	Everton	Huddersfield Town	Orient	Chesterfield
1970/1	Arsenal	Leicester City	Preston North End	Notts County
1971/2	Derby County	Norwich City	Aston Villa	Grimsby Town
1972/3	Liverpool	Burnley	Bolton Wanderers	Southport
1973/4	Leeds Utd	Middlesbrough	Oldham Athletic	Peterborough Utd
1974/5	Derby County	Manchester United	Blackburn Rovers	Mansfield Town
1975/6	Liverpool	Sunderland	Hereford Utd	Lincoln City
1976/7	Liverpool	Wolverhampton Wndrs	Mansfield Town	Cambridge Utd
1977/8	Nottingham Forest	Bolton Wanderers	Wrexham	Watford
1978/9	Liverpool	Crystal Palace	Shrewsbury Town	Reading
1979/80	Liverpool	Leicester City	Grimsby Town	Huddersfield Town
1980/1	Aston Villa	West Ham Utd	Rotherham Utd	Southend Utd
1981/2	Liverpool	Luton Town	Burnley	Sheffield Utd
1982/3	Liverpool	Queen's Park Rangers	Portsmouth	Wimbledon
1983/4	Liverpool	Chelsea	Oxford Utd	York City

FA CUP

The birth of the FA Challenge Cup, the oldest knockout football tournament in the world, can be traced back to 20 July 1871, eight years after the formation of the Football Association itself. On that day, at an FA meeting held at the offices of *The Sportsman* in London, the FA Secretary Charles Alcock first mooted the idea of a challenge cup competition open to all FA members. Alcock's idea was well received, and on 16 October of that year the plan to stage a Cup competition was formally adopted.

Only 15 teams entered the first competition in 1872, and all but two of them were from the London area. The first Final, played at the Kennington Oval cricket ground, saw Wanderers beat the Royal Engineers 1-0 in front of a mere 2,000 spectators. To Matthew Betts of Wanderers went the distinction of scoring the first-ever Cup Final goal. Wanderers won the tournament again in 1873. As holders they were exempt from competing until the Final, when they beat Oxford University. The following season, with the exemption rule scrapped, they lost to Oxford in an early round; the University went on to win the Cup.

Southern amateur sides were to dominate the early years of Cup competition and it was not until 1882 that a northern side – Blackburn Rovers – reached the Final. They lost 1-0 to Old Etonians, who were the last amateur side ever to win the Cup. Henceforward, until the end of the century, the Cup was to become a monopoly of the professionals from the north.

In 1883 Old Etonians reached the Final again, but lost to the first northern winners, Blackburn Olympic. Blackburn Rovers (no relation) then won the Cup three years running, in their first two Finals beating the amateur Glasgow side Queen's Park before winning the first all-professional Final, against West Bromwich Albion, in 1886. Three years later, the Cup went to Preston North End, who in the same season also won the inaugural Football League Championship. That 'double', the first of only four ever achieved, was the more remarkable in the fact that Preston went through their entire League and Cup campaign without losing a game – a feat without parallel.

It was not until 1901 that the Cup came south once more, when it was won by Tottenham Hotspur, then of the Southern League. The trophy, however, was not the original FA Cup. That had been stolen – as the posters of the time proclaimed – 'between the hours of 9.30 pm on Wednesday, the 11th of September and 7.30 am on Thursday 12th 1895 from the shop window of W. Shillcock, Football Outfitter, Newtown Row, Birmingham'. A £10 reward for the Cup's return was offered, but the trophy was never recovered; so a replica was made, and this was the Cup won by Spurs after a drawn game with Sheffield United at Crystal Palace, watched by over 110,000 spectators – at that time by far the greatest number of people ever to have watched a match. After they had won their replay at Bolton, Spurs created another little piece of football history: they tied ribbons of their white and navy-blue club colours to the Cup's handles

Tottenham Hotspur's FA Cup-winning side of 1901 – the only non-League club to do so. They have won the Cup six times since then, and have never been losing finalists.

Remarkable Cup Runs
Only two teams — Wanderers and Blackburn Rovers — have won the Cup three years running. After Wanderers' third victory in 1878 they were awarded the Cup outright — but returned it to the Football Association. Blackburn were not awarded outright possession of the Cup in 1886, but were given a special trophy to mark their achievement. In modern times, only Arsenal have reached three successive Finals (1978-80), losing two and winning one.

horse Billie in getting the game played. The Wembley authorities had calculated the ground could hold 127,000 spectators. In the event 126,047 passed through the turnstiles — while an estimated 100,000 more made their way into the stadium by less orthodox routes. Not surprisingly, the crowd spilled over onto the pitch in such numbers that it looked for a time as if the game would not be able to take place at all. At that point, enter PC Scorey and Billie, who gently eased the crowds back off the pitch and over the touchlines, enabling the game to get under way at last, only half an hour late. The result, almost an afterthought in view of the preceding drama, was that Bolton won 2-0, with the great David Jack scoring Wembley's first-ever goal.

Four years later, in 1927, the Cup left England for the first and only time in its history, when Cardiff beat Arsenal 1-0. The goal that settled the game was a strange one. A shot from the Cardiff centre-forward Ferguson seemed to have been safely gathered by Arsenal's Welsh international goalkeeper Dan Lewis, but the ball somehow squirmed out of his grasp and trickled into the net. Lewis later blamed the disaster on his shiny new jersey — a bizarre scapegoat for a Cup Final defeat.

The 1938 Final was to provide a moment every bit as dramatic in its own way. Preston and

Left The 1923 Cup Final, the first to be held at Wembley Stadium. PC Scorey on his white horse persuades part of the huge crowd to move back from the goal-line.

Below Ted Drake, Arsenal's centre-forward, in a goalmouth incident in the 1936 Final when he scored the only goal of the game against Sheffield United, then in Division 2. Arsenal had also won the Cup in 1930 and were losing finalists in 1932.

— a tradition that has continued down to this day.

The Cup won by Spurs was destined to have as short a working life as its predecessor, for in 1910 it was awarded to Lord Kinnaird to mark his 21st anniversary as President of the Football Association. The new — and present — FA Cup was made by the Bradford firm of Fattorini and Sons for presentation to the 1911 Cup winners, who, in one of those footballing ironies that run through the game at every level, were Bradford City — the only time they have ever won the Cup.

Until World War I the competition continued to provide an unbroken string of winners from the north and midlands. Only Southampton, then in the Southern League, threatened that dominance — in 1900, when they reached the Final only to lose to Bury, and in 1902, when they lost to Sheffield United. It was not until 1921 that the Cup came south once more — again to Tottenham. That game was one of three interwar Finals played at Stamford Bridge, before the showpiece of the English soccer season was moved to the newly built Wembley Stadium in 1923.

The first Wembley Final, between Bolton Wanderers and West Ham United, passed into soccer folklore as the 'White Horse Final', in recognition of the part played by a mounted policeman, Constable George Scorey, and his

Huddersfield had played out a dour, goal-less 90 minutes and the game had gone into extra time. With just a few moments remaining and a replay the likeliest outcome, Preston's George Mutch was tripped inside the area and a penalty was awarded. Mutch himself took the kick and scored, the ball ricocheting down from the underside of the bar. Ironically, Preston were to lose to a late penalty in the 1954 Final, scored by West Bromwich's Ronnie Allen. But that game, and most other Finals since, pale almost to insignificance when compared with the legendary 1953 Cup Final, arguably the greatest of all.

The man on whom that game centred was Blackpool's (and England's) great winger, Stanley Matthews. Twice before he had played in Finals, and twice he had finished a loser. Now, approaching his 40th birthday, he knew this game against Bolton would almost certainly be his last chance of a winner's medal. That hope seemed a forlorn one, however, when Bolton led 3-1 with only 20 minutes of the match left. At that point, however, Matthews became inspired. His wing play tore the Bolton defence to shreds, and from one of his crosses Blackpool scored their second goal. Time still seemed to be on Bolton's side, but, with just three minutes remaining, Blackpool equalised, England striker Stan Mortensen scoring directly from a free-kick for

Giant Killers

Only eight clubs outside Division 1 have won the Cup since the Football League was founded in 1888: Notts County (1894), Wolves (1908), Barnsley (1912), West Bromwich Albion (1931), Sunderland (1973), Southampton (1976), and West Ham United (1980) were all in Division 2; Tottenham (1901) were in the Southern League at the time – the only non-League club ever to win the Cup.

There have been some remarkable Cup runs by Division 3 sides, though none has yet reached a Final. In 1937 Millwall – then in Division 3 (South) – became the first side from that Division to reach the semi-final, where they lost 2-1 to the eventual winners, Sunderland. Since World War II the following Division 3 sides have reached the semi-finals: Port Vale (1954), York City (1955), Norwich City (1959), Watford (1970), and Crystal Palace (1976). No Division 4 side has reached the semi-finals.

There are many instances in the Cup's history of non-League sides beating League opposition and of teams from the lower Divisions knocking out top Division 1 sides. Perhaps the most famous FA Cup result of all was Walsall 2 Arsenal 0 in the 3rd round on 14 January 1933. Arsenal were at that time the best team in the country and en route to the first of three successive Division 1 championships; Walsall were in Division 3 (North). Since the War, four non-League clubs have reached the Cup's 5th round by defeating League opposition. They are: Colchester United (1948), Yeovil Town (1949), Blyth Spartans (1978), and Telford United (1985).

Above *Stanley Matthews (right) and his captain Harry Johnston are chaired by team-mates after Blackpool had beaten Bolton Wanderers 4-3 in the breathtaking 1953 Final.*

Right *Stan Mortensen (darker shirt) turns away after his team-mate Bill Perry has slotted in the final goal from yet another pinpoint Matthews pass. Mortensen, a formidable England striker, scored Blackpool's other three goals.*

Record Appearances in Final

Newcastle United and Arsenal had, at the start of the 1983/4 season, each appeared in 11 Finals, of which Newcastle had won 6 and Arsenal 5.

Most Wins

Tottenham Hotspur and Aston Villa have each won the Cup 7 times. However, Spurs have never lost a Final, while Villa have finished runner-up on two occasions.

his and his side's third goal. Then, with full-time just seconds away, another magical Matthews surge down the right wing culminated in another pinpoint centre for Perry to slide the ball in and so settle this most emotionally charged of Finals. Even Bolton and their supporters found it hard to begrudge Matthews his moment.

In 1961, exactly 40 years after their last Cup win, Tottenham returned to the Final. This time more than the Cup itself was at stake. As League champions, they were bidding to become the first side since Aston Villa in 1897 to complete the elusive 'double' – a feat they duly achieved by beating Leicester in a drab game before returning to retain the Cup against Burnley the following season. Ten years after Tottenham's 'double' it was the turn of their greatest rivals, Arsenal, who came to Wembley as League champions and won the Cup against Liverpool in extra-time.

Two years later Sunderland, from Division 2, provided the greatest Final upset since World War I by beating mighty Leeds 1-0. That day belonged to their goalkeeper Jim Montgomery and their manager, Bob Stokoe, whose charge across the pitch at the final whistle to embrace his 'keeper remains one of Wembley's abiding memories. In 1976, Southampton further underlined the fact that the Cup is not always a Division 1 prerogative with an equally surprising, though not half as dramatic, victory over Manchester United.

Three years on United returned to face Arsenal. With 85 minutes of the match gone, United were seemingly dead and buried at 2-0 down. Those last five minutes, however, are now a part

Above *1961 Final: Bobby Smith (Tottenham Hotspur, hand on ground), scores the first goal against Leicester. Spurs won 2-0 to complete the Cup and League double.*

Below *1973 Final: Ian Porterfield (Sunderland), in striped shirt second from right, scores the goal that beat hot favourites Leeds United.*

Right *1981 Final: Ricky Villa's virtuoso solo goal for Spurs: he ghosts past Mackenzie, sends Caton the wrong way, and slips the ball under Corrigan.*

Goal-Scoring Records

The individual scoring record in an FA Cup-tie is the nine goals scored by Ted Mac-Dougall for Bournemouth in their 11-0 defeat of Margate on 20 November 1971. The team scoring record is held by Preston North End, who beat Hyde United 26-0 in a 1st-round match in 1887.

Below *1979 Final: Alan Sunderland (Arsenal, nearer yellow shirt) turns after scoring the winning third goal. Beaten goalkeeper Gary Bailey (Manchester United) contemplates the infinite.*

Bottom *1983 Final: Arnold Muhren (Manchester United, 8) scores the penalty in the replay against Brighton.*

of the Cup legend. United scored twice inside a minute to equalise, only to have the game snatched from them by a last-gasp Arsenal winner.

The last three Finals have also had their moments – particularly so in 1981 in the 100th Final, when Tommy Hutchison of Manchester City scored first against Tottenham and then put through his own net to send the game to a replay. The score was 2-2 when Tottenham's Argentinian international Ricardo Villa scored perhaps the best solo goal ever seen in a Wem-bley Final, weaving past three men to slip the ball under the goalkeeper. In 1982 Tottenham equalled Aston Villa's record of seven Cup wins by beating Queen's Park Rangers in another replayed Final – the third such all-London affair since 1967 (before which there hadn't been any at all!). The replay was settled by a penalty, the first single-goal Final to be so decided since George Mutch's spot-kick won the Cup for Preston in 1938.

And so to 1983, with Brighton, about to be relegated to Division 2, beating Liverpool at Anfield on their way to Wembley, where they so nearly won the Cup. With mere seconds remaining, Brighton's Michael Robinson laid the ball invitingly into the path of Gordon Smith, some eight yards from goal with not a defender near him and only the goalkeeper to beat. Smith controlled the ball, steadied himself and shot – only for Manchester United's 'keeper Gary Bailey to scramble the ball away. That lost chance cost Brighton the Cup, for they were beaten 4-0 in the replay. But, with the curious habit the competition seems to have of giving beaten sides a second chance, they may be back at Wembley before too long. A last thought: Liverpool have not won the Cup for a decade.

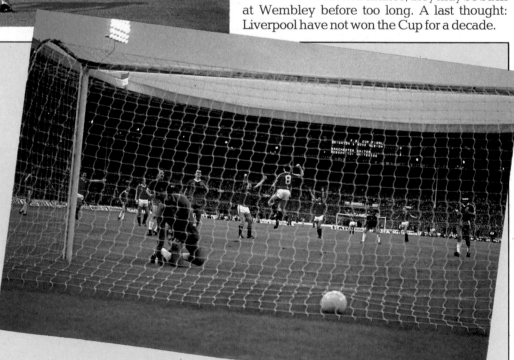

Cup Final Venues
1872 Kennington Oval
1873 Lillie Bridge, London
1874-92 Kennington Oval
1893 Fallowfield, Manchester
1894 Goodison Pk, Liverpool
1895-1914 Crystal Palace
1915 Old Trafford, Manchester
1920-2 Stamford Bridge
1923 onwards Wembley Stadium

Replay Venues
1875 Kennington Oval
1876 Kennington Oval
1886 Derby Co
1901 Burnden Pk, Bolton
1902 Crystal Palace
1910 Goodison Pk, Liverpool
1911 Old Trafford, Manchester
1912 Bramall Lane, Sheffield
1970 Old Trafford, Manchester
1981 onwards Wembley Stadium

FA Cup Finals 1872-1983
(aet = after extra time)

1872 Wanderers 1 Royal Engineers 0
1873 Wanderers 2 Oxford University 0
1874 Oxford University 2 Royal Engineers 0
1875 Royal Engineers 2 Old Etonians 0 (after 1-1 draw)
1876 Wanderers 3 Old Etonians 0 (after 1-1 draw)
1877 Wanderers 2 Oxford University 1 (aet)
1878 Wanderers 3 Royal Engineers 1
1879 Old Etonians 1 Clapham Rovers 0
1880 Clapham Rovers 1 Oxford University 0
1881 Old Carthusians 3 Old Etonians 0
1882 Old Etonians 1 Blackburn Rovers 0
1883 Blackburn Olympic 2 Old Etonians 1 (aet)
1884 Blackburn Rovers 2 Queens Park 1
1885 Blackburn Rovers 2 Queens Park 0
1886 Blackburn Rovers 2 West Bromwich Albion 0
   (after 0-0 draw)
1887 Aston Villa 2 West Bromwich Albion 0
1888 West Bromwich Albion 2 Preston North End 1
1889 Preston North End 3 Wolverhampton Wanderers 0
1890 Blackburn Rovers 6 The Wednesday 1
1891 Blackburn Rovers 3 Notts Co 1
1892 West Bromwich Albion 3 Aston Villa 0
1893 Wolverhampton Wanderers 1 Everton 0
1894 Notts Co 4 Bolton Wanderers 1
1895 Aston Villa 1 West Bromwich Albion 0
1896 The Wednesday 2 Wolverhampton Wanderers 1
1897 Aston Villa 3 Everton 2
1898 Nottingham Forest 3 Derby Co 1
1899 Sheffield Utd 4 Derby Co 1
1900 Bury 4 Southampton 0
1901 Tottenham Hotspur 3 Sheffield Utd 1 (after 2-2 draw)
1902 Sheffield Utd 2 Southampton 1 (after 1-1 draw)
1903 Bury 6 Derby Co 0
1904 Manchester City 1 Bolton Wanderers 0
1905 Aston Villa 2 Newcastle Utd 0
1906 Everton 1 Newcastle Utd 0
1907 The Wednesday 2 Everton 1
1908 Wolverhampton Wanderers 3 Newcastle Utd 1
1909 Manchester Utd 1 Bristol City 0
1910 Newcastle Utd 2 Barnsley 0 (after 1-1 draw)
1911 Bradford City 1 Newcastle Utd 0 (after 0-0 draw)
1912 Barnsley 1 West Bromwich Albion 0 (aet, after 0-0 draw)
1913 Aston Villa 1 Sunderland 0
1914 Burnley 1 Liverpool 0
1915 Sheffield Utd 3 Chelsea 0
1916-19 *No competition*
1920 Aston Villa 1 Huddersfield Town 0 (aet)
1921 Tottenham Hotspur 1 Wolverhampton Wanderers 0
1922 Huddersfield Town 1 Preston North End 0
1923 Bolton Wanderers 2 West Ham Utd 0
1924 Newcastle Utd 2 Aston Villa 0
1925 Sheffield Utd 1 Cardiff City 0
1926 Bolton Wanderers 1 Manchester City 0

1927 Cardiff City 1 Arsenal 0
1928 Blackburn Rovers 3 Huddersfield Town 1
1929 Bolton Wanderers 2 Portsmouth 0
1930 Arsenal 2 Huddersfield Town 0
1931 West Bromwich Albion 2 Birmingham City 1
1932 Newcastle Utd 2 Arsenal 1
1933 Everton 3 Manchester City 0
1934 Manchester City 2 Portsmouth 1
1935 Sheffield Wednesday 4 West Bromwich Albion 2
1936 Arsenal 1 Sheffield Utd 0
1937 Sunderland 3 Preston North End 1
1938 Preston North End 1 Huddersfield Town 0 (aet)
1939 Portsmouth 4 Wolverhampton Wanderers 1
1940-45 *No competition*
1946 Derby Co 4 Charlton Athletic 1 (aet)
1947 Charlton Athletic 1 Burnley 0 (aet)
1948 Manchester Utd 4 Blackpool 2
1949 Wolverhampton Wanderers 3 Leicester City 1
1950 Arsenal 2 Liverpool 0
1951 Newcastle Utd 2 Blackpool 0
1952 Newcastle Utd 1 Arsenal 0
1953 Blackpool 4 Bolton Wanderers 3
1954 West Bromwich Albion 3 Preston North End 2
1955 Newcastle Utd 3 Manchester City 1
1956 Manchester City 3 Birmingham City 1
1957 Aston Villa 2 Manchester Utd 1
1958 Bolton Wanderers 2 Manchester Utd 0
1959 Nottingham Forest 2 Luton Town 1
1960 Wolverhampton Wanderers 3 Blackburn Rovers 0
1961 Tottenham Hotspur 2 Leicester City 0
1962 Tottenham Hotspur 3 Burnley 1
1963 Manchester Utd 3 Leicester City 1
1964 West Ham Utd 3 Preston North End 2
1965 Liverpool 2 Leeds Utd 1 (aet)
1966 Everton 3 Sheffield Wednesday 2
1967 Tottenham Hotspur 2 Chelsea 1
1968 West Bromwich Albion 1 Everton 0
1969 Manchester City 1 Leicester City 0
1970 Chelsea 2 Leeds Utd 1 (aet, after 2-2 draw)
1971 Arsenal 2 Liverpool 1 (aet)
1972 Leeds Utd 1 Arsenal 0
1973 Sunderland 1 Leeds Utd 0
1974 Liverpool 3 Newcastle Utd 0
1975 West Ham Utd 2 Fulham 0
1976 Southampton 1 Manchester Utd 0
1977 Manchester Utd 2 Liverpool 1
1978 Ipswich Town 1 Arsenal 0
1979 Arsenal 3 Manchester Utd 2
1980 West Ham Utd 1 Arsenal 0
1981 Tottenham Hotspur 3 Manchester City 2 (after 1-1 draw)
1982 Tottenham Hotspur 1 Queen's Park Rangers 0 (after 1-1 draw)
1983 Manchester United 4 Brighton & Hove Albion 0 (after 2-2 draw)
1984 Everton 2 Watford 0

LEAGUE/MILK CUP

Although the Milk Cup — as the Football League Cup competition has been known since shortly before the 1982 Final — is now an accepted and integral part of the English football season, in its early days it ran the risk of becoming the biggest white elephant our domestic game has known. Leading Division 1 sides at first refused to enter the competition, and the fact that the first Final was between Division 2 and Division 4 teams seemed to bear out the widely held view that this was very much a second-rate competition for second-rate teams. Even the League Cup winners did not rate their successes very highly. Chelsea, having beaten Leicester City in the 1965 Final, did not even bother to defend the trophy the following season; they argued that, as they had qualified for the Inter-City Fairs Cup by virtue of their League placing, they would be quite busy enough without taking part in another cup competititon.

All that was to change in 1967. League secretary Alan Hardaker, who had been the prime mover behind this new competition, decided to scrap the cumbersome two-leg Final in favour of a single showpiece game at Wembley. More importantly, he persuaded the European Football Union to allow League Cup Winners direct entry into the following season's Inter-City Fairs Cup, provided those winners came from Division 1.

The lure of Wembley and Europe proved sufficiently attractive for 90 out of the 92 League clubs to enter the 1967 tournament, only Liverpool (League champions) and Everton (FA Cup-holders) declining to take part. West Bromwich Albion, Cup-winners in 1966, made it through to Wembley for what must have seemed a formality against Queen's Park Rangers, the first Division 3 side ever to play at Wembley. Rangers, however, were no ordinary Division 3 side; they were just beginning a run that would take them into Division 1 in two seasons. Now they proved good enough to give Albion a two goal start before coming back to snatch an improbable 3-2 win. But although the Cup was theirs, they were denied a place in Europe by the 'Division 1-only' rule.

Two years later, another Division 3 side, Swindon Town, reached Wembley to face Arsenal on a pitch ruined by the ill-advised staging of a show-jumping event shortly before. Swindon scored first, Arsenal equalised and the game went into extra-time, during which Swindon scored twice to win the Cup and leave their lofty opponents humiliated – most notably by the performance of Swindon's winger Don Rogers.

Such Division 3 exploits have never been repeated, although, as in the FA Cup, there have been some remarkable giant-killing feats. From the 1972 competition onwards entry to the League Cup became compulsory, bringing in the big guns who had previously stayed out because of their European commitments. As it turned out, the 1972 Final was hardly the stuff of glamour, but it had its own touch of romance, with ageing ex-England midfielder George Eastham coaxing Stoke City to the only Cup they have ever won – and scoring the winner himself.

As with so many FA Cup Finals, however, League Cup Finals have in the main been unexciting affairs. Historians will note that in 1973 Tottenham's Ralph Coates became the first substitute to score the winner in a Wembley Final; while the twice-replayed affair between Aston Villa and Everton in 1977 set records for longevity and – in the first two games – tedium.

The 1978 Final was a different matter entirely – Nottingham Forest, fielding an untested teenage reserve goalkeeper, Chris Woods, held Liverpool to a goal-less draw before winning the replay with a hotly-contested penalty. Forest won the following season too, becoming the first side to retain the trophy, and then equalled Arsenal's FA Cup performance by reaching Wembley for the third year running – only to lose to unfancied Wolverhampton Wanderers.

There was an air of inevitability about Liverpool's League Cup win in 1981. This was the only domestic trophy they had never won and,

1967 Final: the first single-leg engagement at Wembley.

Below *Queen's Park Rangers' goalkeeper Peter Springett is beaten by West Bromwich winger Colin Clark (left) for the opening goal.*

Bottom *Mark Lazarus (7) turns in triumph after scoring QPR's winning third goal.*

although West Ham fought bravely and took them to a replay, there never seemed much doubt as to the eventual outcome. Liverpool's hold on the trophy, however, looked distinctly shaky the following year. The 1982 Final (re-christened the Milk Cup Final as the result of sponsorship from the Milk Marketing Board) saw Tottenham leading, thanks to a Steve Archibald goal, with just three minutes to play. Then Liverpool equalised, before ploughing Tottenham into the ground during extra-time. Much the same happened in the 1983 final. Norman Whiteside scored first for Manchester United, and Liverpool equalised through Alan Kennedy; the game went to extra-time, where Ronnie Whelan, who had scored twice at Wembley in 1982, again provided the winner.

So the Cup again went to Merseyside – and provided Liverpool with yet another record – the only English team this century to win three successive Cup Finals.

Despite its undoubted commercial success, the competition remains something of an anomaly. The first two rounds are played over two legs, while, at the start of the 1983/4 season, the second round became seeded, ostensibly to give sides from lower divisions the chance of lucrative games against top-class opposition. However, the Final, played as it is in March, always has the flavour of a curtain-raiser to the season's climax – the finals of the European club competitions and, of course, the FA Cup Final, which is still *the* game every English player wants to appear in and win.

Above, left 1983 Final: Ian Rush (Liverpool), having beaten Ray Wilkins (Manchester United), is pursued by Remi Moses (left). Liverpool won 2-1 in extra time.

Below 1983 Final: Liverpool's three Scottish stars celebrate victory – Graeme Souness, Kenny Dalglish and Alan Hansen.

Football League/Milk Cup Finals
(* = team at home in first leg; aet = after extra time)

1961 Aston Villa 3 *Rotherham Utd 2 (aet; 0-2; 3-0)
1962 Norwich City 4 *Rochdale 0 (3-0; 1-0)
1963 *Birmingham City 3 Aston Villa 1 (3-1; 0-0)
1964 Leicester City 4 *Stoke City 3 (1-1; 3-2)
1965 *Chelsea 3 Leicester City 2 (3-2; 0-0)
1966 West Bromwich Albion 5 *West Ham Utd 3 (1-2; 4-1)
1967 Queen's Park Rangers 3 West Bromwich Albion 2
1968 Leeds Utd 1 Arsenal 0
1969 Swindon Town 3 Arsenal 1 (aet)
1970 Manchester City 2 West Bromwich Albion 1 (aet)
1971 Tottenham Hotspur 2 Aston Villa 0
1972 Stoke City 2 Chelsea 1
1973 Tottenham Hotspur 1 Norwich City 0
1974 Wolverhampton Wanderers 2 Manchester City 1
1975 Aston Villa 1 Norwich City 0
1976 Manchester City 2 Newcastle Utd 1
1977 Aston Villa 3 Everton 2 (aet, after 0-0 and 1-1 draws)
1978 Nottingham Forest 1 Liverpool 0 (after 0-0 draw)
1979 Nottingham Forest 3 Southampton 2
1980 Wolverhampton Wanderers 1 Nottingham Forest 0
1981 Liverpool 2 West Ham Utd 1 (after 1-1 draw)
1982 Liverpool 3 Tottenham Hotspur 1 (aet)
1983 Liverpool 2 Manchester Utd 1 (aet)
1984 Liverpool 1 Everton 0 (after 0-0 draw)

SCOTTISH LEAGUE & CUPS

At club level Scotland's football history is one of almost complete Glaswegian domination – initially by the amateurs Queen's Park, and then for most of this century by Rangers and Celtic – although sporadic challenges have come from the Edinburgh clubs Heart of Midlothian and Hibernian, the two Dundee sides, and Aberdeen.

The Scottish FA, which – as in England – pre-dated the League, was formed on 3 March 1873 at Dewar's Hotel, Glasgow. Eight clubs made up the initial membership (see box), and were joined soon after by Kilmarnock, then primarily a rugby club, as the name of the ground – Rugby Park – still proclaims. (Perhaps there was some confusion in the minds of Kilmarnock's members, for on that very same day in 1873 the Scottish Rugby Union was also formed in Glasgow!) Of the eight original Scottish FA members, only Queen's Park and Kilmarnock now survive. Of the others, Third Lanark were the last to fold, in 1967.

Although Queen's Park are now very much a minor force in Scotland, their contribution to the game – which they were the first to 'import' from England – was incalculable. They provided the entire Scottish team for the first international against England, and in the 18 years before the foundation of the Scottish League, more than half the players who represented Scotland came from Queen's Park. In that period, England won only three times.

The influence of Queen's Park also extended to the laws of the game, for they were respons-ible for the introduction of the 'Scottish throw-in'. At that time, English players threw-in from touch one-handed, in a way similar to that of modern Rugby Union players. Queen's Park and Scotland pioneered the now-familiar two-handed throw – and England and the rest of the world followed suit.

As in England, though, the dominance of the amateurs in Scotland was short-lived, especially with the formation of the Scottish League in 1890. Queen's Park, however, remain an ama-teur side to this day: the only first-class club of its type in British football.

League football in Scotland quickly took hold after Rangers and Dumbarton had finished equal on points in the first season and then shared the championship after a drawn play-off. By the time the second season began, there were no fewer than 64 clubs in the League, organised into six divisions – 12 each in the First, the Alliance, and the Federation, 10 each in the Midland and Ayrshire Leagues, and 8 in the Northern League.

Dumbarton won the second championship outright: but then Celtic won six of the next eight titles – a foretaste of things to come. The over-whelming hold that Celtic and Rangers have had on Scottish honours since the last decade of the 19th century is not difficult to explain. Both clubs realised at a very early stage that football had enormous potential not only as a sport but also as a business; and both clubs have been run by astute businessmen.

Whether by accident or design, the clubs capitalised on their religious differences, though just how this aspect of their rivalry started is a matter of debate. Celtic were formed in 1888 by a lay brother in a Catholic teaching order to raise money for the poor children of Glasgow's East End, who were almost all Irish Catholics. Rangers, founded in 1873, were the offshoot of a group of Glasgow oarsmen, who played football after rowing on the Clyde. Celtic have never adopted any form of 'Catholics only' policy; indeed, some of the great names in their history have been Protestants, including half the side that won the European Cup in 1967 and their most celebrated recent manager, Jock Stein. Rangers, on the other hand, practised religious discrimination until quite recently (some allege they still do so). The Rangers purist will tell you that no Catholic has ever played for the club. This is not true, but few Catholics have stayed for long at Ibrox Park. There have even been players who switched from one club to the other, such as Alec Bennett, the right winger in the great Celtic side of the early 1900s; while the

Jimmy McGrory (Celtic, right), the most prolific goal scorer in British football history, averaged more than one goal a game in a career spanning almost 17 years. Here he bears down on Partick Thistle goalkeeper Johnstone in a 1935 League match.

Original Members of Scottish FA	
Clydesdale	Queen's Park
Dumbarton	Third Lanark
Eastern	Vale of Leven
Granville	Volunteer Reserves

Original Members of Scottish League	
Abercorn	Rangers
Cambuslang	Renton
Cowlairs	St Mirren
Celtic	Third Lanark
Dumbarton	Vale of Leven
Heart of Midlothian	

father of Ronnie Simpson, who kept goal for Celtic in the 1967 European Cup Final was Rangers' centre-half in the Thirties. For whatever reasons, and however unfortunate some of its effects, the religious polarisation of Rangers and Celtic has unquestionably been a major factor in the success of both.

In the first decade of the 20th century, Celtic won the title six times in a row with a team built by manager Willie Maley and renowned for its forward line of Bennett, McMenemy, Quinn, Somers, and Hamilton. When that team faded, Rangers won the championship three years running, before Maley rebuilt his Celtic side around McMenemy and one of Scotland's immortals – Patsy Gallagher. They took the championship pennant back to Parkhead four times, before Rangers regained it once more, setting new standards of teamwork and fitness based on the previously unheard-of routine of full-time training.

Between the wars Rangers were supreme, winning the title 15 times to Celtic's four. Motherwell shone briefly for a period, winning

the championship in 1932 and finishing runners-up on four occasions, thanks in the main to two forwards – Bob Ferrier, who scored 32 goals in 37 games during the 1930/31 season, and Willie McFadyen, with 52 goals in 1931/2.

Those exploits, however, pale in comparison with the achievements of one of the greatest forwards – and certainly the greatest goal-scoring forward – in the history of British soccer. Jimmy McGrory is the only British player to have scored more League goals than the number of games in which he appeared – 410 goals in 408 games for Celtic and Clyde and a career total of 550; yet, astonishingly, he was capped only seven times by Scotland. McGrory's career ran from 1922 to 1938, almost parallel with that of another great goal-scoring Scot, Hughie Gallacher, who made his name with Airdrieonians and had already won the first of his 20 Scottish caps before moving to England, where he played for a total of six clubs. Between 1921 and 1939 Gallacher scored 387 League goals. But his record does not touch McGrory's, which is still a legend – as is the man – at Parkhead. While on the subject of goal-scoring feats, we should note that in the 1927/8 season Jimmy Smith of Ayr United scores 66 times – which remains a UK all-time record.

After World War II it was the turn of Edinburgh briefly to challenge Glasgow's domination. Hibernian won the title three times in five years with a forward line – Smith, Turnbull, Reilly, Johnstone, and Ormond – every bit as good as Celtic's of some 50 years before. Between them the 'Famous Five' scored 1,500 goals for Hibs over the years and won 87 caps – yet never once were they selected *en bloc* for Scotland.

Once Hibs' successful years were over, Ran-

Above *Gordon Smith (left), outside-right in Hibernian's brilliantly creative 'Famous Five' forward line, beats a St Mirren defender in a 1950 League match.*

Left *The 'Auld Firm': a Rangers goal against Celtic at Ibrox in November 1983. From left: Danny McGrain, Pat Bonner (Celtic keeper), Paul McStay (on ground), John McDonald (14), Tom McAdam (far right); scorer Sandy Clark is just visible behind McDonald.*

gers, Celtic and Aberdeen all won the championship before Hearts restored Edinburgh's pride with two titles in three years. It was a player Hearts had once rejected, Willie Woodburn, and Scotland's greatest-ever centre-half, George Young, who formed the hub of a Rangers side that won eight championships, five Scottish Cups, and four League cups before first Dundee (1962) and then Kilmarnock (1965) heralded the end of that era and the beginning of Celtic's astonishing run under Jock Stein, which saw them bring the title to Parkhead for an unprecedented nine seasons in a row.

That Celtic side was probably the best Scottish club unit of all time. As a player Stein himself had been plucked from the obscurity of non-League football in Wales and had been a fine centre-half and captain for the club. Within a month of Stein taking over as manager (from Jimmy McGrory, of all people), Celtic won the Scottish Cup as a prelude to that amazing run in the League. Their exploits and players overshadowed the Rangers side of that era which, although starved of League success, and with precious little to show for their efforts in either Cup, was graced by another Scottish immortal – Jim Baxter. Of his 34 international appearances, five were against England and only once was he a loser against the 'auld enemy'.

In 1976 the Scottish League was reorganised into a new élite Premier Division, a First, and a Second. It made little difference initially, with the 'auld firm' of Rangers and Celtic sharing the bulk of the spoils until the end of the decade. In the 1980s, though, there are welcome signs of an East Coast renaissance. Aberdeen have twice won the Cup in the Eighties (not to mention the European Cup Winners' Cup and the European Super Cup), while Dundee United won the championship for the first time in 1983.

SCOTTISH LEAGUE AND CUP WINNERS

League Cup Final 1983: Bobby Russell (Rangers) beats Celtic's Danny McGrain in the air. Celtic won 2-1.

Year	Division 1	Division 2	Cup Winners
1874			Queen's Park
1875			Queen's Park
1876			Queen's Park
1877			Vale of Leven
1878			Vale of Leven
1879			Vale of Leven
1880			Queen's Park
1881			Queen's Park
1882			Queen's Park
1883			Dumbarton
1884			Queen's Park
1885			Renton
1886			Queen's Park
1887			Hibernian
1888			Renton
1889			Third Lanark
1890	**Division 1**		Queen's Park
1891	Dumbarton and Rangers tied		Hearts
1892	Dumbarton		Celtic
1893	Celtic	**Division 2**	Queen's Park
1894	Celtic	Hibernian	Rangers
1895	Hearts	Hibernian	St Bernard's
1896	Celtic	Abercorn	Hearts
1897	Hearts	Partick Thistle	Rangers
1898	Celtic	Kilmarnock	Rangers
1899	Rangers	Kilmarnock	Celtic
1900	Rangers	Partick Thistle	Celtic
1901	Rangers	St Bernard's	Hearts
1902	Rangers	Port Glasgow	Hibernian
1903	Hibernian	Airdrieonians	Rangers
1904	Third Lanark	Hamilton Acad.	Celtic
1905	Celtic	Clyde	Third Lanark
1906	Celtic	Leith Athletic	Hearts
1907	Celtic	St Bernard's	Celtic
1908	Celtic	Raith Rovers	Celtic
1909	Celtic	Abercorn	Cup withheld
1910	Celtic	Leith and Raith tied	Dundee
1911	Rangers	Dumbarton	Celtic
1912	Rangers	Ayr Utd	Celtic
1913	Rangers	Ayr Utd	Falkirk
1914	Celtic	Cowdenbeath	Celtic

	Division 1	Division 2	Cup Winners	League Cup Winners
1915	Celtic	Cowdenbeath	*No competition*	
1916	Celtic	*No competition*	*No competition*	
1917	Celtic	*No competition*	*No competition*	
1918	Rangers	*No competition*	*No competition*	
1919	Celtic	*No competition*	*No competition*	
1920	Rangers	*No competition*	Kilmarnock	
1921	Rangers	*No competition*	Partick Thistle	
1922	Celtic	Alloa Athletic	Morton	
1923	Rangers	Queen's Park	Celtic	
1924	Rangers	St Johnstone	Airdrieonians	
1925	Rangers	Dundee Utd	Celtic	
1926	Celtic	Dunfermline Ath.	St Mirren	
1927	Rangers	Bo'ness	Celtic	
1928	Rangers	Ayr Utd	Rangers	
1929	Rangers	Dundee Utd	Kilmarnock	
1930	Rangers	Leith Athletic	Rangers	
1931	Rangers	Third Lanark	Celtic	
1932	Motherwell	East Stirling	Rangers	
1933	Rangers	Hibernian	Celtic	
1934	Rangers	Albion Rovers	Rangers	
1935	Rangers	Third Lanark	Rangers	
1936	Celtic	Falkirk	Rangers	
1937	Rangers	Ayr Utd	Celtic	
1938	Celtic	Raith Rovers	East Fife	
1939	Rangers	Cowdenbeath	Clyde	
1940-1946	*No competition*			
1947	Rangers	Dundee	Aberdeen	Rangers
1948	Hibernian	East Fife	Rangers	East Fife
1949	Rangers	Raith Rovers	Rangers	Rangers
1950	Rangers	Morton	Rangers	East Fife
1951	Hibernian	Queen of the South	Celtic	Motherwell
1952	Hibernian	Clyde	Motherwell	Dundee
1953	Rangers	Stirling Albion	Rangers	Dundee
1954	Celtic	Motherwell	Celtic	East Fife
1955	Aberdeen	Airdrieonians	Clyde	Hearts
1956	Rangers	Queen's Park	Hearts	Aberdeen
1957	Rangers	Clyde	Falkirk	Celtic
1958	Hearts	Stirling Albion	Clyde	Celtic
1959	Rangers	Ayr Utd	St Mirren	Hearts
1960	Hearts	St Johnstone	Rangers	Hearts
1961	Rangers	Stirling Albion	Dunfermline Ath.	Rangers
1962	Dundee	Clyde	Rangers	Rangers
1963	Rangers	St Johnstone	Rangers	Hearts
1964	Rangers	Morton	Rangers	Rangers
1965	Kilmarnock	Stirling Albion	Celtic	Rangers
1966	Celtic	Ayr Utd	Rangers	Celtic
1967	Celtic	Morton	Celtic	Celtic
1968	Celtic	St Mirren	Dunfermline Ath.	Celtic
1969	Celtic	Motherwell	Celtic	Celtic
1970	Celtic	Falkirk	Aberdeen	Celtic
1971	Celtic	Partick Thistle	Celtic	Rangers
1972	Celtic	Dumbarton	Celtic	Partick Thistle
1973	Celtic	Clyde	Rangers	Hibernian
1974	Celtic	Airdrieonians	Celtic	Dundee
1975	Rangers	Falkirk	Celtic	Celtic

	Premier Division	Division 1	Division 2	Cup Winners	League Cup Winners
1976	Rangers	Partick Thistle	Clydebank	Rangers	Rangers
1977	Celtic	St Mirren	Stirling Albion	Celtic	Aberdeen
1978	Rangers	Morton	Clyde	Rangers	Rangers
1979	Celtic	Dundee	Berwick Rangers	Rangers	Rangers
1980	Aberdeen	Hearts	Falkirk	Celtic	Dundee Utd.
1981	Celtic	Hibernian	Queens Park	Rangers	Dundee Utd
1982	Celtic	Motherwell	Clyde	Aberdeen	Rangers
1983	Dundee Utd	St Johnstone	Brechin City	Aberdeen	Celtic
1984	Aberdeen	Morton	Forfar Ath.	Aberdeen	Rangers

Dundee United's 1982/3 Premier Division-winning squad, with Captain Paul Hegarty holding the trophy. Standing, from left: Hamish McAlpine, David Dodds, Ian Phillip, David Narey, Richard Gough, Derek Stark, John Holt, Eamonn Bannon. Front row: John Reilly, Ralph Milne, Paul Sturrock, Billy Kirkwood, Maurice Malpas. The club suffered only four defeats in 36 games and their 90 goals equalled Celtic's Premier Division record.

N. IRELAND & WALES

Northern Ireland's League and Cup competitions, dating respectively from 1891 and 1881, and for so long the near-exclusive domain of the two big Belfast clubs Linfield and Glentoran, cannot aspire to the standards of their English and Scottish counterparts, but they do at least provide an annual passport to European competition. So, too, does the Welsh Cup, which, although open to *English* clubs on the Welsh borders, somewhat bizarrely provides entry into the European Cup-Winners' Cup only for *Welsh* teams. Consequently, when Shrewsbury Town won the Welsh Cup in 1977 and 1979, it was the (Welsh) runners-up who qualified.

Year	League Champions	Cup Winners
1881		Moyola Park
1882		Queen's Island
1883		Cliftonville
1884		Distillery
1885		Distillery
1886		Distillery
1887		Ulster
1888		Cliftonville
1889		Distillery
1890		Gordon Highlanders
1891	Linfield	Linfield
1892	Linfield	Linfield
1893	Linfield	Linfield
1894	Glentoran	Distillery
1895	Linfield	Linfield
1896	Distillery	Distillery
1897	Glentoran	Cliftonville
1898	Linfield	Linfield
1899	Distillery	Linfield
1900	Belfast Celtic	Cliftonville
1901	Distillery	Cliftonville
1902	Linfield	Linfield
1903	Distillery	Distillery
1904	Linfield	Linfield
1905	Glentoran	Distillery
1906	Cliftonville and Distillery tied	Shelbourne
1907	Linfield	Cliftonville
1908	Linfield	Bohemians
1909	Linfield	Cliftonville
1910	Cliftonville	Distillery
1911	Linfield	Shelbourne
1912	Glentoran	Linfield awarded Cup: Final not played
1913	Glentoran	Linfield
1914	Glentoran	Glentoran
1915	Linfield	Belfast Celtic
1916	Linfield	*No competition*
1917	Glentoran	*No competition*
1918	Belfast Celtic	*No competition*
1919	Linfield	*No competition*
1920	Shelbourne awarded Cup: Final not played	Belfast Celtic
1921	Glentoran	Glentoran
1922	Linfield	Linfield
1923	Linfield	Linfield
1924	Queen's Island	Queen's Island
1925	Distillery	Glentoran
1926	Belfast Celtic	Belfast Celtic
1927	Ards	Belfast Celtic
1928	Willowfield	Belfast Celtic
1929	Ballymena	Belfast Celtic
1930	Linfield	Linfield
1931	Linfield	Glentoran
1932	Glentoran	Linfield
1933	Glentoran	Belfast Celtic
1934	Linfield	Linfield
1935	Glentoran	Linfield
1936	Linfield	Belfast Celtic
1937	Belfast Celtic	Belfast Celtic
1938	Belfast Celtic	Belfast Celtic
1939	Linfield	Belfast Celtic
1940	Ballymena	Belfast Celtic
1941	Belfast Celtic	*No competition*
1942	Linfield	*No competition*
1943	Belfast Celtic	*No competition*
1944	Belfast Celtic	*No competition*
1945	Linfield	*No Competition*
1946	Linfield	*No competition*
1947	Belfast Celtic	*No competition*
1948	Linfield	Belfast Celtic
1949	Linfield	Derry City
1950	Linfield	Linfield
1951	Glentoran	Glentoran
1952	Glenavon	Ards
1953	Glentoran	Linfield
1954	Linfield	Derry City
1955	Linfield	Dundela
1956	Linfield	Distillery
1957	Glenavon	Glenavon
1958	Ards	Ballymena
1959	Linfield	Glenavon
1960	Glenavon	Linfield
1961	Linfield	Glenavon
1962	Linfield	Linfield
1963	Distillery	Linfield
1964	Glentoran	Derry City
1965	Derry City	Coleraine
1966	Linfield	Glentoran
1967	Glentoran	Crusaders
1968	Glentoran	Crusaders
1969	Linfield	Ards
1970	Glentoran	Linfield
1971	Linfield	Distillery
1972	Glentoran	Colraine
1973	Crusaders	Glentoran
1974	Coleraine	Ards
1975	Linfield	Coleraine
1976	Crusaders	Carrick Rangers
1977	Glentoran	Coleraine
1978	Linfield	Linfield
1979	Linfield	Cliftonville
1980	Linfield	Linfield
1981	Glentoran	Ballymena
1982	Linfield	Linfield
1983	Linfield	Glentoran
1984	Linfield	Ballymena

Welsh Cup Winners

Year	Winner	Year	Winner	Year	Winner
1878	Wrexham	1921	Wrexham	1966	Swansea Town
1879	Newtown	1922	Cardiff City	1967	Cardiff City
1880	Druids	1923	Cardiff City	1968	Cardiff City
1881	Druids	1924	Wrexham	1969	Cardiff City
1882	Druids	1925	Wrexham	1970	Cardiff City
1883	Wrexham	1926	Ebbw Vale	1971	Cardiff City
1884	Oswestry	1927	Cardiff City	1972	Wrexham
1885	Druids	1928	Cardiff City	1973	Cardiff City
1886	Druids	1929	Connahs Quay	1974	Cardiff City
1887	Chirk	1930	Cardiff City	1975	Wrexham
1888	Chirk	1931	Wrexham	1976	Cardiff City
1889	Bangor	1932	Swansea Town	1977	Shrewsbury Town
1890	Chirk	1933	Chester	1978	Wrexham
1891	Shrewsbury Town	1934	Bristol City	1979	Shrewsbury Town
1892	Chirk	1935	Tranmere Rovers	1980	Newport County
1893	Wrexham	1936	Crewe	1981	Swansea City
1894	Chirk	1937	Crewe	1982	Swansea City
1895	Newtown	1938	Shrewsbury Town	1983	Swansea City
1896	Bangor	1939	South Liverpool	1984	Shrewsbury Town
1897	Wrexham	1940	Wellington		
1898	Druids	1941	*No competition*		
1899	Druids	1947	Chester		
1900	Aberystwyth	1948	Lovells Athletic		
1901	Oswestry	1949	Merthyr Tydfil		
1902	Wellington	1950	Swansea Town		
1903	Wrexham	1951	Merthyr Tydfil		
1904	Druids	1952	Rhyl		
1905	Wrexham	1953	Rhyl		
1906	Wellington	1954	Flint Town		
1907	Oswestry	1955	Barry Town		
1908	Chester	1956	Cardiff City		
1909	Wrexham	1957	Wrexham		
1910	Wrexham	1958	Wrexham		
1911	Wrexham	1959	Cardiff City		
1912	Cardiff City	1960	Wrexham		
1913	Swansea Town	1961	Swansea Town		
1914	Wrexham	1962	Bangor		
1915	Wrexham	1963	Borough United		
1916-19	*No competition*	1964	Cardiff City		
1920	Cardiff City	1965	Cardiff City		

EUROPEAN CLUB COMPETITIONS

The three major continental knockout competitions for European league clubs are the European Cup, the European Cup-Winners' Cup, and the UEFA Cup (formerly the Inter-City Fairs Cup).

The credit for organising a cup competition for the league champions of all European countries must go to the French sports paper *L'Équipe*, who lobbied first the respective national champions of 1955 and then the European Football Union (UEFA) for the idea to be accepted. Displaying the same sad parochialism they showed when the World Cup was launched, the English authorities advised the then Division 1 champions, Chelsea, not to enter the first European Cup competition; their Scottish counterparts, however, Hibernian did take part and reached the semi-finals, where they lost to the eventual runners-up, Stade de Reims.

The first Final in Paris was won – narrowly – by Real Madrid, whose superlatively talented sides went on to win the next four finals as well. While they were establishing their stranglehold on the tournament, British sides were beginning to come to terms with the different demands of European soccer. Manchester United reached two successive semi-finals, and in 1958 might well have gone on to the Final itself had their wonderful young side not been so cruelly destroyed in the Munich air disaster. Although United were not eligible to enter the European Cup the following year, they were invited to enter by UEFA but shamefully were prevented from doing so by the Football League on the grounds that only Wolverhampton Wanderers, as English champions, had right of entry.

In 1961 Rangers emulated Hibernian by reaching the semi-finals of the European Cup, and the following year they were runners-up in the first European Cup-Winners' Cup Final. They were not, however, the first British side to reach a European final, as is often supposed, for in 1958 a representative London side of near-international strength had made it through to the Final of the Inter-Cities Fairs Cup, a cumbersome competition run on a league basis. In the Final, played over two legs, London were thrashed by Barcelona, who also beat Birmingham City in the next Fairs Cup Final in 1960.

That same year saw perhaps the greatest European Cup Final ever, between Real Madrid and Eintracht Frankfurt. Played at Glasgow's Hampden Park, Real won 7-3, with the legendary Hungarian Ferenc Puskás, playing in his first Final, scoring four and the Argentinian maestro Alfredo Di Stéfano the other three. As it turned out, this was to be the last victory in

Real's astonishing run, but it provided a fitting climax to the years in which they dominated European football (they won again in 1966).

The European Cup was destined to remain in the Iberian peninsula with the great Benfica side for the next two years, but while Britain still waited for a win in the premier European club competition, Tottenham carved out a little piece of history for themselves by defeating the title-holders Atlético Madrid in the 1963 Cup-Winners' Cup Final, although rather flattered by the 5-1 score. Celtic reached the semi-finals of the same competition the following year, and West Ham won it in 1965, beating TSV Munich 1860 2-0, fittingly at Wembley Stadium.

Success in the European Cup however, still obstinately refused to come, even though Tottenham, Dundee, Liverpool, and Manchester United all reached the semi-finals in the early sixties; in the 1965/6 quarter-finals, Manchester United, in one of the supreme performances of any British club in Europe, destroyed the powerful Benfica 5-1 in Lisbon. It wasn't until 1967 that Celtic, competing in the tournament for the first time, made it to the Final and then surprised everyone but themselves and their supporters by winning a memorable game in Lisbon 2-1 against Inter-Milan, going behind to an early penalty before Gemmell equalised midway through the second half and Chalmers got the winner five minutes from time. The records show that 1967 was a good year for Britain: in addition to Celtic's success, Rangers and Leeds reached the Finals of, respectively, the Cup-

Above *European Cup Final 1967: Captain Billy McNeil holds the cup after Celtic had become the first British club to lift Europe's premier club trophy.*

Below *European Cup Final 1960: Alfredo Di Stéfano, probably the greatest centre-forward since World War II, scores the second goal for Real Madrid in their classic triumph against Eintracht Frankfurt.*

European Cup Final 1968: George Best leaves a Benfica defender trailing; Bobby Charlton looks on approvingly. Manchester United's thrilling victory at Wembley became emphatic only in extra time, when they scored three times.

United reached the Final of the Cup-Winners' Cup, but were narrowly beaten by AC Milan.

The following year we drew a blank – the first time since 1966 that Britain had failed to win anything in Europe. Spurs lost a two-legged UEFA Cup Final to Feyenoord in Rotterdam amidst scenes of disgraceful crowd violence provoked by visiting supporters; Celtic lost in the semi-finals of the European Cup to the eventual runners-up, Atlético Madrid. In the Cup-Winners' Cup, meanwhile, Glentoran provided a rare taste of success for Northern Ireland in Europe by reaching the quarter-finals, where they were overwhelmed by Borussia Mönchengladbach.

The decline continued in 1975: no wins, although Leeds United managed to reach the Final of the European Cup, where they lost a thoroughly ill-tempered game in Paris to the reigning champions Bayern Munich, who the season before had taken over the mantle of Europe's best side from Ajax. Bayern won the Cup again in 1976, a year in which West Ham reached the Cup-Winners' Cup Final, only to lose to a very good Anderlecht side; Liverpool flexed their muscles for exploits to come by winning the UEFA Cup, beating Bruges in the Final.

Liverpool came back in 1977 to start a British

Winners' Cup and the Fairs Cup; both were beaten, but the fact that British teams had for the first time contested all three Finals in a single season proved we had arrived as a major European soccer force.

As if to underline that Celtic's win was no fluke, Manchester United marked the 10th anniversary of Munich by rewarding their manager Matt Busby with an emotional European Cup win over Benfica by 4-1 after extra time at Wembley; while Leeds United squeezed to the narrowest of Fairs Cup wins over the Hungarians Ferencvaros. In 1969 the Fairs Cup remained in Britain with Newcastle United, while in 1970 the successes of 1967 were emulated, with Arsenal winning the Fairs Cup and Manchester City the Cup-Winners' Cup; Celtic, a shade unluckily, lost the European Cup Final in extra time against Feyenoord.

Two more trophies came Britain's way in 1971, with Leeds winning the Fairs Cup for the second time and Chelsea, belying their underdog status, achieving a 2-1 Cup-Winners' Cup victory over Real Madrid, after an initial 1-1 draw. Celtic, meanwhile, were going out of the European Cup at the quarter-final stage to the brilliant young Ajax side, led by the incomparable Johan Cruyff. Ajax duly went on to the Final at Wembley and beat the Greeks of Panathinaikos – the first of their three successive European Cup victories.

For the third year running 1972 saw two of the three European trophies come to Britain. Tottenham won the first UEFA (ex-Fairs) Cup, beating Wolves in the only all-British European final to date, while Rangers at last emerged from Celtic's shadow by travelling to Barcelona for the Cup-Winners' Cup Final and returning with the Cup – but without quite a number of their violent supporters – after a 3-2 victory over Moscow Dynamo. In 1973 Britain had to make do with just a single trophy, as Liverpool relieved Tottenham of the UEFA Cup; Leeds

run of European Cup domination that no other nation has equalled. Their victory over Borussia Mönchengladbach by 3-1 in Rome was a personal triumph for Kevin Keegan, who ran the Borussia defence ragged and eventually forced them to concede the penalty that sealed Liverpool's win.

In 1978 Liverpool won again, but their 1-0 victory over a boring, ultra-defensive Bruges side bore no comparison to the previous Final. The only goal came from Kenny Dalglish, signed from Celtic to replace the Hamburg-bound Kevin Keegan.

The following season Liverpool had the misfortune to be drawn against and then eliminated by reigning League champions Nottingham Forest, suffering the humiliation of a 1st round exit from the competition. Forest went on to win the Cup in a dreary Final against Malmö. The goal that settled this game in a way justified the £1 million that Forest had paid Birmingham for Trevor Francis, for he scored the winner with a diving far-post header on the stroke of half-time. A rather less expensive player, Scottish international John Robertson, hit a speculative shot that went in off a post to settle the 1980 Final against Kevin Keegan's SV Hamburg. More exciting – eventually – was that year's Cup-Winners' Cup Final between Arsenal and

Above *European Cup Final 1977: Tommy Smith rifles in a superbly directed header from Steve Heighway's corner kick to score Liverpool's second goal against Borussia Mönchengladbach. This was Liverpool's first and, to date, most exciting win in the Final.*

Left *European Cup Final 1979: Nottingham Forest's Trevor Francis scores from John Robertson's left-wing cross to beat Malmö in a game lacking quality or excitement.*

Valencia. With both normal and extra-time failing to produce a goal, the fate of the Cup was decided on penalties. Valencia scored five, Arsenal four – their talented midfielder Graham Rix fluffing the kick that would have kept his side's hopes alive.

In 1981 it was a return to two trophies for Britain, as defender Alan Kennedy scored the late goal which enabled Liverpool to win their third European Cup at the expense of Real Madrid, while Ipswich, after years of trying, finally got their hands on a European title by winning the UEFA Cup, although they nearly squandered a 3-0 home win by losing the return to Alkmaar 2-4.

Not many people fancied Aston Villa's chances against Bayern Munich in the 1982 European Cup Final, especially as Villa soon after the start were forced by injury to bring on an untried 19-year-old reserve goalkeeper, Nigel Spink, and Bayern's captain and main striker, Karl-Heinz Rummenigge, was at the time European Footballer of the Year. Spink, however, coped magnificently, while at the other end, Peter Withe scored the only goal of the game to give Villa the Cup and England an unprecedented six-year hold on Europe's premier club competition.

All that was to end in 1983, however, Villa and Liverpool both going out in the quarter-finals. It was left to Aberdeen to bring the Cup-Winners' Cup to Scotland for the first time since Rangers in 1972 with a thrilling 2-1 extra-time win over Real Madrid, the decisive goal coming from their young substitute Hewitt. In the meantime, SV Hamburg were at last winning the European Cup, at the expense of the hugely talented but tactically timid Juventus; while Anderlecht eased past once-great Benfica to take the UEFA Cup.

No one nation has yet won all three of the European Club trophies in a single season, though Britain has come closest, with those two wins and a runner-up in 1970.

EUROPEAN CLUB COMPETITIONS

European Cup Finals

(aet = after extra time)

1956 (Paris) Real Madrid 4 Stade de Reims 3
1957 (Madrid) Real Madrid 2 AC Fiorentina 0
1958 (Brussels) Real Madrid 3 AC Milan 2 (aet)
1959 (Stuttgart) Real Madrid 2 Stade de Reims 0
1960 (Glasgow) Real Madrid 7 Eintracht Frankfurt 3
1961 (Berne) Benfica 3 Barcelona 2
1962 (Amsterdam) Benfica 5 Real Madrid 3
1963 (London) AC Milan 2 Benfica 1
1964 (Vienna) Internazionale-Milan 3 Real Madrid 1
1965 (Milan) Internazionale-Milan 1 Benfica 0
1966 (Brussels) Real Madrid 2 Partizan Belgrade 1
1967 (Lisbon) Celtic 2 Internazionale-Milan 1
1968 (London) Manchester United 4 Benfica 1 (aet)
1969 (Madrid) AC Milan 4 Ajax Amsterdam 1
1970 (Milan) Feyenoord 2 Celtic 1 (aet)
1971 (London) Ajax Amsterdam 2 Panathinaikos 0
1972 (Rotterdam) Ajax Amsterdam 2 Internazionale-Milan 0
1973 (Belgrade) Ajax Amsterdam 1 Juventus 0
1974 (Brussels) Bayern Munich 4 Atlético Madrid 0
    (after 1-1 draw)
1975 (Paris) Bayern Munich 2 Leeds United 0
1976 (Glasgow) Bayern Munich 1 St Etienne 0
1977 (Rome) Liverpool 3 Borussia Mönchengladbach 1
1978 (London) Liverpool FC Bruges 0
1979 (Munich) Nottingham Forest 1 Malmö FF 0
1980 (Madrid) Nottingham Forest 1 SV Hamburg 0
1981 (Paris) Liverpool 1 Real Madrid 0
1982 (Rotterdam) Aston Villa 1 Bayern Munich 0
1983 (Athens) SV Hamburg 1 Juventus 0
1984 (Rome) AS Roma 1 Liverpool 1 (aet: Liverpool
    won 4-2 on penalties)

European Cup-Winners' Cup Finals

1961 AC Fiorentina 4 Rangers 1 (aggregate score over two legs)
1962 (Stuttgart) Atlético Madrid 3 AC Fiorentina 0 (after 1-1 draw)
1963 (Rotterdam) Tottenham Hotspur 5 Atlético Madrid 1
1964 (Antwerp) Sporting Lisbon 1 MTK Budapest 0 (after 3-3 draw)
1965 (London) West Ham United 2 TSV Munich 1860 0
1966 (Glasgow) Borussia Dortmund 2 Liverpool (aet)
1967 (Nuremberg) Bayern Munich 1 Rangers 0 (aet)
1968 (Rotterdam) AC Milan 2 SV Hamburg 0
1969 (Basle) Slovan Bratislava 3 Barcelona 2
1970 (Vienna) Manchester City 2 Gornik Zabrze 1
1971 (Athens) Chelsea 2 Real Madrid 1 (after 1-1 draw)
1972 (Barcelona) Rangers 3 Moscow Dynamo 2
1973 (Salonika) AC Milan 1 Leeds United 0
1974 (Rotterdam) FC Magdeburg 2 AC Milan 0
1975 (Basle) Dynamo Kiev 3 Ferencvaros 0
1976 (Brussels) Anderlecht 4 West Ham United 2
1977 (Amsterdam) SV Hamburg 2 Anderlecht 0
1978 (Paris) Anderlecht 4 Austria-Vienna 0
1979 (Basle) Barcelona 4 Fortuna Düsseldorf 3 (aet)
1980 (Brussels) Valencia 0 Arsenal 0 (aet; Valencia won 5-4
    on penalties)
1981 (Düsseldorf) Dynamo Tbilisi 2 Carl Zeiss Jena 1
1982 (Barcelona) Barcelona 2 Standard Liège 1
1983 (Gothenburg) Aberdeen 2 Real Madrid 1 (aet)
1984 (Basle) Juventus 2 Porto 1

Inter-Cities Fairs Cup Finals

(* = team at home in first leg; score in each leg in parentheses)
1958 Barcelona 8 *London 2 (2-2; 6-0)
1960 Barcelona 4 * Birmingham City 1 (0-0; 4-1)
1961 AS Roma 4 *Birmingham City 2 (2-2; 2-0)
1962 *Valencia 7 Barcelona 3 (6-2; 1-1)

1963 Valencia 4 *Dynamo Zagreb 1 (2-1; 2-0)
1964 (Barcelona) Real Zaragoza 2 Valencia 1
1965 (Turin) Ferencvaros 1 Juventus 0
1966 *Barcelona 4 Real Zaragoza 3 (0-1; 4-2)

1967 *Dynamo Zagreb 2 Leeds United 0 (2-0; 0-0)
1968 *Leeds United 1 Ferencvaros 0 (1-0; 0-0)
1969 *Newcastle United 6 Ujpest Dozsa 2 (3-0; 3-2)
1970 Arsenal 4 *Anderlecht 3 (1-3; 3-0)
1971 Leeds United 3 *Juventus 3 (2-2; 1-1. Leeds won on
    away goals)

UEFA Cup Finals

1972 Tottenham Hotspur 3 *Wolverhampton Wanderers 2
    (2-1; 1-1)
1973 *Liverpool 3 Borussia Mönchengladbach 2 (3-0; 0-2)
1974 Feyenoord 4 *Tottenham Hotspur 2 (2-2; 2-0)
1975 *Borussia Mönchengladbach 5 Twente Enschede 1
    (0-0; 5-1)
1976 *Liverpool 4 FC Bruges 3 (3-2; 1-1)
1977 *Juventus 2 Athletic Bilbao 2 (0-1; 2-1. Juventus won
    on away goals)
1978 PSV Eindhoven 3 *Bastia 0 (0-0; 3-0)
1979 Borussia Mönchengladbach 2 *Red Star Belgrade 1
    (1-1; 1-0)
1980 Eintracht Frankfurt 3 *Borussia Mönchengladbach 3
    (2-3; 1-0. Frankfurt won on away goals)
1981 *Ipswich Town 5 AZ 67 Alkmaar 4 (3-0; 2-4)
1982 *IFK Gothenburg 4 SV Hamburg 0 (1-0; 3-0)
1983 * Anderlecht 2 Benfica 1 (1-0; 1-1)
1984 Tottenham Hotspur 2 *Anderlecht 2 (1-1, 1-1 aet:
    Tottenham won on penalties)

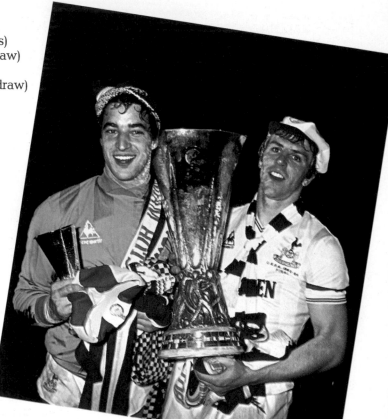

*UEFA Cup Final 1984: Spurs' heroes against Anderlecht,
goalkeeper Tony Parks (left) and captain Graham
Roberts.*

BRITISH CLUBS IN EUROPE

RU = Runners-up (losing finalist)
SF = Semi-finalists
QF = Quarter-finalists

	European Cup	European Cup-Winners' Cup	Inter-Cities Fairs Cup
1956	Hibernian (SF)		
1957	Manchester Utd (SF)		
	Rangers (1st rnd)		
1958	Manchester Utd (SF)		London (RU)
	Rangers (1st rnd)		Birmingham City (SF)
	Glenavon (prelim. rnd)		
1959	Wolverhampton Wanderers (1st rnd)		
	Ards (prelim. rnd)		
	Heart of Midlothian (prelim. rnd)		
1960	Rangers (SF)		Birmingham (RU)
	Wolverhampton Wanderers (QF)		Chelsea (QF)
	Linfield (prelim. rnd)		
1961	Burnley (QF)	Rangers (RU)	Birmingham City (RU)
	Heart of Midlothian (prelim. rnd)	Wolverhampton Wanderers (SF)	Hibernian (SF)
	Glenavon withdrew		
1962	Tottenham Hotspur (SF)	Dunfermline Athletic (QF)	Sheffield Wednesday (QF)
	Rangers (QF)	Leicester City (2nd rnd)	Heart of Midlothian (2nd rnd)
	Linfield (prelim. rnd)	Swansea Town (1st rnd)	Hibernian (2nd rnd)
		Glenavon (1st rnd)	Birmingham City (2nd rnd)
			Nottingham Forest (1st rnd)
1963	Dundee (SF)	Tottenham Hotspur (Winners)	Hibernian (QF)
	Ipswich Town (1st rnd)	Rangers (2nd rnd)	Dunfermline Athletic (2nd rnd)
	Linfield (prelim. rnd)	Portadown (2nd rnd)	Glentoran (1st rnd)
		Bangor City (1st rnd)	Everton (1st rnd)
			Celtic (1st rnd)
1964	Rangers (prelim. rnd)	Celtic (SF)	Partick Thistle (2nd rnd)
	Everton (prelim. rnd)	Manchester Utd (QF)	Arsenal (2nd rnd)
	Distillery (prelim. rnd)	Linfield (2nd rnd)	Sheffield Wednesday (2nd rnd)
		Borough Utd (2nd rnd)	Heart of Midlothian (1st rnd)
		Tottenham Hotspur (2nd rnd)	Glentoran (1st rnd)
1965	Liverpool (SF)	West Ham Utd (Winner)	Manchester Utd (SF)
	Rangers (QF)	Cardiff City (QF)	Dunfermline Athletic (3rd rnd)
	Glentoran (prelim. rnd)	Dundee (2nd rnd)	Everton (3rd rnd)
		Derry City (1st rnd)	Celtic (2nd rnd)
			Kilmarnock (2nd rnd)
1966	Manchester Utd (SF)	Liverpool (RU)	Leeds Utd (SF)
	Derry City (1st rnd)	Celtic (SF)	Chelsea (SF)
1966	Kilmarnock (1st rnd)	West Ham Utd (SF)	Dunfermline Athletic (QF)
		Cardiff City (1st rnd)	Heart of Midlothian (3rd rnd)
		Coleraine (1st rnd)	Everton (2nd rnd)
			Glentoran (1st rnd)
			Hibernian (1st rnd)
1967	Celtic (Winner)	Rangers (RU)	Leeds Utd (RU)
	Linfield (QF)	Everton (2nd rnd)	Kilmarnock (SF)
	Liverpool (2nd rnd)	Glentoran (1st rnd)	Burnley (QF)
		Swansea Town (1st rnd)	Dundee Utd (3rd rnd)
			West Bromwich Albion (3rd rnd)
			Dunfermline Athletic (2nd rnd)
1968	Manchester Utd (Winners)	Cardiff City (SF)	Leeds Utd (Winners)
	Celtic (1st rnd)	Aberdeen (2nd rnd)	Dundee (SF)
	Glentoran (1st rnd)	Tottenham Hotspur (2nd rnd)	Rangers (QF)
		Crusaders (1st rnd)	Hibernian (3rd rnd)
			Liverpool (3rd rnd)
			Nottingham Forest (2nd rnd)
			Linfield (1st rnd)

	European Cup	European Cup-Winners' Cup	Inter-Cities Fairs Cup
1969	Manchester Utd (SF)	Dunfermline Athletic (SF)	Newcastle Utd (Winners)
	Celtic (QF)	West Bromwich Albion (QF)	Rangers (SF)
	Manchester City (1st rnd)	Crusaders (1st rnd)	Leeds Utd (QF)
	Glentoran (1st rnd)	Cardiff City (1st rnd)	Hibernian (3rd rnd)
			Aberdeen (2nd rnd)
			Chelsea (2nd rnd)
			Liverpool (1st rnd)
			Linfield (1st rnd)
			Morton (1st rnd)
1970	Celtic (RU)	Manchester City (Winners)	Arsenal (Winners)
	Leeds Utd (SF)	Rangers (2nd rnd)	Newcastle Utd (QF)
	Linfield (1st rnd)	Cardiff City (2nd rnd)	Dunfermline Athletic (3rd rnd)
		Ards (1st rnd)	Southampton (3rd rnd)
			Kilmarnock (3rd rnd)
			Liverpool (2nd rnd)
			Coleraine (2nd rnd)
			Dundee Utd (1st rnd)
			Glentoran (1st rnd)
1971	Celtic (QF)	Chelsea (Winners)	Leeds Utd (Winners)
	Everton (QF)	Manchester City (SF)	Liverpool (SF)
	Glentoran (1st rnd)	Cardiff City (QF)	Arsenal (QF)
		Linfield (1st rnd)	Hibernian (3rd rnd)
		Aberdeen (1st rnd)	Newcastle Utd (2nd rnd)
			Coleraine (2nd rnd)
			Dundee Utd (2nd rnd)
			Coventry City (2nd rnd)
			Rangers (1st rnd)
			Kilmarnock (1st rnd)

	European Cup	European Cup-Winners' Cup	UEFA Cup
1972	Celtic (SF)	Rangers (Winners)	Tottenham Hotspur (Winners)
	Arsenal (QF)	Liverpool (2nd rnd)	Wolverhampton Wndrs (RU)
	Linfield (1st rnd)	Chelsea (2nd rnd)	Dundee (3rd rnd)
		Cardiff City (1st rnd)	St Johnstone (3rd rnd)
		Distillery (1st rnd)	Aberdeen (2nd rnd)
			Leeds Utd (1st rnd)
			Southampton (1st rnd)
			Glentoran (1st rnd)
1973	Derby Co (SF)	Leeds Utd (RU)	Liverpool (Winners)
	Celtic (2nd rnd)	Hibernian (QF)	Tottenham Hotspur (SF)
		Wrexham (2nd rnd)	Stoke City (1st rnd)
			Manchester City (1st rnd)
			Aberdeen (1st rnd)
			Partick Thistle (1st rnd)
1974	Celtic (SF)	Glentoran (QF)	Tottenham Hotspur (RU)
	Liverpool (2nd rnd)	Sunderland (2nd rnd)	Ipswich Town (QF)
	Crusaders (1st rnd)	Rangers (2nd rnd)	Leeds Utd (3rd rnd)
		Cardiff City (1st rnd)	Wolverhampton Wndrs (2nd rnd)
			Aberdeen (2nd rnd)
			Hibernian (2nd rnd)
			Ards (1st rnd)
1975	Leeds Utd (RU)	Liverpool (2nd rnd)	Derby Co (3rd rnd)
	Celtic (1st rnd)	Dundee Utd (2nd rnd)	Portadown (2nd rnd)
	Coleraine (1st rnd)	Cardiff City (1st rnd)	Hibernian (2nd rnd)
		Ards (1st rnd)	Dundee (1st rnd)
			Ipswich Town (1st rnd)
			Stoke City (1st rnd)
			Wolverhampton Wndrs (1st rnd)
1976	Derby Co (2nd rnd)	West Ham Utd (RU)	Liverpool (Winners)
	Rangers (2nd rnd)	Celtic (QF)	Ipswich Town (2nd rnd)
	Linfield (1st rnd)	Wrexham (QF)	Dundee Utd (2nd rnd)
		Coleraine (1st rnd)	Hibernian (1st rnd)
			Everton (1st rnd)
			Aston Villa (1st rnd)
			Glentoran (1st rnd)

	European Cup	European Cup-Winners' Cup	UEFA Cup
1977	Liverpool (Winners) Rangers (1st rnd) Crusaders (1st rnd)	Southampton (QF) Heart of Midlothian (2nd rnd) Carrick Rangers (2nd rnd) Cardiff City (1st rnd)	Queen's Park Rangers (QF) Derby Co (2nd rnd) Manchester Utd (2nd rnd) Hibernian (2nd rnd) Manchester City (1st rnd) Glentoran (1st rnd) Celtic (1st rnd)
1978	Liverpool (Winners) Celtic (2nd rnd) Glentoran (2nd rnd)	Manchester Utd (2nd rnd) Rangers (1st rnd) Coleraine (1st rnd) Cardiff City (1st rnd)	Aston Villa (QF) Ipswich Town (3rd rnd) Newcastle Utd (2nd rnd) Manchester City (1st rnd) Glenavon (1st rnd) Dundee Utd (1st rnd) Aberdeen (1st rnd)
1979	Nottingham Forest (Winners) Rangers (QF) Liverpool (1st rnd) Linfield (1st rnd)	Ipswich Town (QF) Aberdeen (2nd rnd) Ballymena Utd (1st rnd) Wrexham (1st rnd)	Manchester City (QF) West Bromwich Albion (QF) Arsenal (3rd rnd) Everton (2nd rnd) Hibernian (2nd rnd) Glentoran (1st rnd) Dundee Utd (1st rnd)
1980	Nottingham Forest (Winners) Celtic (QF) Liverpool (1st rnd) Linfield (prelim rnd)	Arsenal (RU) Rangers (2nd rnd) Wrexham (1st rnd) Cliftonville (1st rnd)	Leeds Utd (2nd rnd) Ipswich Town (2nd rnd) Dundee Utd (2nd rnd) Aberdeen (1st rnd) Everton (1st rnd) West Bromwich Albion (1st rnd) Glenavon (1st rnd)
1981	Liverpool (Winners) Aberdeen (2nd rnd) Nottingham Forest (1st rnd) Linfield (1st rnd)	West Ham Utd (QF) Newport Co (QF) Celtic (1st rnd) Crusaders (1st rnd)	Ipswich Town (Winners) St Mirren (2nd rnd) Dundee Utd (2nd rnd) Manchester Utd (1st rnd) Wolverhampton Wndrs (1st rnd) Ballymena Utd (1st rnd)
1982	Aston Villa (Winners) Liverpool (QF) Glentoran (2nd rnd) Celtic (1st rnd)	Tottenham Hotspur (SF) Rangers (1st rnd) Swansea City (1st rnd) Ballymena Utd (1st rnd)	Dundee Utd (QF) Aberdeen (3rd rnd) Arsenal (2nd rnd) Southampton (2nd rnd) Ipswich Town (1st rnd) West Bromwich Albion (1st rnd) Linfield (1st rnd)
1983	Aston Villa (QF) Liverpool (QF) Celtic (2nd rnd) Linfield (1st rnd)	Aberdeen (Winners) Tottenham Hotspur (2nd rnd) Swansea City (2nd rnd) Coleraine (1st rnd)	Dundee Utd (QF) Rangers (2nd rnd) Manchester Utd (1st rnd) Southampton (1st rnd) Ipswich Town (1st rnd) Arsenal (1st rnd) Glentoran (1st rnd)
1984	Liverpool (Winners) Dundee Utd (SF) Linfield (1st rnd)	Aberdeen (SF) Manchester Utd (SF) Rangers (2nd rnd) Glentoran (1st rnd) Swansea City (prelim. rnd)	Tottenham Hotspur (Winners) Nottingham Forest (SF) Celtic (3rd rnd) Watford (3rd rnd) Aston Villa (2nd rnd) St Mirren (1st rnd) Coleraine (1st rnd)

HOME INTERNATIONALS

International football began at the West of Scotland cricket ground, Partick, on St Andrew's Day 1872, when 4,000 people paid one shilling each to watch what turned out to be a goal-less draw between Scotland and England. Given the number of forwards in each team, it was a surprising scoreline, but enough interest was aroused for the fixture to become an annual event, staged alternately in Glasgow and London (where Kennington Oval was the venue).

Within four years the Welsh, too, had a national association and a team to represent it: their first international was a 0-4 defeat at Glasgow in March 1876. And when the Irish FA was formed four years later, an international championship was just a few logical steps away.

Ireland's first game was in 1882, a 0-13 drubbing by England, which, followed by a 1-7 defeat by the Welsh at Wrexham, emphasised that they were a little way behind the rest. But they gallantly agreed to take part in the first championship two years later, when the results fairly reflected the four countries' respective strengths:

Feb 9 (Wrexham) Wales 6 Ireland 0
Feb 23 (Belfast) Ireland 1 England 8
Mar 15 (Glasgow) Scotland 1 England 0
Mar 17 (Wrexham) Wales 0 England 4
Mar 26 (Belfast) Ireland 0 Scotland 5
Mar 29 (Glasgow) Scotland 4 Wales 1

England v. Scotland, Wembley 1928. The Wembley Wizards dismantled England as comprehensively as did the Hungarians a quarter of a century later. In the picture centre-forward Hughie Gallacher (left) watches as right-winger Alex Jackson's shot beats England 'keeper Hufton to put the Scots one up. The two England defenders in the picture are the captain Goodall (centre) and left-back Jones, who was hit on the head and knocked cold by the ferociously struck ball with which inside-left Alex James scored his second goal.

Final Table

	P	W	D	L	F	A	Pts
Scotland	3	3	0	0	10	1	6
England	3	2	0	1	12	2	4
Wales	3	1	0	2	7	8	2
Ireland	3	0	0	3	1	19	0

Goal average is included in the above table only out of interest: from the start it was decided that, in the event of two countries finishing level on points, the title would be shared. That happened in the third season when England managed what was then a rare draw against the Scots, whose superior team-work and passing in those early years became a model for the others to copy. Between 1874 and 1887 England won only one of 14 matches against Scotland.

But from the time that England won 5-0 in Glasgow in 1888, the pattern was set for the next 100 years: the two oldest enemies playing what were usually close games to decide the championship, with Wales (in 1907) and Ireland (in 1914) managing only the odd historic success.

Wales had a particularly good period between the wars, beginning with a title win in 1920 when the legendary Billy Meredith, playing his last international at the age of 45, inspired a 2-1 win over England at Highbury. Wales also topped the table in 1924, 1928, 1933, 1934, and 1937 – but failed to do so thereafter, even in the heyday of the brothers Allchurch and Charles.

England v. Scotland, Wembley 1951. Tom Finney, Preston's great goal-scoring winger, lobs the ball over Scotland 'keeper Jimmy Cowan for England's second goal. Behind Finney, and too late to get in his tackle, is Scotland's captain George Young. Scotland won 3-2.

And even two of these dates will be remembered less for Welsh triumphs than for events surrounding England and Scotland. In 1928 an England side with Dixie Dean at centre-forward achieved the unlikely feat of losing to Ireland in Belfast, to Wales at Burnley – and then (without Dean) to Scotland's 'Wembley Wizards' by five goals to one. Right-winger Alex Jackson scored a hat-trick for a Scottish side containing nine changes after losing to Ireland; in addition to Jackson the forward line – probably the greatest ever to represent Scotland – included Hughie Gallacher at centre forward, Alex James (who scored the other two goals) at inside left, and Alan Morton on the left wing. The year 1937 was notable for an attendance figure at Hampden Park for the Scotland-England game of 149,547 – believed to be the largest-ever anywhere in Europe.

From the Second World War until the end of the tournament in 1984, England were the dominant force. Scotland were unable to beat them between 1951 and 1961 and between 1967 and 1973, and won the title outright only seven times in 37 years. In 1955 they suffered a 2-7 defeat, Dennis Wilshaw scoring four of England's goals; and in 1961 poor goalkeeper Frank Haffey immortalised himself in the history of the oldest international by conceding nine.

The Scots had their moments, of course, especially at Wembley, which up to 70,000 of them invaded every two years. In 1967 the team inspired by Dennis Law and Jim Baxter became the first to beat England since Bobby Moore had held up the World Cup. Within a decade, after Scots fans had torn up the goalposts to celebrate one success, the FA secretary Ted Croker tried to stop them getting tickets altogether – not one of his more successful ideas.

While the England-Scotland fixture re-

BRITISH HOME INTERNATIONAL CHAMPIONSHIP WINNERS 1883-1984

Until 1980 the title was shared when teams finished with the same number of points. Since then it has been decided on goal difference when necessary.

1883-4 Scotland	1919-20 Wales	1956-7 England
1884-5 Scotland	1920-1 Scotland	1957-8 England, N. Ireland
1885-6 England, Scotland	1921-2 Scotland	1958-9 England, N. Ireland
1886-7 Scotland	1922-3 Scotland	1959-60 England, Scotland, Wales
1887-8 England	1923-4 Wales	
1888-9 Scotland	1924-5 Scotland	1960-1 England
1889-90 England, Scotland	1925-6 Scotland	1961-2 Scotland
1890-1 England	1926-7 England, Scotland	1962-3 Scotland
1891-2 England	1927-8 Wales	1963-4 England, Scotland, N. Ireland
1892-3 England	1928-9 Scotland	
1893-4 Scotland	1929-30 England	1964-5 England
1894-5 England	1930-1 England, Scotland	1965-6 England
1895-6 Scotland	1931-2 England	1966-7 Scotland
1896-7 Scotland	1932-3 Wales	1967-8 England
1897-8 England	1933-4 Wales	1968-9 England
1898-9 England	1934-5 England, Scotland	1969-70 England, Scotland, Wales
1899-00 Scotland	1935-6 Scotland	
1900-1 England	1936-7 Wales	1970-1 England
1901-2 Scotland	1937-8 England	1971-2 England, Scotland
1902-3 England, Ireland, Scotland	1938-9 England, Scotland, Wales	1972-3 England
		1973-4 England, Scotland
1903-4 England	1939-46 *no competition*	1974-5 England
1904-5 England	1946-7 England	1975-6 Scotland
1905-6 England, Scotland	1947-8 England	1976-7 Scotland
1906-7 Wales	1948-9 Scotland	1977-8 England
1907-8 England, Scotland	1949-50 England	1978-9 England
1908-9 England	1950-1 Scotland	1979-80 N. Ireland
1909-10 Scotland	1951-2 England, Wales	1980-1 not completed
1910-11 England	1952-3 England, Scotland	1981-2 England
1911-12 England, Scotland	1953-4 England	1982-3 England
1912-13 England	1954-5 England	1983-4 N. Ireland
1913-14 Ireland	1955-6 England, Scotland, N.Ireland, Wales	
1914-19 *no competition*		

Above *Wales v. Scotland, Cardiff 1956. Welsh maestro John Charles climbs above a Scottish defender to direct a powerful header past the goalkeeper.*

Below *England v. Northern Ireland, Wembley 1959. Captains Ronnie Clayton (England, left) and Danny Blanchflower, both of them wing-halves. Blanchflower, probably Northern Ireland's greatest post-war captain, was an inspiring leader and a shrewd tactician – qualities that helped him lead Tottenham to the League and Cup double two years later.*

ENGLAND v SCOTLAND
Official Internationals 1872-1984

Month	Year	Venue	E	S	Month	Year	Venue	E	S	Month	Year	Venue	E	S
Nov	1872	Glasgow	0	0	April	1907	Newcastle	1	1	April	1953	Wembley	2	2
March	1873	Kennington	4	2	April	1988	Glasgow	1	1	April	1954	Glasgow	4	2
March	1874	Glasgow	1	2	April	1909	Crystal Pal.	2	0	April	1955	Wembley	7	2
March	1875	Kennington	2	2	April	1910	Glasgow	0	2	April	1956	Glasgow	1	1
March	1876	Glasgow	0	3	April	1911	Everton	1	1	April	1957	Wembley	2	1
March	1877	Kennington	1	3	March	1912	Glasgow	1	1	April	1958	Glasgow	4	0
March	1878	Glasgow	2	7	April	1913	Chelsea	1	0	April	1959	Wembley	1	0
April	1879	Kennington	5	4	April	1914	Glasgow	1	3	April	1960	Glasgow	1	1
March	1880	Glasgow	4	5	April	1920	Sheffield	5	4	April	1961	Wembley	9	3
March	1881	Kennington	1	6	April	1921	Glasgow	0	3	April	1962	Glasgow	0	2
March	1882	Glasgow	1	5	April	1922	Aston Villa	0	1	April	1963	Wembley	1	2
March	1883	Sheffield	2	3	April	1923	Glasgow	2	2	April	1964	Glasgow	0	1
March	1884	Glasgow	0	1	April	1924	Wembley	1	1	April	1965	Wembley	2	2
March	1806	Glasgow	1	1	April	1925	Glasgow	0	2	April	1966	Glasgow	4	3
March	1887	Blackburn	2	3	April	1926	Manchester	0	1	April	1967	Wembley	2	3
March	1888	Glasgow	5	0	April	1927	Glasgow	2	1	Feb	1968	Glasgow	1	1
April	1889	Kennington	2	3	March	1928	Wembley	1	5	May	1969	Wembley	4	1
April	1890	Glasgow	1	1	April	1929	Glasgow	0	1	April	1970	Glasgow	0	0
April	1891	Blackburn	2	1	April	1930	Wembley	5	2	May	1971	Wembley	3	1
April	1892	Glasgow	4	1	March	1931	Glasgow	0	2	May	1972	Glasgow	1	0
April	1893	Richmond	5	2	April	1932	Wembley	3	0	Feb	1973	Glasgow	5	0
April	1894	Glasgow	2	2	April	1933	Glasgow	1	2	May	1973	Wembley	1	0
April	1895	Everton	3	0	April	1934	Wembley	3	0	May	1974	Glasgow	0	2
April	1896	Glasgow	1	2	April	1935	Glasgow	0	2	May	1975	Wembley	5	1
April	1897	Crystal Pal.	1	2	April	1936	Wembley	1	1	May	1976	Glasgow	1	2
April	1898	Glasgow	3	1	April	1937	Glasgow	1	3	June	1977	Wembley	1	2
April	1899	Birmingham	2	1	April	1938	Wembley	0	1	May	1978	Glasgow	1	0
April	1900	Glasgow	1	4	April	1939	Glasgow	2	1	May	1979	Wembley	3	1
March	1901	Crystal Pal.	2	2	April	1947	Wembley	1	1	May	1980	Glasgow	2	0
May	1902	Birmingham	2	2	April	1948	Glasgow	2	0	May	1981	Wembley	0	1
April	1903	Sheffield	1	2	April	1949	Wembley	1	3	May	1982	Glasgow	1	0
April	1904	Glasgow	1	0	April	1950	Glasgow	1	0	June	1983	Wembley	2	0
April	1905	Crystal Pal.	1	0	April	1951	Wembley	2	3	May	1984	Glasgow	1	1
April	1906	Glasgow	1	1	April	1952	Glasgow	2	1	May	1985	Glasgow	0	1

Unofficial Internationals

			E	S				E	S				E	S
April	1902	Glasgow	1	1	May	1941	Glasgow	3	1	Feb	1944	Wembley	6	2
April	1919	Everton	2	2	Oct	1941	Wembley	2	0	April	1944	Glasgow	3	2
May	1919	Glasgow	4	3	Jan	1942	Wembley	3	0	Oct	1944	Wembley	6	2
August	1935	Glasgow	2	4	April	1942	Glasgow	4	5	Feb	1945	Aston Villa	3	2
Dec	1939	Newcastle	2	1	Oct	1942	Wembley	0	0	April	1945	Glasgow	6	1
May	1940	Glasgow	1	1	April	1943	Glasgow	4	0	April	1946	Glasgow	0	1
Feb	1941	Newcastle	2	3	Oct	1943	Manchester	8	0					

Notes: Until March 1884 the matches were all friendlies; all matches thereafter were in the home international championship, except these unofficial internationals and the match in February 1973 (which celebrated the Scottish FA centenary). In addition, the games in 1950 and 1954 also counted as World Cup qualifying matches, and the games in 1967 and 1968 counted as European Championship qualifiers.

mained the be-all and end-all for many Scots, others became aware that international football existed outside the gates of Hampden and Wembley. In 1950 and 1954 the home international championship was used as a qualifying group for the World Cup, and in 1966-8 for the European Championship. England qualified on all three occasions, the Scots refusing to go to the 1950 World Cup finals with them because they had finished only second!

The England-Scotland fixture will live on, probably as long as the sport itself. This is no consolation to Ireland and Wales, who believe they have done more than just made up the numbers since 1884 and whose associations have depended greatly on the fixtures for their income. It was appropriate that one of them should take a title in the modern era. The Irish did so by winning at Cardiff in 1980; and they claimed another (unsuccessfully) the following year, when England and Wales declined to visit Belfast, leaving the tournament unfinished for the first and only time.

The importance of genuinely international, rather than just British, football, and the need to prepare for international competition as thoroughly as possible, meant that the match between Scotland and England in Glasgow in May 1984 marked the end of the Home Championship, 100 years after it had begun.

Scotland v. England, Hampden Park 1974. Jimmy Johnstone gets an assisted take-off from England back Mike Pejic. Johnstone, often a matchwinner for Celtic, was in the Scotland tradition of small, fast wingers with the sort of ball control that could tie defences into knots. On this occasion he helped Scotland beat the 'auld enemy' for the first time in seven years.

EUROPEAN CHAMPIONSHIP

Originally known as the European Nations' Cup, the tournament was launched in 1960. It did not get off to the best of starts, with only 18 nations competing and one of those (Spain) withdrawing at the quarter-final stage rather than face the USSR. True to form, in view of their past suspicion of the World Cup and European club tournaments, the four UK nations declined to take part. The Republic of Ireland entered but did not last long, being eliminated by the Czechs in a preliminary-round tie despite winning in Dublin. The Final, between the USSR and Yugoslavia, was not a particularly memorable affair: Netto put through his own goal to give Yugoslavia the lead, only for Metreveli to equalise and Ponedelnik to score the winner in extra-time. France, who had scored freely in the tournament's early stages, lost an extraordinary semi-final to the Yugoslavs and ultimately were denied even the satisfaction of third place by the Czechs.

From this relatively inauspicious beginning, the tournament began to take shape. A format was agreed whereby the preliminary qualifying stages would be played in the two years immediately following the World Cup finals, with the last stages taking place prior to the start of the build-up to the next World Cup. England, Wales, and Northern Ireland all entered the 1964 championship; Scotland, for reasons that presumably made sense to them, did not.

As in the previous tournament, progress was on a straightforward knockout basis. In the 1st round England were paired with France, drawing the home leg 1-1, only to be thrashed 2-5 in Paris – a defeat that led to the Football Association replacing manager Walter Winterbottom with Alf Ramsey. Wales fared little better, losing 1-3 away to Hungary and only drawing the return 1-1; but Northern Ireland at least made it to the 2nd round, beating Poland 2-0 both at home and away before going out by the narrowest margin against Spain, drawing the away leg 1-1 only to lose 0-1 in Belfast. Spain went on to win the championship, beating the USSR in Madrid, while the Hungarians finished third.

For the next championships, in Rome in 1968, qualifying groups were introduced for the first time. England, by virtue of their World Cup success in 1966, were the clear favourites to win. The Home Championship became the qualifying group, which England made rather heavy work of winning, losing 2-3 to Scotland at Wembley, but getting the draw they needed to qualify in the game at Hampden. In the quarter-finals, England justified their position as tournament favourites by beating Spain both at home and away, but their semi-final against Yugoslavia is remembered not for the loss to the great winger Dragan Dzajic's late goal, but for the sending-off of Alan Mullery, who thus achieved the dubious distinction of becoming the first player in history to receive his marching orders while wearing an England shirt.

In 1972 England reached the quarter-finals without losing a game, although they allowed Switzerland the glory of a 1-1 draw at Wembley; Greece and Malta, the other opposition, provided few problems. Wales, faced with Czechoslovakia, Romania and Finland, beat the latter at home and away, but lost all their other games. Northern Ireland, in another tough qualifying group with the USSR, Spain and Cyprus, coped with the last easily enough and held both Spain and the USSR to 1-1 draws in Belfast—fine results, but not good enough to qualify. Scotland fancied their chances against Belgium, Portugal, and Denmark, but after opening their campaign with a laboured 1-0 home win against the Danes, lost three successive away games, including the return to Denmark, to go out of contention.

England's bid to emulate the feats of 1968 came sadly unstuck at Wembley, however, where West Germany avenged their 1966 World Cup Final defeat with a Günter Netzer-inspired 3-1 win that was even more emphatic than the score suggests. The 1-1 draw England managed in the return was not enough to save

Final 1976: Antonin Panenka (Czechoslavakia) turns away after scoring the fifth, and decisive, penalty against West Germany in the shoot-out after the extra-time score deadlocked at 2-2.

them. The Germans then got the better of Belgium in the semi-finals before sweeping past the USSR in the Final, with Gerd Müller scoring two of their three goals.

England opened their 1976 campaign with a 3-0 victory at Wembley against the Czech side destined to become champions of Europe; but—as later results showed—they lost their chance of qualifying for the quarter-finals by allowing Portugal to draw 0-0 at Wembley. The next home game, against Cyprus, was won 5-0 and enabled England centre-forward Malcolm Macdonald to claim a record of sorts by scoring all five goals – the first Englishman to achieve such a feat since Willie Hall in 1938. Scotland, too, fell by the wayside. Grouped with Denmark, Spain and Romania, they beat the Danes home and away, but failed to win another game. Northern Ireland performed bravely, beating the ultimate qualifiers, Yugoslavia, in Belfast and winning in Sweden; but a home defeat by the Swedes and an away loss to Norway put paid to their chances.

No such problems for Wales, though, who achieved a minor miracle to win a qualifying group containing Austria, Hungary, and Luxembourg. Their luck ran out against Yugoslavia in the quarter-finals, however, when they lost 2-0 away and managed only to draw the return 1-1. Most neutral football followers were hoping for a repeat of the 1974 World Cup Final, and their wishes seemed to have been granted when both West Germany and Holland were

kept apart by the semi-final draw. Inexplicably, the Dutch lost in extra-time to Czechoslovakia, while West Germany were also taken to extra-time by Yugoslavia. That the Germans eventually won, however, made them hot favourites in the Final.

That Final produced one of football's more satisfying upsets. The Czechs seemed to have the game won before Holzenbein's late equaliser sent the game into a scoreless extra-time. That thoroughly unsatisfactory modern invention, the penalty shoot-out, was used to settle the outcome, and thanks to some uncharacteristic nervousness on the part of the Germans and some fine goalkeeping by the Czechs' Ivo Viktor, the underdogs won the penalties 5-3. Holland, meanwhile, recovered their composure and, although taken once more to extra-time, beat Yugoslavia 3-2 to take third place.

The format for the 1980 championships was changed again, with two four-team leagues, the winners of which would contest the Final, replacing the quarter- and semi-final stages. England qualified in decisive style, winning all their games except for a 1-1 away draw in the Republic of Ireland, although they were given an almighty fright in Denmark before winning 4-3. Scotland once again performed lamentably, beating Norway at home and away, but failing to make any impression against Austria, Portugal or Belgium. Wales had the misfortune to be paired with West Germany, and although the Germans suffered from two goal-less draws

Quarter Finals 1972: West Germany completely outclassed England at Wembley, the score of 3-1 doing scant justice to their superiority. From left, in this England attack: Alan Ball, Gerd Müller, Colin Bell, Francis Lee, Paul Breitner, Martin Chivers, Franz Beckenbauer, Günther Netzer.

Group 2, 1980: Trevor Brooking and his Belgian counterpart Wilfried van Moer. The match ended in a 1-1 draw.

away to Malta and Turkey in that group, they were still powerful enough to qualify. Northern Ireland, in the same group as England, the Republic of Ireland, and Denmark, suffered two heavy defeats at English hands – 1-5 in Belfast and 0-4 at Wembley.

In the final stages, with the knock-out element removed, the league play-offs were tedious affairs, particularly in the group containing England, Italy, Spain and Belgium. Italy, placing faith in their superb defence, contrived to score just once in three games – good enough for the third place match, but not for the Final, which was reached from that group by Belgium.

The other group at least produced goals, though the issue became a foregone conclusion once West Germany had won their two opening matches and Czechoslovakia had surrendered any lingering hopes they might have held with a 1-1 draw with Holland.

The Final itself was not a game to linger in the memory. The Belgian defence was not good enough to contain the Germans, for whom the giant Hrubesch scored twice. Van der Eycken replied for Belgium, but that was to be their only response. Italy meanwhile received their comeuppance in an eccentric penalty decider against the Czechs after a 1-1 draw in the third place match. Awakening memories of their shoot-out against West Germany four years previously, the Czechs won this one too, although it took them rather longer, 9-8 being the eventual outcome.

THE EUROPEAN CHAMPIONSHIP
1960: FRANCE

(* = team at home in first leg; score in each leg in parentheses; aet = after extra time)

Quarter finals
Yugoslavia 6 *Portugal 3 (1-2; 5-1)
*France 9 Austria 4 (5-2; 4-2)
Czechoslovakia 5 *Romania 0 (2-0; 3-0)
USSR had walkover (Spain withdrew)
Semi-finals
Yugoslavia 5 France 4

USSR 3 Czechoslovakia 0
Third place match
Czechoslovakia 2 France 0
Final
USSR 2 Yugoslavia 1

1964: SPAIN
Quarter-finals
Denmark 6 *Luxembourg 5 (2-2; 3-3; 1-0)
*Spain 7 Republic of Ireland 1 (5-1; 2-0)
Hungary 5 *France 2 (3-1; 2-1)
USSR 4 *Sweden 2 (1-1; 3-1)
Semi-finals
USSR 3 Denmark 0
Spain 2 Hungary 1
Third place match
Hungary 3 Denmark 1 (aet)
Final
Spain 2 USSR 1

1968: ITALY
Quarter-finals
*England 3 Spain 1 (1-0; 2-1)
Italy 4 *Bulgaria 3 (2-3; 2-0)
Yugoslavia 6 *France 2 (1-1; 5-1)
USSR 3 *Hungary 2 (0-2; 3-0)
Semi-finals
Yugoslavia 1 England 0
Italy 0 USSR 0 (aet; Italy won on toss of coin)
Third place match
England 2 USSR 0
Final
Italy 2 Yugoslavia 0 (after 1-1 draw)

1972: BELGIUM
Quarter-finals
West Germany 3 *England 1 (3-1; 0-0)
Belgium 2 *Italy 1 (0-0; 2-1)
*Hungary 5 Romania 4 (1-1; 2-2; 2-1)
USSR 3 *Yugoslavia 0 (0-0; 3-0)
Semi-finals
USSR 1 Hungary 0
West Germany 2 Belgium 1
Third place match
Belgium 2 Hungary 1
Final
West Germany 3 USSR 0

1976: YUGOSLAVIA
Quarter-finals
West Germany 3 *Spain 1 (1-1; 2-0)
*Yugoslavia 3 Wales 1 (2-0; 1-1)
*Czechoslovakia 4 USSR 2 (2-0; 2-2)
*Holland 7 Belgium 1 (5-0; 2-1)
Semi-finals
Czechoslovakia 3 Holland 1 (aet)
West Germany 4 Yugoslavia 2 (aet)
Third place match
Holland 3 Yugoslavia 2 (aet)
Final
Czechoslovakia 2 West Germany 2 (aet; Czechoslovakia won 5-3 on penalties)

1980: ITALY
Group 1
West Germany 1 Czechoslovakia 0
Holland 1 Greece 0
West Germany 3 Holland 2
Czechoslovakia 3 Greece 1

Czechoslovakia 1 Holland 1
West Germany 0 Greece 0

	P	W	D	L	F	A	Pts
West Germany	3	2	1	0	4	2	5
Czechoslovakia	3	1	1	1	4	3	3
Holland	3	1	1	1	4	4	3
Greece	3	0	1	2	1	4	1

Group 2
Belgium 1 England 1
Spain 0 Italy 0
Belgium 2 Spain 1
Italy 1 England 0
England 2 Spain 1
Italy 0 Belgium 0

	P	W	D	L	F	A	Pts
Belgium	3	1	2	0	3	2	4
Italy	3	1	2	0	1	0	4
England	3	1	1	1	3	3	3
Spain	3	0	1	2	2	4	1

Third place match
Czechoslovakia 1 Italy 1 (aet; Czechoslovakia
won 9-8 on penalties)
Final
West Germany 2 Belgium 1

1984: FRANCE

Four years later, the tournament staged in
France was as uplifting as the Italian one had
been depressing. Britain was unfortunate – in
every sense – not to have a single representative
among the eight qualifiers. Northern Ireland
finished second to West Germany on goal difference despite beating them at home and away
(Norman Whiteside's goal securing a famous
victory in Hamburg); Wales failed when Yugoslavia scored a last-minute goal to beat Bulgaria;
England had the best goal difference of all 32
teams (23 against 3) but the penalty converted by
Allan Simonsen at Wembley ultimately gave
Denmark victory in the group. Only Scotland
were consistently feeble, winning just one of
their six games against Belgium, East Germany
and Switzerland to finish bottom of their group.

In the championship finals the individual and
team skills displayed by France, Denmark and
Portugal in particular were a tonic. From the time
the first two opened Group 1 with a single-goal
victory to the French, it looked as though they
could go on and meet again in the final itself.
Denmark shrugged off that defeat (and the loss
of Simonsen with a broken leg) to demolish
Yugoslavia 5-0 and then came from behind to
beat Belgium 3-2. The host country matched
each performance exactly, beating Belgium 5-0
and then Yugoslavia 3-2, with the irresistible
Michel Platini scoring a hat-trick in each game –
from midfield!

The other group, featuring West Germany,
Spain, Portugal and Romania, was much tighter,
with the first three games drawn, then three
single-goal victories. A goal by Antonio Maceda
gave Spain a critical win over the Germans, who
failed to progress further when Nene's goal for
Portugal beat Romania.

So the Iberian peninsula had both countries
through as underdogs in the semi-finals, where
they found France and Denmark feeling the
strain. France were lifted by a crowd of 56,000 at
Marseille, where they came from 1-2 down in
extra-time to beat Portugal in probably the best
and certainly the most exciting match of the
tournament. Denmark could only draw with
Spain, who then won the penalty 'shoot-out' by
5-4.

The 'dream final', then, did not materialise,
and it was something of an anti-climax as the
weary French deservedly but laboriously beat
Spain with goals by Platini and Bruno Bellone. At
least the best team won the competition; and
Platini – unquestionably the star of the tournament – finished with nine goals, scoring at least
once in every game he played.

Group 1
France 1 Denmark 0; Belgium 2 Yugoslavia 0;
France 5 Belgium 0; Denmark 5 Yugoslavia 0;
France 3 Yugoslavia 2; Denmark 3 Belgium 2

	P	W	D	L	F	A	Pts
France	3	3	0	0	9	2	6
Denmark	3	2	0	1	8	3	4
Belgium	3	1	0	2	4	8	2
Yugoslavia	3	0	0	3	2	10	0

Group 2
W. Germany 0 Portugal 0; Romania 1 Spain 1;
Portugal 1 Spain 1; West Germany 2 Romania 1;
Portugal 1 Romania 0; West Germany 0 Spain 1

	P	W	D	L	F	A	Pts
Spain	3	1	2	0	3	2	4
Portugal	3	1	2	0	2	1	4
W. Germany	3	1	1	1	2	2	3
Romania	3	0	1	2	2	4	1

Semi-finals
France 3 Portugal 2 (aet)
Spain 1 Denmark 1 (aet: Spain won 5-4 on pens.)

Final
France 2 Spain 0

Below Final, 1984: first goal.
Michel Platini (blue shirt), the
greatest European footballer of
the mid-1980s, bends his free
kick around the Spanish wall.
Luis Arconada, Spain's keeper,
had the ball covered but
inexplicably allowed it to slip
through his hands. Bruno
Bellone added a second goal to
seal France's well-deserved
victory.

WORLD CUP

1930: URUGUAY

A variety of reasons led to Uruguay being chosen as host nation for the inaugural World Cup tournament: Uruguay had been the 1924 and 1928 Olympic champions; they promised to build a new stadium especially for the event, and to pay all the expenses of visiting teams; and 1930 also marked Uruguay's centenary as a nation. The event attracted only 13 countries. The four UK nations were not at that time members of FIFA – the International Federation of Football Associations, the game's governing body – and were therefore ineligible. Uruguay came through the entire competition undefeated to beat their dearest rivals Argentina, whom they had also beaten in the 1928 Olympic Final.

Group 1
France 4 Mexico 1
Argentina 1 France 0
Chile 3 Mexico 0
Chile 1 France 0
Argentina 6 Mexico 3
Argentina 3 Chile 1

	P	W	D	L	F	A	Pts
Argentina	3	3	0	0	10	4	6
Chile	3	2	0	1	5	3	4
France	3	1	0	2	4	3	2
Mexico	3	0	0	3	4	13	0

Group 2
Yugoslavia 2 Brazil 1
Yugoslavia 4 Bolivia 0
Brazil 4 Bolivia 0

	P	W	D	L	F	A	Pts
Yugoslavia	2	2	0	0	6	1	4
Brazil	2	1	0	1	5	2	2
Bolivia	2	0	0	2	0	8	0

Group 3
Romania 3 Peru 1
Uruguay 1 Peru 0
Uruguay 4 Romania 0

	P	W	D	L	F	A	Pts
Uruguay	2	2	0	0	5	0	4
Romania	2	1	0	1	3	5	2
Peru	2	0	0	2	1	4	0

Group 4
USA 3 Belgium 0
USA 3 Paraguay 0
Paraguay 1 Belgium 0

	P	W	D	L	F	A	Pts
USA	2	2	0	0	6	0	4
Paraguay	2	1	0	1	1	3	2
Belgium	2	0	0	2	0	4	0

Semi-finals
Argentina 6 USA 1
Uruguay 6 Yugoslavia 1
Final
Uruguay 4 Argentina 2

1934: ITALY

A qualifying tournament was held for the first time, but defending champions Uruguay, in retaliation to the poor European response to the 1930 finals, boycotted the event. The four UK nations, who still had not joined FIFA, were once again absent. The format adopted in 1934 was a straightforward knock-out competition. Although Italy needed a replay to beat Spain in the second round, the host nation duly reached the Final and, despite falling behind, came back to equalise and then to win in extra time.

First round
Italy 7 USA 1
Czechoslovakia 2 Romania 1
Germany 5 Belgium 2
Austria 3 France 2 (aet)
Spain 3 Brazil 1
Switzerland 3 Holland 2
Sweden 3 Argentina 2
Hungary 4 Egypt 2
Second round
Germany 2 Sweden 1
Austria 2 Hungary 1
Italy 1 Spain 1 (aet)
Czechoslovakia 3 Switzerland 2
Replay: Italy 1 Spain 0
Semi-finals
Czechoslovakia 3 Germany 1
Italy 1 Austria 0
Third place match
Germany 3 Austria 2
Final
Italy 2 Czechoslovakia 1 (aet)

1938: FRANCE

Although still not members of FIFA, England were invited to participate in place of Austria, who had withdrawn for political reasons; the offer, however, was declined. Once the first round had been laboriously completed, France – who had been awarded the tournament as a tribute to FIFA President and World Cup mentor Jules Rimet (whose name the trophy was to bear until 1970) – succumbed to Italy, who then disposed of a talented Brazilian side in the semi-

Uruguay 1930: Jules Rimet presenting the trophy that bears his name to the president of Uruguay FA after the Uruguayans' victory in the first-ever World Cup.

finals before comfortably beating Hungary, to record their second successive tournament victory.

First round
Switzerland 1 Germany 1 (aet)
Cuba 3 Romania 3 (aet)
Hungary 6 Dutch East Indies 0
France 3 Belgium 1
Czechoslovakia 3 Holland 0 (aet)
Brazil 6 Poland 5 (aet)
Italy 2 Norway 1 (aet)
Replays: Switzerland 4 Germany 2
       Cuba 2 Romania 1
Second round
Sweden 8 Cuba 0
Hungary 2 Switzerland 0
Italy 3 France 1
Brazil 1 Czechoslovakia 1 (aet)
Replay: Brazil 2 Czechoslovakia 1
Semi-finals
Italy 2 Brazil 1
Hungary 5 Sweden 1
Third place match
Brazil 4 Sweden 2
Final
Italy 4 Hungary 2

1950: BRAZIL

With the UK nations at last members of FIFA, the Home Championship became a qualifying group, with the first two to go through. Scotland maintained they would enter the World Cup only as British champions; they ended as runners-up to England, and so did not participate. In the event, England might have wished they had followed suit: their inaugural World Cup ended with an ignominious 1-0 defeat by the United States. The results of a final group, which replaced the knock-out format, saw Brazil go into their last game against Uruguay needing only a draw to become world champions. A crowd of 200,000 in Rio's Maracaná Stadium watched Brazil score first, only for Uruguay to score twice to record an improbable win and their second World Cup.

Group 1
Brazil 4 Mexico 0
Yugoslavia 3 Switzerland 0
Yugoslavia 4 Mexico 1
Brazil 2 Switzerland 2
Brazil 2 Yugoslavia 0
Switzerland 2 Mexico 1

	P	W	D	L	F	A	Pts
Brazil	3	2	1	0	8	2	5
Yugoslavia	3	2	0	1	7	3	4
Switzerland	3	1	1	1	4	6	3
Mexico	3	0	0	3	2	10	0

Group 2
Spain 3 USA 1
England 2 Chile 0
USA 1 England 0
Spain 2 Chile 0
Spain 1 England 0
Chile 5 USA 2

	P	W	D	L	F	A	Pts
Spain	3	3	0	0	6	1	6
England	3	1	0	2	2	2	2
Chile	3	1	0	2	5	6	2
USA	3	1	0	2	4	8	2

Group 3
Sweden 3 Italy 2
Sweden 2 Paraguay 2
Italy 2 Paraguay 0

	P	W	D	L	F	A	Pts
Sweden	2	1	1	0	5	4	3
Italy	2	1	0	1	4	3	2
Paraguay	2	0	1	1	2	4	1

Above *France 1938: Guiseppe Meazza (left), captain and star of the Italian side shakes hands with the Hungarian captain Scarosi before the start of the Final. Meazza had also been a member of the victorious Italian side in 1934.*

Left *Brazil 1950: Zair (Brazil) heads over the bar with Maspoli, the Uruguay keeper, helpless in the last Final Group match of the tournament. Uruguay won 2-1 to take the trophy.*

Group 4
Uruguay 8 Bolivia 0

Final Group
Uruguay 2 Spain 2
Brazil 7 Sweden 1
Uruguay 3 Sweden 2
Brazil 6 Spain 1
Sweden 3 Spain 1
Uruguay 2 Brazil 1

	P	W	D	L	F	A	Pts
Uruguay	3	2	1	0	7	5	5
Brazil	3	2	0	1	14	4	4
Sweden	3	1	0	2	6	11	2
Spain	3	0	1	2	4	11	1

Winners Uruguay

1954: SWITZERLAND

World champions Uruguay thrashed Scotland and then comfortably disposed of England, who earlier had wasted a 3-1 lead over Belgium. Despite the South American threat, however, Hungary – fresh from their 6-3 and 7-1 annihilations of England – were the hot favourites. They boasted a superlatively gifted forward line consisting of Czibor, Kocsis, Hideguti, Puskás, and Toth, and played by far the most exciting football of any team in the tournament. But their overwhelming victory over West Germany in a Group 2 match was achieved against a deliberately weakened side who – had goal-average or goal-difference then been in operation – would have been eliminated, but who instead were faced with the simple task of beating Turkey in a play-off. Hungary's captain, Ferenc Puskás, the 'Galloping Major', had been injured in the first game against the Germans. He came back, only half-fit, for the Final and scored the opening goal. Hungary went on to lead 2-0, only for West Germany to equalise before half-time, and then score the winner in a second-half during which Hungary had a third goal disallowed. Kocsis was the tournament's top scorer with 11 goals.

Switzerland 1954: Morlock (West Germany) puts the ball past the Hungarian goalkeeper Grosics to cut the Hungarians' two-goal lead in the Final. Two goals by Helmut Rahn won the match for the Germans against a Hungarian team that had not been defeated for over four years.

Group 1
Yugoslavia 1 France 0
Brazil 5 Mexico 0
France 3 Mexico 2
Brazil 1 Yugoslavia 1 (aet)

	P	W	D	L	F	A	Pts
Brazil	2	1	1	0	6	1	3
Yugoslavia	2	1	1	0	2	2	3
France	2	1	0	1	3	3	2
Mexico	2	0	0	2	2	8	0

Group 2
Hungary 9 Korea 0
West Germany 4 Turkey 1
Hungary 8 West Germany 3
Turkey 7 Korea 0

	P	W	D	L	F	A	Pts
Hungary	2	2	0	0	17	3	4
West Germany	2	1	0	1	7	9	2
Turkey	2	1	0	1	8	4	2
Korea	2	0	0	2	0	16	0

Play-off: West Germany 7 Turkey 2

Group 3
Austria 1 Scotland 0
Uruguay 2 Czechoslovakia 0
Austria 5 Czechoslovakia 0
Uruguay 7 Scotland 0

	P	W	D	L	F	A	Pts
Uruguay	2	2	0	0	9	0	4
Austria	2	2	0	0	6	0	4
Czechoslovakia	2	0	0	2	0	7	0
Scotland	2	0	0	2	0	8	0

Group 4
England 4 Belgium 4 (aet)
England 2 Switzerland 0
Switzerland 2 Italy 1
Italy 4 Belgium 1

	P	W	D	L	F	A	Pts
England	2	1	1	0	6	4	3
Italy	2	1	0	1	5	3	2
Switzerland	2	1	0	1	2	3	2
Belgium	2	0	1	1	5	8	1

Play-off: Switzerland 4 Italy 1

Quarter-finals
West Germany 2 Yugoslavia 0
Hungary 4 Brazil 2
Austria 7 Switzerland 5
Uruguay 4 England 2
Semi-finals
West Germany 6 Austria 1
Hungary 4 Uruguay 2 (aet)
Third place match
Austria 3 Uruguay 1
Final
West Germany 3 Hungary 2

1958: SWEDEN

For the first and only time all four UK nations qualified. Scotland again sank without trace; Northern Ireland, increasingly beset by injuries, performed heroically before running out of steam against the brilliant French; Wales were no less admirable, disposing of a Hungarian side that had lost many of its stars after the 1956

uprising, and losing their quarter-final only to a Brazilian goal scored by the still unknown 17-year-old, Pelé. England succeeded where others failed in preventing Brazil scoring, but were a little unluckily eliminated by the USSR. The Final saw the birth of a legend, both nationally – as Brazil recorded their first win – and personally – with two goals from Pelé. France also added lustre to the tournament, with Raymond Kopa and Juste Fontaine brilliant. Fontaine's 13 goals remains a World Cup record.

Group 1
West Germany 3 Argentina 1
Northern Ireland 1 Czechoslovakia 0
West Germany 2 Czechoslovakia 2
Argentina 3 Northern Ireland 1
West Germany 2 Northern Ireland 2
Czechoslovakia 6 Argentina 1

	P	W	D	L	F	A	Pts
West Germany	3	1	2	0	7	5	4
Czechoslovakia	3	1	1	1	8	4	3
Northern Ireland	3	1	1	1	4	5	3
Argentina	3	1	0	2	4	10	2

Play-off:
Northern Ireland 2 Czechoslovakia 1 (aet)

Group 2
France 7 Paraguay 3
Yugoslavia 1 Scotland 1
Yugoslavia 3 France 2
Paraguay 3 Scotland 2
France 2 Scotland 1
Yugoslavia 3 Paraguay 3

	P	W	D	L	F	A	Pts
France	3	2	0	1	11	7	4
Yugoslavia	3	1	2	0	7	6	4
Paraguay	3	1	1	1	9	12	3
Scotland	3	0	1	2	4	6	1

Group 3
Sweden 3 Mexico 0
Hungary 1 Wales 1
Wales 1 Mexico 1
Sweden 2 Hungary 1
Sweden 0 Wales 0
Hungary 4 Mexico 0

	P	W	D	L	F	A	Pts
Sweden	3	2	1	0	5	1	5
Hungary	3	1	1	1	6	3	3
Wales	3	0	3	0	2	2	3
Mexico	3	0	1	2	1	8	1

Play-off: Wales 2 Hungary 1

Group 4
England 2 USSR 2
Brazil 3 Austria 0
England 0 Brazil 0
USSR 2 Austria 0
Brazil 2 USSR 0
England 2 Austria 2

	P	W	D	L	F	A	Pts
Brazil	3	2	1	0	5	0	5
England	3	0	3	0	4	4	3
USSR	3	1	1	1	4	4	3
Austria	3	0	1	2	2	7	1

Play-off: USSR 1 England 0

Quarter-finals
France 4 Northern Ireland 0
West Germany 1 Yugoslavia 0
Sweden 2 USSR 0
Brazil 1 Wales 0

Semi-finals
Brazil 5 France 2
Sweden 3 West Germany 1

Third place match
France 6 West Germany 3

Final
Brazil 5 Sweden 2

Sweden 1958: Pelé scores Brazil's third goal in the final against Sweden. He and Garrincha – the two supreme virtuosos of Brazilian football – reduced to tatters a Swedish defence that had conceded only two goals in the previous rounds.

Chile 1962: Zito celebrates scoring Brazil's second goal in the final against Czechoslovakia. The Czechs, marshalled by the great midfielder Josef Masopust and with Garrincha kept on a tight rein by left back Novak, had more than their share of the action until goalkeeper error allowed Vavá to tap in Brazil's third goal about 10 minutes from the end.

1962: CHILE

With goal average at last replacing the outmoded play-off system, England carried the flag – albeit haltingly – into the quarter finals, where Brazil thrust them aside with little difficulty. Brazil were now without Pelé, injured in their second match, against Czechoslovakia. But with Zito and Didi in midfield, and with the amazing Garrincha devouring defences at will on the right wing, they had talent enough to cruise through to the Final. That the Czechs had earlier held them to a goal-less draw prompted some thoughts of an upset; but goalkeeper Marian Schroiff, who had excelled in the first game, had a nightmare match and, although Josef Masopust scored first for Czechoslovakia, Amarildo, Zito and Vavá gave the Brazilians their second World Cup win. Top scorer was Jerkovic (Yugoslavia) with 5 goals.

Group 1
Uruguay 2 Colombia 1
USSR 2 Yugoslavia 0
Yugoslavia 3 Uruguay 1
USSR 4 Colombia 4
USSR 2 Uruguay 1
Yugoslavia 5 Colombia 0

	P	W	D	L	F	A	Pts
USSR	3	2	1	0	8	5	5
Yugoslavia	3	2	0	1	8	3	4
Uruguay	3	1	0	2	4	6	2
Colombia	3	0	1	2	5	11	1

Group 2
Chile 3 Switzerland 1
West Germany 0 Italy 0
Chile 2 Italy 0
West Germany 2 Switzerland 1
West Germany 2 Chile 0
Italy 3 Switzerland 0

	P	W	D	L	F	A	Pts
West Germany	3	2	1	0	4	1	5
Chile	3	2	0	1	5	3	4
Italy	3	1	1	1	3	2	3
Switzerland	3	0	0	3	2	8	0

Group 3
Brazil 2 Mexico 0
Czechoslovakia 1 Spain 0
Brazil 0 Czechoslovakia 0
Spain 2 Mexico 0
Brazil 2 Spain 1
Mexico 3 Czechoslovakia 1

	P	W	D	L	F	A	Pts
Brazil	3	2	1	0	4	1	5
Czechoslovakia	3	1	1	1	2	3	3
Mexico	3	1	0	2	3	4	2
Spain	3	1	0	2	2	3	2

Group 4
Argentina 1 Bulgaria 0
Hungary 2 England 1
England 3 Argentina 1
Hungary 6 Bulgaria 1
Argentina 0 Hungary 0
England 0 Bulgaria 0

	P	W	D	L	F	A	Pts
Hungary	3	2	1	0	8	2	5
England	3	1	1	1	4	3	3
Argentina	3	1	1	1	2	3	3
Bulgaria	3	0	1	2	1	7	1

Quarter-finals
Yugoslavia 1 West Germany 0
Brazil 3 England 1
Chile 2 USSR 1
Czechoslovakia 1 Hungary 0

Semi-finals
Brazil 4 Chile 2
Czechoslovakia 3 Yugoslavia 1

Third place match
Chile 1 Yugoslavia 0

Final
Brazil 3 Czechoslovakia 1

1966: ENGLAND

An inauspicious goal-less draw against Uruguay gave little hint of the glory to come England's way, despite the unswerving insistence of manager Alf Ramsey that his side *would* win the Cup. A typical Bobby Charlton piledriver and a Roger Hunt effort disposed of Mexico; then Hunt scored twice against France. Elsewhere, North Korea became folk heroes by beating Italy; Brazil were eclipsed first by Hungary and then by a Portuguese side, built around the excellent Benfica team, which combined superlative football with the successful determination to kick Pelé out of the tournament.

Geoff Hurst, replacing the injured Jimmy Greaves, scored England's quarter-final goal against Argentina, whose captain – Antonio Rattín – was sent off; the Koreans gave Portugal the fright of their collective lives, at one stage leading 3-0 before sheer inexperience and four goals by the great Eusebio consigned them once more to soccer's backwaters. Eusebio's semi-final penalty was the first goal scored against England in the tournament, but Bobby Charlton replied with two to send England into a Final against an ominously impressive West German side containing some prodigious talents, including a precocious Franz Beckenbauer, already the scorer of four goals en route to Wembley. Within 15 minutes Helmut Haller had put the Germans one-up, only for Hurst to equalise almost immediately. A second-half Martin Peters goal seemed to have settled matters until Wolfgang Weber scored in the very last second of normal time. The extra-time drama is now history. Arguments still rage as to whether, in Hurst's second goal and England's third, the ball *did* cross the line after rebounding from the bar, but there was no doubt at all about the goal that gave Hurst his hat-trick (still the only one to be scored in a World Cup Final), and earned a vindicated Alf Ramsey his knighthood.

Group 1
England 0 Uruguay 0
France 1 Mexico 1
Uruguay 2 France 1
England 2 Mexico 0
Uruguay 0 Mexico 0
England 2 France 0

	P	W	D	L	F	A	Pts
England	3	2	1	0	4	0	5
Uruguay	3	1	2	0	2	1	4
Mexico	3	0	2	1	1	3	2
France	3	0	1	2	2	5	1

Group 2
West Germany 5 Switzerland 0
Argentina 2 Spain 1
Spain 2 Switzerland 1
Argentina 0 West Germany 0
Argentina 2 Switzerland 0
West Germany 2 Spain 1

	P	W	D	L	F	A	Pts
West Germany	3	2	1	0	7	1	5
Argentina	3	2	1	0	4	1	5
Spain	3	1	0	2	4	5	2
Switzerland	3	0	0	3	1	9	0

Group 3
Brazil 2 Bulgaria 0
Portugal 3 Hungary 1
Hungary 3 Brazil 1
Portugal 3 Bulgaria 0
Portugal 3 Brazil 1
Hungary 3 Bulgaria 1

	P	W	D	L	F	A	Pts
Portugal	3	3	0	0	9	2	6
Hungary	3	2	0	1	7	5	4
Brazil	3	1	0	2	4	6	2
Bulgaria	3	0	0	3	1	8	0

Group 4
USSR 3 North Korea 0
Italy 2 Chile 0
Chile 1 North Korea 1
USSR 1 Italy 0
North Korea 1 Italy 0
USSR 2 Chile 1

	P	W	D	L	F	A	Pts
USSR	3	3	0	0	6	1	6
North Korea	3	1	1	1	2	4	3
Italy	3	1	0	2	2	2	2
Chile	3	0	1	2	2	5	1

Quarter-finals
England 1 Argentina 0
West Germany 4 Uruguay 0
Portugal 5 North Korea 3
USSR 2 Hungary 1

Semi-finals
West Germany 2 USSR 1
England 2 Portugal 1

Third place match
Portugal 2 USSR 1

Final
England 4 West Germany 2 (aet)

England 1966: Captain Bobby Moore triumphantly holds aloft the trophy after England had beaten West Germany in extra time. From left: Nobby Stiles and Jack Charlton, Gordon Banks, Alan Ball, Martin Peters, Geoff Hurst, Moore, Ray Wilson, George Cohen, Bobby Charlton; out of the picture was Roger Hunt.

1970: MEXICO

Having squeezed through to the quarter-finals, England squandered a brilliantly taken 2-0 lead against West Germany, losing in extra time. Undoubtedly affected by Mexico City's high altitude, the Germans finally ran out of steam in an extra-time thriller against Italy, who themselves then succumbed in the Final to arguably the best of Brazil's World Cup-winning sides, with Pelé, Gerson and Tostão, at the height of their powers and Rivelino a fearsome dead-ball striker. This victory – the Brazilians' third – gave them outright possession of the Jules Rimet Trophy. The tournament's leading scorer was the great West German striker Gerd Müller, with 10 goals.

Group 1
Mexico 0 USSR 0
Belgium 3 El Salvador 0
USSR 4 Belgium 1
Mexico 4 El Salvador 0
Mexico 1 Belgium 0

	P	W	D	L	F	A	Pts
USSR	3	2	1	0	6	1	2
Mexico	3	2	1	0	5	0	5
Belgium	3	1	0	2	4	5	2
El Salvador	3	0	0	3	0	9	0

Group 2
Uruguay 2 Israel 0
Italy 1 Sweden 0
Uruguay 0 Italy 0
Israel 1 Sweden 1
Sweden 1 Uruguay 0
Israel 0 Italy 0

	P	W	D	L	F	A	Pts
Italy	3	1	2	0	1	0	4
Uruguay	3	1	1	1	2	1	3
Sweden	3	1	1	1	2	2	3
Israel	3	0	2	1	1	3	2

Mexico 1970: Tostão (9) in a near miss for Brazil in the final against Italy. The free-scoring Brazilians (they totalled 19 for the tournament) were more than a match for the cautious Italians and overwhelmed them in the second half with an exhilarating display of attacking football.

Group 3
England 1 Romania 0
Brazil 4 Czechoslovakia 1
Romania 2 Czechoslovakia 1
Brazil 1 England 0
Brazil 3 Romania 2
England 1 Czechoslovakia 0

	P	W	D	L	F	A	Pts
Brazil	3	3	0	0	8	3	6
England	3	2	0	1	2	1	4
Romania	3	1	0	2	4	5	2
Czechoslovakia	3	0	0	3	2	7	0

Group 4
Peru 3 Bulgaria 2
West Germany 2 Morocco 1
Peru 3 Morocco 0
West Germany 5 Bulgaria 2
West Germany 3 Peru 1
Bulgaria 1 Morocco 1

	P	W	D	L	F	A	Pts
West Germany	3	3	0	0	10	4	6
Peru	3	2	0	1	7	5	4
Bulgaria	3	0	1	2	5	9	1
Morocco	3	0	1	2	2	6	1

Quarter-finals
Uruguay 1 USSR 0 (aet)
Italy 4 Mexico 1
Brazil 4 Peru 2
West Germany 3 England 2 (aet)
Semi-finals
Italy 4 West Germany 3 (aet)
Brazil 3 Uruguay 1
Third place match
West Germay 1 Uruguay 0
Final
Brazil 4 Italy 1

1974: WEST GERMANY

Scotland, qualifying for the first time since 1958, carried Britain's hopes after England, who had hopelessly underestimated a very good Polish

Group 2

Brazil 0 Yugoslavia 0
Scotland 2 Zaire 0
Brazil 0 Scotland 0
Yugoslavia 9 Zaire 0
Scotland 1 Yugoslavia 1
Brazil 3 Zaire 0

	P	W	D	L	F	A	Pts
Yugoslavia	3	1	2	0	10	1	4
Brazil	3	1	2	0	3	0	4
Scotland	3	1	2	0	3	1	4
Zaire	3	0	0	3	0	14	0

Group 3

Holland 2 Uruguay 0
Sweden 0 Bulgaria 0
Holland 0 Sweden 0
Bulgaria 1 Uruguay 1
Holland 4 Bulgaria 1
Sweden 3 Uruguay 0

	P	W	D	L	F	A	Pts
Holland	3	2	1	0	6	1	5
Sweden	3	1	2	0	3	0	4
Bulgaria	3	0	2	1	2	5	4
Uruguay	3	0	1	2	1	6	1

Group 4

Italy 4 Haiti 1
Poland 3 Argentina 2
Argentina 1 Italy 1
Poland 7 Haiti 0
Argentina 4 Haiti 1
Poland 2 Italy 1

	P	W	D	L	F	A	Pts
Poland	3	3	0	0	12	3	6
Argentina	3	1	1	1	7	5	3
Italy	3	1	1	1	5	4	3
Haiti	3	0	0	3	2	14	0

Second Round
Group A

Brazil 1 East Germany 0
Holland 4 Argentina 0
Holland 2 East Germany 0
Brazil 2 Argentina 1
Holland 2 Brazil 0
Argentina 1 East Germany 1

	P	W	D	L	F	A	Pts
Holland	3	3	0	0	8	0	6
Brazil	3	2	0	1	3	3	4
East Germany	3	0	1	2	1	4	1
Argentina	3	0	1	2	2	7	1

Group B

Poland 1 Sweden 0
West Germany 2 Yugoslavia 0
Poland 2 Yugoslavia 1
West Germany 4 Sweden 2
Sweden 2 Yugoslavia 1
West Germany 1 Poland 0

	P	W	D	L	F	A	Pts
West Germany	3	3	0	0	7	2	6
Poland	3	2	0	1	3	2	4
Sweden	3	1	0	2	4	6	2
Yugoslavia	3	0	0	3	2	6	0

Final

West Germany 2 Holland 1

West Germany 1974: Paul Breitner (arms raised) cancels out Holland's first minute penalty with one for West Germany. Brilliantly organized by Franz Beckenbauer and Dieter Bonhof and with right back Bertie Vogts closely shadowing Johan Cruyff, the Germans were able to counter the quicksilver spontaneity of the Dutch, and held out against almost overwhelming pressure in the second half.

side in their qualifying group, failed to make it through to the finals. The Scots well marshalled by Bremner and inspired by some brilliant performances from David Hay, were unluckily shaded out on goal difference, holding Brazil to a goal-less draw and ultimately not losing a match. The Brazilians themselves – in a period of transition and lacking effective strikers – were to fall to a wonderfully gifted Dutch team built around the incomparable Johan Cruyff in the second group of round-robin matches. The Final provided a contrast of styles: West Germany's Beckenbauer-directed *libero* system against Holland's media-dubbed 'total football'. A first-minute Dutch penalty, converted by Neeskens, failed to demoralise the Germans, who equalised through another penalty by Breitner, before that arch goal-scorer Gerd Müller provided the winner just before half-time. Leading scorer of the tournament was Lato (Poland) with 7 goals; the Poles beat Brazil in the play-off for third.

First Round
Group 1

West Germany 1 Chile 0
East Germany 2 Australia 0
West Germany 3 Australia 0
East Germany 1 Chile 1
East Germany 1 West Germany 0
Chile 0 Australia 0

	P	W	D	L	F	A	Pts
East Germany	3	2	1	0	4	1	5
West Germany	3	2	0	1	4	1	4
Chile	3	0	2	1	1	2	2
Australia	3	0	1	2	0	5	1

Argentina 1978: At left, part of the ticker-tape-scattering, streamer-throwing, banner-waving, horn-blowing multitude at the final between Argentina and Holland.
At right, Daniel Bertoni scores Argentina's third and final goal in extra-time: Mario Kempes (10), the tournament's outstanding striker and top-scorer, watches as Holland's goal-keeper Jongbloed (8) tries to intercept the ball.

1978: ARGENTINA

Scotland, sole UK representatives, were ludicrously ill-prepared. An excellent victory over the Dutch (highlighted by a marvellous solo goal by Archie Gemmill) came too late to save them. Argentina, surviving an early loss to Italy, reached the Final on goal difference, swamping a tired Peru to edge out a strong but uninspired Brazil. Holland, meanwhile, although without Cruyff, got better with each game, but the holders West Germany, without Beckenbauer and Müller from 1974, were pale shadows of the side that had won four years previously. The Final nearly provided an upset, with the Dutch in the main successfully coping with Argentina's twin strikers Kempes and Luque. Although Kempes scored first, Naninga equalised for Holland nine minutes from time. A Rensenbrink shot in the dying moments scraped a post, and the effort was to prove Holland's last chance: first Kempes and then Bertoni scored in extra-time to give Argentina her first-ever World Cup win. Man of the tournament was Mario Kempes, who was top scorer with 6 goals.

Group 1
Italy 2 France 1
Argentina 2 Hungary 1
Italy 3 Hungary 1
Argentina 2 France 1
France 3 Hungary 1
Italy 1 Argentina 0

	P	W	D	L	F	A	Pts
Italy	3	3	0	0	6	2	6
Argentina	3	2	0	1	4	3	4
France	3	1	0	2	5	5	2
Hungary	3	0	0	3	3	8	0

Group 2
West Germany 0 Poland 0
Tunisia 3 Mexico 1
Poland 1 Tunisia 0
Poland 3 Mexico 1
West Germany 0 Tunisia 0

	P	W	D	L	F	A	Pts
Poland	3	2	1	0	4	1	5
West Germany	3	1	2	0	6	0	4
Tunisia	3	1	1	1	3	2	3
Mexico	3	0	0	3	2	12	0

Group 3
Austria 2 Spain 1
Brazil 1 Sweden 1
Austria 1 Sweden 0
Brazil 0 Spain 0
Spain 1 Sweden 0
Brazil 1 Austria 0

	P	W	D	L	F	A	Pts
Austria	3	2	0	1	3	2	4
Brazil	3	1	2	0	2	1	4
Spain	3	1	1	1	2	2	3
Sweden	3	0	1	2	1	3	1

Group 4
Peru 3 Scotland 1
Holland 3 Iran 0
Scotland 1 Iran 1
Holland 0 Peru 0
Peru 4 Iran 1
Scotland 3 Holland 2

	P	W	D	L	F	A	Pts
Peru	3	2	1	0	7	2	5
Holland	3	1	1	1	5	3	3
Scotland	3	1	1	1	5	6	3
Iran	3	0	1	2	2	8	1

Group A
West Germany 0 Italy 0
Holland 5 Austria 1
Italy 1 Austria 0
Holland 2 West Germany 2
Holland 2 Italy 1
Austria 3 West Germany 2

	P	W	D	L	F	A	Pts
Holland	3	2	1	0	9	4	5
Italy	3	1	1	1	2	2	3
West Germany	3	0	2	1	4	5	2
Austria	3	1	0	2	4	8	2

Group B
Brazil 3 Peru 0
Argentina 2 Poland 0
Poland 1 Peru 0
Argentina 0 Brazil 0
Brazil 3 Poland 1
Argentina 6 Peru 0

	P	W	D	L	F	A	Pts
Argentina	3	2	1	0	8	0	5
Brazil	3	2	1	0	6	1	5
Poland	3	1	0	2	2	5	2
Peru	3	0	0	3	0	10	0

Third place match
Brazil 2 Italy 1

Final
Argentina 3 Holland 1 (aet)

1982: SPAIN

With the final stages of the tournament expanded to include 24 qualifiers instead of 16, progress from the European preliminary groups was made much easier. Scotland, Northern Ireland, and England all qualified – although England's presence in Spain owed less to her own efforts than to the failures of others in her qualifying group. The Scots were early casualties, eliminated for the third World Cup running on goal difference – the penalty for allowing New Zealand to score two late goals against them. In her first match England caught France cold and won her qualifying group easily, albeit with increasingly stodgy performances. The Irish, rising to the occasion as they had done in their last finals appearance in 1958, performed minor miracles to defeat the host nation and so win their qualifying group.

Elsewhere, Algeria provided the ultimate World Cup upset with their 2-1 victory over West Germany, and there was more than a hint of the 'old-pals act' about West Germany's 1-0 win over Austria: a result that sent both those sides through to the competition's next stage at Algeria's expense. Italy, meanwhile, looked anything but World Cup winners with three sterile draws in their opening games.

The second phase presented England with a clear-cut task in her last match: she had to better West Germany's 2-1 win over Spain to clinch a semi-final place. England's inability either to create or to score goals against a well-organised, defensively minded team was exposed once more, and the Germans qualified. Northern Ireland's aim was similarly clear-cut: a victory over France would put them in the semis. The French, however, had put that early setback against England behind them and were emerging as one of the most exciting teams of the tournament; the margin of their victory over the Irish was a clear indication of their superiority.

Faced first with Argentina and then with Brazil, Italy at last proved they were capable of playing attacking football when the occasion demanded; the latter game in particular was a marvellous affair in which the Italian centre-forward Paolo Rossi scored a hat-trick. Rossi then scored the two semi-final goals against Poland that put Italy into the Final, while France and West Germany played out a quite extraordinary match in which the Germans recovered from a 3-1 deficit to pull level and then win a penalty shoot-out 5-4. The Final itself was almost no-contest. The Italians, revelling in their new-found attacking confidence, were comfortable winners, and their captain and goalkeeper Dina Zoff was provided with a storybook ending to his career: a World Cup winner at the age of 40!

Group 1
Italy 0 Poland 0
Peru 0 Cameroon 0
Italy 1 Peru 1
Poland 0 Cameroon 0
Poland 5 Peru 1
Italy 1 Cameroon 1

	P	W	D	L	F	A	Pts
Poland	3	1	2	0	5	1	4
Italy	3	0	3	0	2	2	3
Cameroon	3	0	3	0	1	1	3
Peru	3	0	2	1	2	6	2

Group 2
Algeria 2 West Germany 1
Austria 1 Chile 0
West Germany 4 Chile 1
Austria 2 Algeria 0
Algeria 3 Chile 2
West Germany 1 Austria 0

	P	W	D	L	F	A	Pts
West Germany	3	2	0	1	6	3	4
Austria	3	2	0	1	3	1	4
Algeria	3	2	0	1	5	5	4
Chile	3	0	0	3	3	8	0

Group 3
Belgium 1 Argentina 0
Hungary 10 El Salvador 1
Argentina 4 Hungary 1
Belgium 1 El Salvador 0

Right, above *Spain 1982: Italy's Paolo Rossi and Gabriele Oriali tussle with West Germany's Paul Breitner and (left) Wolfgang Dremmler. Italy, having brilliantly disposed of Argentina and Brazil in Group C (quarter-final) matches, had little trouble beating the Germans in the Final.*

Right, below *Spain 1982: Northern Ireland, with Watford 'reject' Gerry Armstrong and Division 3 veteran Billy Hamilton in starring roles, surprised many in Spain with their commitment and refusal to fear nominally better sides. Here Hamilton outpaces Spain's Miguel Tendillo during Northern Ireland's stunning victory over the host country.*

Below *Spain 1982: Trevor Francis scores from a corner against Czechoslovakia in England's second match in Group 4. England conceded only a single goal in five games, but their attack proved conspicuously unable to trouble either West Germany or even the feeble Spanish side in the crucial Group B matches.*

Belgium 1 Hungary 1
Argentina 2 El Salvador 0

	P	W	D	L	F	A	Pts
Belgium	3	2	1	0	3	1	5
Argentina	3	2	0	1	6	2	4
Hungary	3	1	1	1	12	6	3
El Salvador	3	0	0	3	1	13	0

Group 4
England 3 France 1
Czechoslovakia 1 Kuwait 1
England 2 Czechoslovakia 0
France 4 Kuwait 1
France 1 Czechoslovakia 1
England 1 Kuwait 0

	P	W	D	L	F	A	Pts
England	3	3	0	0	6	1	6
France	3	1	1	1	6	5	3
Czechoslovakia	3	0	2	1	2	4	2
Kuwait	3	0	1	2	2	6	1

Group 5
Spain 1 Honduras 1
Northern Ireland 0 Yugoslavia 0
Spain 2 Yugoslavia 1
Honduras 1 Northern Ireland 1
Yugoslavia 1 Honduras 0
Northern Ireland 1 Spain 0

	P	W	D	L	F	A	Pts
Northern Ireland	3	1	2	0	2	1	4
Spain	3	1	1	1	3	3	3
Yugoslavia	3	1	1	1	2	2	3
Honduras	3	0	2	1	2	3	2

Group 6
Brazil 2 USSR 1
Scotland 5 New Zealand 2
Brazil 4 Scotland 1
USSR 3 New Zealand 0
Scotland 2 USSR 2
Brazil 4 New Zealand 0

	P	W	D	L	F	A	Pts
Brazil	3	3	0	0	10	2	6
USSR	3	1	1	1	6	4	3
Scotland	3	1	1	1	8	8	3
New Zealand	3	0	0	3	2	12	0

Group A
Poland 3 Belgium 0
USSR 1 Belgium 0
Poland 0 USSR 0

	P	W	D	L	F	A	Pts
Poland	2	1	1	0	3	0	3
USSR	2	1	1	0	1	0	3
Belgium	2	0	0	2	0	4	0

Group B
England 0 West Germany 0
West Germany 2 Spain 1
Spain 0 England 0

	P	W	D	L	F	A	Pts
West Germany	2	1	1	0	2	1	3
England	2	0	2	0	0	0	2
Spain	2	0	1	1	1	2	1

Group C
Italy 2 Argentina 1
Brazil 3 Argentina 1
Italy 3 Brazil 2

	P	W	D	L	F	A	Pts
Italy	2	2	0	0	5	3	4
Brazil	2	1	0	1	5	4	2
Argentina	2	0	0	2	2	5	0

Group D
France 1 Austria 0
Northern Ireland 2 Austria 2
France 4 Northern Ireland 1

	P	W	D	L	F	A	Pts
France	2	2	0	0	5	1	4
Austria	2	0	1	1	2	3	1
Northern Ireland	2	0	1	1	3	6	1

Semi-finals
Italy 2 Poland 0
West Germany 3 France 3 (aet; West Germany
   won penalty shoot-out 5-4)
Third place match
Poland 3 France 2
Final
Italy 3 West Germany 1

1986: MEXICO

Colombia was originally chosen to host the 1986 finals but, faced with the dauntingly high cost of staging the tournament, was forced to withdraw. Mexico, as the new host nation, will automatically qualify for the final stages, as will Italy as holders. Once again, 24 nations will take part in the 1986 World Cup, the qualifying draw for which, made on 7 December 1983, is as follows.

Europe
Group 1: Poland, Belgium, Greece, Albania
Group 2: West Germany, Czechoslovakia, Sweden, Portugal, Malta
Group 3: England, Northern Ireland, Romania, Turkey, Finland
Group 4: France, Yugoslavia, East Germany, Bulgaria, Luxembourg
Group 5: Austria, Hungary, Holland, Cyprus
Group 6: USSR, Denmark, Republic of Ireland, Switzerland, Norway
Group 7: Spain, Scotland, Wales, Iceland
The winners of all groups will qualify for the finals, together with the runners-up in Groups 2, 3, 4 and 6.

The runners-up in Groups 1, 5 and 7 will also play-off for another qualifying place; the runner-up from this second play-off group will meet the winner of the Oceania qualifying tournament for a place in the finals.
South America
Group 1: Argentina, Peru, Colombia, Venezuela
Group 2: Uruguay, Chile, Ecuador
Group 3: Brazil, Paraguay, Bolivia
The winner of each group qualifies.
The second- and third-placed sides in Group 1 and the runners-up in Groups 2 and 3 will play off for another qualifying place.
Oceania
Australia, New Zealand, Taiwan, Israel.
The winner of this group will enter a two-match play-off against the runner-up from the supplementary European qualifying group for a place in the finals.
Asia
Group 1
Sub-Group 1: Saudi Arabia, United Arab Emirates, Oman
Sub-Group 2: Iraq, Lebanon, Qatar, Jordan
Group 2
Sub-Group 1: Kuwait, North Yemen, Syria
Sub-Group 2: Bahrain, Iran, South Yemen
Group 3
Sub-Group 1: Malaysia, Nepal, South Korea
Sub-Group 2: Thailand, India, Bangladesh, Indonesia
Group 4
Sub-Group 1: China, Hong Kong, Macao, Brunei
Sub-Group 2: Japan, Singapore, North Korea
Two teams from these groups will qualify for the finals.
North and Central America and Caribbean
Group 1
El Salvador v Puerto Rico
Canada v Jamaica
Dutch Antilles v USA
Group 2
Barbados v Costa Rica
Panama v Honduras
Guatemala: bye
Group 3
Trinidad & Tobago v Grenada
Antigua v Haiti
Surinam v Guyana
One team from these groups will qualify for the finals.
Africa
Group 1
Egypt v Zimbabwe
Kenya v Ethiopia
Mauritius v Malawi
Zambia v Uganda
Madagascar v Lesotho
Tanzania v Sudan
Group 2
Sierra Leone v Morocco
Libya v Niger
Benin v Tunisia
Group 3
Togo v Guinea
Ivory Coast v Gambia
Nigeria v Liberia
Angola v Sénégal
Algeria, Cameroon, and Ghana all receive byes into the second qualifying phase, from which two teams will qualify for the finals.

Spain 1982: Paolo Rossi raises the cup in triumph at the end of the Final. Recapturing his finest form in the later stages of the finals, Rossi was the tournament's top scorer.

SOUTH AMERICA

Above *Brazil's Zico, a wonderfully gifted creative force in midfield, with a fearsome repertoire of dead-ball ploys, took Flamengo to the World Club championship in 1981; more recently he has struggled without success to turn Udinese, of the Italian League, into something better than a run-of-the-mill side.*

Below *Pelé, the incomparable, seen here in his heyday with Santos, with whom he won two World Club championships. Supreme in all the arts of both striker and midfielder, he was the perfect expression of what he himself called the 'beautiful game'.*

For most football fans in the world outside, South American football conjures up images of a particular kind of creative excitement – the explosive brilliance of Pelé, the darting elusiveness and strength of Diego Maradona, the prodigious goal-hunger of Fernando Morena. But to talk in terms of a South American style is to deny the true nature of football in the sub-continent: the game there varies from country to country quite as much as it does in Europe. In Brazil individual skill remains the supreme art; in Argentina, superb technique is harnessed to sophisticated tactical awareness; the Uruguayans, at their best, have long been known as brilliant 'counter-punchers'. Chile, Peru, Paraguay, Bolivia, Ecuador and Colombia all have their own traditions, famous clubs, and superstars. The world record for international appearances, for instance, is held by the Peruvian captain and central defender Hector Chumpitaz, who played for his country 127 times.

BRAZIL

Unrivalled at their best for the beauty and excitement of their play, the Brazilians are also among the most successful footballers at international and club levels. Wherever Brazil go they set precedents. They are the only country to have appeared in the final rounds of every World Cup, from the inaugural competition in 1930. Their win in Sweden in 1958 remains the only occasion when a nation from outside the continent of the host country has taken the game's greatest prize. In 1970 their right winger Jairzinho became the only player to have scored in every game of every round of the finals up to and including the Final itself. Also in 1970 Brazil became the first country to win the World Cup three times, adding to their victories in 1958 and 1962.

Strangely, the Brazilians were introduced to the game by an Englishman, Charles Miller. The son of English residents in São Paulo, Miller set the fuse for the Brazilian football explosion by bringing two footballs with him on his return from study in England in the 1890s. The first properly organised match in Brazil took place in São Paulo on 15 April 1895. The two teams represented the local gas company and the São Paulo railway, for whom Miller played at centre-forward. The word quickly spread. Other clubs were formed. In Río de Janeiro admirers of the game persuaded members of their sailing club to form a team – from which humble beginnings evolved Flamengo, South American and world club champions of 1981.

One of the great incidental triumphs of football in Brazil was in breaking down racial and class barriers. Most important of all in leading the movement towards social equality was Artur Friedenreich, a mulatto, whose extraordinary feats – he scored well over 1,300 goals between 1910 and 1930 – earned him the admiration and respect of all classes and all races in a country that already was intoxicated with football. Friedenreich retired before the advent of the World Cup. But it was indirectly due to him that one particular black star was accepted as everyone's football hero in the 1930s. That man was Leonidas da Silva, a centre forward renowned for his mid-air acrobatics in pursuit of goals (he pioneered the overhead scissors kick). He created a sensation in the 1938 World Cup, scoring eight of Brazil's 14 goals.

Leonidas opened the floodgates: behind him came a torrent of star names. The inside-forward trio of Jair, Ademir, and Zizinho starred in the 1950 World Cup in Brazil. Then along came two fine, creative full-backs, Djalma and Nilton Santos (unrelated), and a great midfield creator named Waldyr Pereira, better known to the world of football by his nickname, Didi.

In 1958 these were joined by two of the greatest footballers of all time – the irresistible goal-scoring winger Garrincha ('Little Bird'), master of the banana shot, and a 17-year-old inside-left named Edson Arantes do Nascimento, otherwise Pelé. He scored two wonderful goals in the 5-2 victory over Sweden in the 1958 World Cup Final, and went on to become the most famous footballer of all.

Pelé made his club, Santos, world-famous too. In recent years they have faded, since the great man's retirement to New York, and the power in Brazilian club football has reverted to Río, and particularly to Flamengo. Under former national team boss Claudio Coutinho (later drowned in a skin-diving accident) and inspired by the goals of Zico, Flamengo dominated in the late 1970s and early 1980s. And even when they slipped from the world pinnacle, there were Gremio, of

Pôrto Alegre in the south, ready to pick up the baton and regain for Brazil the prime club awards in South America and the world.

ARGENTINA

To a greater extent, perhaps, than any other nation in the history of football, Argentina has been an exporter of football talent. Literally hundreds of fine players – and many indisputably great ones – have made their reputations with clubs such as River Plate, Boca, Independiente, Racing Club, and San Lorenzo, and have then gone on to greater glory in Europe, lured by the princely wages and fringe benefits offered by the wealthier Italian and Spanish clubs. Centre-half Luisito Monti and winger Raimundo Ursi were members of the Argentine team beaten in the first World Cup Final by Uruguay in 1930; four years later, after changing nationality, they were members of the Italian team that won the 1938 World Cup Final against Hungary. To achieve such a wealth of talent over the years, Argentina has drawn on all the immigrant peoples to have settled there.

As in Brazil, the moving spirit behind the early popularization of the game in Argentina at the turn of the century was a Briton – a schoolteacher named Alexander Hutton. And it was an English high school team, Alumni, that won the original (amateur) championship 10 times in 11 seasons. Professionalism soon caught on, and the game developed rapidly in terms of both organization and the quality of play. Star players from all over South America were attracted to play for Buenos Aires clubs in the 1930s and 1940s. This was the great age of Argentine football, the age when River Plate's forward line proved so lethal they were nicknamed La Maquina (The Machine).

A star among stars in the late 1940s was the centre-forward Alfredo Di Stéfano. In the early 1950s, however, he and many others left, first to join the pirate league in Colombia (which Stoke City and England centre-half Neil Franklin also joined), then for Europe. And Argentinian football drifted in the doldrums for a decade.

It took clubs such as Independiente to lead a revival. They proved as outstandingly talented in the Copa de los Libertadores (the South American club competition) as rivals Estudiantes proved violent. The national side gradually improved – a process that culminated in Argentina's victory in the World Cup in 1978. Under the exceptionally astute managership of César Menotti they frequently displayed a blend of toughness and attacking flair that would not have disgraced the great sides of an earlier era.

URUGUAY

For a nation of only three million people Uruguay's record is remarkable. They won the World Cup in 1930 and 1950, were placed fourth in both 1954 and 1970, and reached the quarter-finals in 1966. Peñarol and Nacional, their two top clubs, have been frequent winners of the South American and world club championships, and their players have performed with great success for clubs in Spain, Italy, France, Greece and Austria.

The domestic league is a perpetual two-horse race. Since 1931 Nacional or Peñarol have won the title each year apart from 1976, when unfashionable Defensor sprang a major surprise. But it is a measure of the success of Peñarol, in particular, that this year (1984) is only the third occasion that they have failed to qualify to compete in the continental club championship, the Copa de los Libertadores. Peñarol have benefited during the past decade (apart from a three-year interruption while he was in Spain) from the scoring exploits of centre-forward Fernando Morena. He has scored more than 600 goals in top competition; and it is a measure of his importance to Peñarol that they endured a disastrous league season in 1983 after Morena suffered a serious leg fracture while playing for his country in the South American championship.

THE REST

Given the records of Brazil, Argentina, and Uruguay in the World Cup, it is perhaps surprising to realise that they have not always been able to claim mastery of their own continent.

Paraguay, for example, have a proud football tradition. In the 1930s it was a Paraguayan centre-forward, Arsenio Erico, who set a long-standing scoring record in the Argentine league. Years later, in 1979, Paraguay reached a pinnacle of achievement: league club Olímpia of Asunción won the South American and world club crowns and Paraguay's national team won the continental championship.

Chile, too, have not been without their great moments. As hosts they finished third in the 1962 World Cup finals; and in recent years the emergence as a major force of Cobreloa, based on the Andean copper-mining town of Calama, shows every indication of shifting the balance of power in top-level club football in South America. Among the greatest of Chilean stars, Elías Figueroa was voted South American player of the year three years running in 1974-6.

Peru, World Cup quarter-finalists in 1970 and second-round finalists in 1978, have always been a threat to the Big Three. Any country which can produce forwards of the quality of Teófilo Cubillas and clubs of the stature of Alianza and Sporting Cristal of Lima can never be a pushover. Scotland discovered that to their cost during the 1978 World Cup.

The unpredictable Ecuador and Venezuela, as well as Colombia – briefly an off-limits El Dorado to the World's players at the turn of the 1950s – have all had their moments of glory; while Bolivia – where visiting teams have to play at high altitude – are always likely to surprise, or at least outlast, their opponents.

Above *Scourge of South American defences for more than a decade, Peñarol's Fernando Morena was possibly the deadliest striker in the world until his accident in 1983.*

Below *Teófilo Cubillas, the Peruvian master, almost beat Scotland on his own in the 1978 World Cup finals, scoring two goals with shots combining great power with remarkable accuracy. He was later lured to the short-lived bonanza of the NASL.*

A DECADE OF CLUB CHAMPIONS

The following tables list the 'league' champions of all the countries in the confederation over the past 10 years. The 'national championships' of Argentina and Brazil are the nearest equivalent to our FA Cup; they are organised not on a simple knock-out basis but on series of 'round-robin' group matches between qualifiers from the various senior provincial leagues.

ARGENTINA
First Division
1975 River Plate
1976 Boca Juniors
1977 River Plate
1978 Quilmes
1979 River Plate
1980 River Plate
1981 Boca Juniors
1982 Estudiantes
1983 Independiente
1984 Argentinos Juniors
National championship
1975 River Plate
1976 Boca Juniors
1977 Independiente
1978 Independiente
1979 River Plate
1980 Rosario Central
1981 River Plate
1982 F C Oeste
1983 Estudiantes
1984 Ferro Carril Oeste

BOLIVIA
1975 Guabira
1976 Bolívar
1977 The Strongest
1978 Bolívar
1979 Oriente Pétrolero
1980 Jorge Wilsterman
1981 Jorge Wilsterman
1982 Bolívar
1983 Bolívar
1984 Blooming

BRAZIL
Carioca (Río de Janeiro) championship
1975 Fluminense
1976 Fluminense
1977 Vasco da Gama
1978 Flamengo
1979 Flamengo
1980 Fluminense
1981 Flamengo
1982 Vasco da Gama
1983 Fluminense
1984 Fluminense
Paulista (São Paulo) championship
1975 São Paulo
1976 Palmeiras
1977 Corinthians
1978 Corinthians
1979 Corinthians
1980 São Paulo
1981 São Paulo
1982 Corinthians
1983 Corinthians
1984 Santos
National championship
1974 Vasco da Gama
      (Pôrto Alegre)
1976 Internacional
1977 São Paulo
1978 Guarani
1979 Internacional
1980 Flamengo
1981 Gremio
      (Pôrto Alegre)
1982 Flamengo
1983 Flamengo
1984 Fluminense

CHILE
1975 Unión Española
1976 Everton
1977 Unión Española
1978 Palestino
1979 Colo Colo
1980 Cobreloa
1981 No competition
1982 Colo Colo
1983 Cobreloa
1984 Universidad Catolica

COLOMBIA
1975 Independiente Santa Fé
1976 Nacional Medellin
1977 Atlético Junior (Barranquilla)
1978 Millionarios (Bogotá)
1979 America Cali
1980 Atlético Junior
1981 Nacional
1982 America Cali
1983 America Cali
1984 America Cali

ECUADOR
1975 Liga Deportivo Universitario
1976 Nacional (Quito)
1977 Nacional
1978 Nacional
1979 Emelec
1980 Barcelona (Guayaquil)
1981 Barcelona
1982 Nacional
1983 Nacional
1984 Nacional

PARAGUAY
1975 Olímpia (Asunción)
1976 Libertad
1977 Cerro
1978 Olímpia
1979 Olímpia
1980 Olímpia
1981 Olímpia
1982 Olímpia
1983 Olímpia
1984 Guarani

PERU
1975 Alianza
1976 Unión Huaráz
1977 Alianza
1978 Alianza
1979 Sporting Cristal
1980 Sporting Cristal
1981 Melgar
1982 Universitario
1983 Sporting Cristal
1984 Sport Boys

URUGUAY
1975 Peñarol
1976 Defensor
1977 Nacional
1978 Peñarol
1979 Peñarol
1980 Nacional
1981 Peñarol
1982 Peñarol
1983 Nacional
1984 Central Español

VENEZUELA
1975 Portuguesa
1976 Portuguesa
1977 Portuguesa
1978 Portuguesa
1979 Táchira
1980 Estudiantes Mérida
1981 Táchira
1982 San Cristóbal
1983 Universidad de los
      Andes
1984 Deportivo Táchira

CAMPEONATO SUDAMERICANO DE FÚTBOL

This championship, competed for by national teams of the South America confederation, was launched in 1917 and has been held, with some interruptions, at intervals since; at present it takes place every four years. At various times since the 1920s a number of unofficial championships have been held, but the winners of these have been excluded from the list below.

1917 Uruguay	1926 Uruguay	1949 Brazil	1975 Championship
1919 Brazil	1927 Argentina	1953 Paraguay	Semi-finals - Colombia bt Uruguay 3-0, 0-1
1920 Uruguay	1929 Argentina	1955 Argentina	Peru bt Brazil 1-3, 2-0
1921 Argentina	1936/7 Argentina	1957 Argentina	Final - Peru bt Columbia 0-1, 2-0, 1-0
1922 Brazil	1939 Peru	1959 Argentina	Semi-finals - Chile bt Peru 2-1, 0-0 Paraguay bt Brazil 2-1, 0-0
1923 Uruguay	1942 Uruguay	1963 Bolivia	Final - Paraguay bt Chile 3-0, 0-1
1924 Uruguay	1947 Argentina	1967 Uruguay	1983 Championship
1925 Argentina			Semi-finals - Uruguay bt Peru 1-0, 1-1
			Brazil bt Paraguay 1-1, 0-0
			(toss of coin)
			Final - Uruguay bt Brazil 2-0, 1-1

COPA DE LOS LIBERTADORES

This tournament, the South American club championship, is competed for by the two top teams of the preceding season from each country in the confederation. The winner qualifies to meet the winner of the European Cup to decide the World Club championship.

1960 Peñarol (Uru)	1967 Racing Club (Arg)	1974 Independiente	1981 Final: Flamengo (Br) bt Cobreloa (Ch) 2-2, 0-1, 2-0 (play-of)
1961 Peñarol	1968 Estudiantes (Arg)	1975 Independiente	1982 Final: Peñarol bt Cobreloa 0-0, 1-0
1962 Santos (Br)	1969 Estudiantes	1976 Cruzeiro (Br)	1983 Final: Gremio (Br) bt Peñarol 1-1, 2-1
1963 Santos	1970 Estudiantes	1977 Boca Juniors (Arg)	1984 Final: Independiente bt Gremio 1-0, 0-0
1964 Independiente (Arg)	1971 Nacional (Uru)	1978 Boca Juniors	
1965 Independiente	1972 Independiente	1979 Olímpia (Par)	
1966 Peñarol	1973 Independiente	1980 Nacional	

WORLD CLUB CHAMPIONSHIP

When Gremio of Brazil outlasted SV Hamburg in extra time in Tokyo in December 1983 they were simply confirming what most football observers have come to expect: that the World Club Cup (or the Toyota Cup, as it is now called) spends more time in South America than in Europe. The destination of the cup is decided every year by an encounter between the holders of the European Cup and its South American equivalent, the Copa de los Libertadores.

The World Club championship has its origins in the enterprise of the great Uruguayan club Peñarol. The Copa de los Libertadores was launched in 1960, the South American football confederation having been greatly impressed by the prestige (not to mention financial rewards) generated by the European Cup, then in its fifth season. The first winners of the Copa were Peñarol, who promptly issued a challenge to the European champions, Real Madrid.

If the World Club Cup was conceived at the end of football's romantic era, it came to maturity in an age when success has counted for much more than the manner in which it has been achieved, and when stopping the other team playing has often seemed the first priority for even the most gifted sides. The competition was in only its fourth season when violence broke out between Santos (Pelé's club) and AC Milan in Río de Janeiro's vast Maracaná stadium.

For the next two years Internazionale of Milan and Independiente of Argentina played out gruelling, highly disciplined, tactically craven matches. They were followed by Peñarol, making a fine comeback against Real Madrid.

In 1967, however, violence flared once more. The bad feeling created between Argentina and Britain by the sending off of Antonio Rattín in the 1966 World Cup quarter-final between England and Argentina spilled over when Racing Club of Buenos Aires met Celtic: no fewer than six players were sent off in the play-off in Montevideo (Uruguay). Even worse was to come in the next three years from perhaps the most cynical of all the South American champions, Estudiantes de la Plata, also of Argentina. When they played Manchester United in 1968 Nobby Stiles (in Buenos Aires) and George Best (at Old Trafford) were sent off, the victims of extreme provocation and feigned injury.

It took a long time to rebuild the trust between the continents. For several seasons, indeed, the future of the tournament was in doubt. Then salvation arrived from an unlikely source: the Japanese soccer federation, backed by a massive injection of capital by sponsors Toyota, offered to stage the event as a single-match contest in Tokyo. It was an offer that could not be refused: not only would the financial rewards be immense for each club taking part, staging the match in a neutral stadium on the other side of the world would remove much of the violent passion from the event, allowing the teams to concentrate on showing the best in football styles from the Old World and the New.

It has not always worked out that way since

Nuñez scores Flamengo's second goal in the 3-0 defeat of Liverpool in 1981. Inspiringly led by Zico, the Brazilians played the finest football yet seen in the Toyota Cup series.

1980, when the first match was held in Tokyo. But in general the move to neutral territory and to a single-match formula has been amply vindicated – not least in 1981 when Liverpool, plausibly regarded then as the finest side in Europe, were thrillingly overwhelmed by a Zico-inspired Flamengo eager to display all the arts of the Brazilian game.

WORLD CLUB CHAMPIONS

1960   Real Madrid (Sp) bt Peñarol 0-0, 5-1
1961   Peñarol bt Benfica (Port) 0-1, 5-0, 2-1
1962   Santos (Br) bt Benfica 3-2, 5-2
1963   Santos bt AC Milan (It) 2-4, 4-2, 1-0
1964   Internazionale (It) bt Independiente (Arg) 0-1, 2-0, 1-0
1965   Internazionale bt Independiente 3-0, 0-0
1966   Peñarol bt Real Madrid 2-0, 2-0
1967   Racing Club (Arg) bt Celtic 0-1, 2-1, 1-0
1968   Estudiantes (Arg) bt Manchester United 1-0, 1-1
1969   AC Milan bt Estudiantes 3-0, 1-2
1970   Feyenoord (Hol) bt Estudiantes 2-2, 1-0
1971   Nacional (Uru) bt Panathinaikos (Gr) 1-1, 2-1
1972   Ajax Amsterdam (Hol) bt Independiente 1-1, 3-0
1973   Independiente bt Juventus (It) 1-0 (in Rome)
1974   Atlético Madrid (Sp) bt Independiente 0-1, 2-0
1975   *no competition*
1976   Bayern Munich (W. Ger) bt Cruzeiro (Br) 2-0, 0-0
1977   Boca Juniors (Arg) bt Borussia Mönchengladbach (W. Ger) 2-2, 3-0
1978   *no competition*
1979   Olímpia (Paraguay) bt Malmö FF (Sw) 1-0, 2-1
1980   Nacional bt Nottingham Forest 1-0
1981   Flamengo (Br) bt Liverpool 3-0
1982   Peñarol bt Aston Villa 2-0
1983   Gremio (Br) bt SV Hamburg (W. Ger) 2-1
1984   Independiente bt Liverpool 1-0

NORTH AMERICA

As a spectator sport in North America, soccer ranks a poor fourth behind American gridiron football, baseball, and basketball. It owes its now-precarious existence mainly to two men: NASL Commissioner Phil Woosnam (formerly of West Ham and Wales), who was in at NASL's birth when two rival leagues merged in 1968; and the immortal Pelé, who became the focus of unprecedented media and spectator interest when he was lured out of retirement in 1975 by a two-year contract worth $5 million to play for the New York Cosmos. Pelé's impact on North American soccer can hardly be overstated. At the end of NASL's first season in 1968, 12 of the competing 17 clubs withdrew: by 1979 the entry had peaked at 24. (As of late-1983, however, only nine teams were scheduled to start the 1984 season.)

Pelé's arrival did, however, have one significant detrimental effect on the American game. It prompted other clubs to look for star imports instead of nurturing native talent. The two biggest captures were Franz Beckenbauer, who arrived in New York to fill the void left by Pelé's second retirement in 1977; and Johan Cruyff, who went to Los Angeles. Elsewhere, a host of good players in the twilight of their careers, and younger men not quite good enough for the top grade in their own countries, flooded in from Europe and South America, thus blocking the progress of promising American players.

Hasty rule changes to the effect that clubs were allowed to field only two foreign imports led merely to adoption of American nationality by the incomers. Meanwhile, on-field changes in the laws of the game, designed to make scoring easier – and so make matches more entertaining for spectators – resulted in a curious hybrid version of soccer at odds with the game played elsewhere.

The public did attend in large numbers, however, most notably in New York, where crowds of over 70,000 during the Pelé-Beckenbauer era at the Cosmos were common. But as star players retired and were not replaced, attendances dwindled once more; which in the autumn of 1983 even prompted the by now desperate Cosmos to offer 43-year-old Pelé another $5m to play for them in 1984. Sensibly, he refused.

The NASL has effectively collapsed and professional soccer in the United States is confined to a hybrid indoor version of the game. Although the genuine article is very popular at school and college level, the professional outdoor game seems unable to attract the crowds – or TV sponsorship.

New York Cosmos' cheerleaders go through their routine at the NASL Soccer Bowl.

PREVIEW 1985/6

In the aftermath of Bradford and Brussels it is easy to get carried away with visions of doom. But if the headline writers' predictions of the 'Death of the Game' may prove exaggerated, there is little doubt that England football begins this season under a huge cloud and that it will be struggling for survival, never mind respectability. It does not need a Cassandra to suspect that gates will take a marked drop, as a sense of disenchantment and disgust affects more and more of the genuine fans and also as radically more effective methods of keeping the thugs out of the stadia begin to take effect.

We go into the season knowing that there will be no English clubs in European competitions or in friendly matches there or anywhere else in the world. Such bans will have repercussions beyond the big clubs directly involved: in football, when Manchester United sneeze, Oldham Athletic are likely to catch cold. And unless the Government, which takes so much money out of the game, shows a wholly unexpected generosity, the need to bring safety standards and crowd-control measures to acceptable levels could deal the final financial blow which sends some small clubs into liquidation.

At the time of writing the Government measures to try to stamp out the violence which has disfigured the innocent game for the last two decades have yet to be crystallised, so it is impossible to forecast their efficacy. But unless the sort of interpretation of the rules which permitted the police to turn back striking Kentish miners on their way to Nottingham is also applied to English football fans – whether travelling from London to Manchester, or going abroad on the pretext of supporting a Scottish team in Europe – it is difficult to see how the criminal element can be kept out of the grounds. Even if the new measures are successful, the fear must be that a lot of innocent people will be discouraged from attending the game, and the sport itself, already the biggest victim of social forces beyond its control, will be further damaged.

Against such a backcloth, Bobby Robson – and hopefully Billy Bingham, Mike England, and Jock Stein, too – will be preparing their sides for the World Cup. It will not be the easiest of tasks, but the loss of European club competition commitments for most of their leading players will at least have the effect of lessening the load on them, and that offers some compensation.

For the leading clubs that loss will have taken some of the zest from the season. It is especially hard on Everton, who won the league so brilliantly while completing their first successful foray into Europe. It is even worse for Norwich City, who had counted on European competition offering some consolation, in terms of cash as well as morale, for their unfortunate relegation. If they can make a swift return to the top flight – and the standard of Division 2, Leeds United apart, suggests it should be within their compass – then every neutral will be delighted.

Gary Lineker (right) a welcome recruit to the England squad and joint highest League-goal scorer (with Kerry Dixon) in Division 1 in 1984/5, was lured from Leicester City to Everton at the end of the season. With his new signing, and with Adrian Heath's long-term injury on the mend, Howard Kendall deemed Goodison's front line strong enough to allow Andy Gray to move to Aston Villa.

LAWS OF THE GAME

LAW 1

THE FIELD OF PLAY

(1) **Dimensions** The field of play shall be rectangular, its length being not more than 130 yards nor less than 100 yards and its breadth not more than 100 yards nor less than 50 yards. (In International Matches the length shall be not more than 120 yards nor less than 110 yards and the breadth not more than 80 yards nor less than 70 yards.) The length shall in all cases exceed the breadth.

(2) **Marking** The field of play shall be marked with distinctive lines, not more than 5 inches in width, not by a V-shaped rut, in accordance with the plan, the longer boundary lines being called the touch lines and the shorter the goal-lines. A flag on a post not less than 5 feet high and having a non-pointed top, shall be placed at each corner; a similar flag-post may be placed opposite the halfway-line on each side of the field of play, not less than 1 yard outside the touch-line. A halfway-line shall be marked out across the field of play. The centre of the field of play shall be indicated by a suitable mark and a circle with a 10 yards radius shall be marked round it.

(3) **The Goal-Area** At each end of the field of play two lines shall be drawn at right-angles to the goal-line, 6 yards from each goal-post. These shall extend into the field of play for a distance of 6 yards and shall be joined by a line drawn parallel with the goal-line. Each of the spaces enclosed by these lines and the goal-line shall be called a goal-area.

(4) **The Penalty-Area** At each end of the field of play two lines shall be drawn at right-angles to the goal-line, 18 yards from each goal-post. These shall extend into the field of play for a distance of 18 yards and shall be joined by a line drawn parallel with the goal-line. Each of the spaces enclosed by these lines and the goal-line shall be called a penalty-area. A suitable mark shall be made within each penalty area, 12 yards from the mid-point of the goal-line, measured along an undrawn line at right angles thereto. These shall be the penalty-kick marks. From each penalty-kick mark an arc of a circle, having a radius of 10 yards, shall be drawn outside the penalty-area.

(5) **The Corner-Area** From each corner flag-post a quarter circle, having a radius of 1 yard, shall be drawn inside the field of play.

(6) **The Goals** The goals shall be placed on the centre of each goal-line and shall consist of two upright posts, equidistant from the corner-flags and 8 yards apart (inside measurement), joined by a horizontal cross-bar the lower edge of which shall be 8 ft from the ground. The width and depth of the goal-posts and the width and depth of the cross-bars shall not exceed 5 inches (12 cm). The goal-posts and the cross-bars shall have the same width.

Nets may be attached to the posts, cross-bars and ground behind the goals. They should be appropriately supported and be so placed as to allow the goalkeeper ample room.

INTERNATIONAL BOARD DECISIONS

1. In International Matches the dimensions of the field of play shall be: maximum 110 metres × 75 metres; minimum 100 metres × 64 metres.

2. National Associations must adhere strictly to these dimensions. Each National Association organizing an International Match must advise the Visiting Association, before the match, of the place and the dimensions of the field of play.

3. The Board has approved this table of measurements for the Laws of the Game.

Imperial		Metric	Imperial		Metric
130 yd	.. ..	120m	1 yd	.. ..	1m
120 yd	.. ..	110m	8 ft	.. ..	2.44m
110 yd	.. ..	100m	5 ft	.. ..	1.50m
100 yd	.. ..	90m	28 in	.. ..	0.71m
80 yd	.. ..	75m	27 in	.. ..	0.68m
70 yd	.. ..	64m	9 in	.. ..	0.22m
50 yd	.. ..	45m	5 in	.. ..	0.12m
18 yd	.. ..	16.50m	½ in	.. ..	12.7mm
12 yd	.. ..	11m	⅜ in	.. ..	10mm
10 yd	.. ..	9.15m	14 oz = 396 g		
8 yd	.. ..	7.32m	16 oz = 453 g		
6 yd	.. ..	5.50m	9 lb/sq in = 600g/cm^2		
			10.5 lb/sq in = 700 g/cm^2		

4. The goal-line shall be marked the same width as the depth of the goalposts and the cross-bar so that the goal-line and the goal-posts will conform in the same interior and exterior edges.

5. The 6 yards (for the outline of the goal-area) and the 18 yards (for the outline of the penalty-area) which have to be measured along the goal-line must start from the inner sides of the goal-posts.

6. The space within the inside areas of the field of play includes the width of the lines marking these areas.

7. All Associations shall provide standard equipment, particularly in International Matches, when the Laws of the Game must be complied with in every respect and especially with regard to the size of the ball and other equipment which must

Field of Play

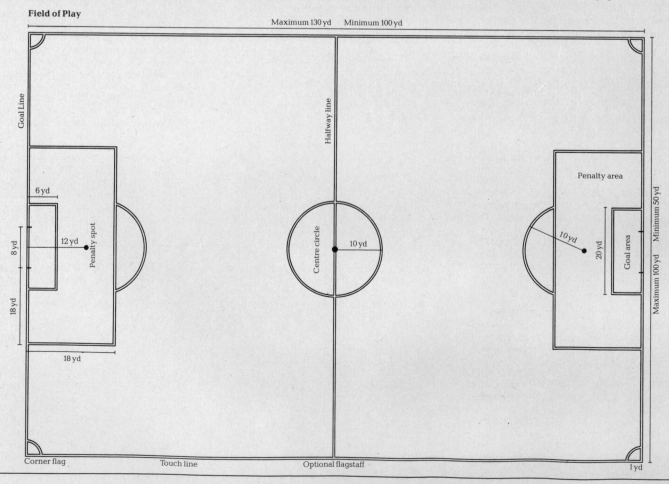

Maximum 130 yd   Minimum 100 yd

Goal Line · Halfway line · 6 yd · 12 yd · Penalty spot · 8 yd · 18 yd · 18 yd · Centre circle · 10 yd · Penalty area · 10 yd · 20 yd · Goal area · Maximum 100 yd · Minimum 50 yd · Corner flag · Touch line · Optional flagstaff · 1 yd

conform to the regulations. All cases of failure to provide standard equipment must be reported to FIFA.

8. In a match played under the rules of a competition, if the cross-bar becomes displaced or broken play shall be stopped and the match abandoned unless the cross-bar has been repaired and replaced in position or a new one provided without such being a danger to the players. A rope is not considered to be a satisfactory substitute for a cross-bar.

In a friendly match, by mutual consent, play may be resumed without the cross-bar provided it has been removed and no longer constitutes a danger to the players. In these circumstances, a rope may be used as a substitute for a cross-bar. If a rope is not used and the ball crosses the goal-line at a point which in the opinion of the Referee is below where the cross-bar should have been he shall award a goal.

The game shall be restarted by the Referee dropping the ball at the place where it was when play was stopped.

9. National Associations may specify such maximum and minimum dimensions for the cross-bars and goal-posts, within the limits laid down in Law 1, as they consider appropriate.

10. Goal-posts and cross-bars must be made of wood, metal or other approved material as decided from time to time by the International FA Board. They may be square, rectangular, round, half round, or elliptical in shape. Goal-posts and cross-bars made of other materials and in other shapes are not permitted.

11. 'Curtain-raiser's to International Matches should only be played following agreement on the day of the match, and taking into account the condition of the field of play, between representatives of the two Associations and the Referee (of the International Match).

12. National Associations, particularly in International Matches, should restrict the number of photographers around the field of play, have a line ('photographers' line') marked behind the goallines at least 2 metres from the corner-flag going through a point situated at least 3.5 metres behind the intersection of the goal-line with the line marking the goal area to a point situated at least 6 metres behind the goal-posts, prohibit photographers from passing over these lines and forbid the use of artificial lighting in the form of 'flashlights'.

LAW 2
THE BALL

The ball shall be spherical; the outer casing shall be of leather or other approved materials. No material shall be used in its construction which might prove dangerous to the players.

The circumference of the ball shall be not more than 28 inches and not less than 27 inches. The weight of the ball at the start of the game shall not be more than 16 oz nor less than 14 oz. *The pressure shall be equal to 0.6-1.1 atmosphere (= 600-1,100 g/cm^2) at sea level.* The ball shall not be changed during the game unless authorized by the Referee.

INTERNATIONAL BOARD DECISIONS

1. The ball used in any match shall be considered the property of the Association or Club on whose ground the match is played, and at the close of play it must be returned to the Referee.

2. The International Board, from time to time, shall decide what constitutes approved materials. Any approved material shall be certified as such by the International Board.

3. The Board has approved these equivalents of the weights specified in the Law:

14 to 16 oz = 396 to 453 g

4. If the ball bursts or becomes deflated during the course of a match, the game shall be stopped and restarted by dropping the new ball at the place where the first ball became defective.

5. If this happens during a stoppage of the game (place-kick, goal-kick, corner-kick, free-kick, penalty-kick or throw-in) the game shall be restarted accordingly.

LAW 3
NUMBER OF PLAYERS

(1) A match shall be played by two teams, each consisting of not more than eleven players, one of whom shall be the goalkeeper.

(2) Substitutes may be used in any match played under the rules of an official competition at FIFA, Confederation or National Association level, subject to the following conditions:

   (a) that the authority of the International Association(s) or National Association(s) concerned has been obtained;

   (b) that, subject to the restriction contained in the following paragraph (c), the rules of a competition shall state how many, if any, substitutes may be used; and

   (c) that a team shall not be permitted to use more than two substitutes in any match.

(3) Substitutes may be used in any other match, provided that the two teams concerned reach agreement on a maximum number, not exceeding five; and that the terms of such agreement are intimated to the Referee before the match. If the Referee is not informed, or if the teams fail to reach agreement, no more than two substitutes shall be permitted.

(4) Any of the other players may change places with the goalkeeper, provided that the Referee is informed before the change is made, and provided also that the change is made during a stoppage in the game.

(5) When a goalkeeper or any other player is to be replaced by a substitute, the following conditions shall be observed:

   (a) the Referee shall be informed of the proposed substitution before it is made;

   (b) the substitute shall not enter the field of play until the player he is replacing has left, and then only after having received a signal from the Referee;

   (c) he shall enter the field during a stoppage in the game, and at the halfway-line;

   (d) a player who has been replaced shall not take any further part in the game;

   (e) a substitute shall be subject to the authority and jurisdiction of the Referee whether called upon to play or not.

Punishment

   (a) Play shall not be stopped for an infringement of paragraph (4). The players concerned shall be cautioned immediately the ball goes out of play.

   (b) If a substitute enters the field of play without the authority of the Referee, play shall be stopped. The substitute shall be cautioned and removed from the field or sent off according to the circumstances. The game shall be restarted by the Referee dropping the ball at the place where it was when he stopped play.

   (c) For any other infringement of the Law, the player concerned shall be cautioned, and if the game is stopped by the Referee to administer the caution, it shall be re-started by an indirect free-kick, to be taken by a player of the opposing team, from the place where the ball was when play was stopped. If the free-kick is awarded to a team within its own goal area, it may be taken from any point within that half of the goal area in which the ball was when play was stopped.

INTERNATIONAL BOARD DECISIONS

1. The minimum number of players in a team is left to the discretion of National Associations.

2. The Board is of the opinion that a match should not be considered valid if there are fewer than seven players in either of the teams.

3. A competition may require that the Referee shall be informed, before the start of a match, of the names of not more than five players from whom the substitutes (if any) must be chosen.

4. A player who has been ordered off before play begins may be replaced only by one of the named substitutes. The kick-off must not be delayed to allow the substitute to join his team.

A player who has been ordered off after play has started may not be replaced. A named substitute who has been ordered off, either before or after play has started, may not be replaced. (This decision relates only to players who are ordered off under Law 12. It does not apply to players who have infringed Law 4.)

LAW 4

PLAYERS' EQUIPMENT

A player shall not wear anything which is dangerous to another player. Footwear (boots or shoes) must conform to the following standard:

   (a) Bars shall be made of leather or rubber and shall be transverse and flat, not less than half an inch in width and shall extend the total width of the sole and be rounded at the corners.

   (b) Studs which are independently mounted on the sole and are replaceable shall be made of leather, rubber, aluminium, plastic or similar material and shall be solid. With the exception of that part of the stud forming the base, which shall not protrude from the sole more than one quarter of an inch, studs shall be round in plan and not less than half an inch in diameter. Where studs are tapered, the minimum diameter of any section of the stud must not be less than half an inch. Where metal seating for the screw type is used, this seating must be embedded in the sole of the footwear and any attachment screw shall be part of the stud. Other than the metal seating for the screw type of stud, no metal plates even though covered with leather or rubber shall be worn, neither studs which are threaded to allow them to be screwed on to a base screw that is fixed by nails or otherwise to the soles of footwear, nor studs which, apart from the base, have any form of protruding edge rim, or relief marking, or ornament, should be allowed.

   (c) Studs which are moulded as an integral part of the sole and are not replaceable shall be made of rubber, plastic, polyurethene or similar soft materials. Provided that there are no fewer than ten studs on the sole, they shall have a minimum diameter of three-eighths of an inch (10 mm). Additional supporting material to stabilize studs of soft materials, and ridges which shall not protrude more than 5 mm from the sole and moulded to strengthen it, shall be permitted provided that they are in no way dangerous to other players. In all other respects they shall conform to the general requirement of this law.

   (d) Combined bars and studs may be worn, provided the whole conforms to the general requirements of this law. Neither bars nor studs on the soles shall project more than three-quarters of an inch. If nails are used they shall be driven in flush with the surface.

The goalkeeper shall wear colours which distinguish him from the other players and from the referee.

Punishment

For any infringement of this Law, the player at fault shall be sent off the field of play to adjust his equipment and he shall not return without first reporting to the Referee, who shall satisfy himself that the player's equipment is in order; the player shall re-enter the game only at a moment when the ball has ceased to be in play.

INTERNATIONAL BOARD DECISIONS

1. The usual equipment of a player is a jersey or shirt, shorts, stockings and footwear. In a match played under the rules of a competition, players need not wear boots or shoes, but shall wear jersey or shirts, shorts, or track-suit or similar trousers, and stockings.

2. The Law does not insist that boots or shoes must be worn. However, in competition matches Referees should not allow one or a few players to play without footwear when all the other players are so equipped.

3. In International Matches, International Competitions, International Club Competitions and friendly matches between clubs of different National Associations, the Referee, prior to the start of the match, shall inspect the players' footwear, and prevent any player whose footwear does not conform to the requirements of this Law from playing until such time as it does comply.

The rules of any competition may include a similar provision.

4. If the Referee finds that a player is wearing articles not permitted by the Laws and which may constitute a danger to other players, he shall order him to take them off. If he fails to carry out the Referee's instruction, the player shall not take part in the match.

5. A player who has been prevented from taking part in the game or a player who has been sent off the field for infringing Law 4 **must** report to the Referee during a stoppage of the game and may not enter or re-enter the field of play unless and until the Referee has satisfied himself that the player is no longer infringing Law 4.

6. A player who has been prevented from taking part in a game or who has been sent off because of an infringement of Law 4, and who enters or re-enters the field of play to join or rejoin his team in breach of the conditions of Law 12, shall be cautioned.

If the Referee stops the game to administer the caution, the game shall be restarted by an indirect free-kick, taken by a player of the opposing side, from the place where the ball was when the Referee stopped the game. If the free-kick is awarded to a side within its own goal area, it may be taken from any point within that half of the goal area in which the ball was when play was stopped.

LAW 5
REFEREES

A Referee shall be appointed to officiate in each game. His authority and the exercise of the powers granted to him by the Laws of the Game commence as soon as he enters the field of play.

His power of penalizing shall extend to offences committed when play has been temporarily suspended, or when the ball is out of play. His decision on points of fact connected with the play shall be final so far as the result of the game is concerned.

He shall:

(a) Enforce the Laws.

(b) Refrain from penalizing in cases where he is satisfied that, by doing so, he would be giving an advantage to the offending team.

(c) Keep a record of the game; act as timekeeper and allow the full or agreed time, adding thereto all time lost through accident or other cause.

(d) Have discretionary power to stop the game for any infringement of the Laws and to suspend or terminate the game whenever, by reasons of the elements, interference by spectators, or other cause, he deems such stoppage necessary. In such a case he shall submit a detailed report to the competent authority, within the stipulated time, and in accordance with the provisions set up by the National Association under whose jurisdiction the match was played. Reports will be deemed to be made when received in the ordinary course of post.

(e) From the time he enters the field of play, caution any player guilty of misconduct or ungentlemanly behaviour and, if he persists, suspend him from further participation in the game. In such cases the Referee shall send the name of the offender to the competent authority, within the stipulated time [in England, within two days, Sunday not included] and in accordance with the provisions set up by the National Association under whose jurisdiction the match was played. Reports will be deemed to be made when received in the ordinary course of post.

(f) Allow no person other than the players and Linesmen to enter the field of play without his permission.

(g) Stop the game if, in his opinion, a player has been seriously injured; have the player removed as soon as possible from the field of play; and immediately resume the game. If a player is slightly injured, the game shall not be stopped until the ball has ceased to be in play. A player who is able to go to the touch- or goal-line for attention of any kind shall not be treated on the field of play.

(h) Send off the field of play any player who, in his opinion, is guilty of violent conduct, serious foul play, or the use of foul or abusive language.

(i) Signal for recommencement of the game after all stoppages.

(j) Decide that the ball provided for a match meets with the requirements of Law 2.

INTERNATIONAL BOARD DECISIONS

1. Referees in International Matches shall wear a blazer or blouse the colour of which is distinctive from the colours worn by the contesting teams.

2. Referees for International Matches will be selected from a neutral country unless the countries concerned agree to appoint their own officials.

3. The Referee must be chosen from the official list of International Referees. This need not apply to Amateur and Youth International matches.

4. The Referee shall report to the appropriate authority misconduct or any misdemeanour on the part of spectators, officials, players, named substitutes or other persons which take place either on the field of play or in its vicinity at any time prior to, during, or after the match in question so that appropriate action can be taken by the authority concerned.

5. Linesmen are assistants of the Referee. In no case shall the Referee consider the intervention of a Linesman if he himself has seen the incident and, from his position on the field, is better able to judge. With this reserve, and the Linesman neutral, the Referee can consider the intervention and if the information of the Linesman applies to that phase of the game immediately before the scoring of a goal, the Referee may act thereon and cancel the goal.

6. The Referee, however, can reverse his first decision only so long as the game has not been restarted.

7. If the Referee has decided to apply the advantage clause and to let the game proceed, he cannot revoke his decision if the presumed advantage has not been realized, even though he has not, by any gesture, indicated his decision. This does not exempt the offending player from being dealt with by the Referee.

8. The Laws of the Game are intended to provide that games should be played with as little interference as possible, and in this view it is the duty of Referees to penalize only deliberate breaches of the Law. Constant whistling for trifling and doubtful breaches produces bad feeling and loss of temper on the part of the players and spoils the pleasure of spectators.

9. By par. (d) of Law 5 the Referee is empowered to terminate a match in the event of grave disorder, but he has no power or right to decide, in such event, that either team is disqualified and thereby the loser of the match. He must send a detailed report to the proper authority, which alone has power to deal further with this matter.

10. If a player commits two infringements of a different nature at the same time, the Referee shall punish the more serious offence.

11. It is ithe duty of the Referee to act upon the information of neutral Linesmen with regard to incidents that do not come under the personal notice of the Referee.

12. The Referee shall not allow any person to enter the field until play has stopped, and only then if he has given him a signal to do so; nor shall he allow coaching from the boundary lines.

LAW 6
LINESMEN

Two Linesmen shall be appointed, whose duty (subject to the decision of the Referee) shall be to indicate:

(a) When the ball is out of play.

(b) Which side is entitled to a corner-kick, goal-kick or throw in,

(c) When a substitution is desired.

They shall also assist the Referee to control the game in accordance with the Laws. In the event of undue interference or improper conduct by a Linesman, the Referee shall dispense with his services and arrange for a substitute to be appointed. (The matter shall be reported by the Referee to the competent authority.) The Linesmen should be equipped with flags by the Club on whose ground the match is played.

INTERNATIONAL BOARD DECISIONS

1. Linesmen where neutral shall draw the Referee's attention to any breach of the Laws of the Game of which they become aware if they consider that the Referee may not have seen it, but the Referee shall always be the judge of the decision to be taken.

2. National Associations are advised to appoint official Referees of neutral nationality to act as Linesmen in International Matches.

3. In International Matches, Linesmen's flags shall be of a vivid colour – bright reds and yellows. Such flags are recommended for use in all other matches.

4. A Linesman may be subject to disciplinary action only upon a report of the Referee for unjustified interference or insufficient assistance.

LAW 7
DURATION OF THE GAME

The duration of the game shall be two equal periods of 45 minutes, unless otherwise mutually agreed upon, subject to the following:

(a) Allowance shall be made in either period for all time lost through accident or other cause, the amount of which shall be a matter for the discretion of the Referee.

(b) Time shall be extended to permit of a penalty kick being taken at or after the expiration of the normal period in either half.

At half-time the interval shall not exceed five minutes except by consent of the Referee.

INTERNATIONAL BOARD DECISIONS

1. If a match has been stopped by the Referee, before the completion of the time specified in the rules, for any reason stated in Law 5 it must be replayed in full unless the rules of the competition concerned provide for the result of the match at the time of such stoppage to stand.

2. Players have a right to an interval at half-time.

LAW 8

THE START OF PLAY

(*a*) **At the beginning of the game** choice of ends and the kick-off shall be decided by the toss of a coin. The team winning the toss shall have the option of choice of ends or the kick-off.

The Referee having given a signal, the game shall be started by a player taking a place-kick (i.e., a kick at the ball while it is stationary on the ground in the centre of the field of play) into his opponents' half of the field of play. Every player shall be in his own half of the field and every player of the team opposing that of the kicker shall remain not less than 10 yards from the ball until it is kicked-off; it shall not be deemed in play until it has travelled the distance of its own circumference. The kicker shall not play the ball a second time until it has been touched or played by another player.

(*b*) **After a goal has been scored** the game shall be restarted in like manner by a player of the team losing the goal.

(*c*) **After half-time**. When restarting after half-time, ends shall be changed and the kick-off shall be taken by a player of the opposite team to that of the player who started the game.

Punishment

For any infringement of this Law, the kick-off shall be retaken, except in the case of the kicker playing the ball again before it has been touched or played by another player; for this offence, an indirect free-kick shall be taken by a player of the opposing team from the place where the infringement occurred, unless the offence is committed by a player in his opponents' goal-area, in which case the free-kick shall be taken from a point anywhere within the half of the goal-area in which the offence occurred. A goal shall not be scored direct from a kick-off.

(*d*) **After any other temporary suspension**. When restarting the game after a temporary suspension of play from any cause not mentioned elsewhere in these Laws, provided that immediately prior to the suspension the ball has not passed over the touch- or goal-lines, the Referee shall drop the ball at the place where it was when play was suspended, and it shall be deemed in play when it has touched the ground; if, however, it goes over the touch- or goal-lines after it has been dropped by the Referee, but before it is touched by a player, the Referee shall again drop it. A player shall not play the ball until it has touched the ground. If this section of the Law is not complied with the Referee shall again drop the ball.

INTERNATIONAL BOARD DECISIONS

1. If, when the Referee drops the ball, a player infringes any of the Laws before the ball has touched the ground, the player concerned shall be cautioned or sent off the field according to the seriousness of the offence, but a free-kick cannot be awarded to the opposing team because the ball was not in play at the time of the offence. The ball shall therefore be again dropped by the Referee.

2. Kicking-off by persons other than the players competing in a match is prohibited.

LAW 9

BALL IN AND OUT OF PLAY

The ball is out of play:

(*a*) when it has wholly crossed the goal-line or touch-line, whether on the ground or in the air;

(*b*) when the game has been stopped by the Referee.

The ball is in play at all other times from the start of the match to the finish including:

(*a*) if it rebounds from a goal-post, cross-bar or corner-flag post into the field of play;

(*b*) if it rebounds off either the Referee or Linesmen when they are in the field of play;

(*c*) in the event of a supposed infringement of the Laws, until a decision is given.

INTERNATIONAL BOARD DECISIONS

1. The lines belong to the areas of which they are the boundaries. In consequence, the touch-lines and the goal-lines belong to the field of play.

LAW 10

METHOD OF SCORING

Except as otherwise provided by these Laws, a goal is scored when the whole of the ball has passed over the goal-line, between the goal-posts and under the cross-bar, provided it has not been thrown, carried or intentionally propelled by hand or arm, by a player of the attacking side, except in the case of a goalkeeper who is within his own penalty area.

The team scoring the greater number of goals during a game shall be the winner; if no goals, or an equal number of goals are scored, the game shall be termed a 'draw'.

INTERNATIONAL BOARD DECISIONS

1. Law 10 defines the only method according to which a match is won or drawn; no variation whatsoever can be authorized.

2. A goal cannot in any case be allowed if the ball has been prevented by some outside agency from passing over the goal-line. If this happens in the normal course of play, other than at the taking of a penalty-kick, the game must be stopped and restarted by the Referee dropping the ball at the place where the ball came into contact with the interference.

3. If, when the ball is going into goal, a spectator enters the field before it passes wholly over the goal-line, and tries to prevent a score, a goal shall be allowed if the ball goes into goal, unless the spectator has made contact with the ball or has interfered with play, in which case the Referee shall stop the game and restart it by dropping the ball at the place where the contact or interference occurred.

LAW 11

OFF-SIDE

(1) A player is in an off-side position if he is nearer to his opponents' goal-line than the ball, unless:

(*a*) he is in his own half of the field of play; or

(*b*) there are at least two of his opponents nearer their own goal-line than he is.

(2) A player shall be declared off-side, and penalized for being in an off-side position, only if, at the moment the ball touches, or is played by, one of his team, he is , in the opinion of the Referee

(*a*) interfering with play or with an opponent, or

(*b*) seeking to gain an advantage by being in that position.

(3) A player shall not be declared off-side by the Referee

(*a*) merely because of his being in an off-side position, or

(*b*) if he receives the ball directly from a goal-kick, a corner-kick, a throw-in, or when it

has been dropped by the Referee.

(4) If a player is declared off-side, the Referee shall award an indirect free-kick, which shall be taken by a player of the opposing team from the place where the infringement occurred, unless the offence is committed by a player in his opponents' goal-area, in which case the free-kick shall be taken from a point anywhere within that half of the goal-area in which the offence occurred.

INTERNATIONAL BOARD DECISIONS

1. Off-side shall not be judged at the moment the player in question receives the ball, but at the moment when the ball is passed to him by one of his own side. A player who is not in an off-side position when one of his colleagues passes the ball to him or takes a free-kick, does not therefore become off-side if he goes forward during the flight of the ball.

LAW 12

FOULS AND MISCONDUCT

A player who intentionally commits any of the following nine offences:

(*a*) Kicks or attempts to kick an opponent;

(*b*) Trips an opponent, i.e., throwing or attempting to throw him by the use of the legs or by stooping in front of or behind him;

(*c*) Jumps at an opponent;

(*d*) Charges an opponent in a violent or dangerous manner;

(*e*) Charges an opponent from behind unless the latter be obstructing;

(*f*) Strikes or attempts to strike an opponent or spits at him;

(*g*) Holds an opponent;

(*h*) Pushes an opponent;

(*i*) Handles the ball, i.e., carries, strikes or propels the ball with his hand or arm (this does not apply to the goalkeeper within his own penalty-area)

shall be penalized by the award of a **direct free-kick** to be taken by the opposing side from the place where the offence occurred, unless the offence is committed by a player in his opponents' goal-area, in which case, the free-kick shall be taken from a point anywhere within that half of the goal-area in which the offence occurred.

Should a player of the defending side intentionally commit one of the above nine offences within the penalty-area he shall be penalized by a **penalty-kick**.

A penalty-kick can be awarded irrespective of the position of the ball, if in play, at the time an offence within the penalty area is committed.

A player committing any of the following five offences:

1. Playing in a manner considered by the Referee to be dangerous, e.g., attempting to kick the ball while held by the goalkeeper;

2. Charging fairly, i.e., with the shoulder, when the ball is not within playing distance of the players concerned and they are definitely not trying to play it;

3. When not playing the ball, intentionally obstructing an opponent, i.e. running between the opponent and the ball, or interposing the body so as to form an obstacle to an opponent;

4. Charging the goalkeeper except when he

(*a*) is holding the ball,

(*b*) is obstructing an opponent, or

(*c*) has passed outside his goal-area;

5. When playing as a goalkeeper and within his own penalty-area

(*a*) from the moment he takes control of the ball with his hands, he takes more than four steps in any direction whilst holding, bouncing or throwing the ball in the air and catching it again, without releasing it into play, or, having released it into play before, during or after the four steps, he touches it again with his hands, before it has been touched or played by another player, or

(b) indulges in tactics which, in the opinion of the Referee, are designed merely to hold up the game and thus waste time and so give an unfair advantage to his own team

shall be penalized by the award of an **indirect free-kick** to be taken by the opposing side from the place where the infringement occurred, unless the offence is committed by a player in his opponents' goal-area, in which case, the free-kick shall be taken from a point anywhere within that half of the goal-area in which the offence occurred.

A player shall be **cautioned** if:

(j) he enters or re-enters the field of play to join or re-join his team after the game has commenced, or leaves the field of play during the progress of the game (except through accident) without, in either case, first having received a signal from the Referee showing him that he may do so. If the Referee stops the game to administer the caution the game shall be restarted by an indirect free-kick taken by a player of the opposing team from the place where the ball was when the Referee stopped the game. If the free-kick is awarded to a side within its own goal-area it may be taken from any point within that half of the goal-area in which the ball was when play was stopped. If, however, the offending player has committed a more serious offence he shall be penalized according to that section of the law he infringed;

(k) he persistently infringes the Laws of the Game;

(l) he shows by word or action, dissent from any decision given by the Referee;

(m) he is guilty of ungentlemanly conduct.

For any of these last three offences, in addition to the caution an **indirect free-kick** shall also be awarded to the opposing side from the place where the offence occurred, unless a more serious infringement of the Laws of the Game was committed. If the offence is committed by a player in his opponents' goal-area, a free-kick shall be taken from a point anywhere within the half of the goal-area in which the offence occurred.

A player shall be **sent off the field of play** if, in the opinion of the Referee, he:

(n) is guilty of violent conduct or serious foul play;

(o) uses foul or abusive language;

(p) persists in misconduct after having received a caution.

If play be stopped by reason of a player being ordered from the field for an offence without a separate breach of the Law having been committed, the game shall be resumed by an **indirect free-kick** awarded to the opposing side from the place where the infringement occurred unless the offence is committed by a player in his opponents' goal-area, in which case, the free-kick shall be taken from a point anywhere within that half of the goal-area in which the offence occurred.

INTERNATIONAL BOARD DECISIONS

1. If the goalkeeper either intentionally strikes an opponent by throwing the ball vigorously at him, or pushes him with the ball while holding it, the Referee shall award a penalty-kick if the offence took place within the penalty-area.

2. If a player deliberately turns his back to an opponent when he is about to be tackled, he may be charged but not in a dangerous manner.

3. In case of body-contact in the goal area between an attacking player and the opposing goalkeeper not in possession of the ball, the Referee, as sole judge of intention, shall stop the game if, in his opinion, the action of the attacking player was intentional, and award an indirect free-kick.

4. If a player leans on the shoulders of another player of his own team in order to head the ball, the referee shall stop the game, caution the player for ungentlemanly conduct and award an indirect free-kick to the opposing side.

5. A player's obligation when joining or rejoining his team after the start of the match to 'report to the Referee' must be interpreted as meaning to 'draw the attention of the Referee from the touchline'. The signal from the Referee shall be made by a definite gesture which makes the player understand that he may come into the field of play; it is not necessary for the Referee to wait until the game is stopped (this does not apply in respect of an infringement of Law 4), but the Referee is the sole judge of the moment in which he gives his signal of acknowledgement.

6. The letter and spirit of Law 12 do not oblige the Referee to stop a game to administer a caution. He may, if he chooses, apply the advantage. If he does apply the advantage, he shall caution the player when play stops.

7. If a player covers up the ball without touching it in an endeavour not to have it played by an opponent, he obstructs but does not infringe Law 12, para. 3, because he is already in possession of the ball and covers it for tactical reasons whilst the ball remains within playing distance. In fact, he is actually playing the ball and does not commit an infringement; in this case, the player may be charged because he is in fact playing the ball.

8. If a player intentionally stretches his arms to obstruct an opponent and steps from one side to the other, moving his arms up and down to delay his opponent, forcing him to change course, but does not make 'bodily contact' the Referee shall caution the player for ungentlemanly conduct and award an indirect free-kick.

9. If a player intentionally obstructs the opposing goalkeeper in an attempt to prevent him from putting the ball into play in accordance with Law 12, 5(a), the Referee shall award an indirect free-kick.

10. If after a Referee has awarded a free-kick a player protests violently by using abusive or foul language and is sent off the field, the free kick should not be taken until the player has left the field.

11. Any player, whether he is within or outside the field of play, whose conduct is ungentlemanly or violent, whether or not it is directed towards an opponent, a colleague, the referee, a linesman or other person, or who uses foul or abusive language, is guilty of an offence, and shall be dealt with according to the nature of the offence committed.

12. If in the opinion of the Referee a goalkeeper intentionally lies on the ball longer than is necessary, he shall be penalized for ungentlemanly conduct and

(a) be cautioned, and an indirect free-kick awarded to the opposing team;

(b) in case of repetition of the offence, be sent off the field.

13. The offence of spitting at officials or other persons, or similar unseemly behaviour, shall be considered as violent conduct within the meaning of section (n) of Law 12.

14. If, when a referee is about to caution a player, and before he has done so, the player commits another offence which merits a caution, the player shall be sent off the field of play.

LAW 13
FREE-KICK

Free-kicks shall be classified under two headings: 'Direct' (from which a goal can be scored directly against the **offending side**), and 'Indirect' (from which a goal cannot be scored unless the ball has been played or touched by a player other than the kicker before passing through the goal).

When a player is taking a direct or an indirect free-kick inside his own penalty-area, all of the opposing players shall be at least 10 yards (9.15 m) from the ball and shall remain outside the penalty-area until the ball has been kicked out of the area. The ball shall be in play immediately it has travelled the distance of its own circumference and is beyond the penalty-area. The goalkeeper shall not receive the ball into his hands, in order that he may thereafter kick it into play. If the ball is not kicked direct into play, beyond the penalty-area, the kick shall be retaken.

When a player is taking a direct or an indirect free-kick outside his own penalty-area, all of the opposing players shall be at least 10 yards from the ball until it is in play, unless they are standing on their own goal-line, between the goal-posts. The ball shall be in play when it has travelled the distance of its own circumference.

If a player of the opposing side encroaches into the penalty-area, or within 10 yards of the ball, as the case may be, before a free-kick is taken, the Referee shall delay the taking of the kick until the Law is complied with.

The ball must be stationary when a free-kick is taken, and the kicker shall not play the ball a second time until it has been touched or played by another player.

Notwithstanding any other reference in these Laws to the point from which a free-kick is to be taken, any free-kick awarded to the defending side, within its own goal-area, may be taken from any point within that half of the goal-area in which the free-kick has been awarded.

Punishment

If the kicker, after taking the free-kick, plays the ball a second time before it has been touched or played by another player, an indirect free-kick shall be taken by a player of the opposing team from the spot where the infringement occurred, unless the offence is committed by a player in his opponents' goal-area, in which case, the free-kick shall be taken from a point anywhere within that half of the goal-area in which the offence occurred.

INTERNATIONAL BOARD DECISIONS

1. In order to distinguish between a direct and an indirect free-kick, the referee, when he awards an indirect free-kick, shall indicate accordingly by raising an arm above his head. He shall keep his arm in that position until the kick has been taken and retain the signal until the ball has been played or touched by another player or goes out of play.

2. Players who do not retire to the proper distance when a free-kick is taken must be cautioned and on any repetition be ordered off. It is particularly requested of Referees that attempts to delay the taking of a free-kick by encroaching should be treated as serious misconduct.

3. If, when a free-kick is being taken, any of the players dance about or gesticulate in a way calculated to distract their opponents, it shall be deemed ungentlemanly conduct for which the offender(s) shall be cautioned.

LAW 14
PENALTY-KICK

A penalty-kick shall be taken from the penalty-mark and, when it is being taken, all players with the exception of the player taking the kick, and the opposing goalkeeper, shall be within the field of play but outside the penalty-area, and at least 10 yards from the penalty-mark. The opposing goalkeeper must stand (without moving his feet) on his own goal-line, between the goal-posts, until the ball is kicked. The player taking the kick must kick the ball forward; he shall not play the ball a second

Punishment

For any infringement of this Law:

(a) by the defending team, the kick shall be retaken if a goal has not resulted;

(b) by the attacking team, other than by the player taking the kick, if a goal is scored it shall be disallowed and the kick retaken.

(c) by the player taking the penalty kick, committed after the ball is in play, a player of the opposing team shall take an indirect free kick from the spot where the infringement occurred.

If, in the case of paragraph (c), the offence is committed by the player in his opponents' goal-area, the free-kick shall be taken from a point anywhere within that half of the goal-area in which the offence occurred.

INTERNATIONAL BOARD DECISIONS

1. When the Referee has awarded a penalty-kick, he shall not signal for it to be taken until the players have taken up position in accordance with the Law.

2. (a) If, after the kick has been taken, the ball is stopped in its course towards goal by an outside agent, the kick shall be retaken.

(b) If, after the kick has been taken, the ball rebounds into play from the goalkeeper, the cross-bar or a goal-post, and is then stopped in its course by an outside agent, the Referee shall stop play, and restart it by dropping the ball at the place where it came into contact with the outside agent.

3. (a) If, after having given the signal for a penalty-kick to be taken, the Referee sees that the goalkeeper is not in his right place on the goal-line, he shall, nevertheless, allow the kick to proceed. It shall be retaken if a goal is not scored.

(b) If, after the Referee has given the signal for the penalty-kick to be taken, and before the ball has been kicked, the goal-keeper moves his feet, the Referee shall, nevertheless, allow the kick to proceed. It shall be retaken if a goal is not scored.

(c) If, after the Referee has given the signal for a penalty-kick to be taken, and before the ball is in play, a player of the defending team encroaches into the penalty-area, or within 10 yards of the penalty-mark, the Referee shall allow the kick to proceed. It shall be retaken if a goal is not scored.

The player concerned shall be cautioned.

4. (a) If, when a penalty-kick is being taken, the player taking the kick is guilty of ungentlemanly conduct, the kick, if already taken, shall be retaken if a goal is scored.

The player concerned shall be cautioned.

(b) If, after the Referee has given the signal for a penalty-kick to be taken, and before the ball is in play, a colleague of the player taking the kick encroaches into the penalty-area or within 10 yards of the penalty-mark, the Referee shall, nevertheless, allow the kick to proceed. If a goal is scored, it shall be disallowed, and the kick retaken.

The player concerned shall be cautioned.

(c) If, in the circumstances described in the foregoing paragraph, the ball rebounds into play from the goalkeeper, the crossbar or a goal-post, the Referee shall stop the game, caution the player and award an indirect free-kick to the opposing team from the place where the infringement occurred.

5. (a) If, after the Referee has given the signal for a penalty-kick to be taken, and before the ball is in play, the goalkeeper moves from his position on the goal-line, or moves his feet, and a colleague of the kicker en-

croaches into the penalty-area, or within 10 yards of the penalty-mark, the kick, if taken, shall be retaken.

The colleague of the kicker shall be cautioned.

(b) If, after the Referee has given the signal for a penalty-kick to be taken, and before the ball is in play, a player of each team encroaches into the penalty-area, or within 10 yards of the penalty-mark, the kick, if taken, shall be retaken.

The players concerned shall be cautioned.

6. When a match is extended, at half-time or full-time, to allow a penalty-kick to be taken or retaken, the extension shall last until the moment that the penalty-kick has been completed, i.e., until the referee has decided whether or not a goal is scored.

A goal is scored when the ball passes wholly over the goal-line

(a) direct from the penalty-kick,

(b) having rebounded from either goal-post or the cross-bar, or

(c) having touched or been played by the goalkeeper.

The game shall terminate immediately the referee has made his decision.

7. When a penalty-kick is being taken in extended time

(a) the provisions of all the foregoing paragraphs, except paragraphs 2 (b) and 4 (c) shall apply in the usual way, and

(b) in the circumstances described in paragraphs 2 (b) and 4 (c) the game shall terminate immediately the ball rebounds from the goalkeeper, the cross-bar or the goal-post.

LAW 15

THROW-IN

When the whole of the ball passes over the touch-line, either on the ground or in the air, it shall be thrown in from the point where it crossed the line, in any direction, by a player of the team opposite to that of the player who last touched it. The thrower at the moment of delivering the ball must face the field of play and part of each foot shall be either on the touch-line or on the ground outside the touch-line. The thrower shall use both hands and shall deliver the ball from behind and over his head. The ball shall be in play immediately it enters the field of play, but the thrower shall not again play the ball until it has been touched or played by another player. A goal shall not be scored direct from a throw-in.

Punishment

(a) If the ball is improperly thrown in the throw-in shall be taken by a player of the opposing team.

(b) If the thrower plays the ball a second time before it has been touched or played by another player, an indirect free-kick shall be taken by a player of the opposing team from the place where the infringement occurred, unless the offence is committed by a player in his opponents' goal-area, in which case, the free-kick shall be taken from a point anywhere within that half of the goal-area in which the offence occurred.

INTERNATIONAL BOARD DECISIONS

1. If a player taking a throw-in plays the ball a second time by handling it within the field of play before it has been touched or played by another player, the Referee shall award a direct free-kick

2. A player taking a throw-in must face the field of play with some part of his body.

3. If, when a throw-in is being taken, any of the opposing players dance about or gesticulate in a

way calculated to distract or impede the thrower, it shall be deemed ungentlemanly conduct, for which the offender(s) shall be cautioned.

LAW 16

GOAL-KICK

When the whole of the ball passes over the goal-line excluding that portion between the goal-posts, either in the air or on the ground, having last been played by one of the attacking team, it shall be kicked directly into play beyond the penalty-area from a point within that half of the goal-area nearest to where it crossed the line, by a player of the defending team. A goalkeeper shall not receive the ball into his hands from a goal-kick in order that he may thereafter kick it into play. If the ball is not kicked beyond the penalty-area, i.e., direct into play, the kick shall be retaken. The kicker shall not play the ball a second time until it has touched or been played by another player. A goal shall not be scored direct from such a kick. Players of the team opposing that of the player taking the goal-kick shall remain outside the penalty-area until the ball has been kicked out of the penalty-area.

Punishment

If a player taking a goal-kick plays the ball a second time after it has passed beyond the penalty-area, but before it has touched or been played by another player, an indirect free-kick shall be awarded to the opposing team, to be taken from the place where the infringement occurred, unless the offence is committed by a player in his opponents' goal-area, in which case, the free-kick shall be taken from a point anywhere within that half of the goal-area in which the offence occurred.

INTERNATIONAL BOARD DECISIONS

1. When a goal-kick has been taken and the player who has kicked the ball touches it again before it has left the penalty-area, the kick has not been taken in accordance with the law and must be retaken.

LAW 17

CORNER-KICK

When the whole of the ball passes over the goal line, excluding that portion between the goal-posts, either in the air or on the ground, having last been played by one of the defending team, a member of the attacking team shall take a corner-kick, i.e., the whole of the ball shall be placed within the quarter circle at the nearest corner flag-post, which must not be moved, and it shall be kicked from that position.

A goal may be scored directly from such a kick. Players of the team opposing that of the player taking the corner-kick shall not approach within 10 yards of the ball until it is in play, i.e., it has travelled the distance of its own circumference; nor shall the kicker play the ball a second time until it has been touched or played by another player.

Punishment

(a) If the player who takes the kick plays the ball a second time before it has been touched or played by another player, the Referee shall award an indirect free-kick to the opposing team, to be taken from the place where the infringement occurred, unless the offence is committed by a player in his opponents' goal-area, in which case the free-kick shall be taken from a point anywhere within that half of the goal-area in which the offence occurred.

(b) For any other infringement the kick shall be retaken.

INDEX

Acknowledgements

The publishers thank the following organisations and individuals for their permission to reproduce the photographs in this book:
All Sport Photographic (Simon Bruty) 32, (David Cannon) 1, 5 above right, 13, 16, 17, 23, 37 below, 41 below, 47, 56-7, 57, 76, (Tony Duffy) 142 above, (Trevor Jones) 12, 83 above; AFC. Bournemouth 84 below; BBC Hulton Picture Library 158; Berwick Rangers FC 120; Birmingham City FC 83 below; Colorsport 5 above left, 14, 16 below, 20, 21, 24 above, 27, 29, 30, 31, 33, 43, 44, 45, 49, 68, 80-1, 82, 84 above, 85, 86 below, 87, 88, 89, 90, 91, 92, 93, 95, 96-7, 98, 99, 100, 101, 102, 103, 104, 105, 106, 107, 108 above, 109, 110, 112 above, 113 above, 114-5, 117 above, 119, 121, 122, 123, 126, 127 above, 128, 130-1, 132 below, 134 below, 135, 136, 138 below, 142-3, 148 below, 152-3, 153, 160 above, 161, 162, 165, 172, 174-5, 176 left, 176-7, 178 below, 179 below; Ken Coton 94; *Edinburgh Evening News* 125, 147 right; *Glasgow Herald* 146; Hamilton Academical FC 124; Huddersfield Town FC 96 above; *Hull Daily Mail* 26; Howard Jones/Stockport County FC 111 above; *Paisley Daily Express* 129; The Photo Source/Keystone Press Agency 138-9, 140, 144 above, 166, 167 above, 168, 170; Len Pitson 112 below; Popperfoto 134 above, 151 below, 169; Raith Rovers FC 127 below; S.A.M. Paris 51, 61, S.A.M./Machette 181; Sven Simon, Essen 60; Sportapics 147 left, 149; Sporting Pictures (UK) 4-5, 8-9, 72, 118; Stoke City FC 111 below; Syndication International 108 below, 132 above, 133, 141, 144 below, 151 above, 152, 154 centre, 163, 171, 172-3; *Telford Journal & Trader* 38; Bob Thomas Sports Photography 2-3, 4-5, 8-9, 10, 11, 15, 18, 19, 22, 24 below, 25, 34, 35, 36, 37 above, 39, 46-7, 48, 50, 52, 53, 54, 55, 58, 59, 62, 63, 64, 65, 66, 67, 69, 70, 71, 73, 74, 75, 77, 78, 79, 145, 154, 164, 176 right, 177, 178 above, 179 above, 182, 183; J. Tinkler 86 above; Topham Picture Library 139 below, 159, 160 below, 167 below; Tottenham Hotspur FC 113 below; Wimbledon FC 116 above; Whyler Photos, Stirling 42; *Wolverhampton Express & Star* 116 below; York City FC 117 below; *Yorkshire Post* 28.